OXFORD STUDIES IN AFRICAN AFFAIRS

General Editors
JOHN D. HARGREAVES *and* GEORGE SHEPPERSON

CLAN LEADERS AND COLONIAL CHIEFS IN LANGO

CLAN LEADERS AND COLONIAL CHIEFS IN LANGO

The Political History
of an East African
Stateless Society
c. 1800 - 1939

BY

JOHN TOSH

CLARENDON PRESS . OXFORD
1978

Oxford University Press, Walton Street, Oxford OX2 6DP

OXFORD   LONDON   GLASGOW
NEW YORK   TORONTO   MELBOURNE   WELLINGTON
IBADAN   NAIROBI   DAR ES SALAAM   LUSAKA   CAPE TOWN
KUALA LUMPUR   SINGAPORE   JAKARTA   HONG KONG   TOKYO
DELHI   BOMBAY   CALCUTTA   MADRAS   KARACHI

© *Oxford University Press 1978*

British Library Cataloguing in Publication Data
Tosh, John
    Clan leaders and colonial chiefs in Lango.—(Oxford
    studies in African affairs).
    1. Lango (African tribe)—Tribal government
    I. Title   II. Series
    301.5′92′096761   DT433.242   78–40243

ISBN 0–19–822711–6

*Printed in Great Britain by
Western Printing Services Ltd., Bristol*

To my parents
J.C.P.T. and R.E.T.

Preface

UNTIL the relatively recent past, there existed in Africa a large number of societies which functioned without government; that is, they lacked a specialized political leadership in the form of kings or chiefs. These 'stateless' or 'acephalous' societies have been the subject of intense study by social anthropologists. Historians, on the other hand, have largely neglected them, preferring to concentrate on those African peoples which have evolved more formal institutions of political authority. This work is not the first to consider the political history of an African stateless society, but it is the first to do so in a span which covers both the pre-colonial and colonial eras. My purpose has been to step outside the rigid demarcation between pre-colonial and colonial history, which is commonly observed by writers of historical monographs today, and which can so easily place the African past in a false perspective.

My subject is the Langi,[1] one of Uganda's major peoples. The book focuses primarily on the changing forms of political leadership—from the highly informal and parochial clan leadership of the nineteenth century to the powerful, bureaucratic chiefship through which the Langi were administered during the early twentieth century. How this kind of chiefship, so alien to the egalitarian values of the indigenous culture, was established in Lango is a theme which also sheds light on British colonial administration during the heyday of 'Indirect Rule'.

The first four chapters concern the pre-colonial era. In this part of the book I have not adopted a straightforward chronological approach. This is not because stateless societies were static or 'timeless' prior to the colonial period—indeed, it is one of the objects of this book to dispel that myth. The explanation is rather that the diffuseness of political organization in pre-colonial Lango requires a different framework of analysis. After an opening chapter in which

[1] In the past some confusion has surrounded the words *Lango* and *Langi*. In this work I adhere to the current usage of the people themselves. *Langi* denotes the people in the plural, and is employed in no other context. *Lango* denotes an individual member of the tribe and also his language; in addition, it is used as an adjective in both singular and plural. Until very recently, *Lango* was used indiscriminately in the ethnographic literature, and it appears that *Langi* is a relatively recent form.

the emergence of a Lango cultural identity is traced. I examine pre-colonial Lango society at three levels: first the main categories of social organization (Chapter 2), then clan leadership (Chapter 3), and lastly regional leadership (Chapter 4). In each chapter the place in Lango society occupied by the institution in question is described, as well as the changes which it underwent during the nineteenth century. In a purely static analysis, structural factors would predominate; consideration of political changes, apart from their intrinsic importance, allows the deeds of individuals and groups to come to life. To the extent permitted by the sources, I have endeavoured to provide the flesh and blood, as well as the bones of Lango history in the nineteenth century.

By far the most important sources for the pre-colonial period are the oral traditions of the Langi themselves, which I studied during a period of ten months' residence in Lango District in 1969. For reasons which are explained in the Introduction, the traditions are very much stronger on the late nineteenth century than on the earlier period, but within these bounds they cover a rich variety of topics. Apart from oral sources, there are the writings—mostly published—of European travellers who visited northern Uganda from the 1860s onwards. A third group of sources comprises the verified traditions of neighbouring peoples. Finally, there is J. H. Driberg's classic ethnographic account, *The Lango* (1923). Driberg carried out his research while a District Officer, at a time (1912–18) when colonial rule had as yet made little impression; his book is a mine of information on Lango culture just when the old order was coming to an end.[2]

In the second half of the book, I show how Lango was incorporated into the political structure of the Uganda Protectorate, and how that structure was exploited by chiefs recruited from the ranks of the clan leaders. Chapter 5 covers the complex period of 'pacification' (1894–1911), during which the British were obstructed by repeated resistance on the part of the Langi, while at the same time they were beginning to be manipulated by a small minority of clan leaders who grasped the benefits of judicious collaboration. The next two chapters trace the creation of the colonial administrative system in Lango, based on appointed chiefs, and its performance over a period of twenty years

[2] Two more recent works by anthropologists on particular aspects of Lango culture have been found helpful: T. T. S. Hayley, *The Anatomy of Lango Religion and Groups* (Cambridge, 1947), and R. T. Curley, *Elders, Shades, and Women: Ceremonial Change in Lango, Uganda* (Berkeley, 1973).

(1912–33). My main concern is not the policies of successive District Commissioners, but the response of the Lango chiefs. They manipulated the colonial power to their own advantage with consummate skill. The result was a pattern of government which not only contradicted Lango political values, but also confounded the expectations of the British. The final chapter assesses the colonial political order in the light of an over-cautious attempt on the part of officials to remove its abuses in the mid-1930s. No major reforms were accomplished until after the Second World War, by which time it was Britain's intention to prepare Uganda for self-government;[3] that new phase lies beyond the scope of this book, which is concerned with the period during which politics in Lango were dominated by the appointed chiefs.

My preoccupation with the politics of chiefship during the colonial period would be virtually impossible but for the survival in the Lango District Archives of an almost complete set of County Tour Books. Every sub-county in the District was inspected by a District Officer on tour twice, and sometimes three times a year, and at each place entries were made in the appropriate Tour Book; the comments were particularly full on the performance of individual chiefs, their local standing, and their mutual antagonisms. As a result, the County Tour Books are a vital supplement to the more general material relating to Lango which is to be found in the Uganda National Archives at Entebbe and in the Public Record Office, London. In theory, oral sources, in the form of personal reminiscence, ought to be as plentiful for the colonial period as they are for the pre-colonial. In practice, however, most Langi are reluctant to discuss events of the recent past, especially when these are of a political nature.[4] Oral sources do not, therefore, feature as prominently in the second half of the book as they do in the first.

The shape of this work has been affected by the diversity and unevenness of the sources in two obvious ways. In the first place, lacunae in oral tradition have caused the early nineteenth century to receive rather light coverage—an imbalance which further research is most unlikely to rectify. Secondly, the unavoidable switch from oral to documentary evidence as the principal source for the colonial period has resulted in a greater emphasis than I would have liked on

---

[3] The story of these developments in Lango may be followed in Cherry Gertzel's essay, *Party and Locality in Northern Uganda, 1945–62* (London, 1974).

[4] For an explanation of this phenomenon, see below, Introduction.

the official hierarchy of chiefs, at the expense of other, less formal
political institutions. In the case of an African stateless society, it is
perhaps inevitable that problems of this kind should beset a topic
which spans nearly a century and a half of both pre-colonial and
colonial history. The reader must judge for himself how far these
problems have been surmounted in the pages that follow.

My first debt is to the British Institute in Eastern Africa for the
award of a Research Studentship in 1968–9 which made generous
provision for the expenses incurred during fourteen months' research
in Uganda. For additional financial support before and after fieldwork, acknowledgement is due to the Department of Education and
Science, and to the Governing Body of the School of Oriental and
African Studies, London. The final revisions to the manuscript have
been completed since taking up a Research Fellowship at Clare Hall,
Cambridge; I am grateful to the President and Fellows for their
support.

To the Uganda Government I am grateful for permission to consult
their archives and to conduct fieldwork in Lango District; the then
District Commissioner, Mr. Y. B. Mungoma, and his staff were most
helpful in smoothing my path. For making available the books and
documents in their charge, I would like to thank the library staff of
the British Library, the Church Missionary Society, the Institute of
Commonwealth Studies (London), Makerere University, the Royal
Commonwealth Society, and the School of Oriental and African
Studies. I am also indebted to the staff of the Uganda National
Archives in Entebbe and to the Public Record Office in London. Dr.
T. T. S. Hayley kindly showed me the field-notes of his own research
in Lango during the 1930s; Mr. Nasan Engola, Mr. Lazaro Okelo,
and Mr. Yusto Oweno allowed me to make copies of their vernacular
studies of Lango history. Acknowledgement is due to Cambridge
University Press for permission to reproduce in Chapter 8 material
which was previously published in an article of mine in the *Journal of
African History*, 14 (1973), pp. 473–90.

This book began as a Ph.D. thesis which was prepared while I was a
student at the School of Oriental and African Studies and was
approved by the University of London in 1973. As supervisor of my
research, Professor Roland Oliver provided constant encouragement
and guidance without which the work would never have been completed; I am deeply grateful to him. As examiners of the thesis,

Professor Kenneth Ingham and Professor G. N. Sanderson made many helpful suggestions. Dr. Michael Twaddle, whose knowledge of colonial Ugandan history is probably unrivalled, gave me invaluable assistance in Uganda, and since then has been a perceptive critic at every stage of the writing. The text has also benefited from the constructive comments made by Dr. David W. Cohen, Dr. Richard T. Curley, Dr. John Lamphear, and Dr. Andrew Roberts; to each of these scholars I owe a debt extending over several years. Others who have given help include Miss Mildred Browne, Mr. Peter Enin, Professor P. H. Gulliver, Mr. E. B. Haddon, Professor D. A. Low, Dr. Balam Nyeko, Mr. Julius Odurkene, Bishop Angelo Tarantino, and Professor J. B. Webster. For six months in 1968 Professor A. N. Tucker and Mr. J. Olum Oludhe patiently introduced me to the Lango language, thus enabling me to attain some practical command when I began fieldwork.

During my stay in Lango District I was fortunate in enjoying the hospitality of the Verona Fathers of Lira Diocese, the teaching staff of Boroboro Senior Secondary School, David and Sheila Revill, and Hugh and Jan Coleridge. As interpreter and research assistant, Mr. Kassim Ochen worked with me for seven months, and I owe much to his zeal and industry. My greatest debt is to the people of Lango District. Their courtesy and readiness to communicate their historical knowledge made my stay in their country a very happy one, and without them this book could not have been written.

There is one other debt of a less tangible kind which I wish to place on record, and that is to my mother and father: since the beginning of the project they have given help and encouragement in innumerable ways. This book is dedicated to them.

Clare Hall, Cambridge   JOHN TOSH
November 1977

Contents

List of Maps

A Note on Lango Orthography

IN THE writing of Lango proper names, I have aimed at consistency in the use of Standard Lwo Orthography. Thus, I write *Iceme* rather than *Icheme*, and *Okelo* rather than *Okello*. However, Standard Orthography was devised mainly with reference to the Acholi dialect, and it is not entirely suited to Lango. Most of the difficulties arise in the rendering of colloquial speech rather than the writing of individual names, but one point must be mentioned. In the Lango dialect —unlike most other forms of Lwo—the lengthening of consonants is often very important. I have taken account of this feature by doubling the consonant where appropriate: thus, *Okadde*, *Olwa Abelli*.

Ng in Lango is always pronounced as in *singer*, never as in *ingot*.

Abbreviations

ADA	Acholi District Archives, Gulu
CMS	Church Missionary Society
CO	Colonial Office
CS	Chief Secretary
DC	District Commissioner
EPMP	Eastern Province Minute Paper
FO	Foreign Office
LDA	Lango District Archives, Lira
LDMP	Lango District Minute Paper
NPMP	Northern Province Minute Paper
PCEP	Provincial Commissioner, Eastern Province
PCNP	Provincial Commissioner, Northern Province
PRO	Public Record Office, London
SMP	Secretariat Minute Paper
TB	Tour Book (in LDA unless otherwise stated)
TDA	Teso District Archives, Soroti
UNA	Uganda National Archives, Entebbe

Introduction:
Stateless Societies and the Historian in
Africa

'STATELESS societies have political action, which is universal, but they do not have either purely or even primarily political institutions or roles.'[1] So runs a recent and authoritative definition. The notion of the stateless or acephalous society is evidently based on a negative quality, namely the absence of a state or 'head'. Yet social anthropologists today are less certain of the value of a dichotomy between 'state' and 'stateless' than their predecessors of twenty or thirty years ago. This is partly because research in the field has revealed a bewildering continuum rather than a clear distinction between the two categories.[2] More fundamentally, it is because in recent years social anthropologists have realized that a preoccupation with the typology of political systems skirts the issue of how political goals are actually defined and pursued; they have become increasingly concerned with political processes rather than political structures, with events through time rather than static functional models.[3]

This change of emphasis in social anthropology is a very welcome one to historians, who have experienced some difficulty in incorporating into their work the findings of the older structural–functional school, with its rejection of the historical dimension.[4] The more recent attention to political process should at least serve to bring the

[1] A. W. Southall, 'Stateless Societies', in *International Encyclopedia of the Social Sciences*, vol. 15 (New York, 1968), p. 157.

[2] A particularly influential case-study has been the 'segmentary state' of the Alur of Uganda. A. W. Southall, *Alur Society* (Cambridge, 1956).

[3] A seminal work is V. W. Turner, *Schism and Continuity in an African Society* (Manchester, 1957). For general discussions, see M. J. Swartz, V. W. Turner, and A. Tuden (eds.), *Political Anthropology* (Chicago, 1966), editors' Introduction; and M. J. Swartz (ed.), *Local-level Politics* (Chicago, 1968), editor's Introduction.

[4] For a sympathetic consideration of this point of view by a social anthropologist, see E. E. Evans-Pritchard, *Anthropology and History* (Manchester, 1961), reprinted in the same author's *Essays in Social Anthropology* (London, 1962).

The influence of the structural–functional school is one reason why historians of pre-colonial Africa have not been sufficiently alert to *institutional* changes in the societies which they study. D. W. Cohen, 'Pre-Colonial History as the History of the "Society"', *African Studies Review*, 17 (1974), pp. 467–72.

two disciplines closer together. It is less clear, however, whether historians ought to share the social anthropologists' impatience with the state/stateless distinction. This impatience springs in part from the constraints imposed on the social anthropologist during fieldwork by his habitual role as participant-observer: when political processes are analysed in a single village only,[5] the distinction between states and stateless societies may well be of marginal relevance. The historian, on the other hand, usually studies the society as a whole, or a substantial fraction of it, or the wider culture area of which it forms a part; rather than remain in one locality, he needs to travel widely in order to gather the maximum number of variant traditions. Viewed from this angle, the presence or absence of government is a much more significant issue. For the historian of the colonial period, the issue has added importance, since effective local control by the colonial power depended so much on the existence of indigenous authority positions with clearly defined powers and substantial territorial range.

The distinction just made between the historian's focus and the anthropologist's focus begs an important question: how is the political historian's unit of study to be determined? The short answer is that it should be the polity or political community. If this is defined as the largest area within which disputes can be settled according to agreed procedures, then the historian's unit of study in the case of a stateless society will be very small—often not much larger, indeed, than the single village of the anthropologist; in nineteenth-century Lango the political community comprised a small cluster of adjacent clan sections and can seldom have numbered more than a thousand souls. However, such a definition oversimplifies reality. In pre-colonial stateless societies a high proportion of economic, ritual, kinship, and marriage relations extended beyond the confines of the political community, many of them involving a political dimension. The importance of these wider links was reflected in symbols of cultural identity which were acknowledged over a wide area: in Lango, clanship was one such identity of intermediate range; the broadest frame of reference was provided by Lango identity, compared with which loyalty to the political community was parochial indeed.[6] Only within this outermost, 'tribal' perimeter could all the requisites of social life be satisfied. It is in this sense that we may speak of 'Lango society'

[5] Turner's work (op. cit.) on the Ndembu of Zambia is a case in point.
[6] The emergence of this Lango identity is examined in Chapter 1.

prior to the colonial period; politically, this society can be described as a 'multipolity'.[7] The Lango people are taken as the unit of study here, not merely on account of the political weight which this notion —like so many ethnic categories in Africa—acquired during and after the colonial period,[8] but also because without this dimension the political experience of the Langi during the nineteenth century would be misrepresented.

For the purposes of this study, the salient feature of the acephalous society can readily be defined. In societies of this kind, political authority is widely diffused; such authority positions as exist touch only a limited area of the lives of those subject to them; the unit within which disputes can peacefully be settled is small, and it tends to lack constant membership and fixed boundaries.[9] Thus characterized, the stateless society has often struck Western observers as deeply alien. It can all too easily be dismissed as a mere foil to the experience of the West, or as a simple society, requiring no special effort of understanding. In fact it was relatively late in the progress of African ethnography that the stateless society was submitted to searching analysis. This may be said to have begun with the publication in 1940 of *African Political Systems*, a collaborative volume in which eight social anthropologists reported on their findings.[10] Only three of them actually dealt with acephalous societies, but they included the editors of the book, Fortes and Evans-Pritchard, both of whom had made pioneering contributions in precisely this field. Their researches among the Tallensi of northern Ghana and the Nuer of the southern Sudan revealed complex mechanisms of social cohesion, based on segmentary lineage systems.[11] This type of acephalous society has proved a particularly popular subject of anthropological inquiry.[12] But a wide range of societies has been studied since 1940, giving rise

[7] Southall, 'Stateless Societies', pp. 158–9.
[8] For a sensitive consideration of this issue, see M. Twaddle, ' "Tribalism" in Eastern Uganda', in *Tradition and Transition in East Africa*, ed. P. H. Gulliver (London, 1969), pp. 193–208.
[9] These features are adapted from those enumerated in R. Horton, 'Stateless Societies in the History of West Africa', in *History of West Africa*, vol. I (London, 1971), eds. J. F. A. Ajayi and M. Crowder, p. 78.
[10] M. Fortes and E. E. Evans-Pritchard (eds.), *African Political Systems* (London, 1940).
[11] The full results of their researches were published in: E. E. Evans-Pritchard, *The Nuer* (Oxford, 1940), and M. Fortes, *The Dynamics of Clanship among the Tallensi* (London, 1945).
[12] See J. Middleton and D. Tait (eds.), *Tribes Without Rulers* (London, 1958) for a representative sample of this kind of research.

to a large body of literature on both the actual working of stateless societies and their implications for social theory.

This literature has provided an indispensable groundwork for any historical inquiry. But, with the notable exception of Balandier's work on the Fang of Gabon,[13] it did not by and large tackle questions of a historical kind. The overriding priority was to establish how stateless societies managed to hold together at all, partly because this was of major concern to the colonial governments which financed so much anthropological research during the 1940s and 1950s, and partly because of the widespread use made by British social anthropologists of static functional models based on equilibrium theory.[14] Most studies were set in the 'ethnographic present', which in practice meant the society as the anthropologist experienced it, minus the alien accretions of colonial rule.[15]

It was not until the 1960s that professional historians followed in the wake of social anthropologists, and even then their interest in stateless societies was somewhat hesitant. Their early reluctance may be explained by the limited stock of knowledge of any kind about stateless societies. But by the 1950s this condition no longer applied. More important were the aims and preconceptions of historians themselves. Scholars who turned, after the Second World War, from European or colonial history to the study of Africa were almost entirely preoccupied with the development of indigenous states— Ashanti, Dahomey, Kongo, Buganda, and the rest. This predilection was reflected both in their choice of research subjects and in the broad surveys of African history which were written at that time.[16] There were sound practical reasons for this emphasis, at least as far as the pre-colonial era was concerned. Historians with an orthodox training in Western history naturally felt better equipped to deal with African societies which possessed recognizable institutions of government. There was also the distribution of sources to be considered. African states tended to be more fully covered by contemporary European documents than other polities were, since it was in the

[13] G. Balandier, *The Sociology of Black Africa* (London, 1970). The original French edition was published in 1955.

[14] For an early and influential attack on this ahistorical approach, see E. R. Leach, *Political Systems of Highland Burma* (London, 1954), especially pp. 7, 282–5.

[15] J. Goody, *The Social Organisation of the LoWiili*, 2nd edition (London, 1967), pp. 4–5.

[16] e.g. R. Oliver and J. D. Fage, *A Short History of Africa* (Harmondsworth, 1962).

states that African commerce was concentrated; and the oral traditions of states were richer and more easily retrieved than those of non-centralized polities.[17]

Recent critics, however, have tended to explain the preoccupation with states in terms of an ideological bias, seldom explicit but no less powerful for that. Like other students of the African scene, historians have been much affected by the anti-colonial revolution which has taken place in their own lifetime. They have interpreted the emergence of independent African states as not just a significant event for this day and age, but the culmination of Africa's evolution over several centuries. Once this event is accepted as the grand climacteric, it follows that state-building and 'enlargement of scale' are the aspects of the past most worthy of attention. Individual polities, instead of being considered on their merits, are assessed according to their potential for state development. Even the Atlantic slave trade has been spared total condemnation on the grounds that it created or enlarged several powerful kingdoms in West Africa.[18] Christopher Wrigley, in an eloquent critique, has described the preoccupation with state formation as a kind of historicism, amounting to an obsession,[19] and he has not been the only writer to question current orthodoxy.[20] Of course, it would be foolish to deny that the ebb and flow of states is an important aspect of African history; what is being questioned is its claim to hold the field. The overriding concern with states not only ignores large areas of the continent which have never known government; it also discounts the fact that the capacity to lead an ordered life in a stateless society is one of Africa's more interesting contributions to the sum of human experience, with a value

[17] J. Vansina, R. Mauny, and L. V. Thomas (eds.), *The Historian in Tropical Africa* (London, 1964), pp. 64, 86.
It is equally the case that those social anthropologists with a strong interest in history have not, by and large, considered acephalous societies. See I. M. Lewis (ed.), *History and Social Anthropology* (London, 1968), and the important works cited therein by J. A. Barnes, I. Cunnison, G. I. Jones, and M. G. Smith. The major exception is Balandier, op. cit.

[18] J. D. Fage, 'Slavery and the Slave Trade in the context of West African History', *Jl. African History*, 10 (1969), pp. 393–404.

[19] C. C. Wrigley, 'Historicism in Africa: Slavery and State Formation', *African Affairs*, 70 (1971), pp. 113–24. This article was provoked by Fage's piece, cited in the preceding footnote.

[20] B. A. Ogot, 'Some Approaches to African History', *Hadith*, 1 (1968), pp. 1–9; J. D. Omer-Cooper, 'Kingdoms and Villages: a Possible New Perspective in African History', *African Social Research*, 14 (1972), pp. 301–10. For a stimulating critique on a closely related theme, see D. Denoon and A. Kuper, 'Nationalist Historians in search of a Nation', *African Affairs*, 69 (1970), pp. 329–49.

independent of any place it may occupy in a chain of social evolution.

The attack on the 'historicist' approach has followed hard upon the efforts of the first group of scholars to investigate the pre-colonial history of stateless societies. Most of them have worked in East Africa, though with varying emphases. B. A. Ogot in his pioneering work on the Southern Luo, published in 1967, dealt almost exclusively with migration and settlement.[21] G. S. Were in his account of the Abaluyia of Kenya concentrated mainly on the same themes,[22] while Godfrey Muriuki has examined the history of the Kikuyu from the political angle, as well as tracing the development of their settlement patterns.[23] Perhaps most impressive of all has been John Lamphear's work on the Jie, a small semi-pastoral people of north-eastern Uganda, whose emergence as a political community he has traced over a span of some two hundred years of pre-colonial history.[24] Together these scholars have shown that it is possible to find serviceable oral sources in acephalous societies; they have exploded the myth that such societies are 'timeless' and hence without a history; and they have begun to shift the balance away from states and chiefdoms in the historiography of pre-colonial Africa.[25]

In recent years, if rather more slowly, a beginning has also been made in writing the colonial history of stateless societies. Historians now recognize that the process whereby acephalous peoples were adapted to the institutions and standards of European administration was marked by subtle interaction between rulers and ruled which can only be uncovered by painstaking fieldwork. John Lonsdale's work on

[21] B. A. Ogot, *History of the Southern Luo*, vol. I (Nairobi, 1967).

[22] G. S. Were, *A History of the Abaluyia of Western Kenya* (Nairobi, 1967).

[23] G. Muriuki, *A History of the Kikuyu, 1500–1900* (Nairobi, 1974).

[24] J. Lamphear, *The Traditional History of the Jie of Uganda* (Oxford, 1976). A major work on the nineteenth-century history of the Masai of Kenya is being prepared by Richard Waller. For a social anthropologist's interpretation of the Masai past, see A. H. Jacobs, 'The Traditional Political Organization of the Pastoral Masai', unpublished D.Phil. thesis, Oxford University, 1965.

[25] The preliminary findings of a number of other researchers working on pre-colonial stateless societies in northern and eastern Uganda have been published in J. B. Webster and others, *The Iteso during the Asonya* (Nairobi, 1973), and J. M. Onyango-ku-Odongo and J. B. Webster (eds.), *The Central Lwo during the Aconya* [*sic*] (Nairobi, 1976). See also R. S. Herring, 'A History of the Labwor Hills', unpublished Ph.D. dissertation, University of California, Santa Barbara, 1974.

An important study on central Africa, completed since this chapter was written, is T. I. Matthews, 'The Historical Tradition of the Gwembe Valley, Middle Zambezi', unpublished Ph.D. thesis, London University, 1976.

western Kenya marked a beginning,[26] and more localized studies have since been completed on the Kamba of Kenya by J. Forbes Munro, on the Tiv of central Nigeria by David Craig Dorward, and on the Lugbara of Uganda by Anne King.[27] A common feature of all these works, however, is that they take as their starting point the arrival of the colonial administration and give only a perfunctory account of pre-colonial politics and society.[28] As a result, it is not easy to see the colonial period as an episode in the total historical development of the societies in question.[29] It is one of the objects of this book to illuminate the colonial experience of an African stateless society by setting it in a deeper time-scale.

Stateless societies were, until recently, excluded from their due place in African historiography because they were belittled and de-valued by historians. This was not, however, the only reason for their neglect. There have also been major reservations on the question of sources: assuming that the pre-colonial past of stateless societies is a valid subject of inquiry, is it practicable? The central issue is whether stateless societies possess oral traditions, and if so whether these traditions can yield answers to questions of a historical kind. When in 1961 Jan Vansina expressed his conviction that research in stateless societies would reveal more about their past than was then thought

[26] J. M. Lonsdale, 'A Political History of Nyanza, 1883–1945', unpublished Ph.D. thesis, Cambridge University, 1964. A. E. Afigbo, *The Warrant Chiefs: Indirect Rule in Southeastern Nigeria* (London, 1972) is a more narrowly admini-strative study.

[27] J. F. Munro, *Colonial Rule and the Kamba* (Oxford, 1975); D. C. Dorward, 'A Political and Social History of the Tiv of Northern Nigeria, 1900–1939', un-published Ph.D. thesis, London University, 1971; A. King, 'A History of West Nile District, Uganda', unpublished D.Phil. thesis, Sussex University, 1971. An ambitious comparative approach is attempted in R. L. Tignor, *The Colonial Trans-formation of Kenya: The Kamba, Kikuyu and Maasai from 1900 to 1939* (Princeton, 1976). A work of major importance on the acephalous peoples of eastern Uganda during the colonial period by Dr. Michael Twaddle is eagerly awaited.

[28] In the case of King, op. cit., the starting point is the 1860s, when West Nile was brought within the trading frontier of the Sudanese on the White Nile, and pre-colonial society receives somewhat greater coverage than in the other works of colonial history mentioned above. E. Isichei, *A History of the Igbo People* (London, 1976) is a somewhat unsatisfactory brief survey of Igbo history from early times to the present day; see also the same author's *The Ibo People and the Europeans* (London, 1973).

[29] This tendency for pre-colonial and colonial history to be placed in separate compartments and to be handled by different specialists is not, of course, peculiar to stateless societies; it affects the historian's approach to most aspects of Africa's past.

possible, he pointed out that the experiment had yet to be made.[30] Since then Vansina's hunch has been fully vindicated by the work of Ogot and others in East Africa.[31] It would, nevertheless, be idle to pretend that research into the history of stateless societies is now a straightforward matter. The oral traditions of these societies present serious problems, many of them rather different from those encountered in centralized polities. I turn now to consider the general character of these problems and the particular shape which they assume in Lango.

In a society which traditionally has lacked state organization and chiefs, oral tradition—like political authority—is widely distributed. This is not to say that the oral tradition of centralized societies is necessarily, or even usually, confined to court histories; David W. Cohen's recent study of Busoga has demonstrated the wealth of local, non-official traditions which exist there away from the seats of power.[32] Nevertheless, the fact remains that most historians of centralized societies have depended primarily on authorized traditions of kingship or chiefship, since the development of these institutions has been their main interest.[33] In practice it has tended to be the historians of stateless societies who have worked at the problems posed by widely distributed oral tradition.

One of the most daunting of these problems is the limited geographical horizon of the traditions themselves; they normally concern not the society as a whole, but merely that fraction of it which constitutes (or constituted) the political community—be it village or clan. Those traditions which do purport to be valid for the entire society are much the least reliable and informative.[34] In Lango, historical traditions pertain exclusively to the clan section, the largest localized descent group and the principal arena of political action during the nineteenth century. There are today many hundreds of clan sections

---

[30] J. Vansina, *Oral Tradition* (London, 1965), p. 173. (The original edition, *De la tradition orale*, was published in 1961.)

[31] For a confident affirmation of the reliability of oral traditions in stateless societies, see J. Lamphear and J. B. Webster, 'The Jie-Acholi War: oral evidence from two sides of the battle front', *Uganda Jl.* 35 (1971), pp. 23–42.

[32] D. W. Cohen, *The Historical Tradition of Busoga* (Oxford, 1972). See also E. J. Alagoa, 'Oral tradition among the Ijo of the Niger Delta', *Jl. African History*, 7 (1966), pp. 405–19.

[33] For a cogent defence of this approach, see A. D. Roberts, *A History of the Bemba* (London, 1973), pp. 12–37. S. Feierman, in *The Shambaa Kingdom* (Madison, 1974), has used both court and local traditions.

[34] Lamphear, op. cit., pp. 30–1.

in Lango, and the traditions which they recount are unlikely to interest any Lango who is not a member of the clan section concerned. The wide distribution of historical knowledge in stateless societies, combined with its parochial focus, presents the historian with a severe practical difficulty. Strictly speaking, the history of a whole society can only be written if all the groups within it who hold traditions are canvassed. Some societies are sufficiently small and concentrated to allow near-comprehensive coverage, such as Lamphear achieved in the case of the Jie.[35] But in many societies this would be the work of a lifetime. Lango, with its population of half a million, is one of these. Some kind of selection on the part of the researcher is therefore indicated. If viable results are to be obtained, then clearly the selection of informants cannot be random or arbitrary; it must be based on a working knowledge of the society and a set of clearly defined research objectives. By these criteria I decided in Lango to single out a handful of localities for extended treatment and to ignore the rest almost completely. This procedure enabled me to assemble several case-studies of political history during the pre-colonial and early colonial periods, at that level of their society which the Langi see as the politically operative one—the localized clan section.[36]

Once the historian has overcome these problems of wide distribution and narrow focus, however, he is likely to find that the traditions which he has gathered are free from certain pitfalls of interpretation. The court traditions of a pre-literate state may be easily retrieved, but they can be extremely difficult to evaluate. The ruling élite may have an articulate awareness of the past,[37] but this is partly because they realize its political significance for their own time. Events which reflect adversely on the ruling dynasty may be expunged from the record, and the king's credentials may be strengthened by falsification and exaggeration. In an acephalous society, on the other hand, traditions are not so badly distorted. The incentive to 'politicize' them is not so strong; and, while there is likely to be some bias, this can be checked by reference to the traditions of equivalent groups within the same society.

The kind of bias is determined by the nature of the social groups which transmit the traditions from one generation to the next. In the case of Lango, the only group which counts is the clan section.[38]

---

[35] Ibid., p. 53.
[36] For a description of my fieldwork methods, see Appendix 2.
[37] Vansina, Mauny, and Thomas, op. cit., p. 64.   [38] See below, Chapter 2.

Although the clan section has been superseded in everyday social organization by the territorially-defined 'neighbourhood' (*wang tic*), it is still the sole repository of tradition. Since clan sections in Lango are very small, virtually any tradition recounted by one clan section —typically of migration, settlement, and inter-clan warfare—impinges on the history of a neighbouring section, and can therefore be tested. The existence of several independent bodies of clan tradition in the same locality allowed me to reconstruct the history of that locality with some confidence. Further difficulties arise if the clan sections—or whichever groups transmit traditions—are distinguished according to rank or status, but in Lango this problem does not arise. In any given area, clan sections vary in size and political influence, so that one of them may occupy a dominant position. This indeed was the basis of the nineteenth-century political system; but the dominance of one clan section over its neighbours was never secure, and it was nowhere formalized by a distinction between 'royal' and 'commoner' clans, as happened among other Nilotic peoples.[39] The historian in Lango does not, therefore, have to take account of 'official' histories, or of undue influence by one clan section over the traditions of another.[40]

The historical traditions of acephalous societies differ from court traditions in another important respect: they tend to be much less 'literary' in character. Just as state traditions may be distorted by political considerations, so too they may have to adapt to a stylistic form which compels changes in content. This distortion makes the traditions more attractive, and for that reason more likely to survive over many generations, but it also limits their historical value. To say that non-centralized societies have less oral literature than do large chiefdoms is perhaps too sweeping a generalization, but it certainly seems that in the former the connection between history and literature is more tenuous. Lango culture itself is very poorly endowed with oral literature. Virtually the only form current today is the folk-tale, which is concerned to instil socially approved standards of conduct and is devoid of historical content.[41] The Langi perform several rituals

[39] A. W. Southall, 'Rank and Stratification among the Alur and other Nilotic Peoples', in *Social Stratification in Africa*, ed. A. Tuden and L. Plotnicov (New York, 1970), pp. 31–46.

[40] For comparable observations with regard to the Kikuyu, see Muriuki, op. cit., p. 8.

[41] M. J. Wright, 'Lango folk-tales—an analysis', *Uganda Jl.* 24 (1960), pp. 99–113; J. p'Bitek Okot, 'Oral Literature and its Social Background among the Acholi and Lango', unpublished B.Litt. thesis, Oxford University, 1963, pp. 394–5.

requiring the recitation of verbal formulae and songs; but the only ones to contain historical material—the age-set songs—are no longer used, and such records as we possess suggest that they contained only the most perfunctory allusions to war-leaders of old.[42] Historical traditions in Lango belong almost exclusively to the clan sections. They make no claim to literary appeal. They are pedestrian and un-adorned, and these features make them an excellent historical source.

The informal character of oral traditions in stateless societies applies not only to their style, but usually to their mode of trans-mission as well. The handing-down of traditions from one generation to the next is seldom controlled by any set procedures; it does not have to coincide with specific rituals, nor is it done in secret.[43] In Lango within the setting of the clan section there are—and were—no ceremonies during which traditions are passed on by the elders, nor is knowledge of the past restricted to a small number of people. Almost every elder has absorbed something of his clan section's history; how much he remembers or cares to communicate depends on personal qualities, such as interest and intelligence, rather than on social factors like genealogical or ritual status. Traditions are trans-mitted piecemeal in any domestic setting which brings people together round a beer-pot or hearth. As a result, the history of a clan section is practically never presented as a whole; it is conceived in an episodic way, and when recounted to an audience is less like a recitation than a response to questions and promptings.

Spontaneous and informal transmission of this kind has an im-portant bearing on the time-depth of oral tradition. In the case of dynastic traditions, which are of considerable importance to the ruling family, transmission tends to be carefully controlled in the interests of accuracy and style. Both the most ancient and relatively recent traditions are treated with respect, and the result is an im-pressive depth, which in the interlacustrine kingdoms amounts to some four hundred years.[44] In acephalous societies, by contrast, the

[42] J. H. Driberg, *The Lango* (London, 1923), pp. 254–60; Okot, op. cit., pp. 174–5.

[43] cf. Were, op. cit., p. 14, and Muriuki, op. cit., p. 8. Cf. also Vansina, op. cit., p. 52: 'The fundamental distinction is that between traditions which are trans-mitted at random from one generation to the next, and those which are trans-mitted according to certain rules, and with the aid of special techniques.'

[44] D. W. Cohen, 'A Survey of Interlacustrine Chronology', *Jl. African History*, 11 (1970), pp. 177–201. Cohen advances a chronology extending back to the fourteenth century; from the sixteenth century it is corroborated by an impressive number of tie-ins between the traditions of different kingdoms. For a critique, see

haphazard way in which traditions are usually handed down tends to restrict the number of generations over which the original content of a tradition can survive intact.

Just how short the period of survival is varies considerably from one stateless society to another, according to two factors. In the first place, much depends on what kind of chronological framework the traditions are set in. In East Africa those societies whose social organization is based on age-sets or generation-sets provide the historian with an invaluable tool. Normally the sets are named groups which follow each other in a fixed cycle at regular intervals, and historical events are ascribed in oral tradition to the time of one set or another. In this way Masai chronology extends back to the late eighteenth century, Jie chronology to the early eighteenth century, and Kikuyu chronology to the seventeenth century.[45] In stateless societies where age-groups are not prominent, lineage genealogy provides the only internal chronological framework. This is a less satisfactory tool from the historian's point of view because, in contrast to the overarching nature of an age-set organization, most societies possess a multiplicity of independent genealogies, none of which applies to more than a small proportion of that society's members.

Even so, these genealogies may extend back a long way. Whether or not they actually do so depends on a second factor, which is the social function of the traditions themselves. In the case of sedentary agricultural peoples the crucial issue would seem to be land occupancy. They are mostly interested in the events which tie them to their current locality—how long ago and why they settled there, how they have related to their immediate neighbours, and so on. Where settlement occurred a long time ago, the genealogies too may be very deep; this has been strikingly demonstrated in the case of the Kenya Luo, whose genealogies evidently span some fifteen generations back to the sixteenth century.[46] Such depth is exceptional, and many stateless societies have achieved stability of settlement only within the last two hundred years. The Langi belong to the opposite end of the spectrum from the Luo. Although the main migrations of the Langi were over by the beginning of the nineteenth century, 'secondary' migration within the confines of Lango country continued until near

D. P. Henige, 'Reflections on Early Interlacustrine Chronology: an Essay in Source Criticism', *Jl. African History*, 15 (1974), pp. 27–46.

[45] A. H. Jacobs, 'A Chronology of the Pastoral Maasai', *Hadith*, 1 (1968), pp. 10–31; Lamphear, op. cit., pp. 32–52; Muriuki, op. cit., pp. 14–24.

[46] Ogot, op. cit., pp. 26–8, 151–2.

the end of the century. The settlement of clan sections in their present-day localities dates back no further than the period from about 1860 to 1890.[47] The late nineteenth century sets the limit within which detailed historical traditions are retained, and it is rare for an elder to recall names and relationships beyond the third ascending generation. Traditions which are firmly implanted in a genealogical or generational context are not the only ones current in acephalous societies, but they are much the most useful to the historian. Stories of tribal origin are a popular theme, often embellished with lively detail. But they exist in a timeless vacuum outside all chronological control, and they are highly stereotyped regardless of the disparate historical origins represented in the one society.[48] They have more the character of a 'mythical charter', which serves to justify the social order or to provide a symbol of cultural identity. Such traditions need not be dismissed out of hand, but it is not easy to extract from them the kernel of historical truth.[49] In between these tales of origin and traditions about the relatively recent past there is an intervening period for which oral evidence, if it exists at all, is scanty and hard to place in context. What might be called 'middle-period amnesia' is a familiar problem to students of oral tradition in Africa.[50] It applies also to the Langi, in spite of the short span which their entire history covers. Traditions concerning the decisive phase in the formation of the Lango people (about 1780 to 1820) conform to a stereotype, in which the divergent experience of submerged groups is suppressed in favour of a single tribal origin. Detailed clan-section traditions set in the framework of family genealogies only make their appearance in the 1860s and 1870s, and in many areas later still.

Finally, the historian must take account of the distortions in oral tradition which arise from the colonial experience. Those who are

---

[47] See below, Chapter 1.

[48] cf. Vansina's assessment of oral traditions in acephalous societies: 'great difficulty will be encountered in reconstructing the tribal history because the traditions will be so stereotyped as to be almost meaningless.' Vansina, op. cit., p. 171.

[49] It is curious that Horton, in an otherwise well-balanced survey of stateless societies in West African history, chooses to demonstrate the problems which arise from the interpretation of their oral traditions by referring to traditions of origin in the Niger Delta, rather than to later traditions of settlement history (R. Horton, 'Stateless Societies in the History of West Africa', in *History of West Africa*, vol. 1, ed. J. F. A. Ajayi and M. Crowder (London, 1971), p. 79.) This somewhat intractable material is hardly a fair measure of what stateless societies have to offer.

[50] G. I. Jones, 'Time and Oral Tradition with special reference to Eastern Nigeria', *Jl. African History*, 6 (1965), pp. 153–60; Roberts, op. cit., pp. 22–8.

passing on the traditions today can look back on a lifetime of un-precedented social and political change which inevitably conditions their attitude to the past. One change with potentially immense con-sequences is the spread of literacy. Respect for the written word on the part of the newly literate has meant that undue credence has been accorded by those versed in the past to published bodies of tradition, regardless of their accuracy. This pitfall is a common one in Africa; but in societies whose traditions are devoid of literary form and freely transmitted, contamination by the written word may be particularly widespread and difficult to detect.[51] In Lango this problem is not, as yet, a serious one. Knowledge of the past is strongest among men of sixty years and over, and hardly any Langi within this age bracket can read, since missionary education was available on only a very restric-ted scale before the 1930s. Many elders have heard of Driberg's book, *The Lango*, published in 1923, but their accounts of pre-colonial history show no evidence of contamination by this source.

The colonial experience is responsible for another difficulty in the interpretation of oral tradition. At some period in the last hundred years, all stateless societies in Africa have been absorbed into modern states, and in consequence their political structures have been drastically modified. A key change, especially in British Africa, was the concentration of authority in the hands of individual members of the society, usually with the title of 'chief'. These government func-tionaries occupied quite novel positions, but often—as in Lango—they came from families which had enjoyed privileges under the pre-colonial order, and often the new positions were denoted in the vernacular by terms which had previously applied to much less formal positions in the indigenous political system.[52] There is thus consider-able scope for confusion, and the historian in a stateless society must be particularly quick to detect any tendency among his informants to attribute the powers of a colonial chief to important men of the pre-colonial period. The same care is needed when evaluating tradi-tions about other institutions which have changed greatly since the coming of the Europeans.[53]

Of course, the colonial period itself lives in the minds of today's elders, though as first-hand experience rather than tradition. In theory,

[51] I owe this observation to Dr. Richard Curley.

[52] Thus in Lango a county chief in colonial times (as today) was called *rwot*, the term previously applied to the leader of a clan section.

[53] In Lango this is true of the *wang tic*, or 'neighbourhood'. See below, pp. 216–217, 250.

therefore, oral sources ought to shed as much light on the colonial period as they do on the pre-colonial, but I did not find this to be so in Lango. Informants are happy to talk about the early punitive expeditions and the establishment of administration, but on the colonial period proper they are most unwilling to descend from the level of generalization; they are particularly reluctant to speak of prominent individuals in colonial times, such as the chiefs. This reticence is not difficult to explain. Events in which they were protagonists or spectators are not regarded by the Langi as 'history', which for them concerns only 'olden times' (*kare acon*) before the Europeans came. In fact the colonial period is viewed not as history, but as politics, and with good reason. Whereas the pre-colonial political system is evidently in a different world from today's, no break is perceived at grass-roots level between the colonial era and Independence. The same administrative posts persist, and in many cases the same families continue to fill them. It pays people to be discreet when referring to chiefs of thirty or forty years ago whose clans may still wield influence in the local government now. Undoubtedly this attitude owes much to the fear which oppressive behaviour by the chiefs has inspired in the past.[54] At present there is insufficient comparative evidence to determine whether reticence about the politics of the colonial period is something to which informants in stateless societies are especially prone.

Within their limitations, then, the oral traditions of stateless societies are a viable historical source, requiring critical skills of the same order as do the traditions of states and chiefdoms. There are encouraging signs that this is being increasingly recognized. Certainly in East Africa the last ten years have shown that there is no dearth of scholars prepared to embark on the necessary research. The most pressing need now is for historical studies to be made in other areas of Africa, like the southern Sudan and south-eastern Nigeria, where acephalous peoples are well represented. Nor should inquiries be limited to the political sphere; there is a great deal of work to be done too on economic and religious history.[55] Once progress has been made along these lines, it will become possible for stateless societies to enter the mainstream of African historiography. The result will surely be a more comprehensive view of the African past.

[54] See below, Chapter 7.
[55] An important study of Nuer prophets in the late nineteenth and early twentieth centuries is being prepared by Douglas H. Johnson.

CHAPTER 1

Environment, Economy, and Settlement: The Formation of a Lango Identity

No apology is needed for beginning a historical work of this nature with an account of the physical environment and the indigenous economy. In a society where people live close to the soil and command few technological resources, the political system depends on the nature of the habitat; strict limits are set on the basic forms of social organization and on the political superstructure. At the same time,

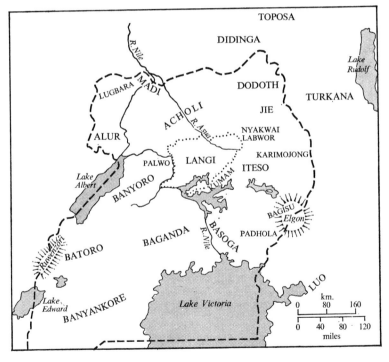

Map 1. Lango and the Wider Region

the dictates of environment and economy are not absolute, as the ethnographic character of northern Uganda makes clear. The peoples of Lango, Acholi, Labwor, and Teso practise a very similar economy in very similar conditions, but their social institutions are far from uniform. How these variations have come about is a complex historical problem which ultimately defies analysis. But it can at least be taken one stage further back in time: the diverse groups which, around the beginning of the nineteenth century, came together to form the Lango people can be identified, and the dynamics of their colonization assessed. On one level, pre-colonial Lango society was determined by environment and economy; on another level, it stemmed from the process of migration and settlement, which was unique to the Langi, and which distinguished them culturally from their neighbours. This chapter deals with both levels of explanation, as an indispensable introduction to the forms of social organization described in Chapter 2.

For so small a country, Uganda encompasses a remarkable diversity of natural environments, ranging from the lush woodland of Buganda and Busoga to the dusty and infertile plain of central Karamoja. Between these two extremes, which are situated in the south and north-east of the country, lies a continuum of intermediate conditions, determined by rainfall and by the course of the Victoria Nile. The region occupied by the Lango people is one such intermediate environment. The Langi today number half a million people.[1] Their homeland coincides very nearly with Lango District, which is about 5,000 square miles in extent. On the south and west the District is bounded by Lake Kyoga and the Nile, which constitute a natural frontier with the Bantu-speaking areas of Busoga, Buganda, and Bunyoro. No such boundaries separate the Langi from the Acholi to the north, or from the Labwor, Iteso, and Kumam to the east, and all these peoples live in comparable conditions of land and climate. Lango country forms part of the extensive plateau north of Lake Kyoga, with an over-all elevation of 3,500 feet. Apart from scattered rock outcrops, there are no dramatic changes of elevation. Away from the Nile, the land rises very gradually towards the water-

[1] The 1969 Census found that Lango District numbered 504,315 people. Since the correspondence between the District and the area actually settled by the Langi is nowadays very close, this figure can be regarded as a fairly accurate indication of the Lango population of Uganda. *Report on the 1969 Population Census*, vol. I (Entebbe, 1971).

shed with the Moroto or Asua river,[2] falling away more abruptly on the other side into the river valley. North of the Moroto, the ground rises again only very slowly, though in the extreme north-east the present extent of Lango settlement is conveniently marked by Otuke Hill, beyond which lie the Labwor Hills of Karamoja.

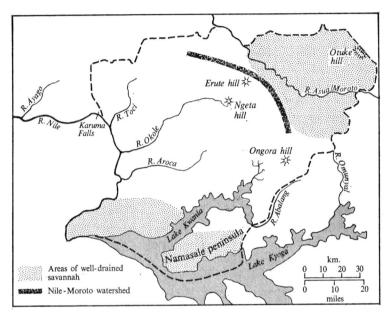

Map 2. Main Physical Features of Lango Country

The Nile–Moroto watershed (Map 2) is the approximate dividing line between two belts of vegetation. South of the watershed, the extreme evenness of elevation is related to the course of the Nile. From the point where it enters Lake Kyoga as far as Karuma Falls— a distance of over one hundred miles—the Nile loses little height and flows very slowly, especially through Lakes Kyoga and Kwania, and for much of this passage the river is concealed from the banks by a thick cover of aquatic vegetation. The Nile and Lake Kwania are fed by numerous streams and rivers from the right bank, of which the most important are the Abalang (now the border between Lango and

[2] On Uganda Government maps, this river usually appears as the Asua, which is a corruption of the Acholi 'Acua'. In Lango, however, it is universally known as the Moroto, which is the name I use here.

Teso), the Aroca, the Okole, and the Toci. These streams too are very slow moving. With the exception of the Toci, no flow of water is perceptible during most of the year, and they have more the appearance of great swamps; indeed, the Langi themselves make no distinction between stream and swamp, but use the same word (*kulu*) for both. Some swamps are more than a mile wide and cannot be crossed at all in the rainy season. Apart from the Nile's main tributaries, there are hundreds of other small swamps which follow the slight declivities of the terrain; they are such a regular feature of the landscape that a Lango in giving directions to a stranger will say that his destination is so-many swamps away. Even in the dry season, few swamps run dry, so that no settlement in these parts is ever far from water; while during the rainy season Lango country is nearly always spared the widespread flooding which so drastically affects the Nilotes of the Southern Sudan. The natural vegetation in this area of Lango is deciduous woodland, the trees growing to a height of sixty feet, not as forest, but close enough together to exclude any cover of long grass underneath.

North of the watershed, the streams run clearer and faster, and they vary considerably in size according to the season. Even the Moroto, which flows north to join the Nile near the Uganda–Sudan border, is liable to become parched during a severe dry season, while at other times of the year its tributaries can swell quite suddenly. The annual rainfall is lower than in the south, and the dry season a little longer. As a result, the vegetation is more characteristic of well-drained savannah: shorter and more scattered trees, thinner soils, and higher grass-cover. On a more restricted scale, these conditions also prevail in the extreme south of the District—in the interior of Namasale peninsula and in the angle formed by the Nile further west. These less favoured areas in the north-east and south-west have the lowest densities of population.[3]

Throughout the period covered in this book, the Lango economy was closely dependent on these geographical factors. Even today such industry as the District possesses is bound up with locally grown crops, which in turn use few artificial aids to combat a tough environment. During the early nineteenth century, when technology was rudimentary and contacts with the outside world minimal, this de-

---

[3] Driberg, *The Lango*, pp. 43–6; I. Langdale-Brown and others, *The Vegetation of Uganda* (Entebbe, 1964); Uganda Government, *Atlas of Uganda* (Entebbe, 1962).

pendence was closer still. For reasons of soil and climate, Lango at that time conformed to the pattern of seed agriculture so prevalent in northern Uganda.[4] This was in contrast to southern Uganda, which for the most part practised a plant agriculture based on the banana. The Lango staple was finger-millet (eleusine), a crop well suited to light soils, high temperature, and uneven rainfall. Second in importance was sorghum which, while more resistant to drought and containing a higher level of protein, is less palatable both as food and when used for making beer. These crops made up the bulk of the diet in Lango.[5] No meal, however, was complete without a relish or sauce. For this purpose, the Langi grew simsim (sesame) for its high oil content, a tasty species of buck-wheat known as *malakwang*, pigeon-peas, and several varieties of bean; ground-nuts were also grown, but did not attain much popularity until the twentieth century.

As an indigenous cropping system, the Lango association of finger-millet, pigeon-peas, and simsim has been judged by one modern authority to be 'the best diet of vegetable protein anywhere in Uganda'.[6] The contrast in physique between the Langi and their Bantu neighbours, who practised a plantain agriculture, often provoked comment by early European observers.[7] However, there was another side to the picture. A millet-based agriculture requires much more labour than one based on the banana. The only perennial crop of the Lango complex was the pigeon-pea, and that was seldom left for more than three years before re-sowing. Millet in particular requires heavy labour every year for clearing the ground, weeding, and harvesting. In Lango, therefore, both men and women were regularly employed in the fields, in contrast to Buganda and Bunyoro where the women did most of the agricultural work.[8]

---

[4] This reconstruction of the nineteenth-century economy rests mainly on (*a*) the observations of Driberg (*The Lango*) at the very beginning of the colonial period, when the traditional economy was as yet untouched; and (*b*) on a large number of passing references to economic matters in the oral traditions which I collected, and which it would be impractical to enumerate here.

[5] The only other staple to be grown on a wide scale before the colonial period was the sweet potato, but this did not appear until mid-century, when it was introduced from Bunyoro (see below, p. 100). Maize and bananas had little impact. Cassava, so popular today, was not introduced until the colonial period.

[6] J. D. Jameson, 'Protein content of subsistence crops in Uganda', *East African Agricultural Jl.* 24 (1958), pp. 67–9.

[7] For the earliest such observation, see C. T. Wilson and R. W. Felkin, *Uganda and the Egyptian Soudan* (London, 1882), vol. II, pp. 53–4.

[8] D. N. McMaster, *A Subsistence Crop Geography of Uganda* (Bude, 1962), pp. 48–50, 83–4.

A further disadvantage for the Langi lay in the yearly distribution of rainfall. In common with other Nilotic-speaking areas, there are effectively two seasons rather than four, the rainfall coming to a single peak, instead of two. The Langi recognized this by dividing the year into one dry season (*oro*) roughly from December to March, and one rainy season (*cwir*) from April to November.[9] By restricting the sowing of most crops to once a year, this two-season pattern limited net harvests and increased the chance of shortage, especially if the dry season was severe.

The agricultural year began at the end of the dry season, with the clearing and digging of the ground in preparation for sowing at the start of the rains. There might be a second sowing in June or July, if the rains let up, as they often do at that time. Harvesting could begin as early as June and continue until November. By the time the dry season began in December, no crops could be expected for six months. It was therefore essential to cultivate the largest possible area, and to store the surplus in granaries; millet is well suited for this, since after careful preparation it can be kept for three years or more.[10]

So far as cultivation goes, the dry season was for the most part a period of enforced leisure. Other activities which were not so dependent on the cycle of seasons tended to be concentrated in this period, for example public rituals and celebrations. Once a certain amount of the harvest had been set aside as a reserve, the remainder was used for beer, and large quantities were made at the beginning of the dry season. No public ritual could be performed without beer being provided, and the same was true of purely leisure pursuits, such as drumming and dancing. All these activities flourished in the relaxed atmosphere after the harvest was complete.[11] Economically, the most important dry-season pursuit was hunting. Lango abounded in elephant, buffalo, rhinoceros, and several species of antelope. Hunting could be organized at any time—for example to protect crops—but it was concentrated in the dry season, partly because conditions were then best suited to the favourite Lango technique of beating out the game by setting fire to the bush, and partly because game meat was a very welcome addition to the diet towards the end

[9] Driberg, *The Lango*, p. 48.
[10] Driberg, *The Lango*, pp. 98–9; McMaster, op. cit.
[11] Driberg, op. cit., p. 129; R. T. Curley, *Elders, Shades and Women: Ceremonial Change in Lango, Uganda* (Berkeley, 1973), p. 71.

of the dry season.[12] In addition, those Langi who lived on the lake-shore or along the principal rivers supplemented hunting with fishing.[13]

Besides cultivation and hunting, there was in the early nineteenth century one other means of subsistence—animal husbandry.[14] Goats were so frequently slaughtered for ritual feats that they constituted an important source of food. Sheep and poultry were also kept. But more important than any of these in Lango eyes were cattle. Until the rinderpest epidemic of the 1890s, the short-horned zebu was kept in large numbers nearly everywhere in Lango.[15] The distribution of permanent swamps and streams was such that, even in the dry season, it was normal for cattle to be pastured near the homesteads of their owners, who therefore had no need to resort to the seasonal trans-humance of peoples like the Jie and the Turkana.[16] As was the case in so much of East Africa, and especially among non-Bantu peoples, cattle were crucial in a wide range of economic and social contexts. They were the principal form of wealth and unit of account. They were also the preferred payment for both bridewealth and com-pensation for offences, and the way in which cattle transferred in these contexts were then distributed among kin was a significant index of social relationships. On important ritual occasions, cattle were slaughtered and eaten ceremonially. However the Lango appetite for meat was satisfied more by game than by domestic animals. In everyday life cattle were an asset not so much for their meat as for their milk, which was drunk curdled or made into butter.[17]

Throughout the nineteenth century the pattern of Lango sub-sistence was made up of crops, livestock, and game, and the balance between them did not shift until the great rinderpest epidemic of the 1890s. The technology with which these resources were exploited was based on iron, and this too hardly changed. Iron spearheads (for hunting game) and iron knives (for preparing meat) were universal. Iron hoes were also used, though it was not until the beginning of the

---

[12] Driberg, *The Lango*, pp. 112–18. For an account of hunting in its social con-text during the nineteenth century, see below, pp. 53–4.

[13] Driberg, *The Lango*, pp. 121–2.

[14] For the earliest reference to the combination of seed agriculture and animal husbandry in Lango, see C. Piaggia, 'Sesto viaggio di Carlo Piaggia sul Fiume Bianco nel 1876', *Bollettino della Società Geografica Italiana*, 14 (1877), p. 389.

[15] The pastoral wealth of the Langi is commented on in S. W. Baker, *Ismailia* (London, 1874), vol. II, pp. 102–3; and in Wilson and Felkin, op. cit., vol. II, p. 55. For the rinderpest, see below, ch. 4.

[16] P. H. Gulliver, *The Family Herds* (London, 1955).

[17] Driberg, op. cit., pp. 91–3.

colonial period that they began to supersede the traditional wooden digging-stick in some parts of Lango.[18] Otherwise Lango technology remained constant.

According to conventional ethnographic classification, the bulk of northern Uganda's population falls into two groups: the Nilotes and the 'Nilo-Hamites',[19] or Para-Nilotes as they are now more widely known.[20] Each of these groups is also represented on a significant scale in Kenya and the Southern Sudan. Although there is a certain amount of linguistic ground common to them all, the Para-Nilotic languages can readily be distinguished as a group from the Nilotic. Each group can be further subdivided along linguistic lines, but in the present context only two subdivisions need to be considered: the Southern Lwo, who are Nilotes, and the Central Para-Nilotes.[21] The Southern Lwo include the Alur, Acholi, and Kenya Luo, and they have become completely separated from the Northern Lwo (e.g. the Shilluk), who live in the Southern Sudan. The Central Para-Nilotes include the Iteso, Karimojong, Dodos, Jie, and Turkana, the last four being generally referred to as the 'Karimojong Cluster'.[22] Close contact between Southern Lwo and Central Para-Nilotes over the last two hundred years or so has made it difficult to attribute precise cultural traits, but broadly speaking Lwo social organization is based

[18] The use of iron in nineteenth century Lango is discussed more fully below, pp. 83–4.

[19] A. Butt, *The Nilotes of the Anglo-Egyptian Sudan and Uganda* (London, 1952); P. and P. H. Gulliver, *The Central Nilo-Hamites* (London, 1953). Both volumes belong to the International African Institute's *Ethnographic Survey of Africa*.

[20] Since not even the Central Para-Nilotes acknowledge a common name for themselves, ethnographers have to fall back on an external linguistic classification. The most plausible alternative yet proposed to the discredited 'Nilo-Hamitic' is 'Para-Nilotic'. A. N. Tucker and M. A. Bryan, *Linguistic Analyses: the Non-Bantu Languages of North-Eastern Africa* (London, 1966).

[21] A. N. Tucker and M. A. Bryan, *The Non-Bantu Language of North East Africa* (London, 1956), pp. 94–117, 149–50. These authors do not actually use the term 'Central Para-Nilotic', but this term corresponds exactly with their 'Teso Language Group' and with the 'Central Nilo-Hamites' as identified in the *Ethnographic Survey of Africa*. (P. and P. H. Gulliver, op. cit.). Recent writers have begun to refer to the Lwo-speaking peoples of Uganda as the 'Central Lwo' (see, for example, J. M. Onyango-ku-Odongo and J. B. Webster (eds.), *The Central Lwo during the Aconya* (Nairobi, 1976)). There appear to be no linguistic grounds for this additional category, though it is convenient for geographical reasons.

[22] P. and P. H. Gulliver, op. cit., p. 9. This term entails somewhat dubious assumptions about the origins of the peoples concerned, but it is a convenient label.

on segmentary systems of descent groups, while the Para-Nilotes have depended more on age or generation groups, and have been even more wedded to pastoral values than their Lwo neighbours. There are several peoples in northern Uganda which cannot confidently be attributed to either group. The Labwor, Nyakwai, and Kumam are cases in point. But much the most important are the Langi, who easily outnumber the other three together. Lango culture contains, in substantial measure, both Nilotic and Para-Nilotic elements. Of the Nilotic, the most significant is language: Lango is classified as one of the Southern Lwo group and is closely related to Acholi.[23] So far as social organization goes, Lango is generally regarded as being closer to the pattern of hereditary clan chiefdoms in Acholi than to the less stratified, more variegated social structure found among the Central Para-Nilotes.[24] Thus language and social organization, which are the principal criteria of conventional ethnographic classification, have caused the Langi to be labelled as Nilotes.[25]

Against this must be set the weight of Lango traditions, which are almost unanimous in pointing to an eastern origin among the present-day speakers of Para-Nilotic.[26] This grass-roots view is supported by linguistic evidence that the Langi once spoke a Para-Nilotic tongue;[27] by several features of ritual practice also found in Teso; and by a number of important clan names with a clear eastern provenance.[28] Particularly significant is the fact that other Lwo-speaking peoples do not regard the Langi as being Lwo at all. Thus the Alur regard the Acholi and the Jopadhola as fellow Lwo, sharing in some degree a common history, but they see the Langi as an alien stock—a sentiment which is fully reciprocated. The rich store of Lwo traditions has little place in Lango folklore, and if well-known Lwo stories are recounted in Lango, they are seldom placed in a historical context.[29]

[23] Tucker and Bryan, *Non-Bantu Languages*, pp. 103–4.
[24] See below, chapters 2 and 3.   [25] Butt, op. cit.; *Atlas of Uganda*, op. cit.
[26] A. Tarantino, 'The Origin of the Lango', *Uganda Jl.* 10 (1946), pp. 12–16. The traditions set out by Tarantino are fully corroborated in the traditions which I collected.
[27] A. N. Tucker, 'Some problems of junction in Lango', *Mitteilungen des Instituts Für Orientforschung*, 6 (1958), p. 142. Professor Tucker has not yet published his evidence for this assertion.
[28] These clans are Atek, Arak, Okarowok, and Otengoro.
[29] For an interesting exception, see N. Engola, 'Olden times in northern Lango', translation of undated vernacular MS, Department of History, Makerere University. This author uses the story of the bead, the spear and the elephant to describe a supposed split between the Langi and the Jopadhola. The original version of the story is found in J. P. Crazzolara, *The Lwoo*, 3 parts (Verona, 1950–4), pp. 62–6.

This combination of diverse cultural traits suggests that the Langi, far from having a single origin, represent a fusion between different groups. The evidence afforded by oral traditions collected in Lango and the surrounding areas leaves little doubt that this was in fact the case, and the composition of these groups and the sequence of their migrations are now reasonably clear.[30]

Chronologically the problem begins with the Lwo migration of the fifteenth century. The history of human settlement in Lango did not, of course, begin at this point, but in the present state of archaeological research any discussion of the earlier period would be wholly speculative. By contrast, the remarkable consistency of traditions among all Southern Lwo groups—from the Alur in the west to the Kenya Luo in the east—has allowed historians to reconstruct with some confidence the migrations which brought the Southern Lwo from their cradleland in the Sudan. During the fifteenth century they began to advance southwards from a halting-place in the Nile valley, near Nimule (on the Uganda–Sudan border), splitting up and dispersing as they went. Over a period of some two hundred years, increasing numbers of Lwo settled in northern Uganda with their herds of cattle along the Nile and its tributaries, where they practised a mixed economy of seed-agriculture and pastoralism. The Lwo made their strongest impact in Alurland, western Acholi, and Padhola, and also in eastern Bunyoro, where as Jopalwo or 'Chope' they maintained an identity separate from the Bantu world around them. The indigenous peoples were assimilated both linguistically and politically, and there emerged a number of small chiefdoms, dominated in most cases by a royal clan of Lwo origin and ruled by a *rwot*.[31]

Present-day Lango was part of the broad stage across which the Lwo were migrating and settling between about 1500 and 1700. Dense and permanent settlement, however, appears to have been confined to three areas. Of greatest importance was the right bank of the Nile on either side of Karuma Falls, including the Toci and Aroca rivers. The second zone was the region of Lake Kwania, where the Lwo estab-

---

[30] The evidence for the conclusions presented here is complex, and in the past has given rise to conflicting interpretations. Since these matters are not directly relevant, detailed discussion is reserved for Appendix 1, and only an outline is given here.

[31] Crazzolara, op. cit., parts 1 and 2; R. Oliver, 'Discernible developments in the interior c. 1500–1840' in *History of East Africa*, vol. I, ed. R. Oliver and G. Mathew (Oxford, 1963), pp. 171–80; Ogot, *History of the Southern Luo*, vol. I, pp. 40–7.

lished themselves in large numbers, especially on the eastern side. Lastly, there was the valley of the Moroto, together with the Lira area to the south; this zone seems to have attracted the least settlers. It can be seen from Map 3 that the Lwo settled in just those areas which they might have been expected to prefer: well-watered locations near rivers and lakes. They avoided the drier regions of the north-east and extreme south-west. There seems to have been no population pressure or intense rivalry for resources. Even along the main watercourses the population was probably sparse and village communities widely spaced.

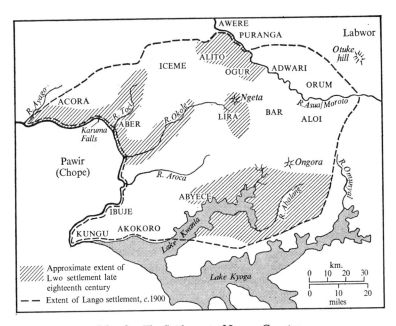

Map 3.   The Settlement of Lango Country

Had the Lwo contribution been confined to these Lwo settlements established before 1750 in Lango country, it would scarcely explain the strong Nilotic elements in Lango culture, and particularly the Lango language. In fact the Lwo also played a vital role in the migrations into Lango from the north-east, which began towards the end of the eighteenth century and were the final stage in the formation of the Lango people. Much light has been shed on these migrations by

Lamphear's recent research among the Jie, a Para-Nilotic people who live in central Karamoja.[32] This area is today predominantly—though not exclusively—a pastoral one, but it only became so around the middle of the eighteenth century, when newcomers entered Jieland from above the Rift Valley Escarpment in the east. Up to that time the existing Para-Nilotic population was predominantly an agricultural one, dependent on millet, sorghum, and simsim. It was this group, known as the Iseera, which began the migrations into Lango. When the pastoralists from the east reached Jieland, a significant proportion of the Iseera migrated south-westwards into Labwor. Then, towards the end of the eighteenth century, a disastrous famine in Labwor caused many of the Iseera to resume their migration, which took them on into present-day Lango. By this time, however, the Iseera themselves were a hybrid group. For many years Lwo had been infiltrating from the west, to such an extent that the Iseera were already bilingual before their departure from Jieland. During their migration to the south-west, they encountered and absorbed still more Lwo communities along the rivers of Labwor. By the time the migrants reached the vicinity of Otuke hill, on the borders of Lango country, they already spoke a language approximating to the modern Lango variant of Lwo. In other words, the basic assimilation between Lwo and Para-Nilotes had been achieved before the easterners reached Lango.[33]

The advance of the Langi from Otuke into their present homeland did not take the form of one migration along a single route.[34] One group, appreciably ahead of the rest, quickly advanced westwards as far as the Nile in about 1780. The movement of the main body began around 1800, and the dispersion from Otuke seems to have continued into the early nineteenth century.[35] The Langi left Otuke at different times and by different routes, some continuing along the north side of the Moroto river for the time being, while others went south immediately. From clan migration traditions it is evident that certain places in Lango were important as dispersion points. One of these places—and the best known today—is said to have been Ngeta rock, near

[32] J. Lamphear, *The Traditional History of the Jie of Uganda* (Oxford, 1976). The extent of my debt to Dr. Lamphear will be evident from Appendix 1.

[33] For a more comprehensive account and a consideration of the evidence, see Appendix 1.

[34] The accounts of both Driberg (*The Lango*, p. 32) and Tarantino ('Notes on the Lango', *Uganda Jl.*, 13 (1949), pp. 146–7) are misleading in this respect.

[35] Driberg, *The Lango*, pp. 26–9, 31; Crazzolara, op. cit., pp. 88, 564.

Lira. Another was Ongora rock, near Abako, and the nearby complex of swamps north of Lake Kwania.[36]

These traditions about concentrations and dispersals refer to the early nineteenth century, when the new arrivals from the north-east seem to have been, in effect, prospecting potential areas of settlement without putting down roots. Secondary migration within Lango country was not, however, restricted to the early part of the century, but continued on a massive scale until the 1880s, and to a more limited extent until the early years of this century. For it is a striking fact that, in most parts of Lango, continuous settlement by the present occupants dates back no further than the second half of the century, approximate dates being: Aloi, 1840–50; Bar, 1850–60; Dokolo, 1870; Acora, late 1870s; Abyece, 1880–85; Iceme, early 1880s; Akokoro, 1888–90 (Map 3).[37] As for the migrations which immediately preceded permanent settlement—and these are the migrations remembered today—there was a wide range of possible motives. Sometimes the deciding factor was political or social, such as tension within the clan, or between clans.[38] But economic considerations were quite as important; a localized drought, a cattle epidemic, or an outbreak of smallpox could cause migration.

One factor predominated over all others, and that was the quest for wild game. Discussion of the different modes of subsistence in northern Uganda tends to turn on seed agriculture and animal husbandry. This focus is justified today in view of the almost total disappearance of big game outside the reserves. Seen historically, however, the stress on food production to the exclusion of hunting is misleading. The present-day decline of wild animals is due precisely to the importance which hunting until recently occupied in the subsistence economy. There is abundant evidence of this in the case of Lango. The outstanding physique of the Langi was attributed by early European observers as much to their high consumption of game as to their happy combination of crops.[39] The 'courage and

---

[36] The migration traditions of some forty clans have been collected to date, by Canon Ogwal and by the present writer. R. Ogwal, untitled vernacular MS., translated as 'A History of Lango Clans', mimeo, Department of History, Makerere University, 1969.

[37] These dates are calculated from the oral traditions which I collected in each of these localities, assisted in some instances by European travel literature of the time.

[38] See below, Chapter 2.

[39] Wilson and Felkin, op. cit., vol. II, pp. 53–4; Driberg, The Lango, p. 104.

perseverance' of the Langi were compared favourably with the less dedicated approach to hunting shown by the Acholi.[40] There were five recognized methods of hunting, and very few wild animals were subject to ritual prohibitions.[41] Several accounts say that the Langi first got to know their present country through hunting expeditions from afar.[42] This pattern continued throughout the nineteenth century. Time and again, settlement traditions explain that clans moved to fresh localities because there was plentiful game there which, in many cases, had already been hunted during dry-season forays from the old home. The Ibuje area on the Nile was not settled until about 1880, but we know from J. W. Grant's account that Lango hunters were going there as early as 1862.[43] Hunting expeditions even crossed Lake Kwania by canoe to try their luck in Namasale peninsula.[44]

This preoccupation with game offers the most convincing explanation for the speed with which a relatively small population colonized so large an area—5,000 square miles in less than a hundred years. So rapid an expansion cannot be accounted for by the pattern of agricultural land use. The rotational bush-fallow cultivation practised in Lango required that fields be allowed to revert to bush after three or four years' cultivation, but so far as can be told from observations made during the first half of this century the population was seldom so dense or good land so scarce as to demand more than a small adjustment in the location of the homestead.[45] On the other hand, a community accustomed to a regular supply of game meat would soon reach the point when its requirements were better served by hunting in new tracts, than by exploiting the diminishing assets of the immediate

[40] C. A. Sykes, *Service and Sport on the Tropical Nile* (London, 1903), p. 177. Sykes's comment is interesting in view of his scorn for the Langi in every other respect, and his own skill as a big game hunter.

[41] Driberg, *The Lango*, pp. 104, 112–18. Hunting methods are described below, pp. 53–4.

[42] Tarantino, 'Notes on the Lango', p. 147; Driberg, op. cit., p. 27; Ogwal Ajungu, untitled vernacular history (1936–7), MS. in the possession of Dr. T. T. S. Hayley, para. 1.

[43] J. W. Grant, *A Walk Across Africa* (London, 1864), p. 303. Interviews: Okelo Abak, Anderea Ogwang, Yakobo Gaci.

[44] Interview: Becweri Ongebo (conducted by J. A. Otima, as part of the undergraduate research scheme of the History Department of Makerere University in 1969).

[45] Driberg, op. cit., pp. 96, 98; J. D. Tothill (ed.), *Agriculture in Uganda* (London, 1940), pp. 47–8. Cf. W. Allan, *The African Husbandman* (Edinburgh, 1965), p. 187.

neighbourhood. The survival well into the colonial period of big game even in the longest settled parts of Lango is not inconsistent with this interpretation: what counted was the disparity, which must quickly have arisen, between the game resources of a settled area and those of an unsettled or more sparsely-populated area.

If the impetus for migration was most often provided by hunting, the actual choice of settlement sites was determined by agricultural considerations. It is said that the earliest Lango settlers on the northern shores of Namasale peninsula tested the fertility of the soil by sowing seed there during their hunting expeditions across Lake Kwania; only then did they decide to migrate south of the lake.[46] The swampy terrain of much of Lango was certainly unfamiliar to the migrants from Otuke, but they realized soon enough that Lango's agricultural potential lay in the marshy areas.[47] The new population was concentrated along the watercourses, particularly in western Lango where it was densest along the Aroca, Okole, and Toci; as late as 1910 the country between those rivers was very sparsely populated.[48] The ideal site was a rise or ridge above a swamp, but any place with surface water near at hand was acceptable. By 1910 the Langi were very much more evenly distributed than their predecessors had been. In the south, excluding Namasale and the extreme south-west, the density of population had resulted in the almost complete clearance of woodland, and its replacement as natural cover by the characteristic 'elephant-grass', eight to ten feet high.[49]

The areas which attracted the most Lango settlers were, of course, precisely those riverain localities which the Lwo had made their own during the previous three hundred years. One would therefore suppose that from the early nineteenth century contact between the two groups was intensive. Lango tradition, while admitting to such contact, limits it to the Lwo along the Toci and Okole, and stresses the aggressive aspect. Some of the Lwo are said to have been pushed into Chope (the Lwo-speaking enclave in Bunyoro) and Acholi by the Lango vanguard around 1800, and others were expelled by later

---

[46] Interview: Becweri Ongebo (conducted by J. A. Otima).

[47] The unfamiliarity of the terrain is delightfully conveyed in the following story. When the Langi first reached the edge of their present country, they walked gingerly, fearing that the soft earth would swallow them up. They did not resume their normal gait until they saw a hartebeest running at a great pace in front of them. (Ogwal Ajungu, op. cit., para. 1.)

[48] Tufnell, Map of Lango District, Oct. 1910, UNA SMP/519/09.

[49] Driberg, The Lango, p. 44.

settlers in the 1860s and 1870s.[50] There is no doubt that such forcible expulsions did occur,[51] but they are not the whole story. Despite the universal Lwo opinion that the Langi are an alien stock, the new-comers from the east cannot have seemed so very strange, with their Lwo language and their mixed subsistence economy; there is no reason for thinking that this encounter differed from the earlier peaceful assimilation between Lwo and Iseera in Jieland and Labwor. The comparatively high density of population in the Toci valley would certainly suggest a continued Lwo presence there.[52] As for more direct indications, some Lango accounts admit that trade and intermarriage took place,[53] and—more important—the occurrence in north-western Lango of composite clan names which mix Para-Nilotic with Lwo roots is strong evidence that Lwo groups were absorbed into Lango clans.[54] As a discrete element, the Lwo survived longest west of the Toci. In 1880 Emin Pasha found Lwo and Lango villages intermingled in Acora (near the Ayago river) and on the north side of Karuma Falls, and this pattern was still discernible in the 1920s.[55] Elsewhere in Lango, the evidence about early contacts with the Lwo is far more slender. Lango traditions are understandably reticent on the subject, and the details of assimilation remain obscure.

Map 3 shows the extent of Lango settlement on the eve of the colonial period. Most of this territory had been taken over by the Langi early in the nineteenth century, but the extremities had been settled much more recently and some were still untouched. In the west, the expansion of the Langi had taken them as far as the Ayago river by 1880, and as far as Kungu in the angle of the Nile by 1900. In the south, no attempt had yet been made to penetrate the inhospit-able centre of Namasale peninsula,[56] but further east most of the fertile region between Lakes Kwania and Kyoga had been colonized.[57]

[50] Driberg, *The Lango*, p. 26; Crazzolara, op. cit., pp. 88–9. Interviews: Bartolomayo Okori, Leoben Okodi, Yakobo Olugo, Suleman Ikwe.
[51] Acholi traditions indicate as much. R. S. Anywar, *Acholi ki ker megi* (Kampala, 1954), p. 135.
[52] This density was first noted in 1900. Anderson to Johnston, 21.3.00, UNA A4/27.
[53] Interviews: Erisa Olugo, Misaki Oki.
[54] Examples of such clan names are: Okarowok me Acore, Arak me Alwaa.
[55] G. Schweinfurth and others (ed.), *Emin Pasha in Central Africa* (London, 1888), pp. 280–1, 286–7; Rubie, entry for 2.9.25 in Paranga TB (1925–6), ADA.
[56] C. E. Fishbourne, 'Lake Kioga (Ibrahim) Exploration Survey, 1907–8', *Geographical Jl.*, 33 (1909), p. 195.
[57] Ormsby, Sketch of Umiru, October 1908, UNA SMP/1822/08; Jervoise, undated entry in Kioga TB (1912–13), TDA.

The extreme north-east, across the Moroto river, was one of the last major areas of permanent settlement; despite its proximity to the eighteenth-century homeland of the Langi, the dry country between Orum and Otuke was still empty.[58] With these exceptions, the confines of Lango country at the turn of the century were roughly as they are today.

The pattern of migration and settlement outlined above was the foundation of Lango tribal identity during the nineteenth century. Internally, there was little institutional basis for a sense of 'Langoness'. Lango society not only lacked the cohesion of a central political authority; it also exhibited considerable variation in the *forms* of social organization.[59] The Langi owed their collective identity not to any internal consistency, but to a historical experience which set them apart from their neighbours. Above all, they were distinguished by the particular way in which Lwo and Iseera groups had combined in Karamoja towards the end of the eighteenth century. Several neighbouring peoples can, of course, be analysed in terms of these same two constituents, but there the 'mix' has taken different forms. In the case of the Labwor, Iteso, and Kumam, these different forms are reflected linguistically, with Para-Nilotic traits of speech much more to the fore. Between the Langi and the Acholi the distinction is not so clear-cut linguistically, but it is reflected in other ways, notably in the contention by both peoples that the Acholi are 'Lwo' while the Langi are not. In this respect the Otuke tradition plays a crucial role. Very few Langi will admit today that their own ancestors did not come from Otuke hill, notwithstanding the contrary evidence afforded by some of their clan-names and by the migration traditions of neighbouring peoples. Those Lwo groups who were living in Lango country before the easterners arrived, and who were then assimilated, subsequently expressed their new identity as Langi by subscribing to the Otuke tradition. The migration from Jieland at the end of the eighteenth century was the central historical experience of the majority, and in time it came to be the defining attribute of Lango identity.

That this identity was a reality during the nineteenth century is shown by what is known of the history of the word 'Lango'. Many tribal names in East Africa originate in the labels—often derogatory

---

[58] Interview: Ogwel Okolla. Driberg, entry for 12.2.18, in Moroto TB (1918–26), LDA.

[59] See below, Chapters 2 and 3.

—which were attached to them by their neighbours and then taken over by badly informed governments. The term 'Lango' certainly lends itself to this kind of interpretation since it was commonly used by Lwo groups when referring to non-Lwo, including the Langi.[60] However the writings of European travellers of the late nineteenth century show that the Langi acknowledged the name as their own, though its origin is obscure. The earliest accounts are those of Speke and Grant, who journeyed down the Victoria Nile in 1862; they referred to the Langi as 'Kidi', a corruption of the label 'Bakedi' which the Banyoro applied to the Langi.[61] Travellers approaching from the north normally referred to the Langi by their modern name,[62] but this might simply be due to the use of Acholi informants who would have described any non-Lwo as 'Lango'. Much more significant is the use of the term by the missionary R. W. Felkin; he approached Lango in 1879 from the Bantu-speaking south, where the word 'Lango' had no meaning.[63] Comparable weight should be attached to the use of the term by Casati, who was resident at the royal court of Bunyoro from 1886 to 1888.[64] These references apply only to the extreme west of Lango country, near the Nile. However, in 1899 the first British officer to traverse southern Lango reported that 'the inhabitants invariably call themselves "Lango" '.[65] Since then the only development has been the popularization of the variant 'Langi' during the last thirty years. Evidently 'Lango' as an ethnic label was not an invention of the colonial period; the word has an indigenous ancestry as the expression of a cultural identity. The question which cannot be answered is just how early in the nineteenth century this identity gained common acceptance.

[60] Thus the Acholi referred to the Central Para-Nilotes as 'Lango-dyang' and to the Langi as 'Lango-omiru'. The Acholi were, on the other hand, responsible for pinning the name 'Lango' on to the small Para-Nilotic tribe of this name who live near the Agoro mountains of the Southern Sudan; there is in fact no connection between this group and the Langi of Uganda. C. G. and B. Z. Seligman, *Pagan Tribes of the Nilotic Sudan* (London, 1932), p. 346; L. F. Nalder (ed.), *Tribal Survey of Mongalla Province* (Oxford, 1937), p. 82.

[61] J. H. Speke, *Journal of the Discovery of the Source of the Nile* (London, 1863), p. 500; Grant, op. cit., pp. 290, 303.

[62] The earliest example is Baker, *Ismailia*, vol. II, p. 220 (referring to 1872).

[63] Wilson and Felkin, op. cit., vol. II, p. 53.

[64] G. Casati, *Ten Years in Equatoria* (London, 1891), vol. II, p. 31.

[65] Evatt to Ternan, 10.5.99, UNA A4/17.

According to information received by Driberg, disagreement as to which side was entitled to the honoured name 'Lango' was one of the causes of fighting between the Langi and Kumam in pre-administration days. Driberg, undated entry in Dokolo TB (1913–26, part 1), LDA.

CHAPTER 2

Social Groups in Nineteenth-Century Lango

OF the anthropological studies made of stateless peoples in Africa over the last forty years, a high proportion has concerned peoples whose social organization is based on segmentary lineage systems. Among the Nuer, the *locus classicus* of this kind of social organization, the political community, or tribe, comprises several levels of territorial segmentation. Each segment is identified with a nuclear lineage, round which other lineages are clustered, and these nuclear lineages constitute a pyramidal genealogical structure, so that relations between territorial segments are conceptualized by the Nuer as relations between lineages. Equivalent segments will co-operate as part of a larger segment or oppose one another according to the issues of the moment. These complementary processes of fission and fusion mean that social cohesion is maintained without violating the egalitarian values to which the Nuer are so deeply committed; the political system is best characterized, in Evans-Pritchard's vivid phrase, as an 'ordered anarchy'.[1] A number of other African peoples conform to modified versions of the Nuer type, and these peoples have exercised a considerable influence on African ethnography. Indeed, to read some of the standard works of political anthropology, one would suppose that segmentary lineage systems accounted for the majority of stateless societies in Africa.[2] This is far from being the case. Segmentary lineage systems have received extensive coverage in the literature, not because they are of frequent occurrence on the ground, but because of the considerable theoretical interest which they hold for social scientists.

Two recent classifications have taken more account of the diversity of social systems which actually exists in Africa. They are the work of social anthropologists, but—interestingly enough—what prompted each of them was a request from historians for a convenient

---

[1] Evans-Pritchard, *The Nuer*, p. 6.

[2] Fortes and Evans-Pritchard, *African Political Systems*. Middleton and Tait, *Tribes Without Rulers*.

ethnographic guide. Horton distinguishes three broad categories of stateless society in West Africa. Firstly, the segmentary lineage system; secondly, the dispersed, territorially-defined community, in which co-residence carries more weight than genealogical ties; and thirdly, the large compact village in which cross-cutting institutions such as age-grades or secret societies predominate over kinship relations.[3] Elizabeth Colson, surveying the entire continent on the eve of the colonial period, offers a broadly similar threefold typology.[4] Societies based on associations such as age-sets or secret societies constitute the first type; then come the segmentary lineage systems; and lastly, 'there were large areas that depended upon an amorphous network of personal relationships for the ordering of public life'.[5] In these 'amorphous' societies the local community typically numbered some five hundred persons, and the wider mobilization which both the other two types could occasionally achieve was out of the question. This last category has attracted little attention from anthropologists, Colson's own studies of the Plateau Tonga of Zambia being the principal exception.[6]

It is this 'amorphous' type which corresponds most closely to pre-colonial Lango society. The correspondence is not exact, because Lango society was not static during the nineteenth century. Early in the century an age-organization provided a broader means of social cohesion for most parts of Lango; and large-scale military combinations were able to repulse slave-raiders at home and to go on expeditions in the interlacustrine kingdoms. But these were precarious combinations which depended less on institutional ties than on personal leadership, and by the 1890s they had collapsed.[7] In all save exceptional circumstances, the political community amounted to no more than a cluster of clan sections distributed over a handful of villages, and numbering between 200 and 500 adult males. These villages lacked the wider affiliations of a segmentary lineage system; nor, by the end of the nineteenth century, was the age-organization strong enough to offset their parochial focus.

Limitations of evidence for pre-colonial Lango preclude the level

---

[3] Horton, 'Stateless societies in the history of West Africa', in *History of West Africa*, vol. I, pp. 78–119.

[4] E. Colson, 'African society at the time of the scramble', in *Colonialism in Africa, 1870–1960*, vol. I, ed. L. H. Gann and P. Duignan (Cambridge, 1969), pp. 27–65.   [5] Ibid., p. 48.

[6] E. Colson, *The Plateau Tonga of Northern Rhodesia: Social and Religious Studies* (Manchester, 1962).   [7] See below, Chapter 4.

of sophistication which social anthropologists achieve in their analysis of present-day societies and those of the very recent past. But one aspect of their method is inescapable, and that is to begin the analysis at the bottom of society with the most basic associations of kinship and neighbourhood. In one sense, such groups are the foundations on which all societies rest, but in a stateless society they are especially so, since many social institutions of a non-political appearance in fact fulfil important political functions. No analysis of an acephalous society can therefore proceed far which does not take kinship and residential groups as its point of departure. This chapter defines the nature of these groups—their composition, range, and cohesion, and the extent to which territorial and descent groups were coterminous. Other groupings of a wider territorial range and a more specialized role, including the age-organization, are described at the end of the chapter. How the political community was organized and how it operated in practice are questions reserved for Chapter 3.

In kinship terms, Lango society during the nineteenth century could be labelled as patrilineal, virilocal, and polygynous.[8] Descent was reckoned in the male line, the descendants of a male ancestor constituting an exogamous descent group, which was a social as well as a genealogical reality; that is, its members shared common interests. From the point of view of his position in society, the individual's most important links were with his agnates—those to whom he was closely related in the male line. Ideally, agnates lived together, and they were bound to each other by mutual obligations of labour and property. They regarded their descent group as having a permanence of its own, irrespective of the fate of the individual members; they therefore shared a common preoccupation with both deceased and unborn members of the group. The first preoccupation was expressed in ancestor rites,[9] and the second in the regulation of marriage. All descent groups were concerned to ensure their survival and expansion. To this end, a woman was required on marriage to associate herself

---

[8] For many of the general statements about Lango society in this chapter it is impractical to give source references. 135 Lango informants were interviewed, and few of them did not contribute in some way to my understanding of the issues discussed here. In the pages which follow, informants are only cited on points of specific detail. Otherwise references are confined to published works, and to unpublished writings accessible to scholars.

[9] Ancestor worship as such played little part in Lango religion, but relations with the dead were important in a number of ways. See below, pp. 54–6.

with her husband's descent group. Apart from leaving her own family, the most important way in which she associated herself with her husband's group was by upholding its ritual observances, or taboos (*kwer*).[10] Most commonly these prohibited the eating of certain animals or the touching of certain plants. In a few instances all members of the clan and their wives were included under the prohibition; more typically, boys before puberty were affected. But the majority of taboos in Lango applied only to women who had married into the clan, and the rules were particularly strict with regard to the pregnant woman; the prohibitions stressed her new loyalties and her well-being at those times when she was able by childbirth to contribute most to her husband's descent group.[11] Her daughters were given in marriage to other descent groups, and the bridewealth surrendered in exchange was used to procure wives for her own sons and so ensure the future of their group. The more children a wife had, the greater her worth in the eyes of her husband and his agnates.

Just as it was desirable for a woman to bear many children, so it was desirable for a man to marry many wives. If a man was rich in livestock, the best way in which he could serve the interests of his descent group was to use them as bridewealth for himself, his sons, or his immediate agnates. Polygyny was the ideal, but since the marriageable age for both sexes was nearly the same, the ideal was not widely attainable. All the same, polygynous households were by no means rare. Among important men, three to five wives were common.[12] The polygynous husband established for each wife a separate household with its own fields, and he directed his marital attentions and his labour to each in turn.

The Langi distinguished between two levels of descent group: the lineage (*doggola*) and above that the clan (*atekere*). Both the lineage and the clan were named groups whose members were referred to as, for example, Jo Elwia ('The Elwia people', a lineage) or Jo Arak ('The Arak people', a clan). If a clan was small, compact, and of recent origin, its members might make no further distinction, in which case clan and lineage would be one and the same. Usually, though, clans

---

[10] There is some doubt as to whether the prohibitions correspond to the strictest definition of the word 'taboo', but I have chosen to follow the most recent anthropological authority on the Langi. Curley, *Elders, Shades, and Women*, p. 41.

[11] For a list of taboos, see Driberg, *The Lango*, pp. 192–204.

[12] For example, Akaki of Akokoro (*c*. 1850–1936) had five wives and at least nine sons who grew to maturity. Interview: Yakobo Adoko.

included two or more lineages, and the number tended to increase as the clan expanded in size. In everyday life the lineage was the more important of the two. It varied in size, but the essential point was that there should be reasonable agreement among members as to the composition of their lineage and the genealogical relationships within it—even if these were sometimes based on fictional descent. The generation-depth of the lineage was defined by the common acknowledgement of an ancestor from whom all members of the lineage could in theory trace their descent. The knowledge which the members had of their lineage was usually based on the fact that they lived close together, within easy reach of one another for assistance, consultation, and participation in the round of domestic ceremonies concerned with birth and marriage. If members migrated far away from their lineage, they were likely to be assimilated to another lineage of their clan or in time to constitute a new lineage altogether.[13]

Once the individual travelled out of his immediate neighbourhood, his clan affiliations became more important to him than his lineage, both with regard to distant kinsmen and in his relations with total strangers. The clan was usually too large for all its members to be known personally to each other or to have any idea of how they were related, and these difficulties were increased if the clan was broken up into a number of territorially separated sections. Thus, while lineage membership could be taken for granted and needed little formal expression, clan membership was defined by various symbols. Each clan had its own clan cry which was uttered during ceremonies, in battle, and while hunting.[14] Cattle were branded with markings according to the clan membership of their owners.[15] The most important symbolic expression of clan membership was the taboo, which was the attribute of the clan, rather than the lineage, and applied to every household, regardless of lineage. Despite the everyday importance of the lineage, it was with the clan that the values of patrilineal kinship were associated, and it was the clan which evoked

---

[13] T. T. S. Hayley, *The Anatomy of Lango Religion and Groups* (Cambridge, 1947), p. 52; Curley, *Elders, Shades, and Women*, pp. 34–40.
Curley introduces the further concept of the 'local lineage', as against the *doggola* or maximal lineage, the first being localized and the second dispersed. This is a useful distinction in terms of present-day social realities, but there is no evidence that the *doggola* was commonly a dispersed group prior to the colonial period.
[14] Hayley, op. cit., pp. 42–3; Ogwal, 'A History of Lango Clans', p. 3.
[15] J. H. Driberg, *Engato the Lion Cub* (London, 1933), p. 29.

the strongest loyalty. A man identified himself by referring not to his lineage, still less to his village, but to his clan.

Respect for the corporate rights of the clan was strongest in the case of livestock. Cattle were regarded as the property of the clan, as is indicated by the practice of cattle-branding. This concept of clan ownership was quite logical in view of the role played by cattle in marriage transactions, which provided for the future of the clan. But in practice, cattle were individually owned and their products individually consumed. The rights of the lineage were most strongly asserted over the inheritance of property. A man could bequeath his property, but his wishes were subject to the decision of his lineage after the burial, and the final arrangements had to stay within certain limits. The wives of the deceased were usually inherited by his brothers. On the other hand, livestock and land under cultivation generally passed to the eldest son, who was then under an obligation to make provision for his uterine brothers and his half-brothers. Only if the lineage was dying out could property pass to kin outside the clan.[16]

From birth through marriage until death, lineage and clan loomed large in the daily life of the individual Lango, but they did not serve all his requirements. As a sedentary farmer he was a member of other groups, which were defined territorially rather than on kinship principles. The composition of these groups depended in the first instance on the requirements of co-operative labour. The system of subsistence agriculture practised in Lango—then as now—could only work satisfactorily if labour sources were pooled. Seed agriculture based on finger-millet involves seasonal peak demands on labour for sowing, weeding, and harvesting; moreover, the annual cycle of only two seasons means that there is great pressure to cultivate the largest possible area in order to supply food all the year round; as McMaster has put it, 'Northern Uganda faces the problem of concentrating agricultural activity to meet the requirements of the convergence of the rainfall regime towards a single peak'.[17] The response of the Langi to this situation was to arrange for the heaviest tasks to be performed by a work-group which attended each member's plot in turn, thus ensuring that at crucial points in the year, labour resources were used to the best advantage. This co-operative principle did not extend to land tenure or consumption, but in the labour context it was, and still is, integral to Lango culture.

[16] Driberg, *The Lango*, pp. 173–5; Hayley, op. cit., p. 46.
[17] McMaster, *A Subsistence Crop Geography of Uganda*, p. 16.

At the most rudimentary level, work-groups comprising a handful of households carried out the less exacting parts of the farming routine such as weeding. These groups, called *alea*, were very informal, and they included women as well as men. The core of the system, however, was the *wang tic*, or work-group proper. This comprised a much larger number of households with a fixed membership and a territorial identity. The work-group was concerned with the heaviest agricultural tasks, above all with clearing the ground before sowing. The basis of the group was reciprocity of labour, but the man whose land was being worked was also expected to provide beer for his fellows at the end of the day. All married men and fully grown boys took part as a matter of course, failure to do so being tantamount to opting out of the community. The work-group controlled not only labour but also land-use, since land was of little value without access to labour which was conferred by membership of the work-group. The elders of the work-group were the people who approved the marking-out of new fields and allocated abandoned land.[18]

The size of the work-group is not easy to determine. Nowadays it varies from twenty to forty homesteads, twenty-five being regarded as the ideal number of active members.[19] But these figures cannot be assumed to be valid for the nineteenth century, since patterns of land-use and settlement have changed so much during the last fifty years. For the same reason, elders have difficulty in giving detailed descriptions of the physical lay-out of settlements before the colonial era. The estimates that we have suggest that the work-group is larger today than it used to be. Driberg, writing of the period 1912–18, regarded twenty as the maximum number of active participants.[20]

Estimating the size of the work-group would be easier if it had been consistently reflected in residential patterns. But during the nineteenth century this was by no means the case. The work-group was not the same as the village (*paco*). Sometimes the two did coincide exactly, but in fact the size and situation of the village were determined by factors other than by labour. The village was by definition a concentration of households. Villages were sometimes built according to a

[18] The best description of the *wang tic* is Curley's (Curley, *Elders, Shades, and Women*, pp. 20–7); this, however, relates to the period 1965–7. For earlier though less detailed accounts, see Driberg, *The Lango*, p. 97, and Hayley, op. cit., pp. 58–9.

[19] A. C. Curley, 'Social Process: Clanship and Neighbourhood in Lango District, Uganda', unpublished M.A. thesis, Sacramento State College, California, 1971, pp. 4, 103.

[20] Driberg, *The Lango*, p. 97.

linear or circular design, but it is unlikely that they had ever followed a set pattern; Driberg noted a tendency for villages to straggle, the huts of one polygynous family being separated from its neighbour by up to thirty yards.[21] There is no doubt, though, that the Langi found it necessary to live in compact residential groups. This pattern of settlement had little to do with the communal labour system. During the last fifty years, the compact village has vanished from the landscape, its components being dispersed as scattered homesteads, and yet the work-group is as strong as ever. Provided the exact composition of a work-group is recognized, there is after all no reason why its members should all live in one place rather than on their respective holdings. The reason for the village was not economic so much as military. It was intended to provide security against attack, especially at night, and greater protection for cattle which were kept in a single village kraal.[22] Once law and order had been established in Lango by the Protectorate Government, the village ceased to have any purpose, and the dispersed work-group became the basic unit of territorial organization.

Villages varied in size according to several factors. One was the extent of their insecurity: people who lived in fear of raiding tended to congregate more densely. Another factor was the nature of the environment. The villagers needed to be able to reach their own plots easily, and if the amount of cultivable land near by was small, this placed a limit on the number of households in the village. A limit was also set by the site of the village, for in most of Lango the dry land is broken up by swamps into tiny units. This did not restrict cultivation, because there was never an overall shortage of dry land, but the size of individual villages was limited because no part of the village could be built on land likely to be waterlogged. For these reasons, a village could number as few as ten and as many as 150 huts or more.[23] 150 huts did not, of course, mean 150 polygynous households: a married man was obliged to build a house for each wife, and his unmarried sons slept in special bachelor-huts on stilts;[24] so most households

[21] Interviews: Luka Abura, Anderea Ogwang. Driberg, *The Lango*, p. 72.
[22] Ibid, pp. 71, 80.
[23] Lt. H. M. Harries, 'With the Bumiro Force', appendix to Uganda Intelligence Report No. 31, July 1907, PRO CO/536/14; Jervoise, Notes on Kwera, *c.* 1913, Dokolo T.B. (1913–26, part 1), LDA; F. H. Melland and E. H. Cholmeley, *Through the Heart of Africa* (London, 1912), p. 223; Driberg, *The Lango*, p. 71.
[24] This curious feature provoked the first outside record of the Langi, though the information was inaccurate and gathered at secondhand: Speke referred to the Langi as 'a stark-naked people who live up in trees', a description which must

included several huts. Rough calculations made in Adwari north of the Moroto in 1918 indicate that the average village there contained fewer than twenty household heads;[25] villages north of the Moroto, however, tended to be on the small side. By contrast, Tarogali village in south-western Lango was found two years earlier to have seventy-three men.[26] We have no means of telling how representative these figures were, or how far they were applicable to the nineteenth century, but at least they show that villages did not necessarily conform to the requirements of the work-group. A few oral accounts are explicit that some villages contained more than one work-group, while others had to combine in order to muster enough men for a work-group.[27] All individuals were members of both a work-group and a village, and in some instances these two were identical; but in origin and function they were different, the first being an economic and the second a strategic arrangement.

In considering the political organization of nineteenth-century Lango, the point of departure must be the relationship between territorial groups and descent groups. Until the eve of the colonial period and even beyond, almost every Lango village was clustered around a single dominant descent group, which in turn formed part of a more far-flung descent group, namely the clan. Bearing in mind the social organization of other Nilotic-speaking peoples, one might therefore assume that here was another example of a segmentary lineage system, in which the lineage structure was articulated at several levels, each segment being identified with a particular locality. Such an analysis would, however, be wide of the mark.[28] The dominant descent group within a Lango village did not constitute a discrete segment of the lineage structure, nor were its relations with other descent groups belonging to the same clan conceptualized in lineage terms. Its membership typically included more than one lineage, and these lineages were often represented in other localities as well. In other words, the vital category was not the lineage or segment, but simply the aggregate of all a clan's members gathered in one locality,

surely have appealed to the prejudices of his Victorian readership. J. H. Speke, *Journal of the Discovery of the Source of the Nile* (London, 1863), p. 89.

[25] Driberg, entries for 17.2.18 in Moroto TB (1918–26), LDA.

[26] Driberg, entry for 9.3.16 in Maruzi TB (1912–19), LDA.

[27] Interviews: Nasaneri Owino, Luka Abura.

[28] For observations to the same effect, see Curley, *Elders, Shades, and Women*, pp. 38–9, and F. K. Girling, *The Acholi of Uganda* (London, 1960), pp. 208–9.

irrespective of their lineage membership.[29] Such an aggregate is called a *clan section* by A. W. Southall in his analysis of Alur society,[30] and this is the term which best describes the largest localized descent group in pre-colonial Lango. Territorial and descent groups were thus closely related, but without the potential for large-scale co-ordination conferred by a segmentary lineage system.[31]

The reasons for this incoherence in Lango lineage structure can only be understood by more detailed reference to the motives behind Lango expansion during the nineteenth century. The environmental and economic factors examined in the first chapter place the overall expansion of the Langi in context, but they do not directly explain the lack of coherence in their lineage organization. Two closely connected social processes can be detected which, during the nineteenth century, acted as a constant check on the scale of the lineage system and limited its political role. Firstly, the largest grouping with which the individual identified on grounds of descent—namely the clan—was becoming smaller. Secondly, the components of the clan were becoming widely dispersed in such a way as to exclude any correspondence between spatial and genealogical relations.

Oral traditions point to a number of tensions which during the pre-colonial period resulted in clan fission. The various factors cannot be quantified, partly because clan names and the traditions about them seldom furnish precise reasons for a particular cleavage,[32] but a number of causes of common application are mentioned. In the first place, quarrels inside the clan could easily be caused by the allocation of meat at ritual feasts. Clans varied in size, but a practical limit was set on the numbers that could be invited to a feast by the amount of meat which one carcass could provide. For many ritual occasions there seems to have been no commonly accepted limit on the range of kin to be invited, one such ceremony being *kayo cogo* ('biting the

---

[29] For an extended example, see the case-study of Akokoro, below, pp. 50–2.

[30] Southall, *Alur Society*, pp. 38–9.

[31] It is symptomatic of the lack of coherence in the lineage system that among today's elders there is frequent uncertainty as to the full name of a clan, its relationship with other groups of the same or a similar name, and whether these groups fall within the marriage restrictions.

[32] Clan cleavages are often indicated by composite clan names, in which a qualifying name is added to that of the original clan. Qualifying names most commonly refer to the leader under whom the seceding section hived off (e.g. Jo Atek me *Oyaro*), or else they allude obliquely to the circumstances of the split; for example, the name Jo Atek me *Okalodyang* refers to the story that the first leader of this clan vaulted over a great bull (interview: Nekomia Agwa).

bone'), which was held when a young child was seriously ill. Much bad feeling could be caused by persistent slighting over invitations to such ceremonies, and this greatly contributed to tension within the clan.[33]

More serious, however, were the quarrels over livestock, the principal form of movable wealth. The theory of clan ownership of livestock became fact when bridewealth and compensation for offences were due for payment. A man was entitled to expect that, when his son married, other members of the clan would contribute to the bridewealth, on the assumption that the future well-being of the clan as a whole was involved. The same principle of corporate action by the clan applied to its relations with other clans. If a member of the clan was guilty of manslaughter or extramarital intercourse, the whole clan was liable and the compensation, paid in goats or cattle according to the offence, was a shared responsibility. Families or lineages who persistently committed offences caused resentment among their clansmen, who in extreme cases severed their clan ties altogether in order to preserve their goods from further liability.[34] Conversely, compensation for offences belonged not to the injured individual but to the clan, and ill-feeling could easily be caused by the inequitable distribution of compensation.[35]

A formal clan split was marked by the ending of marriage restrictions and by the seceding group taking a new name and new taboos. In some cases, however, a breach of exogamy or a change of taboo was a cause rather than a consequence of the split. A series of theoretically incestuous unions between distantly related clan members could cause the elders to decide on a formal split.[36] A section of the clan might consider that a change of taboo was required. The main function of the taboo was, after all, to protect the unborn progeny of the clan; so a possible response to an abnormally high rate of infant mortality was to change the taboo, in the hope that the children would be better protected. Such a change entailed a total breach with those who continued to observe the old taboos.[37] Clan names which expressly allude to the taboo perhaps indicate a split of this kind.[38]

[33] Interviews: Tomasi Ojuka, Reuben Ogwal. *Kayo cogo* is described in Hayley, op. cit., pp. 91–4 and Curley, *Elders, Shades, and Women*, pp. 130–4.

[34] Ogwal, op. cit., *passim*. Interviews: Tomasi Ojuka, Bartolomayo Okori.

[35] Ogwal, op. cit., pp. 57–8.

[36] Interviews: Yubu Engola, Bartolomayo Okori. Ogwal, op. cit., *passim*.

[37] Interview: Tomasi Ojuka.

[38] For example, Jo Atek me *Okwerawele* indicated that the dove (*awele*) is taboo to this clan (Interview: Anderea Okadde). Nine clan names of this type have been recorded to date.

Whatever the reasons, there is little doubt that clans multiplied fast during the nineteenth century. At the present time, the total number of clans is in the region of 250.[39] In view of the limits set on group migration by the colonial government, it is improbable that the number of clans has increased appreciably since the beginning of this century.[40] A much more difficult problem is to determine the number of Lango clans a hundred years before that. The tradition published by Tarantino that all clans stemmed from three parent clans at Otuke is certainly an over-simplification.[41] But it seems clear that at least a hundred clans—and perhaps as many as two hundred—are derived from a core of six clans,[42] and the Langi do not maintain that the number of clans was anything approaching the current figure during the first westward migrations from Otuke. All available indications are that the rate at which clans multiplied was faster than the rate of population growth; in other words, clans were becoming smaller. Even allowing for serious under-enumeration in the first Census count of the Langi in 1921, the membership of the average clan at the beginning of the colonial period must have been considerably less than one thousand all told, or under three hundred adult males.

This figure must be still further reduced if an estimate is required of the number of clansmen with whom the individual came into regular contact. In everyday life, what counted was not the total strength of the clan, but the number of members concentrated in a given area. By the latter half of the nineteenth century these two were very rarely the same, for most clans were represented in several widely separated localities. Three factors were mainly responsible for the dispersion of the clan into territorial sections. The first was pressure of population on the environment. As a clan grew by natural increase, it exceeded the size that could be supported by its territory. The ideal response to this situation was to colonize the nearest ridge of dry land

[39] Clan lists are found in: Driberg, *The Lango*, pp. 192–204; T. T. S. Hayley, field-notes (1936–7); A. Tarantino, 'Lango Clans', *Uganda Jl.*, 13 (1949), pp. 109–11; J. P. Crazzolara, 'Notes on the Lango-Omiru and on the Labwoor and Nyakwai', *Anthropos*, 55 (1960), pp. 174–214. In addition, I collected a number of clan names which had not previously been recorded.

[40] Driberg made no claim to be comprehensive in his list of 112 clans, which relates to the period 1912–18 (*The Lango*, p. 189).

[41] Tarantino, 'Lango Clans', p. 109.

[42] Without research into each of the clans concerned, it is impossible to be more precise about numbers, since the evidence of clan names is not in itself conclusive. The six clans are: Oki, Bako, Atek (or Atekit), Arak (or Arakit), Ober, and Okarowok.

and so retain contiguity of settlement between all members of the clan. Lango history is full of cases where a clan which initially settled in one or two villages expanded over the years into new villages near by. But often the adjacent land was uncultivable, or else occupied by another group already, in which case a section of the clan migrated away, thus causing a rupture in the neighbourhood ties that bound clansmen together. Such a rupture could more readily be contemplated since in Lango the clan was not tied ritually to a particular site by a clan shrine or a clan burial-ground.

The second factor which caused clan dispersion was antagonism between clans. Inter-clan fighting, so well documented for the last few years of the pre-colonial era,[43] appears to have been a feature of Lango society as far back as traditions recall. Illicit sexual intercourse (*luk*) was one common cause of attacks on nearby clans; another was disputes over hunting rights. Inter-clan fighting was sharply distinguished from battles with non-Langi by certain conventional restraints. The most important of these, observed until the 1890s, banned the use of the spear and so held down the mortality of inter-clan conflict.[44] But this relatively low level of bloodshed did not mean that inter-clan hostility could be accepted with equanimity. For any clan section, a great deal depended on harmonious relations with its neighbours, and if these relations were seriously disrupted it was preferable to move to a new area. Fighting often caused a defeated clan section to migrate, even at the price of settling in a less-favoured environment. This is particularly true of the extreme south-west of Lango, where the positive inducements were not very strong, in view of the irregular rainfall and the prevalence of tsetse-fly.[45] Repeated failure to resist the attacks of other clans could result in a clan section migrating further away from the rest of the clan, so that relations between the dispersed sections could no longer be maintained. In about 1900 the uninhabited angle of the Nile opposite Masindi Port was colonized by a group of Jo Arak me Oyakori; they had previously migrated from Teboke on the Okole river to Tarogali near Ibuje, but from there they were expelled by the Jo Ocukuru in a

[43] See below, pp. 106–7.
[44] Interviews: Anderea Okadde, Yakobo Adoko, Kezekia Okelo, Isaka Ojaba. Ogwal Ajungu, untitled vernacular history (1936–7), MS. in the possession of Dr. T. T. S. Hayley, para. 7; Driberg, *The Lango*, pp. 106–7. For the collapse of these conventional restraints, see below, pp. 101–5.
[45] Interviews: Yakobo Adoko, Matayo Aman, Ciriwano Ojok, Misaki Obala, Yosia Omwa.

battle during which their own leader was killed. As a result of their flight after this battle, they found themselves in one of the most remote and inhospitable parts of Lango, separated from their nearest clan brothers by nearly fifty miles.[46]

There was one other factor which caused the dispersion of clans into territorial sections. This was the pull of kinship ties outside the clan. To talk of kinship ties outside the clan may, in the case of a unilineal society, seem to be a contradiction in terms. In a great many patrilineal societies, however, a marriage is regarded as initiating—or continuing—a relationship between two descent groups, and this is particularly so if men customarily find their wives in the immediate neighbourhood. On marriage, the man enters into a lasting relationship not only with his wife but also with his in-laws, or affines, who will continue to be concerned for their sister's welfare, and also for her offspring. This last point is particularly important, for one generation's affinal ties become blood, or cognatic ties in the next generation. It is commonly recognized in African patrilineal societies that a young man's needs cannot always be met by his father and his father's brothers, for his relationship with them is one of respect and even fear which allows few liberties. From time to time he will wish to turn for psychological or material support to his mother's people and particularly to her brothers. The bonds that exist on the one hand between brothers-in-law, and on the other between mother's brother and sister's son, are a recognition that patrilineal descent groups cannot live in isolation from each other. At the same time, if these bonds are too strong they will endanger the solidarity of the patrilineage itself; in part therefore, the cohesion of lineage systems varies according to the strength of these bonds.

In nineteenth-century Lango both affinal and cognatic bonds were very strong indeed. Lango culture placed great emphasis on resolving the ambiguities of the married woman's role. Every stage from her marriage until well past her child-bearing prime was marked by a domestic ceremony attended by both families. Men were constantly in touch with their in-laws, and great store was set by tranquil affinal relationships.[47] Similarly, the bond between mother's brother, or

---

[46] P. Enin, vernacular MS. (1967), translated as 'The Life of Chief Daudi Odora Arimo of Lango' (typescript), Department of Religious Studies, Makerere University, pp. 1–4; R. Ogwal, 'Bino a Muni kede Mwa i Lango', undated vernacular MS., typescript copy in Makerere University Library, p. 7. Interviews: Peter Enin, Sira Okelo.

[47] Curley, Elders, Shades, and Women, pp. 108–50.

nero, and sister's son, or *okeo*, was very strong. The *okeo* could call upon his maternal uncle for help with bridewealth and he could inherit his uncle's wife if heirs in the male line were lacking.[48]

Affinal or cognatic ties could be so strongly felt as to cause an individual to counter the interests of his own descent group. Before an inter-clan raid, it was not unknown for the victims to receive advance warning from a *nero* who belonged to the attacking clan.[49] Still more important, cognatic and affinal connections often caused people to migrate away from their own clan. A man whose clansmen were too poor to provide him with bridewealth would go and join his *nero*; or, if he inherited the *nero*'s wife, he could go to settle in her village. Such changes of residence are common in patrilineal societies, and they often result in the migrant or his offspring being absorbed by the host descent-group.[50] The striking feature of pre-colonial Lango is that it was not unusual for whole groups of clansmen to go and join their affines or their cognatic kin, and to retain their original clan identity, either in a village of their own or in a village shared with the host clan.[51] Time and again, migration traditions recall that it was marriage links or maternal ties that caused a clan section to settle in its present locality.

The pull of kinship ties outside the clan, pressure of the environment, and inter-clan fighting together explain the constant dispersion of clans. In the long run this dispersion was likely to result in fission, the dispersed sections becoming clans in their own right. Once a clan had become spatially divided, the practical difficulty of getting members together for rituals or consultations reduced the awareness of a common identity among the dispersed sections. Formal fission was not inevitable, however, especially if individual sections were small; and if fission did take place, it was likely to be preceded by an interval during which the clan was represented in two or more localities. To say, therefore, that Lango society on the eve of the colonial period was composed of between 200 and 250 clans, each with a membership

---

[48] Driberg, *The Lango*, p. 174; Hayley, op. cit., pp. 54–6.

[49] Interview: Matayo Ayika.

[50] See, for example, Southall, op. cit., pp. 37–8.

[51] Previous writers have suggested that early in Lango history new clans were sometimes formed when a large clan section migrated to settle near another clan with which it had kinship ties. Clan names such as Okarowok me Oki are said to indicate that a new clan was formed by a migrant group (Jo Okarowok) and a host group (Jo Oki) combining. This is a plausible suggestion, though it appears to rest more on inference than oral evidence. Driberg, *The Lango*, p. 191; Hayley, op. cit., p. 41; Crazzolara, op. cit., p. 182.

of 200 or 300 adult males, does not adequately convey the small scale
of localized descent groups. Lango tradition gives the impression that
most clans at that time were dispersed, and this impression is born out
by Driberg's statement that 'clans and even families are often widely
scattered under the stimulus of war and migration'.[52] An estimate of
100 adult males, or two to three villages, would probably convey the
size of the typical clan section around 1900.

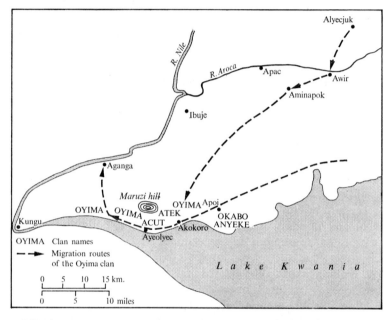

Map 4.   South-western Lango showing the settlement of the Akokoro area
c. 1888–1909

The fragmentation of localized descent groups can best be illustrated by tracing the settlement history of one locality, Akokoro. On
account of its situation on Lake Kwania in the dry country of the
extreme south-west, Akokoro was probably never colonized by the
Lwo, and it was one of the last areas to be settled by the Langi.[53] Its
recent occupation allows the sequence of settlement to be reconstructed with some precision.

[52] Driberg, *The Lango*, p. 71.
[53] The very name Akokoro is said to be an onomatopoeic allusion to the sound
which a spear makes when thrust into the parched ground. Interviews: Suleman
Enoke, Yosia Omwa.

During the 1870s a section of the Jo Oyima clan were living in Alyecjuk, a few miles north of the Aroca river near Aduku. It was in Alyecjuk that Akaki—the grandfather of Milton Obote—grew up, married, and became the leader of his fellow clansmen. In about 1880 fighting in Alyecjuk caused Akaki to lead his clan south-westwards to Awir, in present-day Apac, where there were Jo Oyima already living. However, a quarrel soon arose within the clan and fighting broke out. Akaki was worsted and he migrated to a nearby place called Aminapok which he had first visited while hunting. Soon afterwards, defeat at the hands of another clan caused him to migrate yet again between about 1888 and 1890; this time he settled on the uninhabited lakeshore at Akokoro.[54]

At the core of Akaki's following were his nine brothers, most of whom migrated at the same time to Akokoro. Together with an unknown number of lesser clansmen, they settled in a village about two miles east of the present Akokoro–Ibuje road.[55] On this last stage of migration Akaki was also accompanied by a group of Jo Okarowok me Okabo. The two clans already had close affinal ties, which probably dated back to Alyecjuk, where the Jo Okabo had lived for over twenty years. The Jo Okabo settled in Apoi, a few miles east of Akaki's village.[56]

During the next ten years the two pioneer groups were joined by other clans. The Jo Atek me Okalodyang and the Jo Acut me Ongoda had been forced to leave their previous homes in the north and east, and they already had marriage links with the Jo Oyima.[57] According to one account,[58] they came quietly by night, first the leaders to prospect, and then the main body of twenty or thirty people. Other clans included a small detachment of Jo Atek me Omwara, led by Akaki's *okeo* (sister's son).[59] During the same period, three more sections of the Jo Oyima arrived, all of them belonging to lineages other than Akaki's. One of them settled in Akokoro proper, and the other two further west along the lakeshore.[60] Hitherto it seems that the various groups in Akokoro had coexisted amicably, but one of the later Oyima groups, the Alwa lineage, caused trouble. One source

[54] Interviews: Yakobo Adoko, Matayo Aman, Jorbabel Akora.
[55] Interviews: Yakobo Adoko, Matayo Aman.
[56] Interviews: Suleman Enoke, Yosia Agum.
[57] Interviews: Nekomia Agwa, Samwiri Ade.
[58] Interview: Yakobo Adoko.
[59] Interview: Misaki Obala.
[60] Interviews: Erieza Okelo, Yakobo Adoko.

has it that in a fight over abusive beer-songs, the Jo Alwa killed three men of another clan.[61] But the Jo Alwa also alienated their fellow clansmen of the Jo Oyima, and the upshot was that, shortly before the arrival of the Protectorate Government in 1909, the rest of the Jo Oyima—including Akaki—combined to expel the Alwa lineage, who then migrated to Aganga on the Nile further west. In ridding themselves of the Alwa lineage, the Jo Oyima of Akokoro were helped by another section of their own clan from Apac. Olal, the leader of this section, returned to Apac when the fight was over, but soon afterwards he brought his following southwards to settle at Ayeolyec on the lakeshore.[62] As a result of all these migrations, the adult male population of Akokoro was roughly estimated to be 430 in 1912.[63] Five clans were numerically significant, and there were smaller groups as well. All of them had clan ties outside Akokoro. The largest clan, the Jo Oyima, was made up of several lineages, which had arrived at different times and from different places, and which fell into no overall genealogical pattern (Map 4).

The pattern of clan migration in Lango was such that the juxtaposition of lineages and clan sections did not remain constant. In contrast to other Nilotic peoples such as the Kenya Luo, migration in Lango broke the correspondence between genealogical and spatial relations;[64] to use Bohannan's terminology, it was a case of disjunction rather than expansion.[65] In the late nineteenth century, any locality in Lango of comparable size to Akokoro was inhabited by a number of disparate descent groups which lacked any integrative structure. In most cases, the village could be regarded as belonging to one particular clan section, since the members of other clans were in a small minority. Within a given locality, the clan sections were

---

[61] Interview: Yakobo Adoko.

[62] Interviews: Yakobo Adoko, Erieza Okelo, Anderea Adoko, Yosia Omwa.

[63] Census figures for Akokoro, Maruzi TB (1912–13), LDA.

[64] E. E. Evans-Pritchard, 'Luo Tribes and Clans', *Rhodes–Livingstone Jl.*, 7 (1949), pp. 24–40; A. W. Southall, 'Lineage Formation among the Luo', *International African Institute Memorandum*, 26 (1952); Ogot, *History of the Southern Luo*, vol. I, pp. 110–12.

[65] 'Expansion refers to that type of movement which leads to the enlargement in area of a lineage's territory. It may eventually lead to a change in geographical location of the lineage territory; it does not affect the over-all juxtaposition of lineage areas. Disjunction, on the other hand, characteristically brings about a separation of groups in space and affects not only the geographical position of a lineage territory, but also the juxtaposition of lineage territories.' P. Bohannan, 'The Migration and Expansion of the Tiv', *Africa*, 24 (1956), p. 2. See also Horton, 'Stateless Societies in the History of West Africa', pp. 93–7.

related to each other by the web of affinal and cognatic ties, and they recognized bonds of kinship with their clansmen in other places, but they were in no sense segments of an articulated lineage system.

Everywhere in Lango, however, groups of villages were linked together for certain social purposes, irrespective of clan affiliation. There were three institutional ties which bound together neighbouring villages on an occasional basis and for specific reasons. The first was an economic link determined by hunting requirements. The second and third were ritual links, the one concerned with relations with the dead, and the other involving the allocation of all adult males to corporate age groups. As will become clear shortly, there is some evidence to indicate that one of these ritual links—the age organization—played a very much more integrative role in Lango society during the early nineteenth century; but the age system steadily declined, and by the end of the century the social context of age ceremonies was very limited. This was a restriction which applied still more to the other two institutional links. None of them provided a basis for everyday inter-village co-operation or a framework for the allocation of authority above the village level, but each one contributed to the individual's awareness of a community which transcended his own clan section. No picture of nineteenth-century Lango society would be complete without them.

Among peoples of rudimentary technology, the hunting of big game is necessarily a co-operative venture, for without mass participation personal safety will be at risk and the supply of game meat less sure. Among sedentary agriculturalists the careful regulation of hunting is still more important if crops and homesteads are to be spared needless damage. For the Langi, with their reliance on game meat as an important part of their diet, the organization of hunting was a serious business. The whole of their country was divided up into game tracts, called *arum*. The *arum* varied greatly in size from four to 140 square miles,[66] but it nearly always included more than one village. Such large units were essential if big game was to be efficiently exploited. The most important hunt of the year took place towards the end of the dry season when a fire was lit on one side of the *arum* in order to drive the animals towards a line of hunters armed with spears; if the grass was very dry it was not unknown for 200 square miles to be ravaged by one blaze. Several hundred men could

[66] Driberg, *The Lango*, p. 111.

be involved, and the hunters could cover anything from twenty-five to forty miles a day in pursuit of fugitive game.[67]

Hunting rights over the *arum* were vested in a single individual, the *won arum* or 'master of the hunt'. He chose the day for the hunt, directed the hunters to their positions, and was entitled to a toll of all game killed; during the hunt itself his word was supreme.[68] Such a degree of institutionalized authority was rare in Lango society, but its exercise was very limited. Except when the hunt was in progress, the *won arum* had no authority: he could not, for instance, refuse permission to build or cultivate in his *arum*.[69] In effect, the *won arum* was responsible for organizing hunting in the best interests of the community as a whole. A major hunt entailed co-ordination between groups who lacked a recognized hierarchy, and so there was a clear advantage in concentrating authority in one individual for the occasion. But at all other times, the *won arum* enjoyed no more than the respect due to any clan elder.

The great dry-season hunt was a major expression of the sense of community between neighbouring villages and different clans. But it occurred only once a year, and at other times game was hunted by much smaller groups of men. The co-operation required for rituals, on the other hand, occurred more frequently and related to a greater number of communal concerns. The majority of rituals—then as now —were very small-scale affairs which centred on the individual family; rituals of birth and marriage, for example, were performed by the two family groups concerned. Such occasions should perhaps be called private rituals. From the point of view of neighbourhood ties, the important rituals were those which called for the participation of elders on a territorial basis. These public rituals were of two kinds: ceremonies organized by ritual groups called *etogo*, and ceremonies associated with the age organization.

The *etogo* was the meeting together of elders for the performance of certain rituals which concerned relations between the living and the dead.[70] Like many African peoples, the Langi believed in the power of

---

[67] Driberg, *Engato*, p. 47; *The Lango*, pp. 113, 116.
[68] Driberg, *The Lango*, pp. 113, 116.
[69] Ibid., p. 171.
[70] The account of the *etogo* which follows is drawn from two authorities: Hayley, op. cit., pp. 48–52, 111–26; and Curley, *Elders, Shades, and Women* pp. 51–107. Neither of these two is explicitly concerned with the nineteenth century, but both take account of colonial changes, and Curley pays special attention to the pre-colonial role of the *etogo*.

the dead to bring suffering on the living, either by causing individual sickness or—more seriously—by inflicting drought and other natural disasters. This power was considered to be particularly strong in the case of the recently deceased, and to cope with the danger a series of funeral ceremonies was prescribed by which the spirit or 'shade' (*tipu*) of the dead man was placated. If the continuing malice of a shade was evidenced in chronic sickness, special curing ceremonies were required. The most elaborate ceremony, and the one which expressed most forcibly the link between the shades and the natural elements, was *apuny*, the final funeral rite held every two or three years to commemorate several dead people; it was the ultimate means of placating the shades and ensuring that the rains would fall at the start of the wet season. The interesting feature of Lango attitudes to the dead was the belief that the shades could not be controlled solely by the lineage concerned or by a ritual specialist, but only by the community as a whole—that is, by a number of clan sections acting together. If a shade was badly offended, it was the community which through drought might suffer the consequences. The *etogo* was the practical expression of this belief, and it had responsibility for all funeral ceremonies.

The first essential of the *etogo*, then, was that it should include elders of several different clan sections. By the end of the nineteenth century this was a requirement which could often be met within the confines of a single village; but in fact the *etogo* always included men of different villages, the men of one village being distributed among several *etogo*. In this way, *etogo* affiliations cut across village loyalties.[71] The cross-cutting composition of the *etogo* had an important bearing on social relations in the area from which its members were drawn. Like so many African peoples, the Langi held that good relations with the dead could only be maintained if there was harmony among the living—in this case the *etogo* members. The ideal of good-neighbourliness was explicit in the internal organization of the *etogo*. The central feature of the ceremonies was a ritual feast at which the

The *etogo* is also considered in J. p'Bitek Okot, 'Oral Literature and its Social Background among the Acholi and Lango', unpublished B.Litt. thesis, Oxford University, 1963, pp. 146–54.

[71] Hayley is ambiguous on this point, and other writers without first-hand experience have assumed that *etogo* and village were conterminous: J. E. Goldthorpe, *Outlines of East African Society* (Kampala, 1958), p. 87; Okot, op. cit., p. 150. Curley, however, is in no doubt about the cross-cutting nature of *etogo* membership and its constructive impact on inter-village relations. Curley, *Elders, Shades, and Women*, p. 104.

etogo members were divided into three meat groups, each group consuming a prescribed portion of the animal. A father and his sons could not sit in the same meat group but had to be evenly distributed among all three. Clan ties were thus set aside for the duration of the feast, and within each group an elder had to share the meat with his neighbours rather than his agnatic kin. The *etogo* ceremonies therefore not only allayed anxiety about the shades; they also promoted harmony among men of different villages and clans. While the *etogo* itself had no existence outside the ceremonies, the mutual regard of its members was expected to be maintained at all times. If two villages came to blows, a man was not permitted to fight a member of his *etogo*, and if he did kill him he had to be ritually cleansed before participating in any more ceremonies.

Much of the respect felt for the *etogo* was derived from the belief that its composition was fixed and permanent. The clans involved were believed to have been associated together for ceremonies since time immemorial, and each clan was assumed to have the same *etogo* partners wherever its several components happened to live. This was patently untrue. Sections of the same clan living in widely separated parts of Lango were almost bound to have different neighbours, and it was with them that each section had to associate for *etogo* ceremonies. The belief in the immutability of the *etogo* was a convenient fiction which concealed an essential flexibility. For in fact the composition of the *etogo* was constantly changing as villagers left the neighbourhood and new migrants arrived. On a smaller scale these migrations continue today. When a recently-arrived settler wishes to hold an *etogo* ritual at his home, he will approach his neighbours for help; if they agree to hold the ceremony for him, he will thenceforth consider that his *etogo* comprises the clans who attended the ceremony.[72] Hayley's account, which relates to the 1930s, suggests that the accommodation of new members used to be less straightforward. A first-generation settler could attend the ceremonies of a local *etogo*, but only his sons could in due course become full members.[73] At all events, it is clear that the inclusion of new clans in an *etogo* presented few practical difficulties. In effect, the *etogo* was a means of assimilating new settlers to the village and the wider local community.[74]

[72] Curley, *Elders, Shades, and Women*, pp. 54–61.
[73] Hayley, op. cit., p. 49.
[74] A recent writer on Labwor history has stated that the Lango *etogo* corresponded with the *otem*, the basic unit of political organization in nineteenth century Labwor. The *otem*, like the *etogo*, was a multi-clan community. But it evidently

It is frustrating that some details of the traditional *etogo* organization remain obscure. But these difficulties are small compared with the problem of reconstructing the Lango age-organization, the third institutional link which bound together villages and clan sections. For here the process of decline has been much more devastating. Almost the only source is Driberg's account.[75] By the time that Hayley visited Lango twenty years later, the age-organization had fallen into complete disuse, while among today's elders there is a high degree of ignorance and confusion about an institution which corresponds to very little in their own experience.[76] Driberg's account, based on his own initiation into an age-set in 1915, abounds in colourful detail, but it is not analytically sound. When he assessed his findings he was not able to draw on comparative data of such detail. But since Driberg's day, social anthropologists have shown how very complex East African age-systems can be; the scope for terminological confusion is especially great, since the same vernacular words often refer to structurally distinct elements of an age-system. The position is further complicated by the fact that Driberg withheld some information from publication out of respect for the vow of secrecy which he had taken at his own initiation.[77] Hayley found that memory of the age-organization was already beginning to fade, and such information as he received appeared to differ from Driberg's on some points.[78] The available evidence does, nevertheless, fall into a pattern which carries some conviction in the light of the better documented age-systems of neighbouring peoples.

As the specialized Lango vocabulary shows,[79] and as Driberg himself

had greater cohesion, more territorial precision, and wider social functions than did the *etogo*. R. S. Herring, 'Centralization, stratification, and incorporation: case studies from North-eastern Uganda', *Canadian Jl. African Studies*, 7 (1973), pp. 501, 505–7.

[75] Driberg, *The Lango*, pp. 243–60, and *Engato*, pp. 102–11.

[76] Only 10 per cent of my informants were able to offer any information at all on this subject, and most of this was extremely difficult to interpret. Curley also failed to collect any helpful oral material on the age-organization during eighteen months of fieldwork in eastern Lango (personal communication from Dr. Curley).

[77] This is what Driberg himself told Hayley. Hayley, op. cit., p. 73.

[78] Ibid., pp. 72–3.

[79] More than half the set names were taken from animal names found in Para-Nilotic and not used in any other context in Lango (for example, *amocing*, rhinoceros; *ekori*, giraffe; *engatu*, lion). *Ewor* or *ewuron*, the Lango name for the initiation ceremony, is probably derived from the Ateso, *eigworone*. Driberg observed that the rain-songs taught during the initiation contained many Para-Nilotic words and formulae which even the old men could not understand. *The Lango*, p. 254.

admitted,[80] the Lango age-organization must be considered in the same category as the Para-Nilotic systems further east. If the apparent contradictions between Driberg's and Hayley's accounts are considered in the light of these systems described since their day,[81] then it would appear that the Langi had a cyclical generation-system. According to this interpretation, the basic unit was the *age-set*, a corporate group of age-mates who at puberty or soon afterwards underwent initiation during a single initiation period of about four years, in ceremonies which were co-ordinated throughout Lango.[82] At the end of that period, the set was declared closed, and a fresh one was begun and identified according to an established sequence of animal names. Four sets formed in this way completed a *generation-set*. The break between one generation-set and the next was marked by several years in which no initiations were held, so that a new generation-set began to be formed about twenty-five years after the previous one had been started. Each generation-set passed as a unit through a clearly defined sequence of two or three levels of seniority, or *age-grades*, which were also given animal names. The formation of a new generation-set entailed the promotion of the preceding one to a more senior grade, its duties and privileges changing accordingly.[83]

[80] Driberg, *The Lango*, pp. 253–4.

[81] P. H. Gulliver, 'The Age-Set Organization of the Jie Tribe', *Jl. Rl. Anthrop. Inst.* 83 (1953), pp. 147–68; J. Lamphear, *The Traditional History of the Jie of Uganda* (Oxford, 1976), pp. 34–42. Gulliver, 'The Turkana Age Organisation', *American Anthropologist*, 60 (1958), pp. 900–22; N. Dyson-Hudson, *Karimojong Politics* (Oxford, 1966), pp. 156–204. There is no adequate account of the Teso system, but see A. C. A. Wright, 'Notes on the Iteso Social Organization', *Uganda Jl.* 9 (1942), pp. 57–80.

[82] Driberg's account suggests that each set was further divided into two or three sub-sets which were given animal names associated with the set name. Every initiation ceremony would in this case result in a sub-set being formed. *The Lango*, p. 244; *Engato*, pp. 103–4.

[83] This reconstruction is not explicit in the accounts of Driberg and Hayley, but it explains an important discrepancy between them. According to Driberg, a man remained in the same animal group from initiation until death, while Hayley's informants, drawn from different places in Lango, assured him that as a man grew older his animal name changed. Driberg appears to be referring to age-sets, while Hayley's informants were talking about age-grades. The confusion arises from the fact that the same animal names were used in both contexts.

The generation aspect is strongly indicated by the pause observed at the end of the cycle of age-sets and by the fact that the initiating of a set was conducted by the last group to take the same name (i.e. its namesake in the previous generation); thus the buffalo (*jobi*) set of 1915 was initiated by elders who had been initiated as buffaloes in about 1891 (Driberg, *The Lango*, p. 245). I am grateful to Dr. John Lamphear for his help in analyzing the evidence on Lango age-organization.

The available evidence is so confusing, and the chances of any more coming to light so remote, that the composition of the Lango age-system will probably never be known for sure; so the reconstruction offered here must be regarded as tentative. If the structure of the system were better known, there would be more certainly about its social functions. At the time when Driberg observed the age-organization, these functions had already been attenuated. This was not merely because of the new conditions of colonial rule, for oral traditions indicate that by the 1890s the age-organization was already playing a more limited role than previously.

As Driberg described it, the Lango age-organization had a mainly ritual and symbolic significance. The ceremony of initiation to an age-set, called *ewor* (or *eworon*), was a dramatic introduction to full manhood. For three days the initiates lived in the bush under the direction of the elders; they were made to eat purposely unappetizing food, to go on long marches outside the camp, and to perform hateful sexual practices, the memory of which was expected to act as a deterrent for the rest of their lives.[84] The initiates were also instructed in the customs of the tribe, and above all in the ritual observances of the rain-dance (*myelo kot*). This ceremony was performed once a year early in the wet season and lasted for four days. Roles were allocated according to age- and generation-sets, and the successful performance of the ceremony entailed the correct recitation of songs which were full of difficult archaisms; these songs were taught to the initiates during *ewor*.[85]

There is no evidence that the division of Lango society into age, and generation-sets determined the deployment of warriors in battle-as among the Karimojong,[86] or the hiving-off of agnates to form new settlements, as among the Iteso.[87] But two other functions were fulfilled by the age-organization which were discernible in Driberg's day, though they were already declining in importance. Firstly, initiation to an age-set was the final stage in a young man's training for fighting, the ceremony being immediately followed by a raid on a neighbouring tribe.[88] Secondly, *ewor* appears to have been an occasion for the settlement of inter-clan conflicts and for declarations by the elders against antisocial behaviour such as the killing of

[84] Driberg, *Engato*, pp. 107–10.   [85] Driberg, *The Lango*, pp. 243, 249–53.
[86] Dyson-Hudson, op. cit., pp. 172–3.
[87] J. C. D. Lawrance, *The Iteso* (London, 1957), p. 68.
[88] Driberg, *The Lango*, p. 245; Hayley, op. cit., p. 57.

strangers, or the infringement of hunting rights.[89] The conciliatory and didactic aspects of *ewor* were emphasized by the convention—still observed in Driberg's day—that during the ceremonies a strict truce was kept throughout Lango.[90]

The territorial range of the age-organization gave it an integrative function unique in Lango society. Here Driberg's account is very clear. The whole of Lango country was divided up into four territorial sections. One section, the north-west, did not have formal age-groups, but each of the remaining three sections had a ritual centre, where all the initiates and elders of that section assembled for *ewor* and where the *myelo kot* was also held.[91] Driberg's description is contradicted by several Lango traditions which say that *ewor* could take place in any village.[92] This discrepancy may reflect a distinction between age-set initiation, which was held by each village, and the promotion of a generation from one grade to the next, which was the concern of the entire section acting in concert with the other sections of the tribe;[93] alternatively, the discrepancy may indicate variations of practice between one territorial section and another. It is unlikely that the answer to this question will ever be known for certain. But Driberg's account is sufficiently precise to show that, at one stage in the generation-cycle at least, representatives from a very large number of villages assembled in one place. The co-operation required on this occasion went far beyond the normal range of neighbourhood or kinship ties.

Of the three institutional links which transcended the everyday context of clan and village, the age-organization was plainly the most significant. The impact of the *arum* organization and the *etogo* ceremonies was limited both by their very restricted social context (dry-season hunting and funeral ceremonies) and by their narrowly local basis. By contrast, the age-organization entailed co-operation over a very wide area, and it was specifically concerned with smoothing out inter-clan tensions and enjoining high standards of social conduct. The reason for its decline are therefore of special interest.

---

[89] Interviews: Pilipo Oruro, Isaka Ojaba, Yakobo Gaci, Ibrahim Lodo, Lajaro Obia, Yakobo Adoko.

[90] Driberg, *The Lango*, p. 246.

[91] Ibid., pp. 244–5.

[92] Interviews: Tomasi Ojuka, Lasto Otim, Reuben Ogwal, Adonia Ecun.

[93] This kind of distinction is found among both the Jie and the Karimojong. Gulliver, 'Age-Set Organisation of the Jie Tribe', pp. 149, 153; Dyson-Hudson, op. cit., pp. 188–91.

The age-organization was evidently already in decline by the time of its final suppression by the Baganda Government agents early in the colonial period. The conciliatory and didactic aspects had been much curtailed, and its functions had by Driberg's time become almost exclusively ritual and symbolic. The reasons for this decline are not easy to ascertain, but they should probably be seen in the context of what is clearly a crucial aspect of early Lango history—the fusion of Lwo and Para-Nilotes. On this topic Lango tradition is conspicuously silent, which is hardly surprising if the reconstruction offered in the first chapter is correct—that the fusion of Lwo and Para-Nilotes was well advanced by the time the Langi began to colonize their present country. Although direct oral evidence is lacking, it is nevertheless possible to infer from the social organization of other Lwo and Para-Nilotic peoples the broad outlines of adaption and change among the Langi. The most striking difference between the Lwo and Para-Nilotes lies in the respective importance of lineages and age-groups. Among the Lwo, corporate age-groups are not nearly so important as the segmentary lineage structure.[94] Among the Central Para-Nilotes of the 'Karimojong Cluster', on the other hand, lineage organization is shallow, being entirely overshadowed by the all-embracing age-organization.[95]

The evolution of Lango society during the nineteenth century can up to a point be interpreted in terms of the interplay between these two principles, corresponding to the respective contributions of the Lwo and the Iseera (the principal Para-Nilotic group involved). So far as the age-organization is concerned, it would of course be very misleading to assume an identity of social organization between the Iseera and the present-day peoples of the 'Karimojong Cluster'. Since the latter were so heavily infiltrated by the pastoral Para-Nilotes from the Rift Valley Escarpment, while the agricultural Iseera, who migrated westwards, were hardly affected at all, a substantial discrepancy is more likely.[96] Nevertheless, whatever the ultimate derivation of the Lango age-system may have been, it certainly did not lie with the Lwo. The age-organization is best explained as the distinctive contribution of the Iseera. Its decline can be attributed to the westward expansion of the Langi, which not only

---

[94] Butt, *The Nilotes of the Anglo-Egyptian Sudan and Uganda.*
[95] Gulliver, *The Family Herds*, pp. 76–7, 212; Dyson-Hudson, op. cit., pp. 87–90.
[96] I owe this observation to Dr. Lamphear. Cf. Lamphear, op. cit., p. 130 n. 65.

took them further away from Para-Nilotic influence, but also entailed the absorption of additional Lwo groups already settled in Lango, to whom the age-organization was quite alien.

A similar perspective can be brought to bear upon the problem of the fragmented lineage structure found in nineteenth-century Lango. By the end of the century, clans and lineages were certainly the most important social groups in Lango—much more so than among the Para-Nilotic peoples to the east. But lineage organization in Lango was far removed from the segmentary systems found among the Kenya Luo and the Alur.[97] It provided no social framework above the level of the clan section living in a handful of adjacent villages. As Tarantino has pointed out, the cohesion of the clan in Lango was much less than among other Lwo-speaking peoples, its readiness to break up into separate exogamous units being quite uncharacteristic of the Lwo.[98] This marked dilution of Lwo culture can, like the decline of the age-organization, be seen as a consequence of the combination of Lwo and Iseera groups. As Southall has shown, an age-organization and an extensive segmentary lineage system are fundamentally incompatible; where the two systems do coexist within a single society, neither one is fully developed.[99]

The distinctive aggregate of social institutions in nineteenth-century Lango can hardly be explained in terms of environment or economy, since in these respects Lango did not significantly differ from its neighbours. On the other hand, the process of migration and settlement described in the first chapter was unique. Each group involved in the formation of the Lango people brought its own social institutions, and it was out of these disparate elements that Lango society took shape. The nature of the problem is such that conclusions must depend on reasoned inference, rather than direct evidence; the details are beyond recall, and so is the exact chronology, but the broad pattern is discernible.

Generalization at this level should not, however, imply too great a measure of homogeneity in Lango society. In many ways it is more enlightening to stress the diversity on the ground than to construct a model valid for the whole society. This diversity is striking in two ways. Firstly, localized clan sections varied considerably in size and

---

[97] Southall, 'Lineage Formation among the Luo', and *Alur Society*.
[98] Tarantino, 'The Origin of the Lango', p. 15.
[99] Southall, 'Rank and Stratification among the Alur and other Nilotic Peoples', op. cit., pp. 31–46.

cohesion. A broad distinction can be drawn between east and west, with the east tending towards greater fragmentation. North of the Moroto river, for example, the sparse population was distributed among a multitude of clans on the eve of the colonial period, and this fragmentation was reflected in the small size of villages there.[100] Near the Nile–Toci confluence, on the other hand, the Jo Arak of Aber were the largest clan section in Lango, their members being spread over at least seven large villages.[101] In the second place, there was a comparable regional variation in the strength of the age-organization, though here the continuum followed a north–south, rather than an east–west axis. When Driberg studied the question during the first decade of colonial rule, he found that the further south he travelled in Lango, the more entrenched *ewor* ceremonies appeared to be, while in the north-west they were not practised at all.[102] The existence of these variations shows that within Lango society the fusion of Lwo and Iseera groups was not entirely uniform, but varied according to both local settlement history and geographical position *vis-à-vis* neighbouring peoples.

The essential elements of social organization common to all Lango during the nineteenth century were those described at the beginning of this chapter—the localized clan section, the work-group, and the village. These were the units which dominated the outlook of the ordinary Lango. It was at this level that continuity and consistency were most in evidence, and where the basis of individual political authority was to be found. The crucial stabilizing element was the degree of dominance or subordination which linked one clan section to its neighbours through the medium of clan leadership. So far, the discussion has concerned the nature of social groups in nineteenth-century Lango. It is now necessary to turn instead to the distribution of authority within and between these groups.

---

[100] Interviews: Okelo Olet, Festo Odwe, Adonia Owuco, Yosua Odongo Opio, Joseph Orama, Onyanga Ewoi, Ogwel Okolla. Driberg, entries for 17.2.18 in Moroto TB (1918–26), LDA.

[101] For a full account of pre-colonial Aber, see below, pp. 74–81.

[102] Driberg, *The Lango*, pp. 243, 245, 254. My own experience bears out Driberg's. Of all my Lango informants, those in the north-west (Aber and Iceme) were the most ignorant of the age-organization, even though their historical knowledge in general tended to be above the average for Lango as a whole.

CHAPTER 3

Pre-Colonial Clan Leadership

STATELESS societies are commonly classified according to their varying forms of social organization—segmentary lineages, age-groups, village councils, and so on. We have seen how far Lango society in the nineteenth century corresponded to any of these categories. Yet a political system depends not only on social structure but also on political values. This further dimension is particularly important in determining the role of individual authority. The weight attached to personal leadership varies considerably from one stateless society to another; and it is not determined by the forms of social organization alone, as Robert LeVine has made clear in his comparison of Gusii with Nuer society. Despite close structural similarity (based on the corporate lineage), the two societies exhibit radically opposed attitudes towards authority: while the Nuer are exceedingly open and egalitarian in nearly all their social relationships, the Gusii instinctively defer to elders and to wealthy men.[1] The social institutions described in the last chapter would certainly suggest a prevalence of egalitarian values in nineteenth-century Lango, but it remains to be seen how far political status was differentiated and what role was filled by individual leadership.

Driberg, author of the first ethnographic account of the Langi, was in no doubt about their attitude towards authority at the beginning of the colonial period. They were, he wrote, 'emphatically independent and impatient of control . . . Each man is as good as his neighbour, and disliking interference himself, is equally averse to limiting his own individuality by an acknowledgement of political dependence. They are the last people in the world to be dragooned into any line of thought or action.'[2] Driberg's judgement would appear to have been impaired by the frustrations which he endured as a pioneer administrator. His description suggests an egalitarian—even anarchic—outlook hardly different from that of the Nuer. This is an oversimplifica-

[1] R. A. LeVine, 'The Internalization of Political Values in Stateless Societies', *Human Organization*, 19 (1960), pp. 51–8.

[2] Driberg, *The Lango*, p. 69.

tion, for the Lango attitude to authority was much less straightforward. There is no denying that certain areas of Lango life were conducted in a very egalitarian spirit. Chief of these was the seasonal routine of agricultural work. The *wang tic*, or communal work-group, today functions in a highly open and democratic way;[3] and since the basis of the work-group is co-operation and reciprocity of labour, it can hardly have functioned otherwise during the nineteenth-century: every able-bodied householder possessed equal rights and obligations, regardless of seniority or wealth. In the sphere of ritual, the all-important *etogo* was only slightly less egalitarian. Active participation in the feasting ceremonies was confined to elders, defined as married men whose fathers had died; but beyond that no differentiation of rank or status was made. Indeed, equal sharing of the meat and other tokens of good-neighbourliness were deemed essential if the vengeful interference of the shades was to be averted.[4] Thus in the conduct of their most important public rituals, and in the allocation of labour (and thus also of land), the Langi showed a highly egalitarian tendency. In these spheres, at least, no quarter was given to individual leadership.

This limitation did not, however, apply to every area of social action. In two situations which are central to any consideration of politics, individual leadership played a vital role in nineteenth-century Lango. These situations were the settlement of disputes and the organization of military activities; they were usually handled by the same men, though it was leadership in battle which identified the Lango 'chief' in the eyes of the first European visitors.[5] This concentration of authority, despite its many practical limitations, shows that Lango egalitarianism was far from consistent. The institutional basis of individual authority was not apparent to the earliest observers, and it has been analysed in contradictory ways by twentieth-century writers. Driberg believed that the 'chief' was essentially a war-leader, whose position depended on success in battle and was unrelated to the clan system.[6] Tarantino, on the other hand, has said that

---

[3] The fullest treatment of this theme is A. C. Curley, 'Social Process: clanship and neighbourhood in Lango District, Uganda', unpublished M.A. thesis, Sacramento State College, California, 1971, pp. 96–100, 112–15.

[4] R. T. Curley, *Elders, Shades, and Women*, pp. 51–2, 72–4.

[5] See, for example, E. Linant de Bellefonds, 'Voyage de service fait entre le poste militaire de Fatiko et la capitale de M'tesa roi d'Uganda', *Bulletin Trimestriel de la Société Khédiviale de Géographie du Caire*, I (1876–7), pp. 15–16.

[6] Driberg, *The Lango*, pp. 204–8.

the only chiefs in pre-colonial Lango were the clan heads.[7] The contradiction is explained by a failure to distinguish between two levels of leadership; each combined judicial with military authority, but they differed in territorial range, institutional basis, and stability of tenure. The first category was clan leadership. This was a strictly localized position, though in favourable circumstances it could carry authority over neighbouring clans as well. The second type was regional leadership, which completely transcended the context of clan and village. The basis of this regional authority is much more obscure, but until the 1890s it was a vital element in the military ability of the Langi to impose upon their neighbours and to resist external pressures. This second type of leadership is examined in the next chapter. Here we are concerned only with clan leadership, which was a constant of the political scene throughout the pre-colonial era.

The term 'clan leader' requires immediate qualification in the context of nineteenth-century Lango, since this position in fact seldom carried authority over an entire clan. It reflected the way in which descent groups and territorial groups had become intertwined, and also the fact that most clans were dispersed. The typical 'chief' was not a clan head, or even a lineage head, but the leader of all the members of one clan living in one village, irrespective of lineage, and irrespective of clansmen outside the village; in other words, he was the leader of a clan section.[8] Provided this qualification is borne in mind, the term 'clan leader' is acceptable, and for the sake of simplicity it is employed here.

Clan leadership in Lango was far removed from the stereotype of chiefship popular among European observers of the African scene. There were almost no formal trappings of power. A clan leader had no retainers or 'court'; indeed, his household could seldom be distinguished by its size or position from those of his neighbours. He wore no commonly recognized insignia of office, though in some clans particular ornaments were regarded as his prerogative.[9] Nor was his position even identified by a commonly accepted title. The term *rwot*

---

[7] Tarantino, 'Lango Clans', p. 110.   [8] See above, pp. 43–4.

[9] Driberg (*The Lango*, p. 63) believed that the wearing of ivory ornaments was the universal prerogative of chiefs and their descendants, but there were many places in Lango where any elder could wear ivory. R. H. Johnstone, 'Past Times in Uganda' (1921), MS. in Rhodes House Library, Oxford, p. 16. Interviews: Yakobo Adoko, Luka Abura.

In some places, the wearing of a heavy iron bracelet (*okom*) was a mark of leadership; in others it was a leopard-skin. Interviews: Okelo Abak, Tomasi Ojuka.

was probably the most widely used, but a clan leader was also referred to as *awitong* (spear-leader) or *awimony* (battle-leader).[10]

As for the substance of his authority, the clan leader occupied no special position in the economic life of his locality. This, as we have seen, was the business of the *wang tic*, whose members controlled not only labour, but in effect land-use as well. The fact that land was not controlled by the clan leader represented a considerable restriction on his power, since in many African societies it was special rights with regard to land which enabled such leaders to develop their authority as chiefs.[11] Nor was the clan leader entitled to free labour service or tribute in kind. Any such obligations would have been an affront to the egalitarian values of the *wang tic*; without them, a limit was placed on the hospitality which the leader could dispense, and hence on the following which he could attract. Hunting activities were controlled by the *won arum*, or master of the hunt, in whom considerable authority was on occasion vested.[12] This office was hereditary, the succession being usually limited to the close agnates of the deceased. In some places, the hunting leader was succeeded by his sister's son, thus ensuring the rotation of the office among the clans.[13] Where the office did lie with one clan only, hunting leader and clan leader were very seldom the same man. In Ibuje, for example, the extensive territory of the Jo Ocukuru included during the 1890s two *arum*, and in each case the *won* was a member of the clan without being one of the three clan leaders.[14]

Most significant of all, the exercise of ritual power by chiefs, which was so common a feature of East African society in the nineteenth century, was almost completely absent from Lango.[15] On the one hand, relations with the dead were handled by the *etogo*, an egalitarian body which transcended the clan context.[16] On the other,

[10] Driberg (*The Lango*, p. 206) listed three titles as a hierarchy, according to territorial range: *jago*, *rwot*, and *twon lwak* as the highest. No such classification existed. The terms *jago* and *twon lwak* did not denote formal positions at all. *Jago* appears to have been an importation from Acholi at the beginning of the colonial period. *Twon lwak* ('bull of the crowd') was simply a praise-name, with which any outstanding leader might be complimented.

[11] See, for example, Girling, *The Acholi of Uganda*, pp. 95–6; J. C. Buxton, *Chiefs and Strangers* (Oxford, 1963), pp. 36–91.

[12] See above, p. 54.   [13] Driberg, *The Lango*, p. 175.

[14] Interview: Anderea Ogwang. See also Hayley, *The Anatomy of Lango Religion and Groups*, p. 149.

[15] The only significant exception was the special position enjoyed by the rainmakers of Aduku from about 1860 onwards. See below, pp. 91–2.

[16] See above, pp. 54–6.

communication with the various manifestations of *Jok*, the presiding spirit of the universe, was in the hands of professional diviners, called *ajoka*. These were usually women. They were expected to cure sickness, sterility, and mental disorder, to identify witches, and to determine auspicious moments for dangerous undertakings like hunting, cattle-raiding, and long journeys. Their services were in constant demand, and people were prepared to travel well beyond their normal neighbourhood range in order to consult a good diviner: at the turn of the century, Angwen of Ngai was consulted by men from Aber, twenty miles away.[17] But no practical advantages accrued to the clan leader in whose village the diviner lived. The clan leader had no control over the diviner's activities, still less did he practise divination himself. If the diviner recommended certain ceremonies to be performed, the clan leader might organize them, but he himself had no ritual power.[18] Here again, as in the case of land, the lack of a ritual role deprived the Lango clan leader of one of the most potent sources of chiefly authority.[19]

Taking into account all the restrictions which surrounded the position of *rwot* or clan leader in Lango, it is clearly inappropriate to speak of him as a chief. Writers on other Lwo-speaking peoples such as the Alur and the Acholi normally render the word *rwot* as 'chief'.[20] This translation is probably justified, since in those societies the *rwot* exercised important ritual functions, stood at the head of an aristocratic clan, and received tribute from his people. The Lango *rwot*, on the other hand, enjoyed none of these advantages. Critical aspects of community life were untouched by his authority. His actual functions were twofold. In the first place, as the terms *awitong* and *awimony* imply, he led his clan in battle. Secondly, he took the lead in settling peacefully disputes between members of the clan. Neither of these functions was carried out without some sharing of authority, however. The decision to go on an expedition was generally taken in consultation with the best warriors of the clan; and in the arbitration

[17] Interviews: Nekomia Otwal, Misaki Oki, Ogwang Abura, Barikia Opie. Driberg, *The Lango*, pp. 233–40; Hayley, op. cit., pp. 22–9, 153–69.

[18] I have found no evidence to support the view mentioned to Hayley by Driberg that the clan leader 'incarnated' the power of *Jok* in the clan. Hayley, op. cit., p. 43.

[19] For examples, see Southall, *Alur Society*, pp. 88–97; Girling, op. cit., pp. 98–100; and the several case-studies in A. Roberts (ed.), *Tanzania Before 1900* (Nairobi, 1968).

[20] Southall, op. cit.; Girling, op. cit.; J. M. Onyango-ku-Odongo and J. B. Webster (eds.), *The Central Lwo during the Aconya* (Nairobi, 1976).

of disputes the opinion of the clan elders (*odonge*) was respected, for—whether or not they were still able to fight in battle—they were deeply versed in the clan's affairs and were credited with sound judgement.

The degree of authority which a clan leader was able to exercise depended in the last resort on his personal qualities. If these were outstanding, the processes of consultation would carry less weight. The most important quality was prowess in battle. In so far as skill in hunting added to a man's prestige, this was also an asset.[21] In addition a clan leader was expected to be hospitable and sociable.[22] These were the qualities which on the death of a clan leader influenced the choice of his successor. Clan leadership was in fact based on a combination of ascribed and achieved criteria. The wishes of the deceased were taken into account, and a son usually succeeded, but the final choice lay with the elders of the clan section. Ideally the eldest son was most suitable; he was likely to have amassed greater wealth and married more wives than his younger brothers; he would therefore enjoy greater prestige and be able to dispense more hospitality. But if the eldest son made a poor showing in battle, he was passed over in favour of a younger son, a brother, or even an agnatic cousin of the deceased. In Abyece, for example, Ogwang Owiny, the leader of the Jo Alipa, died prematurely of smallpox in about 1900. His sons were too young and his brother was a weakling; so the leadership devolved on Ogwang's first cousin, Ebek, who had only recently migrated with his brothers to Abyece and inherited a wife there.[23]

In some cases, however, a son of the deceased became clan leader notwithstanding extreme youth. Among the Jo Arak of Aber, Odongo Aja was chosen to succeed his father during the 1870s while still in his twenties; during his early years as *rwot* senior members of the clan guided him until his own success in battle proved the wisdom of their choice.[24] In Iceme, Olwa Abelli, who died in about 1895, was succeeded as *rwot* of the Jo Olwa by his son Olong Adilo, then in his teens. For some years afterwards the effective leader of the clan was Olwa's brother, Okaka, who as late as 1905 was regarded as the local 'chief' by the British. It was only shortly before colonial administration was established in northern Lango in 1910 that Olong Adilo

---

[21] Interviews: Onyanga Ewoi, Yakobo Adoko.
[22] Interviews: Matayo Acut, Sira Okelo.
[23] Interviews: Benedikto Okelo Elwange, Matayo Ojok, Ibrahim Lodo.
[24] Interviews: Matayo Acut, Leoben Okodi.

ceased to defer to his uncle and became clan leader in fact as well as in name.[25]

The normal rules of succession were also bent when a clan leader survived the dangers of battle and disease to become an old man. In such cases the leader usually held a meeting of the elders and with their approval transferred his authority to a son or close agnate.[26] It is possible that stories about transfers of this kind conceal usurpation of clan authority by younger men of outstanding abilities, but no explicit traditions of usurpation have been recorded, and there is no doubt that in the majority of cases clan leaders continued in office until death or old age overtook them.

There was little variation in the content of Lango clan leadership, but the actual power which it conferred varied greatly according to the size of the clan section. Probably the majority of clan sections in the late nineteenth century were each accommodated in one or two villages, but there were many clan sections which required several villages and were able to retain them as a terrible bloc. Sometimes these blocs were the result of one large clan section migrating *en masse*, as in northern Ibuje where in the mid 1880s the Jo Ocukuru arrived in large numbers and settled in three villages.[27] In other cases the first representatives of the clan were quite few, but they were later joined by other sections of the clan who founded villages adjacent to the first; the way in which the commanding position of the Jo Oyima in Akokoro was built up has already been described.[28]

The fact that a clan section was spread over several villages did not cause all the functions of clan leadership to be concentrated in one man. Each village within the complex had its own leader who was head of a lineage or a clan section. Like any other clan leader, he was responsible for the settlement of petty disputes and for the defence of his village. The way in which villages of the same clan responded to each other's needs in an informal way is conveyed in the following

[25] Lazaro Okelo, 'Concerning Our Ancestors', translation of undated vernacular MS., typescript in Department of History, Makerere University, p. 1; Nasan Engola, 'Olden Times in Northern Lango', translation of undated vernacular MS., typescript in Department of History, Makerere University, p. 6. Fowler to Wilson, 9.7.05, UNA A12/6. Interviews: Mohammed Okec, Lazaro Okelo, Ogwang Abura.

[26] Interviews: Suleman Ikwe, Bejaleri Ogwang, Pilipo Oruro, Onyanga Ewoi.

[27] Interviews: Anderea Ogwang, Yakobo Gaci.

[28] See above, pp. 50–2.

account, which refers to the three villages occupied by the Ocukuru clan in Ibuje during the 1880s and 1890s:[29]

When there was trouble in Aduni, a horn was blown there and a drum beaten; then the people here [in Alenga] would run and join the warriors there, and all the Aketo people went along as well. When a fight began here and the leader sounded his horn, the leader of Aketo heard it and sounded his horn as well. And when the people of Aduni heard it, they hurried along, saying, 'Our brothers over there are being attacked!'

In Ibuje there was no single leader recognized as head of all Jo Ocukuru in the area; in the last few years before administration was established there in 1909, two men appear to have exercised almost equal authority.[30] This was an atypical situation. For while village leaders settled disputes in their own villages, they usually recognized the primacy of one of their number as leader of expeditions. In effect, a clan section which occupied several villages needed a single head where relations with other clan sections were concerned. And when these were small and dependent, the single head became a powerful figure.

To a limited extent, nearly all clan leaders ruled men of other clans. For by the end of the century—and probably earlier—most villages in Lango included a handful of non-agnates who had migrated there because of kinship ties or difficulties at home. These strangers, while retaining their original clan identity, were subject to the authority of the leader of the host clan section. The typical Lango 'chief' was thus village headman as well as head of his clan section. This was an interesting gloss on the principle of clan leadership, but in practice it represented hardly any increase in the clan leader's power. The strangers who attached themselves to established clan sections were very seldom numerous enough to provide an additional political resource, as clientage did among the Mandari of the Southern Sudan.[31] On the other hand, above the village level, the acknowledgement of authority outside the clan was the most significant growth point in the Lango political system.

The dominance of one clan section over another seems usually to have been based on primacy of settlement, a clan section being more

---

[29] Interview: Anderea Ogwang.

[30] The two men were Arum of Aduni and Gongi of Aketo. The fact that Arum later became County Chief of Maruzi (1913–30) has caused his pre-colonial eminence to be exaggerated in some quarters. Interviews: Yakobo Gaci, Yakobo Oluma, Anderea Ogwang, Pilipo Omwa Ayo.

[31] Buxton, op. cit., ch. 7.

likely to assert itself if it had been the first to settle in the area. As the last chapter showed, the decision of other clan sections to settle near by was frequently based on affinal or cognatic ties. This was the reason why during the 1890s the Jo Atek me Okalodyang, the Jo Acut me Ongoda, and the Jo Anyeke migrated to the lakeshore in Akokoro. They came from different places and had been obliged to move on for different reasons, but they all had marriage links with Akaki's clan, the Jo Oyima. Once having settled in Akokoro, they regarded Akaki as their leader.[32] Often, however, clan dominance was not based on kinship links in the first instance, though such links were the inevitable result of prolonged residence in the same locality. A migrating clan section could settle near another clan section merely because there was vacant land. If the first clan section was a large one, it was likely all the same to become dominant, either because the new arrivals had to ask for military help in a crisis, or because they preferred to accept a subordinate position rather than risk becoming the target for cattle-raids by the stronger group. The reason for entering into a subordinate relationship was still more compelling if the dominant clan section had already proved its strength by expelling other clan sections from the area. In Abyece for example, a succession of incidents in about 1902 precipitated a clash between Ebek of the Jo Alipa and four small clan sections. By calling on the help of allies from Agwata, Ebek so harassed the other clan sections that they abandoned Abyece altogether and settled south of Lake Kwania.[33] At about the same time, a section of the Jo Arak me Eling settled in western Abyece, and it seems to have been Ebek's military reputation which caused them to accept his leadership in battle and even his views on the succession to their own clan leadership.[34]

The most widespread way in which clan dominance was most commonly expressed was in war. The subject clan sections answered calls to arms by the dominant clan section, or one of them requested military help, but in either case it was the leader of the dominant clan section who commanded the expedition. In some places, this military co-operation was formalized by the gathering together each year of the clan sections concerned for a meeting (amur) at the leader's village, where expeditions during the coming dry season were planned.[35]

[32] Interviews: Yakobo Adoko, Nekomia Agwa, Samwiri Ade, Yosia Omwa.
[33] Interviews: Isaka Ojaba, Ibrahim Lodo, Nasaneri Ongona, Matayo Ojok.
[34] Interviews: Pilipo Oruro, Omara Ekak, Matayo Ojok.
[35] Interviews: Erisa Olugo, Tomasi Ogwete, Yakobo Olugo, Misaki Oki, Barikia Opie, Mohammed Okec, Yakobo Adoko, Yosia Omwa.

In places where the dominant clan section was particularly well established or respected, military leadership was combined with authority to adjudicate in inter-clan disputes. Quarrels within the clan section were generally settled by the clan leader concerned; they were unlikely to involve serious offences, because respect for the solidarity of the clan was so deeply ingrained; but between different clans fewer restraints applied. Personal quarrels were much more likely to result in homicide, and illicit sexual intercourse (*luk*) with wives or unmarried girls was a common cause of friction. Disagreement arose less over the identity of the offender than the extent of his liability for compensation in livestock. At different times there was a fair measure of agreement about what, in theory, the rates of compensation were,[36] but in practice the two parties were unlikely to agree on an exact amount, particularly if the number of cattle in the neighbourhood was fluctuating or a 'free' wife was suggested as an alternative compensation in a homicide case.[37] If the two clan sections concerned were not immediate neighbours linked by affinal and cognatic ties, disputes of this kind often took the form of raiding and counter-raiding. But between neighbouring clan sections, kinship ties placed a limit on violent reprisals. Compensation might be fixed by consultation among the two groups of elders, but the matter was more likely to be settled smoothly if a third party could arbitrate. In this way, the leader of a locally-dominant clan section could become responsible for maintaining good relations between the clans he led in battle. In Akokoro during the time of Akaki, for instance, the leader of the Jo Anyeke settled any disputes that arose within his clan section, but if another clan section was involved he sent to Akaki, either for warriors so that the issue could be determined by force, or to ask him to adjudicate; this Akaki did in a homicide case between the Jo Anyeke and their neighbours, the Jo Akabo.[38]

The subordination of one clan section to another might be interpreted as a form of clientage, particularly in view of the element of protection involved. But it is important to note that, in contrast to other recorded instances,[39] the subordinate group in Lango remained

---

[36] Since about 1890 the usual rate for homicide has been seven head of cattle; it was almost certainly greater before the rinderpest epidemic of the 1890s. Driberg, *The Lango*, pp. 210–11; Curley, *Elders, Shades, and Women*, pp. 36–7.

[37] A. Tarantino, 'Il matrimonio tra i Lango anticamente e al presente', *Anthropos*, 35 (1941), p. 881. Interview: Anderea Okadde.

[38] Interview: Yosia Omwa.

[39] Buxton, op. cit., pp. 93, 102–3.

a discrete entity; it did not merge with the dominant clan section. The relationship between host and client groups was neither institutionalized nor blurred by time, with the result that it was inherently unstable.

The number of clan sections which were militarily or judicially dependent on a dominant clan section varied considerably. One British observer estimated on the basis of his experience of southern Lango in 1899 that a powerful 'chief' ruled up to ten villages[40]—including, of course, the villages of his own clan section. The number of subordinate clans and villages depended ultimately on the strength of the dominant clan section, for the greater its size and reputation, the greater would be the number of groups seeking its protection. This can best be illustrated by an extended case-study of the Jo Arak of Aber. At the beginning of this century, their hegemony enveloped seven substantial clan sections in north-west Lango–the most powerful military combination of its time. The case of the Jo Arak was not typical, but it presents in high relief the strict limitations on individual authority in Lango on the eve of the colonial period.

The area known as Aber lies north of the Nile, astride the River Toci, and it is among the most fertile parts of Lango. It attracted Lwo settlers as well as the earliest Lango migrants from the east. By the 1870s the largest group in Aber was the Jo Arak.[41] This clan was present in very great numbers—indeed, it was the largest single clan concentration anywhere in Lango. By the end of the nineteenth century its members were living in at least seven villages, divided into three groups. North of the Toci was a group of villages called Kamdini, associated with the Elwia lineage. This same lineage was also dominant in a group of four villages called Ocini, due east of Kamdini on the left bank of the Toci, while five miles south-west of Ocini lay Akaka, the village of the Ocola lineage.[42] Early British observers were much impressed by this density of population[43] (Map 5).

Each of the three groups had its own leader, but the leadership of the whole clan section lay with the Elwia lineage in Kamdini. By 1880, Odongo Aja had succeeded to the position of *rwot*, with Owiny Akulo

---

[40] H. J. Madcocks, Wakedi Field Force Intelligence Report, May 1899, PRO FO/403/281.

[41] Interviews: Leoben Okodi, Misaki Oki, Matayo Acut, Yosia Omara.

[42] Interviews: Leoben Okodi, Misaki Oki, Matayo Acut, Nekomia Otwal.

[43] Anderson to Johnston, 21.3.00, UNA A4/27; Jervoise, Report on Masindi District for July 1906, UNA SMP/515/part 1.

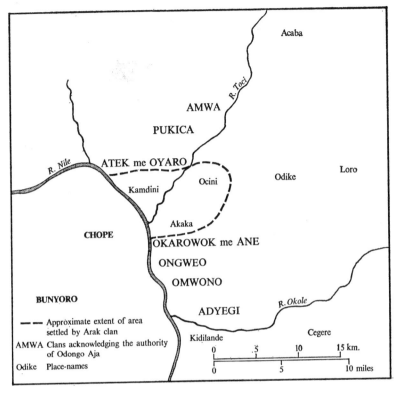

Map 5. Aber on the Eve of the Colonial Period

as leader of Ocini, and Okelo Abong as leader of Akaka.[44] Odongo Aja did not concern himself with the internal affairs of Ocini and Akaka, but he took the lead in organizing raids against other clans. On one occasion when a man of the Ocola lineage led a raid south of the Okole river and was killed, Odongo Aja stepped in to recover the clan's prestige.[45] The only remembered case of a successful expedition not led by Odongo, was Owiny Akulo's attack on Anyeke.[46] After Odongo, Owiny Akulo was the best warrior in the clan; the raid on Anyeke may have occurred during Odongo's last illness in 1906.[47]

[44] Interviews: Leoben Okodi, Matayo Acut, Nekomia Otwal, Kosia Ato.
[45] Interview: Misaki Oki.   [46] Interviews: Kosia Ato, Simon Ogwete.
[47] One of Odongo's last expeditions was against the Jo Olwa of Iceme. He kept in the background, probably because of illness, and in Iceme Odongo's brother, Otwal, and Owiny Akulo are remembered as the leaders of the expedition. Engola, op. cit., p. 7. Interviews: Mohammed Okec, Ogwang Abura.

By that time, Odongo had capitalized on the numerical strength of the Jo Arak to achieve a dominance over all the country from the Okole river in the south to very nearly the Acholi border in the north. Seven substantial clan sections acknowledged his leadership.[48] According to Odongo's son, all those north of the Toci were conquered by force.[49] Another account distinguishes between those clan sections defeated in battle and those who were cowed into submission by Odongo's reputation—those who, as the tradition puts it, 'saw the fire' (*oneno mac*).[50] These explanations exaggerate Odongo's prowess. None of the subject clan sections has a tradition of conquest by the Jo Arak. Their accounts suggest that their subordination dated from, or shortly after, their original settlement. Two closely linked factors can be distinguished. Firstly, such a large concentration of one clan was an attraction for smaller and less secure clan sections seeking protection. At the lowest level, the Jo Arak attracted individual families who had been forced to leave their own settlements. Refugees of this kind are said to have come from as far away as Erute and Aduku in central Lango, and one etymology advanced today for the place-name Aber is that it meant 'the good place' (*aber*) for refugees.[51] In the same way, whole clan sections settled in Aber in order to enjoy the protection of the Jo Arak. This is admitted to have been the case among the Jo Pukica, who seem to have settled north of the Toci around 1890, and it was probably so elsewhere.[52] Secondly, even if other clan sections did not settle near Kamdini explicitly in order to be protected by Odongo Aja, circumstances could quickly oblige them to turn to him for help. It is often said in Aber today that Odongo used to answer appeals from war-leaders who wished to attack a more powerful adversary, or who had already been defeated.[53] Towards the end of his life, Odongo's answers to these appeals took him as far afield as Ngai and Iceme. But before 1900 this was how several clan sections nearer home became dependent on him. When the Jo Okarowok me Omwono settled near Atura, Odongo helped them to expel some of the Lwo there; their dependence on Odongo was increased a few years later when they called on him to secure the release

---

[48] The seven clans were: Adyegi, Ongweo, Okarowok me Omwono, Okarowok me Ane, Atek me Oyaro, Pukica and Amwa. Interviews: Koranima Ayena, Suleman Ikwe, Yosia Okwe, Edwardi Olir, Erisa Olugo, Yakobo Olugo, Tomasi Ogwete.
[49] Interview: Matayo Acut.   [50] Interview: Leoben Okodi.
[51] Interview: Leoben Okodi.   [52] Interview: Yakobo Olugo.
[53] Interviews: Leoben Okodi, Edwardi Olir, Nekomia Otwal.

of their leader who had been captured by a clan section from Cegere.[54] In 1899 the Jo Adyegi, who had recently migrated across the Okole from Cegere, fell out with the clans already there, and Odongo's intervention enabled the Jo Adyegi to expel them.[55]

The price of protection was invariably participation in Odongo's own raids, under his orders. With a view to planning expeditions, all the subject clan sections were required to attend regular meetings at Odongo's home, along with the elders of his own clan section; the only exception to this rule was the Jo Adyegi who lived further away from Kamdini than any other clan section.[56] With this military subordination went an acknowledgement of Odongo's authority as arbitrator in disputes. In the case of the Jo Pukica this authority was even called upon to resolve the constant quarrels between the two component lineages.[57] But Odongo Aja's main interest was in disputes that divided one clan section from another among those he relied on for his military adventures. Thus, the Jo Adyegi asked Odongo to intervene if one of their number was murdered on a path outside his village.[58] In a case of manslaughter, arising from illicit sexual intercourse, which involved the Jo Pukica and a small clan section living near by, Odongo went to the scene and settled the dispute, although both parties had already begun to assemble warriors for a fight.[59] Instead of going himself, Odongo sometimes sent an assistant (*awang rwot*), who was usually a senior member of the Jo Arak, resident in Odongo's own village.[60] But, whoever came brought warriors, and it is plain that some of these missions turned into punitive raids in which the offender was plundered and perhaps even killed.[61]

It will be evident from the foregoing account that the dependence of the subordinate clan sections was primarily on Odongo Aja, rather than on the other two leaders of the Jo Arak. This was so wherever the subordinate clan section was situated. For example, both the Jo

[54] Interview: Suleman Ikwe.

[55] Interview: Koranima Ayena. The dating seems certain because this was one of the first battles in which the guns of the Sudanese mutineers were used (see below, ch. 5) and because it corresponds closely with a major disruption among the Langi within fifteen miles of Foweira, recorded by a British officer in Bunyoro in August 1899: Evatt to Ternan, 8.8.99, UNA A4/20.

[56] Interviews: Erisa Olugo, Yakobo Olugo, Tomasi Ogwete, Nekomia Otwal, Koranima Ayena.   [57] Interview: Yakobo Olugo.

[58] Interview: Koranima Ayena.   [59] Interview: Yakobo Olugo.

[60] The position of *awang rwot* in Lango is in some ways comparable to that of *wang rwot* in nineteenth-century Acholi, though there he normally belonged to a clan other than the *rwot*'s. Girling, op. cit., pp. 96–7.

[61] Interviews: Leoben Okodi, Misaki Oki, Yakobo Olugo, Matayo Acut.

Ongweo and the Jo Adyegi looked to Odongo Aja in Kamdini, and not to Okelo Abong in Akaka, despite the fact that Akaka was much closer.[62] The only authority which Okelo Abong or Owiny Akulo had outside the members of their own clan was over non-agnates living in their own villages. In Owiny Akulo's area of Ocini, this authority was considerable: the minority clan sections were so numerous that one of their elders was made headman of one of the four villages in Ocini.[63] Outside Ocini, however, Owiny Akulo enjoyed great prestige as a warrior, but his authority was not comparable to Odongo Aja's.

On the basis of his strong position in the Jo Arak and among the neighbouring clan sections, Odongo Aja was able to raid far afield during his last years. The assistance which he had given to the Jo Adyegi in 1899 involved him in a feud with one of the groups that had been chased away, the Jo Adok of Kidilande. On one of his raids south of the Okole river in about 1902, Odongo even went as far as Ibuje, to the territory of the Jo Ocukuru, who were allies of the Jo Adok.[64] At about the same time, Odongo went to attack the Jo Olwa of Iceme, and shortly before his death he answered an appeal from the Jo Olwa themselves, who were anxious to defeat one of their northern neighbours, the Jo Ongoda.[65] The main aim of these expeditions was of course plunder, and much livestock was taken from south of the Okole and from the Jo Ongoda.[66] A sizeable proportion of the booty was kept by the rwot, 'for his flag' (me bere), as it was said.[67] Odongo also made a speciality of human captives. Many women and children were taken from the Jo Olwa, including their leader's son who was nearly sacrificed alive.[68] Captives were released in return for a ransom of livestock: a woman of Iceme recalls that her husband paid eight head of cattle to recover her from the Jo Arak a year after her capture.[69]

Towards the end of his life, Odongo's position as rwot was increasingly formalized. At his own village of Ayel in Kamdini he maintained about six warriors called jo kal ('people of the rwot's compound') or

[62] Interviews: Yosia Okwe, Koranima Ayena.

[63] Interview: Leoben Okodi.

[64] Interviews: Yakobo Oluma, Koranima Ayena, Matayo Ayika, Anderea Ogwang. Fowler to Wilson, 27.2.05, UNA A12/6; Knowles to Wilson, 30.5.08, UNA SMP/1005/08.

[65] Engola, op. cit., pp. 5–7. Interviews: Leoben Okodi, Edwardi Olir, Mohammed Okec, Ogwang Abura.

[66] Interview: Erisa Olugo. Engola, op. cit., p. 5.

[67] Interview: Koranima Ayena.   [68] Interview: Mohammed Okec.

[69] Interview: Anna Awor (cf. Leoben Okodi, Matayo Acut).

ogwok rwot ('*rwot*'s guards') who guarded his compound and accompanied him on campaigns, carrying his shield and spears until he required them.[70] During battle, Odongo stayed in the rear to encourage back-sliders; he entered the fray only when his men were hard pressed, the actual attack being led by Owiny Akulo or by Odongo's brother, Otwal.[71] Odongo also carried a baton or sceptre, which was made of wood and decorated with iron rings and incisions.[72] Most important of all, Odongo Aja's position of authority was coming to be defined by the term *ker*. This word was commonly used by the Alur and the Acholi to describe the authority which a *rwot* exercised over his own clan and the subordinate clans. It denoted not the territory of the *rwot*, but the quality of his authority, and can best be translated as 'chiefly power'.[73] *Ker* was used with just the same meaning in Aber.[74]

The concept of *ker* indicates that the leadership of the Jo Arak in Aber was beginning to be seen as an institution, rather than a temporary recognition of one man's outstanding abilities. This impression is strengthened by the turn of events after Odongo Aja's death in 1906.[75] The British official stationed at Masindi (in Bunyoro) reported that Odongo's brother, Otwal, had been 'chosen by his own people' to succeed him.[76] Practically speaking, this was so, but the report concealed an all-important limitation on Otwal's prospects. For the formal successor was not Otwal, but Odongo's own son Itot, who was then only about ten years old. Odongo himself had succeeded his father as a very young man, and it seems that the rule of filial succession was particularly strong in the Jo Arak; but the designation of a mere boy was most unusual, perhaps unprecedented in Lango. Otwal had his own ambitions for the chiefship, but he failed to persuade the other elders that Itot ought to be set aside on account of his extreme youth. Instead, Otwal acted as guardian for his nephew. For the time being he effectively ruled as *rwot* and was recognized as such by the subordinate clan sections; indeed it is sometimes assumed among elders in Aber today that he was Odongo's actual successor. But in

[70] Interviews: Matayo Acut, Leoben Okodi.
[71] Interviews: Leoben Okodi, Fancio Itot.   [72] Interview: Leoben Okodi.
[73] Southall, *Alur Society*, pp. 189–91; Girling, op. cit., pp. 82–91.
[74] Interviews: Fancio Itot, Yosia Omara.
The term *aker*, meaning one invested with *ker*, i.e. a chief, occurs in a Lango proverb, but in no other context. T. R. F. Cox, 'Lango Proverbs', *Uganda Jl.*, 10 (1946), p. 118.
[75] Jervoise, Report on Masindi District for Oct. 1906, UNA SMP/515/part 2.
[76] Ibid.

the Arak clan it was fully understood that Itot would one day take over the powers of his father, for he had been installed as *rwot* in an elaborate ceremony, in which he was ritually 'washed' by the clan elders and declared to have assumed his father's *ker*.[77]

The effectiveness of the new regime cannot easily be assessed, since within three years of Odongo Aja's death, Protectorate rule was established in north-western Lango. But it seems fairly clear that the dominance of the Jo Arak survived Odongo's death. By 1908 the initial fears of British officials that Otwal's influence would not equal Odongo's had been dispelled,[78] and the raids south of the Okole river continued as vigorously as before.[79] It is possible to discern in Aber on the eve of the colonial period the makings of a stable political structure enveloping the Toci valley and the right bank of the Nile over an area equivalent to nearly two modern sub-counties. Had British administration not been established in 1909, the next generation or two might have seen the Arak dominance strengthened by new institutions.

It is as well to be clear just how little inter-clan dominance had been institutionalized in Aber. Odongo Aja exercised no ritual powers, any more than leaders of less populous clan sections did elsewhere. The ascendancy of the Jo Arak had not led to a distinction between an 'aristocratic' clan (*jo kal* or *jo ker*) and 'commoner' clans (*lwak* or *lobong*), as had happened among the Acholi.[80] There was no term to describe the territorial extent of the *rwot*'s authority, and no symbolic expression of his dominance such as a chiefdom shrine or a ceremony attended by all subject clans: even Itot's succession ceremony appears to have been the exclusive concern of the Jo Arak. Nor was there any tendency towards appointive chieftaincy, for the leaders of the subordinate clan sections continued to be chosen by the elders in the traditional way.[81] Odongo's authority was channelled through the

[77] Interviews: Leoben Okodi, Matayo Acut, Fancio Itot (Odongo's successor). According to Okodi, Odongo Aja had also been 'washed' at his succession.

[78] Jervoise, Report on Masindi District for December 1906, UNA SMP/515/ part 2; Knowles to Wilson, 50.5.08, UNA SMP/1005/08. The traditions of the subordinate clans also indicate no diminution of power. Interviews: Koranima Ayena, Oyom Iyim, Yakobo Olugo, Yosia Okwe, Tomasi Ogwete.

[79] Knowles to Wilson, 30.5.08, UNA SMP/1005/08. Interview: Nekomia Otwal.

[80] Crazzolara, *The Lwoo*, pp. 71–2; R. M. Bere, 'Land and Chieftainship among the Acholi', *Uganda Jl.*, 19 (1955), pp. 49–50.

[81] Some of Hayley's informants in the 1930s told him that a *rwot* used to appoint other clan chiefs as his *jagi* or sub-chiefs; but, as Hayley himself pointed out, this was probably due to a confusion with the colonial system of appointive chiefs; the word *rwot* was later used to mean county-chief. Hayley, op. cit., p. 145.

leaders of the other clan sections and did not impinge directly on their clansmen; his was inter-clan rather than supra-clan or territorial authority. In short, politics in Aber on the eve of the colonial period cannot be seen in terms of chiefship values. The individual's political loyalties were to his clan section and village; any obligations beyond that were recognized for practical reasons, and not out of respect for an ideal of chiefly rule.

These qualifications applied with still greater force elsewhere in Lango. The degree of one-clan concentration in Aber was unique. Nowhere else was the disparity in size between a dominant clan section and its subordinates so marked. The special regard for the *rwot*'s position, as shown in the succession ceremony and the notion of *ker*, was found only in north-western Lango.[82] Furthermore, the judicial content of inter-clan authority was more developed in western and central Lango than in the east where, outside his own clan section and village, a *rwot* tended to exercise no more than occasional military leadership. In Omoro at the beginning of this century, for example, there were four major clan sections; two of them, the Jo Otikokin and the Jo Atek me Okwerowe, were close associates, but their alliance was one of equals, and they had no authority over the remaining two, though they did lead some smaller clan sections on cattle raids.[83] Round the present-day town of Dokolo, the leaders of the two most populous clan sections used to combine periodically for attacks on the Kumam during the 1890s, and other clan sections used to join them, but at all other times the authority of the two leaders, Okwanga and Opige, was restricted to their own villages.[84] This distinction between east and west did not escape European observers. It was probably with his previous experience of western Lango in mind that G. P. Jervoise, the first British official to be stationed near Dokolo, remarked that there appeared to have been 'no chiefs

---

[82] Both these elements are found among the Jo Inomo of Loro and the Jo Olwa of Iceme (Interviews: Yosia Omara, Ogwang Abura), but they have not been recorded anywhere else. They were absent, for instance, from Ibuje, Akokoro, and Abyece.

Olyech's description of a traditional clan leader's installation ceremony is applicable only to north-western Lango. E. Olyech, 'The Anointing of Clan Heads among the Lango', *Uganda Jl.*, 4 (1937), pp. 317–18.

[83] Interviews: Nasaneri Owino, Yolam Aliro, Kezekia Okelo, Anderea Okadde, Enoci Bua, Yubu Engola.

[84] Interviews: Tomasi Ojuka, Yeromia Otim, Zedekia Ogwang Abor, Ekoc Opige, Abiramo Okelo Oyanga, Oco Abolli, Amnoni Abura, Alessandro Ocen.

recognized by the Lango' there before his arrival;[85] in Aber, by contrast, Jervoise had been in no doubt that Odongo Aja was a formidable authority.[86]

It is easier to record these variations in political organization on the eve of the colonial period than to account for their roots in terms of divergent experience during the previous century. However, the contrast between east and west is probably to be explained with reference to the uneven influence of Lwo ideas upon the political organization of the Langi. Western Lango, particularly the country along the Nile and its tributaries, had been the area most affected by Lwo settlement during the period from 1600 to 1800. The Lango migrants from Otuke who colonized this area from 1800 onwards not only absorbed more Lwo than their fellow-countrymen to the east, but they were also living in closer proximity to the well-established Lwo populations of Acholi and Chope, and further away from any Para-Nilotic-speaking peoples. These accidents of geography and migration accounted for the more sophisticated clan leadership found in north-western Lango. In eastern Lango, on the other hand, clan sections tended to be smaller, and clan leadership was less freely acknowledged. The chances of an effective inter-clan dominance being built up were therefore much reduced.

The role of clan leadership has up to this point been considered in relation to the internal ordering of Lango society, and in particular as a focus of antagonism or alliance between neighbouring clan sections. It remains to be shown what part clan leaders played in the relations between the Langi and their neighbours during the nineteenth-century. Inter-tribal trade and warfare caused a steady flow of material assets into and out of Lango. To what extent was this flow controlled by clan leaders, and how far were the assets acquired from abroad a political resource?

As in much of sub-Saharan Africa, the most important articles of indigenous trade in pre-colonial Uganda were iron and mineral-salt. Natural deposits of both these essentials were relatively rare, and during the nineteenth-century there was a brisk trade in salt and iron throughout the interlacustrine region and beyond.[87] Mineral-salt does

[85] Jervoise, undated entry in Dokolo TB (1913–26, part 1), LDA.
[86] Jervoise, Report on Masindi District for Oct. 1906, UNA SMP/515/part 2.
[87] For a brief survey of this trade, see J. Tosh, 'The Northern Interlacustrine Region', in R. Gray and D. Birmingham (eds.), Pre-Colonial African Trade (London, 1970), pp. 104–11. For fuller details of the salt traffic, see C. M. Good,

exist in Lango near Lake Kwania, but it was not discovered until the beginning of the colonial period.[88] Salt could be extracted from goat's dung and from certain wild grasses, but the results were not very palatable, and during the nineteenth century there was a demand in Lango for imported mineral-salt from the deposits at Kibero in Bunyoro.[89] Natural deposits of iron-ore are quite common in Lango, and in the northern and eastern parts of the country smelting was practised by the earliest settlers; but the Langi were not good iron-workers, and they preferred to import metalware from their more highly skilled neighbours—the Labwor in the east, and the Banyoro in the west. Bracelets and wire were imported for use as bodily ornament, and also hoes, which were turned into spear-heads as well as put to agricultural use. The iron trade appears to have flourished from the earliest period of Lango settlement onwards, so much so that by the beginning of the twentieth century the indigenous tradition of iron-smelting had almost completely disappeared.[90]

The main commodities given in exchange for salt and ironware were foodstuffs—principally millet, sorghum, and simsim. Goats and poultry were also bartered. Both the Labwor and the Banyoro regarded Lango as an important source of food to supplement inadequate supplies at home; such shortages were very common in Bunyoro, though more irregular in Labwor. By the beginning of the twentieth century imported hoes had begun to replace wooden digging-sticks, especially in those parts within easy reach of the Nile and Lake Kwania, and grain crops were still Lango's main export.[91] This suggests that the Langi produced considerable surpluses of food. In subsistence economies it is common for the farmer to place under cultivation enough land to furnish his subsistence needs if the yield proves bad; in years of good yield he will therefore produce a

'Salt, Trade, and Disease: Aspects of Development in Africa's northern Great Lakes Region', *International Jl. African Historical Studies*, 5 (1972), pp. 543–86.

[88] Jervoise, Report on Bululu District for March 1909, UNA SMP/945/09; unsigned entry for 14.9.17 in Dokolo TB (1913–26, part 1), LDA.

[89] C. T. Wilson and R. W. Felkin, *Uganda and the Egyptian Soudan* (London, 1882), vol. II, p. 54; Ogwal Ajungu, untitled vernacular history (1936–7), MS. in the possession of Dr. T. T. S. Hayley, paragraph 8; Driberg, op. cit., pp. 89–90.

[90] Interviews: Leoben Okodi, Oco Abolli, Lazaro Okelo, Luka Abura, Erieza Oyaka. Grant to Commissioner, 21.3.02, UNA A10/2/1902 (for Labwor). Driberg, op. cit., pp. 44, 62, 81, 87. A. Tarantino, 'Notes on the Lango', *Uganda Jl.*, 13 (1949), p. 149.

[91] Jervoise, Report on Masindi District for Dec. 1906, UNA SMP/515/part 2; Fishbourne, Report on districts round Lake Kyoga, 5.10.08, UNA SMP/549/09.

surplus.[92] It is unlikely, however, that the prevalence of imported hoes can be explained in terms of the 'normal surplus' alone. Almost certainly, there was deliberate production of a market surplus in some parts of Lango, and this impression is strengthened by the reliance which the Protectorate Government was able to place on food exports from Lango during the years 1913–14, when there were severe shortages in Busoga and northern Buganda.[93]

Lango traders were known to travel abroad during the nineteenth century,[94] but most of the barter was conducted by itinerant traders from Bunyoro and from Labwor. The Banyoro were much the more important of the two, since they penetrated every part of Lango except the extreme north-east, and because they came much more frequently than the Labwor did. The most regular traffic from Bunyoro was carried by boat along Lake Kwania and Lake Kyoga, a route which enabled the Banyoro to extend their activities to Kumam country and even to Teso; but the traders also came by land, and by the end of the century they were visiting the Moroto valley. Banyoro traders travelled in small groups, stopping for a few days in one promising locality before moving on to the next. Lango traditions are almost unanimous that the traders did not travel at random, but stayed at the homes of well-known leaders for protection. Such a home could be used either as a base for touring the immediate vicinity, or as a market from which salt and ironware were redistributed in small quantities by individual Langi. No doubt a clan leader's prestige was increased if he played host to foreign traders, but there is no evidence that he controlled either the production of agricultural surpluses or the distribution of the trade goods. Trade with non-Langi involved the humblest cultivators and was in no sense a source of political patronage.[95]

[92] W. Allan, *The African Husbandman* (Edinburgh, 1965), pp. 38–48.

[93] Scott, Report on Lango District for 1913–14, UNA EPMP Z/228/13. Driberg, *The Lango*, pp. 99–100. See also J. Tosh, 'Lango Agriculture during the Early Colonial Period: Land and Labour in a Cash-crop Economy', *Jl. African History*, 19 (1978), in the press.

[94] Interviews: Nekomia Otwal, Leoben Okodi, Isaka Ojaba, Tomasi Ojuka, Yubu Engola, Anderea Okadde, Onyanga Ewoi. G. Schweinfurth and others (eds.), *Emin Pasha in Central Africa*, p. 113; W. Junker, *Travels in Africa During the Years 1882–6* (London, 1892), pp. 470–1.

[95] Knowledge of nineteenth-century trade with the Banyoro is common among Lango elders today. The following were the best informants: Yakobo Adoko, Pilipo Oruro, Yeromia Otim, Yakobo Gaci, Koranima Ayena, Amnoni Abura, Tomasi Ojuka, Lazaro Okelo, Yolam Aliro, Luka Abura. On the Labwor trade, the following were helpful: Erieza Oyaka, Lakana Ekin, Kezekia Ongom, Ogwel

This situation was not radically altered when, with the arrival of Sudanese traders on the Victoria Nile in the 1860s, Lango became tenuously connected with overseas markets for the first time.[96] The Sudanese (also known as Nubians or 'Khartoumers') created a demand for ivory which was passed on to the Langi by Banyoro traders and—to a very limited degree—by the Sudanese themselves. But elephants in Lango continued to be hunted by the long-established communal methods, the tusks falling to the first hunter to spear the elephant.[97] Only among the Jo Arak of Aber was there a successful attempt to extend to Lango the convention current in Acholi, whereby one of the tusks belonged by right to the *rwot*.[98] Nor is there any indication that the commercial possibilities of ivory were sufficiently powerful to bring into being a class of professional elephant hunters, as they evidently were in the Chope region of Bunyoro.[99] In northwestern Lango—the only area where the Sudanese traders operated directly—fire-arms became available in small quantities, probably during the 1880s. Among both the Jo Arak of Aber and the Jo Olwa of Iceme, these fire-arms were concentrated in the hands of the clan leaders,[100] but in not one of the recorded oral traditions about precolonial battles do fire-arms have any place. The possession of guns seems to have been largely a matter of prestige. They were fired during war-dances,[101] and as a means of sounding an alarm before battle,[102] but they had no military impact. In short, neither local trade nor the importing of exotic goods affected the standing or powers of clan leadership. The benefits of trade with the non-Lango world were, for the most part, rapidly dispersed throughout Lango society.

Raiding was as constant a feature of relations between the Langi and their neighbours as trade. Linant de Bellefonds observed in 1875,

Okolla, Anderea Okadde, Amnoni Abura. For nineteenth-century trade in general, see D. A. Low, 'The Northern Interior, 1840–84', in Oliver and Mathew, *History of East Africa*, vol. I, p. 327.

[96] For the wider context of the Sudanese penetration, see R. Gray, *History of the Southern Sudan, 1839–89* (London, 1961), and Low, op. cit., pp. 324–6.

[97] Interviews: Oco Abolli, Tomasi Ojuka, Lazaro Okelo, Yokonia Ogwal.

[98] Interviews: Nekomia Otwal, Leoben Okodi, Misaki Oki, Matayo Acut. For the Acholi, see Girling, op. cit., p. 94.

[99] A. Adefuye, 'Palwo Economy, Society and Politics', *Transafrican Jl. History*, 5 (1976), pp. 1–20.

[100] Interviews: Leoben Okodi, Matayo Acut, Mustio Apunyo, Mohammed Okec, Yokana Engola, Onap Awongo. [101] Interview: Tamali Adur Apio.

[102] 'Whenever the Langi heard a gun go off, they used to regard it as a summons for help.' Interview: Leoben Okodi (in Aber).

with understandable overstatement, that the Langi 'live only by raiding and are the terror of these lands'.[103] During the nineteenth century, the Acholi of Puranga and Patongo, the Iteso, and the Kumam were all regular targets of Lango raiding.[104] From the 1850s onwards Lango campaigns were also fought in Bunyoro and the other interlacustrine states to the south.[105] Sometimes these conflicts were caused by disputed claims to hunting tracts, such as the uninhabited country due north of Karuma Falls during the 1870s.[106] But nearly always the purpose of raids was the acquisition of livestock and human captives. Large numbers of women and children were brought back to Lango, and many important Langi of the late nineteenth century are said to have been born of non-Lango mothers or to have been foreigners captured in infancy.[107]

These spoils of war were not, however, the prerogative of clan leaders, despite their crucial role in the organization and conduct of military campaigns. Both livestock and captives were distributed among the warriors of the clan section. The capture of women and children did not introduce a slave element into the political system, nor did it provide clan leaders with a personal following of uprooted followers. Instead, war captives were rapidly absorbed into the kinship system, and the acquisition of 'sons' and 'daughters' in this way lay within the reach of ordinary clan members. Particular emphasis seems to have been placed on the capture of women and girls, for these allowed the ideal of polygyny to be more widely attained.[108] We do not know on what basis war-captives were allocated, but oral tradition gives no indication that clan leaders controlled the distribution. Successful campaigning contributed to a leader's reputation, but it does not appear to have brought him additional controls over his clansmen.

The picture of clan leadership painted in this chapter is basically a static one. Judging by the examples adduced, it may be objected that the condition of Lango as it was around 1900 has too readily been

[103] Linant de Bellefonds, op. cit., p. 16 (my translation from the French).
[104] For a summary of Lango military activity based on oral tradition, see A. Tarantino, 'Lango Wars', *Uganda Jl.*, 13 (1949), pp. 230–5.
[105] See below, pp. 93–6.   [106] Baker, *Ismailia*, vol. II, pp. 130–1.
[107] Interviews: Yakobo Adoko, Yakobo Obia, Festo Ejok. Driberg, op. cit., pp. 165, 173; Warne, entry for 4.8.13 in Koli TB (1912–14, part 2), LDA.
[108] Interviews: Samwiri Ade, Yakobo Gaci, Onap Awongo, Reuben Ogwal, Yeromia Otim. On the capture of women and children, see Linant de Bellefonds, op. cit., pp. 15–16.

assumed to apply to the previous century. The emphasis on the last generation before colonial rule (c. 1880–1910) is dictated by the principal weakness of Lango oral tradition, which is that detailed clan histories can be pushed no further back than the settlement of clan sections in their final, present-day localities.[109] The lack of evidence for the earlier period inevitably leaves the picture incomplete, so that we have no means of telling how early in Lango history clan leadership took the shape described here. It seems fairly clear, however, that it had done so before the last generation of the pre-colonial era. What distinguished this generation from its predecessors was the intensification of trade and warfare with non-Langi, and there is no evidence that this trend greatly affected the content of clan leadership. The determining factors would rather appear to have been the combination of territorial and descent groups found in Lango, and the pattern of secondary migration and settlement.

The limited scope of clan leadership in nineteenth-century Lango should by now be evident. Spatially, the position involved control over no more than a hundred or so adult males and their wives and children, with in some cases the addition of a few smaller clan sections whose territory was immediately adjacent. In qualitative terms, clan leadership was given little or no symbolic expression, and it carried with it no control over economic resources, whether produced by the clan itself, or brought in from outside through trade and warfare. Control over land and responsibility for communal rituals, which in other African societies have often been the foundation of chiefly power, were in Lango both exercised by broadly-recruited groups rather than individuals. The clan leader's role was limited to command in battle and the settlement of disputes. That these functions were carried out by a leader whose position largely turned on hereditary qualifications, undoubtedly represented an inroad on Lango egalitarianism. But the inroad was nevertheless a small one, in view of the clan leader's need to spread responsibility for decision-making, and the lack of prestige or mystique attached to his office. In the final analysis the characterization of Lango society in the nineteenth century as 'chiefless' must stand.

---

[109] For a fuller discussion of this point, see above, Introduction.

CHAPTER 4

The Zenith and Collapse of Regional Leadership

THE local concentration of a single clan section, or of a group of allied clan sections, constituted the political community in nineteenth-century Lango. Beyond its confines there existed no permanent institutions of social co-operation, nor any agreed procedures for settling disputes without recourse to arms. Nevertheless, political authority was not restricted entirely to clan leadership at this parochial level. The individual clan section, or group of associated clan sections, did not totally dominate the outlook of the individual Lango. In certain situations, and on an occasional basis, clan sections were caught up in very much wider alignments. These alignments were an important feature of Lango society until the early 1890s. Their collapse on the eve of the colonial occupation had a significant bearing on the response of the Langi to their British and Baganda adversaries during the ensuing twenty years of pacification.

The main features of political co-operation above the local level during the nineteenth-century can be summarized under four heads: the exercise of personal leadership at a regional level; the observance of conventions limiting the intensity of inter-clan fighting; a capacity to intervene militarily in neighbouring countries, especially in the interlacustrine world; and a corresponding capacity to defeat the Sudanese slave-raiders who invaded Lango during the 1870s. It is in these areas that the limitations of oral tradition in Lango are most serious. Because regional leadership transcended the familiar context of clan and family, it lies outside the scope of the clan histories which are recounted today; and because it is a vanished institution there are no social groups today with an interest in handing down traditions about it. Those traditions which have survived tend to be confused as regards place and time, since they lack the control of genealogical reckoning; they highlight the problem of middle-period amnesia which was discussed in the Introduction.[1] All the same, when these

[1] See above, p. 13.

traditions are carefully weighed and then set alongside the writings of contemporary European travellers and the known history of neighbouring peoples, they do yield a consistent picture, if not a complete one.

In many parts of Lango, stories are told about great leaders of old who were respected over a wide area—men like Opyene Nyakanyolo, Ngora Akubal, Ogwal Abura, and Agoro Abwango. They are said to have limited the extent of clan warfare at home and to have led the Langi on successful campaigns abroad; in some of the traditions they are described as having presided over mass gatherings at which 'laws' were promulgated and admonitions given to the people.[2] This exalted form of authority is closely linked in tradition with the maintenance of important restraints on fighting within Lango: in the early days of Lango settlement, the use of the spear was confined to hunting and to raids on other tribes; battles between clan sections or villages were fought with sticks or clubs, and with whips made from twisted buffalo-hide. A clear distinction was therefore drawn between Langi and non-Langi in the military sphere. Consequently the participants in a clan battle were less likely to be killed, the chances of a prolonged state of feud were reduced, and clan sections could more easily be mobilized over a wide area for campaigns abroad.[3] There may be elements of a mythical golden age in these stories, but the traditions as a whole need to be taken seriously, since, in one form or another, they are found all over Lango, and also because European accounts substantiate the tradition of large-scale campaigning abroad.[4]

The first requirement is to establish the place of the great leaders of old in Lango social organization. This is no easy task, in view of the tendency for traditions of this period to be divorced from the mainstream of clan histories. It is usually claimed that the authority of these leaders extended all over Lango. A much more probable explanation, however, is that they were figures of regional rather than tribal importance, and this is indicated by the fact that the personalities whose deeds are recounted vary from one part of Lango to another: of the five men mentioned above, the first two are mainly associated with south-western Lango, and the last two with the east.

[2] Interviews: Yakobo Adoko, Jorbabel Akora, Yakobo Gaci, Luka Abura, Lakana Ekin, Adonia Ecun, Erieza Oyaka, Tomasi Ojuka, Lajaro Obia, Kezekia Okelo. Tarantino, 'Lango Clans', p. 110.
[3] Interviews: Anderea Okadde, Yakobo Adoko, Kezekia Okelo, Isaka Ojaba. Ogwal Ajungu, untitled vernacular history (1936–7), para. 7; Driberg, The Lango, pp. 106–7.   [4] See references below in this chapter.

Assuming that their authority was regionally based, it is tempting to see it as in some way dependent on the age-organization. According to this interpretation, the regional leaders were heads of the four territorial sections into which Lango was divided for purposes of the age-ceremonies; they were clan leaders in their own right, who periodically came to prominence during the *ewor* ceremonies, where they took the lead in enforcing the ban on spear-fighting, enjoining good standards of behaviour, and organizing attacks on other tribes.[5] Oral tradition does contain a few positive indications of a link between the great leaders and the age-organization. In western Lango several leaders, notably Opyene Nyakanyolo, were reputedly prominent in the *ewor* ceremonies;[6] while the songs of the buffalo age-set include several references to Ngora Akubal's campaigns against the Madi.[7]

Attractive though this explanation is—and it may be the correct one—it would be unwise to seize upon it too readily. The territorial spread of the age-organization certainly contributed to an atmosphere of inter-clan concord in which regional leadership would have been more easily accepted. But the evidence is far too slender to determine whether there was any closer connection. Furthermore, the ultimate fate of regional leadership would suggest that personal influence was more important than an institutional base. In view of the inadequate sources, it is unlikely that this question will ever be settled. But the practical importance of regional leadership is demonstrated by the record of large-scale Lango campaigns abroad during the nineteenth century, and especially in the period from about 1850 to 1890; on this, there is no room for doubt at all.

Raiding in large combinations and over great distances dates back to the time of the initial westward expansion of the Langi from Otuke. In northern Lango during the second quarter of the nineteenth century, combinations of border clans were led against the Acholi by a warrior named Angulo Orenga, who met his death in the royal village of the *rwot* of Patiko.[8] The period from about 1820 to 1860 was

---

[5] See above, pp. 57–60.

[6] Interviews: Yakobo Adoko, Jorbabel Akora, Yakobo Gaci.

[7] The songs as set down by Driberg, (*The Lango*, pp. 257–60) refer to him as 'Ngora' only, but there is little doubt that this is the Ngora Akubal whose campaigns against the Madi are recorded in other traditions (Tarantino, 'Lango Wars' p. 230). Okot is right to identify one with the other (Okot, 'Oral Literature and its Social Background among the Acholi and Lango', p. 161).

[8] Crazzolara, *The Lwoo*, pp. 236–7; Tarantino, 'The Origin of the Lango', p.12, and 'Lango Wars', p. 232; Girling, *The Acholi of Uganda*, pp. 86, 117.

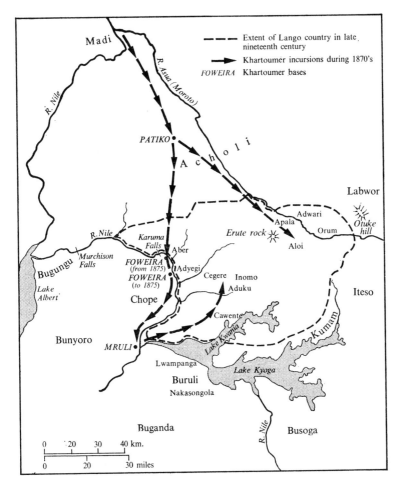

Map 6. The Langi and their Neighbours in the Nineteenth Century

also the time of greatest activity against the Madi of the Albert Nile, to the north-west of Lango, from whom many captives were taken.[9]

One interesting consequence of these raids may be mentioned. The campaigns against the Madi resulted not only in the taking of many

---

[9] Interviews: Yakobo Adoko, Yakobo Obia. Driberg, *The Lango*, p. 165. This dating depends mainly on the place in clan genealogies of known war captives. But for corroboration, see also: Crazzolara, op. cit., p. 366; Tarantino, 'Lango Wars', p. 230; Girling, op. cit., p. 155.

captives, but also in the introduction into Lango of new techniques of rain-making and a tendency towards ritual centralization. On one of these expeditions—probably during the 1840s or 1850s—Oketa, a clan leader of the Jo Ogora, captured a Madi youth who was brought back to Lango with his possessions, including two large rain-stones and a two-mouthed pot. The captured boy was adopted by Oketa and given the name Okelo Maitum; he grew up to become—probably during the 1860s—leader of the clan section at Ikwera, near present-day Aduku, and a noted rain-maker.[10] Among the Madi, a rain-maker or rain-chief was distinguished by his possession of rain-stones made of quartz, which were kept in a special pot.[11] The rain-stones and the ritual power of the rain-makers were much venerated by the Madi, and they seem to have communicated this respect to the Lwo, for the same system was practised among the Acholi of the Sudan–Uganda border.[12] It is hardly surprising, therefore, that Madi techniques proved attractive to the Langi. What is remarkable is the fact that Okelo Maitum and his son Lingo were the only rain-makers in Lango who practised them. So far as is known, theirs were the only rain-stones brought from Madi. As a result they enjoyed immense prestige. They combined the position of rain-maker with leadership of their own section of the Jo Ogora. By the end of the century, Lingo's ceremonies were attended by people from all over south-western Lango.[13] Their prestige as rain-makers allowed the Ogora clan of Aduku to take a lead in other spheres as well. Okelo Maitum convened the age-ceremonies (*ewor*) for the south-western section of Lango (*jo moita*), and in either his time or Lingo's, the other territorial sections of Lango began to acknowledge the south-west as the initiators of both *ewor* and the rain-dance (*myelo kot*).[14] In this way the Jo Ogora constituted a unique exception to the general rule in Lango that ritual and secular authority were not combined in the same persons.

[10] Interview: Yakobo Obia. Hayley, *The Anatomy of Lango Religion and Groups*, pp. 74–5; Tarantino, 'Lango Wars', p. 230.

[11] For rain-makers in Madi, see: J. Middleton, 'Notes on the political organization of the Madi of Uganda', *African Studies*, 14 (1955), pp. 33–5; F. H. Rogers, 'Notes on Some Madi Rain-stones', *Man*, 27 (1927), pp. 81–7.

[12] E. T. N. Grove, 'Customs of the Acholi', *Sudan Notes and Records*, 2 (1919), pp. 172–3; C. G. and B. Z. Seligman, *Pagan Tribes of the Nilotic Sudan*, pp. 130–2.

[13] Interviews: Yakobo Obia, Lajaro Obia, Yosia Omwa, Yakobo Oluma, Isaka Ojaba, Omara Ekak, Pilipo Oruro.

[14] Interviews: Lajaro Obia, Ibrahim Lodo. Driberg, *The Lango*, p. 249; Hayley, op. cit., p. 75.

The most striking evidence of the power of Lango regional leaders is to be found not so much in their campaigns against the Acholi or Madi, as in their activities in the interlacustrine world. The Langi affected the balance of power within the kingdom of Bunyoro itself, and in the conflicts between Bunyoro and Buganda their aid was eagerly sought by both sides. That the Langi were seen in this light by the rulers of aggressive hierarchical states is no small measure of the authority wielded by Lango regional leaders.

Lango traditions, while they stress the dependence of the Banyoro kings on Lango military help, are imprecise as to particular expeditions and over-all chronology. According to Nyoro royal tradition, however, the first significant Lango intervention was in about 1851–2, during the succession war between Kamurasi and Olimi Rwakabale. Kamurasi enlisted Lango help, and in a battle near Lwampanga, on the left bank of the Nile, Olimi was defeated and killed.[15] This early success did not, however, render Kamurasi secure from other challenges. For the kingdom was still suffering from the effects of the breakdown of royal authority during the reign of Kamurasi's grandfather, Kyebambe Nyamatukura, early in the nineteenth century. Not only had the independent kingdom of Toro then been carved out of the Nyoro state; two of Nyamatukura's sons had also tried to use Chope, the Lwo-speaking enclave in eastern Bunyoro, as a base from which to throw off the *omukama*'s authority. During Kamurasi's reign this challenge was continued by Mpuhuka and Ruyonga, sons of the original rebels.[16] By and large, the Langi sided with the rebel princes, both by giving military help and by offering them refuge when they were expelled from Bunyoro.[17] This is hardly surprising,

[15] R. M. Fisher, *Twilight Tales of the Black Baganda* (London, 1911), pp. 153–5; K.W., 'The Kings of Bunyoro–Kitara', part 3, *Uganda Jl.*, 5 (1937), p. 62; J. W. Nyakatura, *Anatomy of an African Kingdom: a History of Bunyoro–Kitara* (New York, 1973), p. 97.

Tarantino ('Lango Wars'), working from Lango sources, also regards this as the first Lango intervention in Bunyoro, and he associates it with the regional leader, Opyene Nyakanyolo. I have found no traditions pertaining explicitly to this succession war.

[16] For the nineteenth-century background in Bunyoro, see: K. W., op. cit.; Nyakatura, op. cit. Their accounts are corroborated in: Linant de Bellefonds to Gordon, 24.3.75, in M. F. Shukry (ed.), *Equatoria under Egyptian Rule* (Cairo, 1953), p. 237; Wilson and Felkin, *Uganda and the Egyptian Soudan*, vol. II, p. 325.

[17] Speke, *Journal of the Discovery of the Source of the Nile*, p. 570; Grant, *A Walk Across Africa*, pp. 284, 312; S. W. Baker, *The Albert N'yanza* (London, 1867), vol. II, pp. 241, 243; K.W., op. cit., p. 62.

since Chope was immediately adjacent to Lango, and its Jopalwo population had close affinities with the Langi, especially with the clans of the Toci and Okole valleys, who had absorbed substantial Lwo elements.[18]

On Kamurasi's death in 1869, there was again a disputed succession and a protracted war between the rivals. Kabarega, the eventual winner, was twice defeated by Kabigumire, his brother, and there is little doubt that Kabigumire's ability to prolong the struggle owed something to his 'strong army of Bachope and Lango warriors'.[19] Kabigumire's death did not halt the challenge to royal authority from the Chope princes and their Lango allies. In 1872 Ruyonga and a Lango force attacked Kabarega at the same time as the Baganda invaded from the south.[20] In 1875 about 3,000 Langi raided Kabarega on behalf of Mupina, the brother and successor of Mpuhuka.[21] A year later Colonel Charles Gordon, Governor of Egypt's Equatoria Province, planned to mobilize 4,000 Langi as part of a major assault on Kabarega, though his plan was never implemented;[22] and in 1878 Mutesa of Buganda also tried to secure the co-operation of Lango leaders.[23]

The Langi were not, however, uniformly hostile to royal authority in Bunyoro. During the 1860s Kamurasi appears to have been receiving many visitors from Lango.[24] Nor is it by any means clear that all Lango war-bands operating in Bunyoro during the succession war of 1869–70 were on the side of Kabigumire.[25] During the 1870s Kabarega was certainly receiving military help from Lango, as this revealing remark of Linant de Bellefonds in 1875 shows:[26] 'It is a strange thing that the same Langos who one day are helping Kabarega

---

[18] On the secessionist challenge in Chope, see A. Adefuye, 'Palwo Economy, Society and Politics', *Transafrican Jl. History*, 5 (1976), pp. 1–20.

[19] K.W., op. cit., pp. 63–4.   [20] Baker, *Ismailia*, vol. II, p. 433.

[21] Linant de Bellefonds, 'Voyage de service fait entre le poste militaire de Fatiko et la capitale de M'tesa roi d'Uganda', pp. 15–16.

Campaigns on Mupina's behalf are well substantiated by traditions in north-western Lango. Interviews: Yakobo Olugo, Mohammed Okec, Yokonani Alyai.

[22] Gordon to Khairy Pasha, 28.9.76, in Shukry, op. cit., p. 366; G. B. Hill (ed.), *Colonel Gordon in Central Africa, 1874–79* (London, 1881), p. 194.

[23] Entries for 31.1.78 and 5.2.78 in 'The Diaries of Emin Pasha—Extracts III', *Uganda Jl.*, 26 (1962), p. 86.   [24] Speke, op. cit., pp. 502–4, 509, 567.

[25] Some Lango traditions speak of intervention on Kabarega's side, but the adversary mentioned, usually 'Abwon', has not been identified. Interviews: Leoben Okodi, Nekomia Otwal.

[26] Linant to Gordon, 24.3.75, in Shukry, op. cit., p. 238 (my translation from the French).

against Rionga return the next day with Rionga against Kabarega.' Quite how much help the king received is more difficult to determine. Kabarega himself made a powerful impression in Lango, perhaps on account of his exile there during the late 1890s.[27] Nowadays Lango traditions tend to see pre-colonial contacts with Bunyoro in terms of a personal relationship with Kabarega, and few Langi will admit that their leaders ever fought against him, although the documentary record on this point is unequivocal. Clearly, then, the estimate made by the Langi themselves of their role in Kabarega's campaigns must be treated with some caution. That Lango war-bands helped Kabarega against the Chope rebels and in border wars against Buganda is not in doubt. It is the claim that the Langi took part in campaigns much further afield which is difficult to assess. The Alur, the Banyankore, and the Bagungu are all recalled as adversaries.[28] Perhaps the most interesting Lango claim relates to Kabarega's reconquest of Toro during the 1870s. The belief that the Langi contributed materially to the reconquest is quite common in Lango.[29] No mention is made of Lango participation in any of the published bodies of Nyoro tradition, but the awareness in Lango tradition of so remote an event as the reconquest of Toro would seem to indicate some form of involvement by the Langi.

The frequency of Lango campaigns in Bunyoro during the 1860s and 1870s raises several important questions. The first is: what precisely was the military role of the Langi in the more sophisticated interlacustrine world? They evidently acted as auxiliaries, quite distinct from the regular troops deployed in Bunyoro. How closely they were supervised by their paymasters, on the other hand, is less clear. Nyoro tradition describes one expedition against Buganda in 1890 when the Langi acted as part of the vanguard, which was led by the second-in-command of Kabarega's army;[30] but it is impossible to generalize from one account. Neither documentary nor traditional sources describe the tactics employed by the Langi when fighting in large numbers. We have to be content with the assurances of European contemporaries that the fighting abilities of the Langi were widely respected.[31]

[27] See below, pp. 112–14.
[28] Tarantino, 'Lango Wars', pp. 233–4. Interviews: Yakobo Adoko, Yakobo Gaci, Suleman Ikwe, Tomasi Ojuka.
[29] Interviews: Yakobo Gaci, Tomasi Ojuka, Anderea Ogwang, Koranima Ayena, Reuben Ogwal.   [30] Nyakatura, op. cit., p. 145.
[31] Speke, op. cit., p. 90; Wilson and Felkin, op. cit., vol. II, p. 53.

There is more evidence about the appeal, in Lango eyes, of campaigning abroad. A successful expedition brought not only plunder from the enemy, in the form of cattle and captives,[32] but often rewards from allies as well, such as hoes, beads, salt, and sweet-potato plants—unknown in Lango at that time.[33] The spoils of war were within the reach of ordinary clan members, who might be in need of bridewealth,[34] and they could be obtained without necessarily disrupting the agricultural routine at home, since warriors did not normally spend more than three months away on an expedition.[35] For as long as foreign expeditions entailed no severe losses of men, the prospect of reward and plunder was a highly attractive one. It seems very likely that the opportunities for easy pickings held out by Kamurasi, Kabarega, Ruyonga, and the rest, contributed greatly to the hold which regional leaders were able to exert over their followings. And this development was not confined to the border clans along the Nile: large war-bands came from as far afield as Aloi, Alito, and Omoro in the Moroto valley.[36]

It was against this background of effective military co-operation abroad that the Langi were confronted by the most serious external threat before the arrival of the British—namely, the Sudanese raiders, or 'Khartoumers', who first became active on the Victoria Nile during the 1860s. Brief mention has been made of the trading activities of these people in north-western Lango.[37] In most of their field of operations, however, the Khartoumers came not so much as traders in the normal sense of the word but as raiders, and it was in this guise that they made their first appearance in Lango. The main requirement of the Khartoumers was ivory, with only a subsidiary interest in slaves; but the ivory trade itself was conducted in a highly irregular fashion. The 'traders' raided the indigenous peoples for cattle and slaves, with which to pay their porters and ivory suppliers. The explorations of J. H. Speke and Samuel Baker exposed these abuses to the outside world, and trade was soon followed by the flag:

---

[32] Linant de Bellefonds, op. cit., pp. 15–16.

[33] Interviews: Ibrahim Lodo, Gideon Odwongo, Lakana Ekin, Yakobo Adoko, Mohammed Okec. Linant de Bellefonds, op. cit., p. 16; Driberg, entry for 3.2.16 at Aloi, in Eruti TB (1915–21), LDA; Tarantino, 'Lango Wars', pp. 233–4.

[34] Interviews: Dominiko Opone, Isaka Ojaba, Yakobo Gaci, Yeromia Otim.

[35] Interviews: Erieza Okelo, Yubu Engola, Lakana Ekin.

[36] Interviews: Anderea Okadde, Yubu Engola, Ogwel Okolla, Yokonia Ogwal. Driberg, entry for 3.2.16 in Eruti TB (1915–21), LDA. The participation of easterners is also confirmed by informants in western Lango: Erisa Olugo, Benedikto Okelo Elwange.   [37] See above, p. 85.

in 1870 Baker returned to the White Nile with instructions from the Egyptian Khedive to set up a province in 'Equatoria'. His intention was to curb the rapacity of the freebooters and to establish instead 'legitimate commerce'. In practice, the problem was too great for Baker and his successors, Gordon and Emin Pasha, to solve with their limited resources. They were unable even to restrain their own Sudanese soldiers and petty officials, who raided the African peoples of the Province for provisions and for goods to trade on their own account.[38]

In northern Uganda, the main victims of the Sudanese were the Acholi, Madi, and Lugbara. The Langi lived further from the main lines of communication, and they were not included in the formal administration of Equatoria Province.[39] All the same, they were well within the range of the Sudanese: before Baker arrived as Governor in 1872, the Khartoumers already had permanent bases at Patiko, in south-western Acholi, and at Foweira, on the left bank of the Nile near the mouth of the Okole river; while later there were Government garrisons at Foweira from 1872 to 1884,[40] and at Mruli, near the Nile–Kafu confluence, from 1876 to 1880. The reason why the Langi suffered less than their neighbours from the Sudanese lay not so much in their geographical remoteness, as in their capacity to defeat the raiders.

In two areas of Lango, the Sudanese suffered major reverses during the 1870s. When Baker reached Acholi in 1872, he was given a graphic account of the first of these reverses which had just occurred. A force of some three hundred Sudanese and Acholi left Patiko for Lango country. They followed the course of the Asua–Moroto river upstream to the south-east, until they reached a well-populated area with large herds of cattle, in what is now Moroto county. Here they were hospitably received and were given seventy head of cattle and

---

[38] For the history of Equatoria, see Gray, *History of the Southern Sudan, 1839 to 1889*, pp. 99–119, 135–51.

[39] Only one case is known of Langi who acknowledged the rule of Equatoria. In 1880 a group of 'chiefs' near Foweira agreed to pay a tax to the Government. Most probably, these were Langi who lived in Kumeri and Acora, west of Karuma Falls, and beyond the control of the powerful Jo Arak in Aber. Entry for 2.11.80, in 'Diaries of Emin Pasha [hereafter D.E.P.]—Extracts IV', *Uganda Jl.*, 26 (1962), p. 134.

[40] In 1875 Foweira fort was moved about twelve miles northwards to a site opposite the Nile–Toci confluence, where it remained until 1884 (Linant de Bellefonds to Gordon, 24.3.75, in Shukry, op. cit., p. 237). For a brief period in 1879–80 the garrison was withdrawn on Gordon's orders.

much ivory; but after a week the Sudanese rounded on their hosts, burning villages, massacring the inhabitants, and capturing women and children who were taken back to Patiko.[41] This sudden and devastating attack caused several clan sections to migrate away from the area altogether.[42] But it also caused those that remained in the Moroto valley to set aside their differences and prepare to resist the next attack. As one tradition current in Adwari puts it:[43]

All the people who were divided by hatreds assembled together and made an agreement. People from Adwari, Orum, Aloi, and Apala [from both sides of the Moroto river] met together. They said, 'Let us put aside our hatreds. These strangers are depleting our people; for take note that when they siezed our cattle, they also captured our best young men and added them to the livestock.'

The Sudanese soon returned. A ruffian named Lazim led another force of 350 Sudanese, together with many Acholi auxiliaries, in order to capture cattle and slaves from the same area. But when the advance-guard of 250 men went ahead to attack a group of villages at dawn, they were ambushed on a narrow path; the Langi attacked them from the high grass on both sides; and before most of them could even load their muskets they were speared; only one survivor regained the main body of the expedition, which returned to Patiko by forced marches, after beating off a further Lango attack. About 250 men had been killed and 103 guns lost. The Moroto valley was never again troubled by the Sudanese (Map 6).[44]

   The second crisis occurred in south-western Lango, in what are now Maruzi and Kwania counties. It was probably this area which was affected by the first recorded Sudanese incursion into Lango in 1864, when Kamurasi of Bunyoro sent a Sudanese trader and eighty of his men to punish Lango villages which had offered help to the rebel, Mphuka.[45] South-western Lango became more seriously exposed when an Egyptian station was established at Mruli in 1876.[46] The garrisons of Government stations tended to live off the land,

[41] Baker, *Ismailia*, II, pp. 102–3.
[42] Reuben Ogwal, 'A History of Lango Clans', pp. 5, 21. Interviews: Yosua Odongo Opio, Yakobo Onya.
[43] Interview: Kezeron Awongo. According to this informant, the Khartoumers had raided the Aloi area several times before. This could well be true; it was not, after all, in the Khartoumers' interest to reveal the full extent of their plundering to Baker.
[44] Baker, *Ismailia*, II, pp. 104–6. Interviews: Kezeron Awongo, Yubu Engola.
[45] Baker, *Albert N'yanza*, II, p. 244.
[46] Gordon to Khairy Pasha, 4.1.76, in Shukry, op. cit., p. 433.

despite official inducements to the troops to grow their own crops, and Mruli was no exception. The country immediately opposite the fort, on the right bank of the Nile, was at this time still uninhabited, but there were Langi living further inland in Cegere, Inomo, and Cawente. On what was probably not the first foraging expedition, 200 men crossed over into Lango in August 1877; they returned to Mruli two weeks later, having lost over eighty men, about thirty women and children, and—as Emin Pasha ruefully remarked—with 'not a dishful of provisions secured'.[47] An avenging expedition the following year captured 800 head of cattle,[48] but it seems that the débâcle of 1877 was an effective deterrent. Between 1879 and the withdrawal of the Patiko and Foweira garrisons in 1884–5, only one further raid is recorded: a fruitless foraging expedition from Foweira in 1882, which lost yet more men and munitions.[49]

Little is known about the Lango response to the raids from Mruli, but, according to one tradition, the threat caused the clans of the south-west to unite under a leader in Inomo, called Abili Obangkwon, who visited a diviner in Bugerere in order to secure protection against the bullets of the Sudanese.[50] It may well have been Abili who organized the decisive rebuff of 1877. At any rate, the oral record on both the Patiko and Mruli raids indicates a co-ordinated, multi-clan response over a wide area, and the very scale of the defeats inflicted on the Sudanese supports this conclusion.

By the end of the 1870s the raids of the Sudanese had been effectively repulsed, and those few who still came to Lango now adopted more conventional methods of trade.[51] For the Langi, the opportunities to campaign in the interlacustrine region continued, and on

[47] Entries for 27.8.77 and 9.9.77 in 'D.E.P.—Extracts II', *Uganda Jl.*, 25 (1961), p. 154.
The fact that the expedition was equipped with rockets, probably for setting fire to the villages of obdurate Langi, suggests previous experience of resistance. Sir John Gray, 'The Lango Wars with Egyptian Troops, 1877–8', *Uganda Jl.*, 21 (1957), p. 114.
[48] Entries for 19.2.78 and 28.4.78, in 'D.E.P.—Extracts III', *Uganda Jl.*, 26 (1962), pp. 86, 93; Wilson and Felkin, op. cit., vol. II, pp. 38–9. Relations between the Mruli garrison and the Langi are minutely examined in two articles by Sir John Gray: 'Gordon's Fort at Mruli', *Uganda Jl.*, 19 (1955), pp. 62–7; and 'Lango Wars with Egyptian Troops'.
[49] Entry for 16.7.82, in 'D.E.P.—Extracts V', *Uganda Jl.*, 27 (1963), p. 2.
[50] Interviewers: Yosia Omwa, Jabulon Okuta (conducted by W. Okot-Chono, as part of the Makerere undergraduate research scheme, 1969). See also, J. N. Odurkene, 'The Langi–Banyoro Relationship and the Career of Chief Daudi Odora, 1850–1931', mimeo. (1968), Department of Religious Studies, Makerere University. [51] See above, p. 85.

much the same pattern as before. During the 1880s Lango war-bands were active on Kabarega's side, as well as on the side of the rebels based in Chope—Ruyonga, Mupina, and their successors.[52] In the late 1880s Kabarega was active against two other adversaries—the Equatoria administration, now on its last legs, and the Baganda—and here too the Langi were involved. When at the end of 1887, Kabarega began to prepare for an attack on Emin Pasha's few remaining posts, his forces included Langi.[53] As for the border wars against Buganda, Lango participation on Kabarega's side is recalled in tradition, being associated with both victory and defeat.[54] It is likely that the Langi took part in Kabarega's greatest success against the Baganda—the battle of Rwengabi in 1886, when an invading army was repulsed with heavy losses and its commander killed.[55]

As a result of the frequent campaigning in Bunyoro, Lango society was exposed to influence from the interlacustrine world over a period of some forty years, from about 1850 to 1890. This influence took both economic and cultural forms. The sweet-potato brought back from Bunyoro proved very popular, and by the turn of the century the new crop was a common sight in north-western Lango.[56] A few captured Ankole cattle were responsible for one characteristic strain of cattle in Lango.[57] The practice of spirit-possession was so greatly influenced by the *kubandwa* cult of the Banyoro, that several features of the Nyoro complex have since become an integral part of Lango religion.[58]

Politically, however, the impact of Bunyoro was less than might be imagined. Once the regional leaders had become able to mobilize their warriors on demand, the Lango political system was remarkably little affected. A centralizing process is implied in the claim sometimes

[52] Entries for 23.3.87 and 9.5.87 in 'D.E.P.—Extracts VII', *Uganda Jl.*, 28 (1964), pp. 82, 90–1.

[53] G. Casati, *Ten Years in Equatoria* (London, 1891), vol. II, pp. 92, 144; entry for 7.1.88 in 'D.E.P.—Extracts VIII', *Uganda Jl.*, 28 (1964), p. 216.

[54] Interviews: Erieza Okelo, Pilipo Oruro, Leoben Okodi, Yakobo Adoko, Yosia Omara, Erisa Olugo, Erieza Oyaka. Tarantino, 'Lango Wars', pp. 233–4.

[55] On this battle, see: K.W., op. cit., p. 64; Nyakatura, op. cit., pp. 134–6; Fisher, op. cit., pp. 170–1; Schweinfurth, *Emin Pasha in Central Africa*, pp. 499, 501. None of these accounts mentions the Langi, but some Lango traditions apparently refer to the battle of Rwengabi. Interviews: Koranima Ayena, Luka Abura.

[56] Delmé-Radcliffe, 'Memorandum on the Physical Features and Animals of the Lango Country' (1901), PRO FO/403/318.

[57] Driberg, *The Lango*, p. 91.

[58] Curley, *Elders, Shades, and Women*, pp. 152–5.

made that military leaders summoned detachments from everywhere in Lango to fight in Bunyoro. But conflicting claims of this kind are made on behalf of several contemporary leaders in different parts of the country, and they can be dismissed as mythical exaggeration. In fact, contact with the state structure of Bunyoro made little impact. This was probably because individual expeditions were relatively brief. Absences of two or three months from home, even if repeated several times over a number of years, gave ordinary Langi little experience of living in a more hierarchical and deferential society. Kamurasi and Kabarega sometimes claimed that they were rulers of Lango,[59] but this claim had absolutely no basis in fact. Probably it was expressed partly in order to impress European visitors, and partly out of sentimental regard for the tradition that the ruling Bito dynasty had, centuries before, originated in Lwo country on the Lango side of the Nile.[60] The only Langi who became absorbed into a centralized state structure were those adventurers who during the 1870s and 1880s enlisted in Kabarega's own army, the *abarasura*.[61] No memory of these men is retained in Lango tradition, so it is likely that they settled permanently in Bunyoro. Certainly their experience made no impression at home.

Politically, the main interest of the Lango campaigns in Bunyoro lies not so much in their effects on Lango society, as in the evidence they afford of an effective military leadership at regional level, able to transcend clan divisions and to mobilize thousands of warriors for expeditions abroad. Yet within ten years of the battle of Rwengabi, regional leadership had been destroyed. The difficulties that stand in the way of any attempt to reconstruct the authority of a man like Opyene Nyakanyolo are due precisely to the fact that this type of authority had disappeared by the time the first European observers began to penetrate deeply into Lango country at the end of the 1890s. The punitive columns which entered Lango at that time were never resisted by groups of more than 200 or 300 warriors at the most.[62] Faced with resistance on such a restricted basis, British officers were

[59] K.W., op. cit., p. 67; Speke, op. cit., pp. 496, 516; Linant de Bellefonds, op. cit., pp. 12, 15; Schweinfurth, op. cit., p. 118.
[60] K.W., op. cit., part 1, p. 160; Crazzolara, op. cit., p. 105.
[61] Baker, *Ismailia*, II, pp. 162–3, 257; Casati, op. cit., pp. 62, 80, 82–3. The Langi were by no means the only non-Banyoro to serve in the *abarasura*; Kabarega evidently made a point of attracting foreigners to his service.
[62] See below, ch. 5.

at a loss to account for the earlier Lango successes against the Khartoumers; they could only fall back on feeble explanations such as the 'treachery' of the Langi and the machinations of Kabarega.[63] Plainly, a dramatic and destructive change occurred in a short space of time.

Lango tradition speaks of two developments, closely linked: the great campaigns abroad came suddenly to an end; and the conventional restraints on inter-clan fighting were overturned. And so the Langi turned their attention from plundering abroad to internecine strife at home. Spears became the normal weapon in all battles; raiding and ambushing were practised without restraint, and lone travellers were likely to be set upon unless well armed.[64] Oral tradition is not very enlightening as to the causes of this deterioration. It is sometimes linked with the personality of Agoro Abwango, who lived in the country between Erute Rock and the Moroto river; his death is said to have removed the one man capable of maintaining peace.[65] Driberg recorded a tradition that it was Akena, a war-leader of Adyegi on the Okole river, who destroyed the traditional conventions.[66] These attempts to attribute a widespread change to one individual are not very convincing. It is necessary to search for more deepset causes. The record of the years 1890–3 provides two such causes.

The first is that at the beginning of the 1890s Lango war-bands fighting in Bunyoro suffered major losses for the first time. It was at this juncture that Kabarega's fortunes took a decisive turn for the worse. In the border war with Buganda which had been intermittently waged since Mwanga's accession to the Ganda throne in 1884, there appears to have been a fairly even balance of loss and gain. But early in 1890, Kabarega suffered a major defeat as a result of his intervention in the Ganda civil war on the side of Mwanga's Muslim rival, Kalema.[67] When Kalema fled to Bunyoro, Kabarega continued to support him; and he was heavily involved on Kalema's side when Lugard and the Baganda Christians defeated the Muslims in May 1891, killing—so it was said—300 of the enemy.[68]

[63] Delmé-Radcliffe to Coles, 10.9.01, PRO FO/403/318.
[64] Interviews: Yakobo Adoko, Luka Abura, Kezekia Okelo, Anderea Okadde; Driberg, *The Lango*, pp. 106–7; Tarantino, 'Lango Clans', p. 110.
[65] Interviews: Luka Abura, Lakana Ekin; Odurkene, op. cit., p. 10.
[66] Driberg, *The Lango*, p. 107.
[67] R. P. Ashe, *Chronicles of Uganda* (London, 1894), pp. 143–4; Fisher, op. cit., pp. 172–3.
[68] M. Perham and M. Bull (eds.), *The Diaries of Lord Lugard*, vol. II (London, 1959), pp. 162–7.

There is contemporary documentation from Buganda to the effect that Kalema's foreign allies during 1890 included Langi as well as Banyoro.[69] And Lango traditions leave little doubt that large numbers were involved, and that they paid dearly for it. Many Langi are said to have been killed south of Nakasongola, in Buruli, among them Agoro Abwango.[70] It is not clear to which of the battles against the Baganda this tradition refers; the Langi may, indeed, have fought in both battles; but there is little doubt that the disaster made a deep impression. After Agoro Abwango's death, it is said, no major expeditions went to Bunyoro.[71] The death of a famous leader and so many other warriors seems to have caused widespread disenchantment with foreign campaigning. Perhaps there was an awareness that, as fire-arms assumed a more important role in interlacustrine warfare, there was less place for Lango fighting techniques. Campaigning abroad was attractive so long as plunder and gifts could be relied upon. The campaigns of 1890–1 destroyed Lango confidence in the rewards of foreign war. The implications for regional leadership can only be conjectured, but they can hardly have been other than serious. Regional leadership, in contrast to clan leadership, was very largely an achieved status: out of the many clan leaders who doubtless aspired to it, only those endowed with outstanding personal qualities stood any chance of attaining it. Any leadership position of this nature depends for its acceptance upon a consistent record of success. On the basis of traditions about expeditions against the Madi, earlier in the nineteenth century, Driberg states that the authority of a major war-leader could not survive defeat in battle.[72] It seems likely, therefore, that at the end of the century the scale of the disaster in Buganda so discredited all the leaders involved as to destroy the whole basis of regional authority in Lango.

Overshadowing the reverses suffered in Buganda, however, was a catastrophe of far greater proportions—the rinderpest epidemic. In 1889 the cattle disease known as rinderpest was first observed on the East African coast. With lightning speed it spread inland during 1890,

[69] Richard Walker (CMS missionary) to family, 4.1.90 and 1.11.90, Walker Papers, CMS Archives. (I am indebted to Dr. Michael Twaddle for these two references.) For corroboration in Nyoro tradition, see Nyakatura, op. cit., p. 145.

[70] Interviews: Leoben Okodi, Pilipo Oruro, Lakana Ekin, Luka Abura, Elia Olet, Yakobo Obia. See also Tarantino, 'Lango Wars', p. 234.

Luwero, Bombo, and Kakogi are among the battle-sites in Buruli and Bulemezi mentioned in these traditions.

[71] Interviews: Lakana Ekin, Yosia Omara. Tarantino, 'Lango Wars', p. 234.

[72] Driberg, The Lango, pp. 206–8.

devastating the herds of the Masai and other cattle-keeping peoples.[73] By the early 1890s the epidemic was wreaking havoc in Lango.[74] The wealth of the Langi in cattle is well documented for the 1870s; indeed, it was the 'vast quantities of the finest cattle' in the Moroto valley which attracted the Khartoumers in 1872.[75] In about 1883 there appears to have been an earlier, unidentified cattle epidemic, and this may have increased competition for cattle between clans.[76] But it was the rinderpest outbreak of about 1891 which inflicted the greatest damage. Some parts of Lango were completely denuded of cattle.[77]

In view of the economic, social, and ritual importance of cattle in Lango society, it would be hard to exaggerate the shock of the epidemic. In the long run the Langi adapted to the new, unwelcome conditions—bridewealth was paid instead in sheep, goats, or hoes.[78] But the immediate result was desperate competition for those cattle that had survived. As an informant from Dokolo put it:[79]

> When the Langi came from Didinga [in the south-eastern Sudan] they had many cattle,—as many as the people of Karamoja do today. One man might possess 100, 500, or even 1000 cattle, and as many goats besides. But then disease killed off the cattle. So it was the shortage of cattle which caused fighting and divisions. If you had livestock, other people would come and rob you; they would attack you and rob your goods. It was this which caused fighting and divisions.

No doubt the Langi engaged in some cattle-raiding among themselves before the 1890s. But in those days cattle had been abundant, and the incentive to steal them was relatively low. After the rinderpest epidemic, cattle-raiding was more a matter of life and death. Clan

[73] The impact of the first great rinderpest on sub-Saharan Africa still awaits comprehensive historical treatment, but for some stimulating introductory observations see J. Ford, *The Role of the Trypanosomiases in African Ecology* (Oxford, 1971), pp. 138–45, 190–2, 296–7, 393–6. See also H. Hjekshus, *Ecology Control and Economic Development in East African History* (London, 1977), pp. 126–32.

[74] Driberg (*The Lango*, p. 91) estimated 1890–1 as the date. This is probably more accurate than the estimate of 1893 by Captain Johnstone, who was in Lango in 1911–12. Johnstone, 'Past times in Uganda', p. 17.

[75] Baker, *Ismailia*, II, pp. 102–3. See also Wilson and Felkin, op. cit., II, pp. 39, 55.

[76] Driberg (*The Lango*, pp. 46, 91) referred to this epidemic as rinderpest also, but in view of the general course of the disease, this is most unlikely. The difficulty is that the Lango word for rinderpest, *ideke*, is applied to several other diseases.

[77] Tarrant to Johnston, 13.11.00, UNA A10/1.

[78] Ibid.; Driberg, *The Lango*, p. 91.

[79] Interview: Tomasi Ojuka. See also Luka Abura (of Bar).

sections which had lost all their cattle urgently needed more stock if their members were to get wives, and if essential rituals were to be performed,—if, in other words, society was to continue functioning at all. Clan sections which lived near the tribal boundaries could attempt to replenish their stock at the expense of neighbouring peoples; it was probably the rinderpest which caused the incessant cattle-raiding between the Langi and the Kumam around the turn of the century.[80] But the Kumam themselves were just as affected by the disease, while in the west the end of the big campaigns after 1891 reduced the flow of captured livestock from the interlacustrine region. For most people, therefore, neighbouring clan sections were the only possible source of cattle.

The result was that all restraints on fighting within Lango were abandoned. Those without livestock used whatever means they could to make good their losses. The spear became the normal weapon in any combat, whereas previously it had only rarely been used in fights between Langi, and the shedding of blood that ensued created implacable hatred between clans. This deterioration in inter-clan relations has its own logic, but it must be stressed that in many other societies with a strong dependence on pastoralism the rinderpest epidemic did not cause a comparable breakdown in social order; in most Para-Nilotic societies, for example, where the economic disruption caused by the rinderpest was even more severe, the limitations on fighting within the tribe survived.[81] In Lango, on the other hand, the strain imposed by the shortage of cattle proved too great, and conventional restraints were cast aside. The authority of regional leaders was totally irreconcilable with this situation. They could no longer lead large combinations in war, nor could they smooth out inter-clan tensions. In effect, the coincidence of the defeats in Buganda with the rinderpest epidemic caused the complete disappearance of regional leadership as a political force during the years 1890 to 1893.

This left as the apex of the political system in Lango the clan leader who enjoyed authority over a handful of subordinate clan sections, amounting to perhaps a dozen villages. Such a leader was responsive to the wider demands of clanship and cognatic kinship,

[80] Interview: Tomasi Ojuka.
[81] I owe this observation to Dr. Lamphear, whose research into Jie history has revealed a quite different reaction to the rinderpest: the Jie resorted to more elephant-hunting, to trade and even emigration, but not to fighting within the tribe (J. Lamphear, *The Traditional History of the Jie of Uganda* (Oxford, 1976), pp. 224–7).

and hence might combine with another clan leader for limited ends. But in general, relations between clan leaders could hardly have been worse, now that the traditional rules of war and the restraining influence of the regional leader had gone. On the eve of the colonial occupation of south-eastern Lango, a British officer who had just toured the area wrote, 'The whole country is divided up into sections, each consisting of a few villages, under petty chiefs whose jealousy, suspicion and resentment of control prevents any organized combination for a common end.'[82] There is no reason to suppose that this report was exaggerated, or that it did not apply with equal force to most parts of Lango.

Oral tradition, personal recollection, and contemporary European accounts together shed a good deal of light on the newly intensified inter-clan warfare which was being waged on the eve of the colonial period. When armed for battle, a Lango warrior usually carried five or six throwing-spears and an oblong shield, made preferably from buffalo-hide.[83] Most fighting was carried on during the dry season, when swamps could be crossed easily and men could be spared from agricultural work, but attacks also occurred during June and July, when the purpose was to destroy the enemy's young crops.[84] On minor raids the object was to surprise the enemy's village, usually just before dawn, in order to carry off their cattle and sometimes to destroy their crops; for this purpose, a band of fifteen or twenty warriors would be sufficient.[85] A major expedition involved the co-operation of several neighbouring clans, and the performance of rituals before the day, in which case the enemy were likely to have had warning; they would summon their warriors by sounding war-horns, and a general mêlée ensued.[86] An expedition of this sort could number 200 or 300 warriors.[87] Each clan was commanded by its own leader, but once battle had been joined in earnest, there was little

[82] Lt. Fishbourne, Report on the Districts round Lake Kyoga, 5.10.08, UNA SMP/549/08. For comparable remarks relating to western Lango, see Anderson to Johnston, 21.3.00, UNA A4/27.
[83] Interviews: Koranima Ayena, Paulo Ajuk, Isaka Ojaba, Matayo Ayika. Tarrant to Johnston, 13.11.00, UNA A10/1; Johnstone, op. cit., p. 17; Driberg, *The Lango*, pp. 81–4.
[84] Paske Smith to Grant, 13.12.09, UNA SMP/1876/09; Johnstone, op. cit., pp. 13–14; Driberg, *The Lango*, p. 111.
[85] Driberg, *The Lango*, p. 109; Curley, op. cit., p. 103.
[86] Sykes, *Service and Sport on the Tropical Nile*, p. 239.
[87] Interviews: Koranima Ayena, Isaka Ojaba, Matayo Ayika; Ogwal Ajungu, op. cit., para. 34; Fishbourne, Report on the Districts round Lake Kyoga, 5.10.08, UNA SMP/549/08.

direction; the warriors did not fight in tightly-knit groups, but stood at several yards' distance from each other.[88] Contact with the enemy was established by long-range spear-throwing. The two sides then closed in hand-to-hand fighting, at the end of which the vanquished were pursued. If the enemy were completely routed, their villages were destroyed, and any women, children, and livestock who had not been sent to safety were captured.[89] An attack on this scale could last from dawn until the afternoon, though the intensive hand-to-hand fighting took much less time.[90]

The numbers killed in inter-clan battles are difficult to assess. Numerical estimates in oral tradition or personal reminiscence are notoriously unreliable. European estimates must also be treated with reserve, since they were nearly always second-hand and were often taken from the defeated side, who were likely to exaggerate their losses in order to press their case for help. European estimates vary from twenty to sixty warriors killed in a single battle.[91] Even this lower figure represents a pretty formidable rate of mortality. There can be little doubt that the chances of an ordinary clan warrior being killed in battle were considerable. The years from 1890 to 1910 were the period when, as some Langi later recalled with a touch of nostalgia, 'a man's grave was in the bush'.[92] Nor were the men alone in this fate. The mortality of inter-clan fighting was increased by the fact that, in the final stages of a successful onslaught, women were not only captured and held to ransom—they were sometimes killed outright.[93]

By the end of the nineteenth-century, therefore, inter-clan fighting was being carried out in deadly earnest. It was subject to as few restraints as inter-tribal fighting; it had become more frequent and more lethal than ever before. Here again satisfactory evidence for the earlier period is lacking, but it does seem that as a result of the deterioration in inter-clan relations, the insecurity of everyday life

[88] Interviews: Koranima Ayena, Yakobo Adoko, Yosia Omwa, Anderea Okadde. Driberg, *The Lango*, p. 109.

[89] Interviews: Nekomia Agwa, Lazaro Okelo. Engola, 'Olden Times', pp. 4–7; Driberg, *The Lango*, p. 109.

[90] Interviews: Koranima Ayena, Isaka Ojaba, Paulo Ajuk.

[91] Knowles to Wilson, 30.5.08, UNA SMP/1005/08; Jervoise to Spire, 28.2.10, UNA SMP/332; Jervoise, Return of murders and raids by natives, 1911, UNA SMP/2020; Driberg, entry for 14.5.16 in Eruti TB (1915–21), LDA.

[92] J. H. Driberg, 'The Lango District, Uganda Protectorate', *Geographical Jl.*, 58 (1921), p. 127.

[93] Ogwal Ajungu, op. cit., para. 7; Engola, op. cit., pp. 5, 6, 7. Interview: Nekomia Agwa.

increased. In south-eastern Lango, for example, the first resident British official reported that no man would have thought of travelling unarmed, or of working in the fields without weapons at his side.[94] Travel outside the neighbourhood was in fact severely limited, and if people wished to visit friends or clansmen at any distance, they travelled in groups, and at night.[95] The daily insecurity is well conveyed by this account of life among the Jo Ocukuru of Ibuje on the eve of the colonial period:[96]

Food used to be gathered from all the houses to one man's house. And while the people ate, others kept a look-out in case enemies should come. . . . Those who lived on the higher ground here ate their food together for fear of enemies. The people at Adak, where the school now is, ate separately, for they had a village of their own. If you went and ate somewhere else, enemies might come and seize your goods while you were away.

On the eve of the colonial period, Lango society was further from being a political unit than it had ever been. Throughout the nineteenth-century, two social developments were constricting the outlook of the individual Lango. On the one hand, the size of localized descent groups was being steadily reduced by the dispersal and fragmentation of clans. On the other, the age-organization was declining as an integrative force.[97] On top of this, the Langi were subjected to the disasters of the early 1890s—the defeats in Buganda, and above all the terrible rinderpest. These reverses resulted in the collapse of regional leadership, an intensification of inter-clan fighting, and an increase in the insecurity of everyday life. Unimpeded travel and redress for wrongs were only possible within the territory of a small number of clan sections, grouped under a clan leader. In western Lango, such an area might approach the size of a modern sub-county; in the east it tended to be still smaller. And everywhere, even this small degree of security was in danger of disruption by raiding, in which villages were burnt and women and children captured or killed.

Theoretically, it would be possible to envisage that, in the course of several more generations, the informal dominance of one clan section over its neighbours might have developed into formal territorial chiefship. To be sure, there was greater potential here than at the level of regional leadership, which the nineteenth-century record shows to

[94] Jervoise to Spire, 8.7.11, UNA SMP/2020.
[95] Interviews: Pilipo Omwa Ayo, Yakobo Adoko, Oco Abolli. Fishbourne, Report on the Districts round Lake Kyoga, 5.10.08, UNA SMP/549/08.
[96] Interview: Anderea Ogwang.   [97] See above, Ch. 2.

have been a precarious institution, geared to external circumstances, rather than integral to Lango society. On the eve of the colonial period, however, there were very few signs of a territorial chiefship developing in this way, and they were limited entirely to north-western Lango. Speculation of this kind is anyway misplaced, since it takes attention away from the resources which Lango society possessed, for all its fragmentation and disorder. The collapse of regional leadership had not resulted in a decline in martial fervour or a reluctance to retaliate against alien intruders. For some twenty years after 1894, the efforts of the colonial power to evolve a new political order among the Langi were held up by persistent and wide-spread resistance on the part of countless clan leaders and their followers. For a colonial power whose representatives were very thin on the ground, this localized resistance was in many ways more taxing than a co-ordinated, uniform response would have been. Lango society hardly measured up to the European stereotype of an African tribe ruled by autocratic chiefs, and for this reason British officials were inclined to dismiss the Lango people as a negligible quantity.[98] They were soon to learn otherwise.

[98] 'Taken at their own valuation they would be formidable foes indeed; in reality . . . they could be very simply dealt with' (Fishbourne, Report on the Districts round Lake Kyoga, 5.10.08, UNA SMP/549/08). See also Fowler to Wilson, 8.3.05, UNA A12/6.

CHAPTER 5

The Politics of Pacification

On the Victoria Nile, the interval between the demise of Egypt's Equatoria Province and the first assertion of British colonial control was a brief one. Barely a year after Emin Pasha had abandoned his few remaining posts in May 1889, the Anglo-German agreement which assigned Uganda to the British sphere was concluded. In April 1890 the first representative of the Imperial British East Africa Company arrived in Buganda from the coast; by a treaty signed in April 1892 the Kabaka acknowledged the Queen's rule, and two years later a British Protectorate was formally declared over Buganda. The implications of this assertion of imperial control were momentous, for potentially the Protectorate Government was infinitely more powerful than any other polity on the Victoria Nile.

Yet the titan was slow to extend itself. The resources invested in the new Protectorate were trifling by imperial standards. Outside Buganda, the range of effective administration was only gradually and haltingly extended. No part of Lango was administered by a British official until 1908, and only in 1918 was the whole of Lango brought under control. The reason for this slow progress lay in the financial stringency imposed by the imperial Government in London. No expenditure could be sanctioned which did not bear directly on the motives behind Britain's original entry into Uganda. The overriding objective had then been to secure the headwaters of the Nile against European rivals; this resolve had been strengthened by public concern in Britain that the Christian missionaries and their converts at the Kabaka's court should be protected, and by Buganda's popular reputation as a haven of order and prosperity. Throughout the 1890s and beyond, the Foreign Office was opposed to any expansion of the Protectorate which did not buttress the security of Buganda, or the maintenance of communications down the Nile. Thus Bunyoro was conquered between 1893 and 1896 because of Kabarega's hostility to Buganda; Toro was occupied at the same time in order to cut off Kabarega's supplies of munitions from German East Africa; and in 1898 a line of forts was established on the Nile below Lake Albert as a precaution against French expansion from the west. But there was no immediate prospect of extending administration north of Lake Kyoga or inland from the Nile valley stations.[1]

Prospects for expansion were still further restricted by the emergency of 1897: a rebellion by Kabaka Mwanga in July was quickly followed by a mutiny among the Government's Sudanese troops. For several months the British position in Uganda lay in the balance. Elaborate and expensive counter-measures were required, including the dispatch of military reinforcements from India. By the time the position had been fully restored in 1899, the imperial Government's grant-in-aid to the Protectorate had soared far beyond the acceptable limit.[2] At the turn of the century, therefore, the prevailing view in the Protectorate capital at Entebbe was that expansion into the peripheries of the British sphere must be delayed on grounds of both retrenchment and security: a forward policy could not be implemented until economic development had produced a healthy balance of tax revenue, and until police and troops could be spared from duties at the centre. Furthermore, when expansion was resumed, areas of genuine economic potential had to take precedence.[3]

It was only in 1905 that officials visiting the borders of Lango became convinced that the costs of administering the country could be quickly recovered from taxation there. Foodstuffs, skins, and ivory were already being exported to Bunyoro in greater quantities every year, and it was expected that the Langi would readily take to the cultivation of cotton for the export market; if carefully managed, both these forms of trade would enable the Government to collect a significant amount of tax.[4] This was a cogent argument in favour of extending administration into Lango, but it was not enough to convince the Secretariat officials in Entebbe. Lango did not loom large in their plans for expansion until 1906, when a steamer service was being

[1] On the British occupation of Uganda, see: R. Robinson and J. Gallagher, *Africa and the Victorians* (London, 1961), ch. 11; M. de K. Hemphill, 'The British Sphere, 1884–94' in *History of East Africa*, vol. I, ed. R. Oliver and G. Mathew (Oxford, 1963), pp. 391–432; D. A. Low, 'Uganda: the Establishment of the Protectorate, 1894–1919', in *History of East Africa*, vol. II, ed. V. Harlow and E. M. Chilver (Oxford, 1965), pp. 57–120.

[2] The best account of the 1897 emergency and its consequences is Low, op. cit., pp. 72–8.

[3] For the debate in Whitehall and Entebbe on expansion during the years 1901–9, see J. Barber, *Imperial Frontier* (Nairobi, 1968), pp. 34–65.

[4] See for example: Fowler to Wilson, 8.3.05, UNA A12/6; Jervoise, Report on Masindi District for Oct. 1906, UNA SMP/515/part 2; Grant to Boyle, 1.7.07, UNA SMP/751/07; Knowles to Wilson, 6.10.08, UNA SMP/1520/08.

planned on Lake Kyoga as part of a water-route linking the north-
west of the Protectorate with the terminus of the Uganda Railway on
Lake Victoria.[5] Once the first government station with responsibility
for the Langi had been opened at Bululu in 1908, the pace of further
advance continued to depend on broader objectives: in 1910 the proposed expansion from the Nile valley into central Lango was recommended to the Colonial Secretary on the grounds that the export of
produce from the new area would be facilitated by the projected
Busoga Railway.[6] In this way, the fortunes of the Langi were tied up
with the economic strategy of the Protectorate as a whole.

There is an important sense, however, in which the colonial era in
Lango can be said to have begun during the 1890s rather than the
years 1908–18. The Government could not afford to ignore Lango
completely, partly because its enemies tended to take refuge there,
and partly because the Langi continued to raid areas which were now
administered. From 1894 onwards, therefore, Lango was penetrated
by British expeditions, which made a stronger impression than any
previous raids, and which were a foretaste of the colonial regime to
come. The long interval between the first appearance of British
officials and the beginning of formal administration allowed the
Langi to devise responses which determined their behaviour when the
Government arrived in strength. For the most part, their response was
resistance to alien incursions; and, despite the highly localized
range of this resistance, it was remarkably effective right up to the
beginning of administration in 1908–9 and beyond. By that time,
certain patterns of accommodation had also emerged, especially in
western Lango. In the context of Lango history, the real significance
of the years from 1894 to 1908 lies in this diversity of contact with—
and response to—the colonial power.

Between 1894 and 1901 the Government was obliged to take action
in Lango on account of the flight there first of Kabarega, and then of
Kabaka Mwanga and the Sudanese mutineers. The brief campaign of
1893–4 ended Bunyoro's independence, and established the British
and their Baganda allies in control; but their position in Bunyoro
remained insecure as long as the *omukama* was at large. Early in
1894 Kabarega crossed into Lango, and his headquarters was almost
continuously there until he was captured five years later in Angai,

[5] Boyle to Deputy Commissioner, 4.7.06, UNA SMP/765/06.
[6] Boyle to Crewe, 4.1.10, PRO CO/536/32.

near Lake Kwania. During his last year of freedom, Kabarega was able to make common-cause with Mwanga and the remainder of the Sudanese mutineers, who escaped to Lango early in 1898 after their defeat in Buganda. Mwanga was captured along with Kabarega. The mutineers established themselves in a fort on the upper Toci, near the confines of Acholi country. They were finally captured during a protracted campaign of several months by government forces under Delmé-Radcliffe in 1901. Delmé-Radcliffe's expedition, though more elaborate than most, was in fact the tenth that had entered Lango since 1894. During that period, much of western and southern Lango had been traversed—the valleys of the Toci and Okole, the right bank of the Nile from Aber up to Namasale peninsula, and the eastern shores of Lake Kwania.[7] In these areas the Langi had not been idle witnesses to others' misfortunes, but had been directly involved.

Some Langi had been actively engaged on the side of the fugitives. Kabarega's purpose in moving to Lango was partly to have a convenient base for sallies against the government forces, but partly also because he hoped that friendly Lango clan sections would provide him with military reinforcements, as well as a place of refuge. On account of the collapse of regional leadership earlier in the decade, Kabarega could no longer rely on the aid of large clan combinations, and no war-bands came from the far east at all; but in south-west Lango, where Kabarega was based from 1894 to 1895, some of the clan sections joined the *abarasura* (royal army) in their raids across the Nile,[8] and when a British column pursued Kabarega northwards along the right bank of the Nile in May 1895, they had to force a passage over the Aroca.[9] Support for Kabarega was strongest in the south-east, probably on account of the vigorous lake trade of the Banyoro. When Kabarega withdrew along Lake Kwania in April 1899, his pursuers were attacked, and Lango warriors were at

[7] The principal sources for these expeditions are as follows: the series A2 and A4 in UNA; the FO series 403/211, 241 and 318 (in the PRO); A. G. Bagshawe, 'Journal of Lango Expedition, April–August 1901', MS. in Makerere University Library; S. Vandeleur, *Campaigning on the Upper Nile and Niger* (London, 1898); Sykes, *Service and Sport on the Tropical Nile*.

[8] Some observers attributed the raids on Bulemezi and Buruli to the Langi alone (Ternan to Commissioner, 5.1.95, UNA A4/4; Pulteney to Commissioner, 16.3.96, UNA A4/4; Vandeleur, op. cit., p. 104). Col. Evatt, whose expedition captured Kabarega in 1899, was of the opinion that Kabarega's followers were solely to blame (Evatt to Ternan, 10.5.99, UNA A4/17). The truth is probably that the Langi took part in raids organized by the Banyoro; they are mentioned together in connection with a raid in February 1895 (Dunning to Commissioner, 13.2.95, UNA A4/1). [9] Vandeleur, op. cit., p. 72.

Kabarega's side when he was captured a few days later. The expedition retaliated by destroying villages and granaries.[10]

Although the Sudanese mutineers lacked any previous connection with the Langi, they too were able to come to an arrangement with local clan leaders. A handful of mutineers stayed with Odongo Aja in Kamdini; they sold him a few fire-arms and instructed some of the Jo Arak how to use them; they also joined Odongo on some of his raids.[11] When Delmé-Radcliffe entered Lango at the mouth of the Toci in April 1901, the mutineers had evidently left Kamdini and Odongo himself was co-operative, but during the course of the expedition he was suspected of complicity with the mutineers, and two of his villages were attacked in August.[12] Most of the mutineers, though, were based at their fort on the upper Toci. They used their surplus of fire-arms to equip local allies, principally the Alwaa clan; mutineers and Langi raided the Acholi, as well as Lango clans hostile to the Jo Alwaa.[13] The clan sections who supported the mutineers were punished accordingly: a small expedition in 1899 fired their villages and crops,[14] and this treatment was repeated on a much larger scale by Delmé-Radcliffe in 1901.[15]

However the injuries inflicted on the Langi during the years 1894–1901 went a good deal further than retribution for supposed offences. During the 1890s, the number of troops in the Protectorate was so small that large numbers of irregulars had to be employed in the pursuit of Kabarega and the mutineers. These irregulars were mostly Baganda whose main objective was to return with as much plunder as possible. The handful of British officers who led the expeditions were usually quite unable to prevent the Baganda from raiding the Lango hinterland for livestock and provisions.[16] In Ocini this behaviour provoked a strong reaction from Owiny Akulo and the Jo Arak; in

---

[10] Evatt to Staff Officer, 8.4.99, UNA A4/16; Evatt to Ternan, 10.5.99, UNA A4/17. Interviews: Gideon Odwongo, Tomasi Ojuka, Reuben Ogwal.

[11] Interviews: Misaki Oki, Kosia Ato, Leoben Okodi, Fancio Itot, Koranima Ayena. Wilson to Johnston, 7.10.00, UNA A12/1.

[12] Delmé-Radcliffe, Diary of Lango Field Force, entries for 26.4.01, 27.4.01, 15.8.01, 16.8.01, PRO FO/403/318; Bagshawe, 'Journal', entry for 17.8.01. Interviews: Juma Arbam, Edwardi Olir.

[13] Anderson to Johnston, 21.3.00, UNA A4/27; Macallister to Johnston, 20.11.00, UNA A16/1. Interviews: Yakobo Olugo, Yokonani Alyai.

[14] Sykes, op. cit., pp. 240–1.

[15] Delmé-Radcliffe, Diary of Lango Field Force, passim; Bagshawe, 'Journal', passim.

[16] See for example: Captain Gibb, Diary of Mruli Expedition, May 1894, UNA A2/2; Vandeleur, op. cit., p. 74.

May 1895 they ambushed and killed 150 Baganda irregulars as they were waiting to be ferried across the Nile.[17] Elsewhere the scale of the clashes between Baganda and Langi was much smaller, but there is little doubt that the depredations of the Baganda at this time made a deep impression.

Map 7. The Colonial Penetration of Lango 1894–1909

It is more difficult to assess Lango attitudes to the colonial regime itself. The material strength of the government forces must have made a considerable impact, and particularly the straits to which Kabarega and Mwanga were reduced.[18] A decisive demonstration of power by the Government could certainly elicit a submissive response; friendly

[17] Vandeleur, op. cit., p. 79; Jackson to Foreign Office, 7.6.95, PRO FO/403/210; Scott, entry for 31.1.14, in Koli TB (1912–14, part 1), LDA. See also Tarantino, 'Lango Wars', p. 234.

[18] The officer commanding the expedition of 1899 was particularly optimistic on this score. Evatt to Ternan, 10.5.99, UNA A4/17.

advances were made around Kamdini in 1896,[19] and also in 1899 near Lake Kwania, where Kabarega's last refuge was revealed by a local clan leader.[20] But these submissions did not entail a resolve to co-operate with the Government in the future; they were merely diplomatic gestures designed to stave off an immediate crisis. The impression of material strength was offset by the fleeting nature of government interventions, for most expeditions were over in a matter of weeks rather than months. The Government might be powerful, but it appeared to have no intention of taking Lango over for good. As a senior official put it in 1903, the Langi 'look upon our action in their country as being always purely transient'.[21]

In the aftermath of Kabarega's capture, the experience of south-east Lango began to diverge markedly from that of the west. The agencies of pacification differed in personnel and attitude. The Government itself regarded south-east Lango in the light of its experience in Bukedi, while western Lango was seen from the point of view of the Bunyoro administration. This distinction did not cease to be drawn with the beginning of formal administration in Lango. Miro District, established in 1908, was supervised from Mbale, while Palango District was set up in 1909 by officials operating from Hoima. Although officials were aware that they were dealing with a single people, they nevertheless maintained the separation of east from west until 1911. It might be tempting to dismiss this arbitrary division as an administrative convenience, with little bearing on the experience of the Langi themselves. In point of fact it had a very great bearing on the local perception of colonial rule. The task of devising a viable political system proved to be more difficult in the south-east than in the west. In part, this was caused by the smaller scale of inter-clan politics there, but it was also due to the divergent experience of east and west during the years from 1899 to 1911. Whereas in the west European officials were actively involved in making contact between Government and Langi before the start of formal administration, in the east this task was left entirely to African intermediaries, whose attitude to the Langi was predatory and vindictive. As a result, when officials eventually took direct responsibility for the south-east, the

[19] Ternan to Berkeley, 20.10.96, UNA A4/6.
[20] Evatt to Ternan, 10.5.99, UNA A4/17.
[21] Wilson to Hayes Sadler, 9.12.03, UNA A12/5. Compare also Delmé-Radcliffe to Coles, 10.9.01, PRO FO/403/318.

atmosphere had been poisoned, and the local reaction was one of sullen indifference or overt resistance. By contrast, the relative restraint with which officials in the west had handled the Langi before 1909 elicited in some quarters a positive response, based on a confidence that the colonial regime could be manipulated by local interests. In order to appreciate this distinction, it is necessary to treat each story separately, and in some detail, up until 1911. In that year the two Districts, having expanded towards a common boundary, were merged to form a single Lango District; and for the first time officials took stock of what they had achieved to date.

The divergent experience of south-eastern Lango originated in the attempt by the powerful Muganda chief, Semei Kakungulu, to carve out a personal fief in the area, with the approval of the Protectorate authorities. This improbable enterprise was determined by two factors: the expansionist energies of the Baganda, and the readiness of the Government to consider any cheap method of extending administration. Kakungulu himself had been one of the outstanding figures in Ganda politics during the civil wars of 1888–93, but it was his rival in the Protestant faction, Apolo Kagwa, who gained most from the settlement in Buganda. Frustrated at home, Kakungulu began to look further afield. His interest in opportunities abroad was shared by many less illustrious Baganda, for whom the advent of the colonial order and the entrenchment of the Christian chiefly élite limited the prospects for promotion, profit, and adventure at home.[22]

When Bunyoro south of the Kafu river was annexed to Buganda in 1894, Baganda were appointed to chiefships in that area. Kakungulu took charge of Bugerere, the province which adjoined the Nile immediately south of Namasale peninsula; the Banyara, who inhabited northern Bugerere, had been an integral part of Kabarega's kingdom. It was while he was reorganizing the administration of Bugerere that Kakungulu became interested in 'Bukedi', by which the Baganda meant all the country to the north and east of Lake Kyoga.[23] His attention was probably directed there in the first instance by the

[22] For the aspirations of Kakungulu and his followers, see M. J. Twaddle, 'Politics in Bukedi, 1900–1939', unpublished Ph.D. thesis, London University, 1967, especially pp. 83–91, 120–6.

[23] The story of Kakungulu's career during the period 1896–1900 is involved and obscure. The following accounts have some relevance: H. B. Thomas, 'Capax Imperii—The Story of Semei Kakunguru', *Uganda Jl.*, 6 (1939), pp. 125–36; Lawrance, *The Iteso*, pp. 17–22; J. M. Gray, 'Kakunguru in Bukedi', *Uganda Jl.*, 27 (1963), pp. 31–59; Twaddle, op. cit. However in the following account I have drawn mainly on discussions with Dr. Twaddle, who has made extensive use of

long-standing trade links between this part of Bunyoro and 'Bukedi'. In about 1896 Kakungulu began to send his own traders north of the Lake. Kaweri island, near Bululu, was taken over as a commercial base, and during the next two years several trading posts were established in the hinterland to the north. Most of the posts were situated in Kumam and Teso country, but the one at Agaya, near the southern tip of Lake Kwania, lay within Lango country, and there is little doubt that Kakungulu's followers were trading with the Langi at this time.

Kakungulu's opportunity for a more decisive expansion came in the middle of 1899. Earlier in the year he had taken part in the expedition which captured Kabarega and Mwanga near Lake Kwania. This experience gave him first-hand acquaintance with Lango country, as well as a claim on the British authorities. He was able to secure a loan of government rifles, and official approval to extend his chiefdom in Bugerere across Lake Kyoga. In June 1899 he established himself at Agaya, with the intention of building up a kingdom on the basis of his trading connections with Lango and Kumam. Trading posts were turned into forts, and additional forts were established in Lango—at Dokolo and at Akabo on the eastern shore of Lake Kwania. Kakungulu achieved some success with the Kumam, who regarded him as a potential ally against the Langi.[24] But in Lango the reaction was almost uniformly hostile.[25] The fort at Agaya was plagued by attacks from the start, and when in September Kakungulu launched a major plundering expedition into Lango, there was a heavy engagement at Dokolo in which his second-in-command was killed. Livestock were seized and settlements burnt, but the Baganda appear to have been prevented from penetrating any deeper than Dokolo, and the expedition was scarcely an encouragement to empire-building in Lango. By the end of 1899 Kakungulu had withdrawn to Bululu, well within Kumam country. The following year he directed the main thrust of his offensive against the Iteso to the east, and he then moved his headquarters away from Lake Kyoga altogether. Until his retirement

Luganda chronicles and personal reminiscences in order to reconstruct Kakungulu's movements at this time; I gratefully acknowledge his assistance.

It should be noted that Lango oral sources are an inadequate guide in this matter, since Kakungulu is frequently confused with later Baganda.

[24] In 1896 a delegation of 'Bakedi' had accompanied Kakungulu to Mengo to request military assistance for operations north of the Lake. These were amost certainly Kumam.

[25] There is only one recorded case of a Lango clan leader visiting Kakungulu; this was Okori of Amac. Jervoise to Spire, 18.4.10, UNA SMP/624.

in 1902, Kakungulu maintained a presence on the lake, with chiefs at Bululu and Akabo, but with no greater success against the Langi. Kakungulu's brief imperial venture earned for the Baganda the deep hatred of the south-eastern Langi. An informant who grew up near Akabo fort gives an account which reflects this hatred, as well as the rough methods of government employed by the Baganda:[26]

While Kakungulu was here, if you were caught doing something wrong, your ears or your lips were cut off, or the ear and the eye on opposite sides of the face were cut off. That's how Kakungulu behaved. Sometimes four poles were stuck in the ground and you were tied onto them; then they lit a fire underneath and dried you out as a wild animal is dried out.

The standing of the Baganda was further compromised by their close association with the Kumam.[27] For the Langi, cattle-raiding against the Kumam became more difficult, and the pressure on the most easterly Lango settlements to withdraw towards the Abalang river, may also have begun in Kakungulu's time.[28]

In 1902 Kakungulu's position on Lake Kyoga was taken over with government approval by the Banyara (the inhabitants of Bugerere), many of whom had joined him in exploiting their traditional connections with the peoples of 'Bukedi'.[29] A leading Munyara, named Musabira, was placed in charge of Bululu. The fort at Akabo had been abandoned by now, and the Banyara appear to have made no great efforts to administer the Langi. But their influence with the Kumam depended on their ability to deter cattle-raids by the Langi, and this was no easy task. Only a year or so after taking charge of Bululu, Musabira met his death when he responded to a Kumam appeal for reprisals against the Jo Arak of Alwa, near the Abalang river.[30] Musabira's kinsman and successor, Kazana, gradually built up his influence among the Kumam.[31] The Langi, on the other hand, proved scarcely more amenable than they had in the time of

[26] Interview: Tomasi Ojuka.
[27] Interviews: Yusufu Erau, Abiramo Okelo Oyanga.
[28] Driberg credited Kakungulu with the expulsion of the Langi from Anyara and Kelle (*The Lango*, p. 35). It is certain, however, that the Abalang only became the effective frontier between the Langi and Kumam after a government station had been established at Bululu in 1908.
[29] Thomas, op. cit., p. 132.
[30] Jervoise, undated entry at Kelle, in Kioga TB (1912–13, part 1), TDA. Interviews: Yeromia Otim, Abiramo Okelo Oyanga, Tomasi Ojuka, Yusufu Erau.
[31] Boyle to Wilson, 6.3.07, UNA SMP/281/07.

Kakungulu. By the middle of 1907 a handful of villages had begun to pay tax,[32] but the over-all pattern of Langi–Banyara relations did not change. The Langi continued to raid the Kumam and Banyara for cattle, goats, and women, burning villages and destroying crops. From time to time Kazana launched reprisals.[33]

This pattern of raiding and counter-raiding between Kazana and the Langi was not in itself very significant. Kazana's importance lies in the fact that European officials assessed the prospects for administration in south-east Lango through his eyes, and incorporated his informal political structure into the Protectorate. Kazana enjoyed from the beginning some official status as the inheritor of Kakungulu's commission to subdue this part of 'Bukedi'. So when in 1906 government officials began to consider the administrative implications of opening steamship communications through Lakes Kyoga and Kwania, Kazana was an important factor in their calculations. The only other candidate to spearhead the advance into Lango was a chief from Buruli named Kabagambe, who had settled on the uninhabited south-western shores of Namasale peninsula in about 1898.[34] Kazana had for some time been discrediting Kabagambe in official quarters, when events played into his hands. In January 1907, a Muganda agent called Bumbakali Kamya was placed at Namasale, partly to supervise supplies for the Nile steamer, but also to keep an eye on Kabagambe.[35] When the agent and sixteen of his followers were murdered in April, Kabagambe was suspected of inciting the Langi to kill them; he was deported to Jinja, and his colony of Baruli was placed under Kazana.[36]

Kamya's murder highlighted the need to provide some security for commerce and communication along Lake Kyoga. Senior officials were also aware that the Government would lose credibility if it continued to ignore attacks by the Langi on Kumam tax-payers.[37] In June 1907, therefore, a major punitive operation was launched against

[32] Grant to Boyle, 1.7.07, UNA SMP/751/07.
[33] Boyle to Wilson, 28.9.06, UNA SMP/1054/06; Grant to Acting Deputy Commissioner, 24.4.07, UNA SMP/549/07. The precise locale of Kazana's counter-raids is not known, but one clan leader in Angai was killed during one of them. Driberg, undated entry in Dokolo TB (1913–26, part 1).
[34] Jervoise, Notes on Namasale, Kioga TB (1913), TDA.
[35] Boyle to Wilson, 29.11.06, UNA SMP/1054/06; Grant to Boyle, 18.2.07, UNA SMP/305/07.
[36] Evidence taken by P. W. Cooper at Kabagambe's, enclosed in Cooper to Grant, 1.5.07, UNA SMP/544/07; Grant to Boyle, 1.7.07, UNA SMP/751/07.
[37] Wilson to Elgin, 16.7.07, and enclosed memorandum, UNA SMP/751/07.

those Langi who lived along the Abalang river and in Namasale peninsula. The Kyoga Expedition was exceptional in the annals of Lango pacification, in that its sole objective was to teach the Langi a sharp and indiscriminate lesson. Every ten miles or so, the expedition set up camp and then scoured the surrounding country; not even those who took refuge in the bush were safe.[38] In effect, a licence to plunder was given to Kumam irregulars, over whom Kazana had little control. On the first day of the campaign, the expedition was attacked by the Jo Palamyek under Opige at Dokolo,[39] but elsewhere there was little overt resistance, as the officer-in-charge admitted. In just over ten days, 163 villages were destroyed and 200 casualties inflicted;[40] between 20,000 and 30,000 Langi were estimated to have been 'dealt with'.[41] The expedition was the climax to an eight-year sequence of violence between the Langi and the Protectorate's unofficial African representatives.

The Government's strategy was to follow up this convincing demonstration of strength with a more conciliatory attitude and a beginning of formal administration. During the next year, arrangements were made for a new district of Miro to be formed, with jurisdiction over the Kumam and the Langi near Lake Kyoga.[42] An Assistant Collector (soon to be renamed Assistant District Commissioner) responsible to Mbale was to administer the District from a station at Bululu, near Kazana's village. In March 1908 G. P. Jervoise arrived there with a complement of thirteen police—soon increased to forty—in order to open the new District,[43] and in May a survey-party covered again the route of the Kyoga Expedition.[44]

The administrative structure of the new District conformed very closely to the 'agent system' then in operation among all acephalous peoples in the Eastern Province of Uganda. The practice of governing through Baganda agents was derived from the informal empire which Kakungulu had set up in Bukedi. When in 1900 Kakungulu had

---

[38] Edwards to Commissioner, 5.7.07, UNA SMP/751/07. Interview: Tomasi Ojuka (an eyewitness as a boy).

[39] Grant to Boyle, 1.7.07, UNA SMP/751/07. Interviews: Tomasi Ojuka, Yeromia Otim, Abiramo Okelo Oyanga.

[40] Edwards to Commissioner, 5.7.07, UNA SMP/751/07.

[41] Grant to Boyle, 1.7.07, UNA SMP/751/07.

[42] For reasons that are not clear, the term used by the Kumam when referring to the Langi was adopted as the name of the District.

[43] Jervoise, Report on Miro District for March 1908, UNA SMP/216/08.

[44] Fishbourne, Preliminary Report on Umiro Country, May 1908, UNA SMP/549/08.

turned his energies from Lango to Teso, Bugwere, and Bugisu, he had been very much more successful, so much so that the Protectorate authorities, who had authorized the venture in the first place, became uneasy. From 1902 onwards, overall control of Kakungulu's 'kingdom' was appropriated by British officials, their efforts culminating in Kakungulu's transfer to Busoga in 1906. At the same time, Kakungulu's vast following was reduced in number and, stage by stage, bureaucratized: by the end of 1905, his chiefs had become salaried agents of the Protectorate government. This somewhat irregular arrangement was justified on the grounds that the agents would accustom the 'Bakedi' to the benefits of ordered government, during the time it would take to train administrative personnel locally. Their job was to punish and prevent breaches of the peace, to build roads with local labour, and to collect taxes.[45]

It was taken for granted that Miro District would be administered along the same lines. The only improvisation lay in the choice of staff for the Kumam area. Kazana was not superseded by a Muganda; instead, his sphere of influence was incorporated as it stood.[46] In Lango itself, a more orthodox arrangement was made. Isaka Nziga, formerly a prominent client of Kakungulu's, and now an agent in Teso, was chosen to be chief agent. He was installed at Dokolo in July 1907 with fifty armed askaris, as an advance party of the incoming government.[47] The intention was that Nziga should visit the places through which the Kyoga Expedition had passed in the previous month; but for the time being his hands were full in Dokolo, where forced labour had to be mobilized in order to build a permanent fort.[48] Towards the end of 1908, Jervoise established three agents' posts at Angai, Kwera, and Bata.[49] Three more posts were set up along the northern shores of Namasale peninsula in 1909,[50] and early in 1910 Agwata and Abyece on the north side of Lake Kwania were taken under administration.[51] (Map 8).

This relative caution in pushing out the frontiers of administration

[45] The best account of the emergence of the agent system is Twaddle, op. cit.
[46] Boyle to Wilson, 11.3.07, UNA SMP/305/07. See also K. Ingham, 'British Administration in Lango District, 1907–35', *Uganda Jl.*, 19 (1955), p. 156.
[47] Coote to Grant, 7.8.07, UNA SMP/279/07; Jervoise, Report on Miro District for March 1908, UNA SMP/216/08; Jervoise, Notes on Dokolo, Dokolo TB (1913–26, part 1).
[48] Interviews: Yeromia Otim, Abiramo Okelo Oyanga.
[49] Jervoise, Report on Miro District for 1908–9, UNA SMP/925/09.
[50] Jervoise to D. C. Mbale, 30.4.09, UNA SMP/359/09.
[51] Jervoise to Spire, 28.2.10. UNA SMP/332.

accorded with the gradualist approach favoured by the Governor, Sir Hesketh Bell:[52]

Instead of compelling the outlying primitive tribes to accept our authority suddenly by force of arms, it appears to me far preferable to effect our object gradually by a policy of peaceful penetration. The officer stationed at Bululu will gently extend his influence among the neighbouring clans, and, little by little, the Lango tribes may be led to appreciate the advantages of our rule and the benefits of an orderly regime.

Yet the prospects of 'peaceful penetration', if they existed at all, depended less on a modest rate of territorial expansion than on caution in saddling the Langi with unfamiliar demands. And here administrators proved less than circumspect. At the close of the Kyoga Expedition in 1907 an experienced official declared that, once a European was on the scene, the Langi would 'be prepared to do whatever they are told.'[53] He could hardly have been more mistaken. What he and other administrators failed to grasp at the outset was that even the most indispensible activities of an administration were unacceptable to the Langi.

As in other newly subjected areas, the Government's immediate priorities were the establishment of law and order and the enlistment of forced labour for public works. The first of these objectives meant in practice an end to inter-tribal and inter-village raiding, and a recognition that the punishment of serious crimes was henceforth the job of the government and those to whom it chose to delegate responsibility. When a cattle-raid was reported, or a clan-leader refused to hand over an alleged murderer, the appearance of a District Officer at the head of a police detachment could easily be construed as a hostile act, to which the villagers responded either by attacking or by decamping into the bush. All too often, officials had little choice but to open fire on the attackers, or to confiscate livestock and burn abandoned settlements.[54] As for forced labour, this was if anything more unpalatable in a society where political authority had never been associated with the right to labour service; inevitably, orders that the Langi should clear roads and build permanent camps tended to be obeyed only when force was used, or at least threatened.[55]

---

[52] Hesketh Bell to Crewe, 8.5.08, UNA SMP/549/08.

[53] Grant to Boyle, 1.7.07, UNA SMP/751/07. Grant had served as Collector at Hoima and Mbale, and in both postings had direct contact with the Langi.

[54] See for example, Jervoise to Coote, 19.3.09, UNA SMP/225/09, for two such incidents in Kwera and Amac.

[55] See for example, Jervoise to Spire, 27.10.09, UNA SMP/1705/09, and Wright to Spire, 15.11.10, UNA SMP/1408.

Nor was the Government content to settle for its most pressing priorities. Reports of plentiful crops and livestock were treated as an excuse for demanding a tax in kind, known as 'hut-tax', which had first been levied from Langi living near Bululu as early as 1906, and was now applied throughout the administered area.[56] At the same time the agricultural routine of the Langi was disrupted by the introduction of compulsory cotton-cultivation in 1909, in the hope that the unwieldy hut-tax would shortly be replaced by a tax in cash on the proceeds of cotton-growing.[57]

The most taxing demand on the south-eastern Langi during the first years of administration was one which they certainly could not have accepted without protest; this was their forcible expulsion from the most recently settled areas: the western shores of Namasale peninsula and the country between the Abalang river and Lake Kyoga. Since the Government had entered the area in the wake of Kazana, local officials felt some responsibility towards the Kumam, many of whom had been paying tax to Kazana for a year or two before Bululu station was opened. One of their first priorities was therefore to provide protection for the Kumam against the menace of Lango cattle-raids.[58] But officials were also aware that in recent years Lango settlement had been steadily gaining ground at the expense of the Kumam between the Abalang and Omunyal rivers. Both Kakungulu and Kazana had made some headway in checking Lango expansion, and during 1909 the Government's success in limiting Lango raids enabled the Kumam to resettle in the no-man's-land round Kaberamaido.[59] Jervoise, however, was not content with 'freezing' the existing boundary; in his view, a fair deal for the Kumam entailed moving all Langi still on the left bank of the Abalang over to the other side.[60] There were several large villages in Alwa, including that of Okwanga, leader of the Dokolo Jo Arak. By

[56] Boyle to Commissioner, 12.4.06, UNA A10/5/1906; Grant to Boyle, 1.7.07, UNA SMP/751/07; Jervoise, Report on Miro District for 1908–9, UNA SMP/925/09.

[57] Jervoise, Report on Miro District for May 1909, UNA SMP/359/09. For exactly how Lango agriculture was affected by the introduction of cotton see J. Tosh, 'Lango Agriculture during the Early Colonial Period: Land and Labour in a Cash-Crop Economy', Jl. African History, 19 (1978), in the press.

[58] The second agent's post in Lango was set up in October 1908 at Angai, near the Abalang river, with precisely this objective in mind. Jervoise, entry for 3.9.12 at Angai, Dokolo TB (1913–26, part 1), LDA.

[59] Jervoise, Report on Miro District for June 1909, UNA SMP/359/09; Jervoise, Notes on Kaberamaido, in Kioga TB (1912–13), TDA.

[60] Jervoise to Spire, 31.12.10, UNA SMP/178.

April 1912 they had all been compelled to leave, and the reluctant ones had been burnt out.[61]

A similar policy was implemented on Namasale peninsula, though here the beneficiaries were the Baruli, to whom the Government also felt obliged. Since Kabagambe's arrival in about 1898, the Baruli had colonized the southern coastline of the peninsula, and by about 1910 had reached Cakwara on the north-western coast. At the same time, Langi from Awelo had been pressing steadily southwards, not into the interior of the peninsula, which was poorly-watered, but along the coast, where they encountered the Baruli. As long as the two populations were intermingled, theft and murder were frequent, and there was much to be said for separating them. For a time, Jervoise toyed with the idea of making the whole of Namasale a Bantu preserve, and the Langi were urged to migrate to the north side of Lake Kwania.[62] By 1913 this plan had been abandoned, and the Government was content with expelling Langi from south of Cakwara. By 1918 almost all of them had been moved north.[63] The converse of this arrangement was that the Bantu-speakers living north of Cakwara were expelled, but the numbers involved were considerably smaller, and can scarcely have mitigated the impact of the restrictions on Lango settlement to the south.[64]

Whether administrative demands took the form of forced labour, restrictions on raiding, tax in kind, compulsory cotton-cultivation, or enforced migration, the difficulty of making them acceptable to the local population was greatly increased by the fact that they were usually channelled through the Baganda. For the average villager, 'the Government' meant not the one or two Europeans based in Kumam country at Bululu, but the nearest agent and his followers. Nziga's men were certainly better armed than Kakungulu's had been, and they were possibly better disciplined, but they were nevertheless Baganda, and quite a few of them must have been veterans of the 1899–1902 episode. It is highly unlikely that the Langi drew any distinction between the two. In the case of Nziga, resistance to the Baganda would appear to have been more sporadic—probably because of the strong impact made by the Kyoga Expedition—and it

---

[61] Jervoise, Notes on Dokolo, in Dokolo TB (1913–26, part 1). Interviews: Tomasi Ojuka, Gideon Odwongo.

[62] Jervoise, Notes on Awelo, 1913, in Kioga TB (1914–19).

[63] Kioga TB (1913–25), *passim*. During the 1920s the Langi began to infiltrate southern Namasale again, and the two communities are inextricably mixed today.

[64] Entries for 26.6.15 and 26.6.16, in Kioga TB (1914–19).

was certainly less successful. All the same, there were over thirty armed clashes between Nziga's followers and the Langi between 1907 and 1911.[65] The most serious opposition was encountered in 1910 in the Abyece area, where the Jo Alipa and their neighbours attacked the stockade five times, and Baganda patrols three times; the agent could do little except remain in the stockade until early in 1911, when Jervoise moved the post to a new site about ten miles away.[66]

When, therefore, the government station at Bululu was closed down and a headquarters for the new Lango District opened at Abyece in 1911, the prospects for administration in the south-east were bleak. From 1899 until 1907 there had been an almost continuous record of violence between the Langi and a succession of alien chiefs on their borders. And, far from implying a fresh start, the beginning of regular administration in 1907 merely formalized the freelance activities of those chiefs. Worse still, the Government took over the prejudices of Kakungulu and Kazana in favour of the Kumam and the Banyara, and the Langi were expelled from disputed areas. By 1911 hardly any attempt had been made to recruit administrative personnel locally. When, as a result of policy changes at Protectorate level, local chiefs were appointed in 1912, the resentment and suspicion built up among the Langi since 1899 added greatly to the difficulties. These points will emerge in higher relief as we turn to consider the contrasting story of western Lango in the same period.

The close interest taken by the Government in western Lango during the 1890s had been aroused by the presence there of Kabarega, Mwanga, and the Sudanese mutineers. However, the rounding up of the last fugitives by Delmé-Radcliffe in 1901 did not end the Government's anxieties. The limelight was henceforward taken by Lango raids into administered territory. During the years 1901–9 there were frequent raids against the Acholi. Lango war-bands were seen as far afield as the Murchison Falls area and around Patiko.[67] Systematic administration of the Acholi away from the Nile did not begin until

[65] Jervoise, Returns of encounters between Isaka Nziga's Baganda Agents and the Miru up to May 1911, UNA SMP/2020.

[66] These incidents are reported individually in UNA SMP/332, 178, 1133, 1408. See also, Jervoise, Notes on Nabieso, in Kwania TB (1913–19). This is the only instance in the whole of Lango where local pressure compelled the administration to alter the site of a post.

[67] Cooper to Wilson, 6.12.04, UNA A16/4. There are several other references to these raids for the years 1902–6 in series A12 and A16. See also A. B. Lloyd, *Uganda to Khartoum* (London, 1906), pp. 193–5, 225.

1910, but the vacillations of official policy since 1899 had resulted in an ill-defined obligation to protect friendly *rwode* (chiefs). British officials were posted temporarily to Lamogi from 1899 to 1901 and to Keyo (near Patiko) from 1906 to 1907. Promises of protection had been made, with the result that, even when the government presence was limited to the Nile valley, complaints about Lango raids were investigated. From time to time local officials advocated punitive operations against Lango leaders such as Okaka of Iceme;[68] but the Entebbe authorities were adamant that expeditions could not be launched on such slender grounds.[69]

The authorities were much more worried about the situation in Bunyoro, which was unequivocally part of the Protectorate, and where strenuous efforts were needed to reconcile the conquered population to colonial rule. As a result of the Baganda depredations of 1895–6, the Langi of Aber were strongly antagonistic to the Government, and Delmé-Radcliffe's campaign had hardly modified their attitude. Early in 1902 they attacked the government post at Foweira,[70] and by 1904 the temporary refuge they offered to tax evaders from eastern Bunyoro was becoming a serious headache.[71] South of the Okole river, the Government found itself in a dilemma over those Banyoro who had settled on the east bank of the Nile. They had done so for a variety of reasons. During the 1890s some had gone to Lango in order to escape from the general insecurity in Bunyoro, and from the excesses of the Baganda who manned a chain of forts along the Nile from 1895 onwards.[72] Others had migrated because of famine in Bunyoro,[73] or in order to evade taxation.[74] Banyoro communities were to be found along the Nile from Kungu as far east as Kwibale, near Maruzi hill. As their numbers increased, they began to pose a threat to the Langi, who were rapidly expanding in this area. By August 1904 there had been six clashes between Langi and Banyoro on the right bank.[75] No doubt officials would have preferred to ignore the right bank completely, but it was difficult to collect tax from the Banyoro on the left bank if those on the right bank were exempt. In

[68] Cooper to Wilson, 14.3.05, UNA A16/4; Fowler to Wilson, 30.9.05, UNA A12/7.
[69] Hayes Sadler to Wilson, 28.8.05 and 14.11.05, UNA A13/2.
[70] Langton to Wilson, Jan. 1902, UNA A12/2.
[71] Speke, Report of Tour in Chopi District, Nov. 1904, UNA A12/5.
[72] Thruston to Ternan, 5.5.97, UNA A4/8. Interview: Yakobo Adoko.
[73] Evatt to Ternan, 8.10.99, UNA A4/21.
[74] Grant to Hayes Sadler, 30.8.04, UNA A12/5.   [75] Ibid.

1903 the Government therefore ordered that tax should be collected from the Banyoro living between Kungu and Kwibale. Yet the Banyoro could hardly be expected to pay up unless they were given protection against Lango raids. Officials in Bunyoro were thus placed in the impossible position of supposedly administering Banyoro across the Nile without being allowed to intervene against the Langi.[76] Not until 1905 did a punitive column under C. W. Fowler, Sub-Commissioner of Western Province, cross the Nile. Fowler tried to solve the problem by evacuating all Banyoro to the left bank, but by 1909 many had returned, including tax evaders.[77]

The Government's difficulties with regard to these Banyoro illustrate very well the contrast between official attitudes to the west and east of Lango. In the east, no essential short-term interests were at stake, and the officials at Mbale—ninety miles from the nearest Lango settlements—were only marginally concerned with how the Baganda and Banyara behaved there; and so between 1899 and 1907 no European official visited the south-eastern Langi. By contrast, western Lango was immediately adjacent to a District of the Protectorate—a District, moreover, the stability of which was a high priority for the Protectorate as a whole. From 1903 onwards a civilian official was resident at Masindi, less than thirty miles from the most westerly part of Lango. The reports submitted by successive Assistant Collectors at Masindi show that considerable thought was given to relations with the Langi, in the light of the long-term problem of pacifying the country east of the Nile.[78] After Fowler's visit in 1905, this interest was quickened by a positive response from some of the Lango clan leaders. As the permanence of the Government's presence in Bunyoro became more obvious, and as officials showed more concern about the right bank of the Nile, so clan leaders in western Lango began to take the Government into account when making political calculations. Overtures were made by Odora of Kungu in 1904, by Arum of Ibuje in 1905, and by the great Odongo Aja in 1906. Accommodating gestures had been made before, but not until 1904

---

[76] Prendergast to Wilson, 8.12.03 and 9.12.03, and attached minutes, UNA A12/5; Prendergast to Wilson, 21.12.03, UNA A12/4; Grant to Wilson, 10.10.04, UNA A12/5.

[77] Fowler to Wilson, 8.3.05, UNA A12/6; Henry, Report on Masindi District for April 1909, UNA SMP/280/09; Jervoise, undated entry, in Maruzi TB (1912–13).

[78] These reports can be found in UNA as follows: A12/5, A12/7, SMP/314/06, SMP/515, SMP/371/07, SMP/34/08, SMP/4/08, SMP/1005/08.

can we identify a response which was determined by a long-term perception of colonial rule rather than the exigencies of an immediate crisis.

These overtures were important in several ways. In the first place, they partly determined the timing of the Government's entry into western Lango. Officials in Bunyoro were quick to see how important the assistance of friendly 'chiefs' would be when the time came to open a station in Lango; they soon realized, too, that if they did not respond quickly, the local standing of 'pro-government' leaders in Lango was likely to be undermined. Such fears were particularly strong at the beginning of 1908;[79] and so in April of that year the Sub-Commissioner was instructed to tour western Lango and to draw up detailed plans for its administration.[80] Thus, whereas the timing of the Government's entry into Miro was affected by the increasing menace of Lango raids, in the west the Government acted when the momentum of conciliation appeared to be endangered. Psychologically the difference was considerable. In the second place, the personal acquaintance which officials had had with individual clan leaders before 1909 meant that they began to administer western Lango with at least some grasp of local politics, and with some confidence that indigenous 'chiefs' could be used, in marked contrast to the pattern in the south-east. Finally, in Lango itself the contacts with the administration during the years 1904–8 ensured that the initial response to colonial rule was not entirely negative or passive; a handful of clan leaders at least were prepared to play the Government along and to manipulate it in their own interests.

The advances made by Lango leaders from 1904 onwards therefore repay careful attention. The first, and unquestionably the most skilful, was made by Odora Arimo of Kungu. For this reason alone, Odora's story merits a closer look. Furthermore, a unique combination of contemporary documentation and oral reminiscence allows his life to be reconstructed in some detail. In the account that follows, each stage by which he rose to an extremely influential position in 1909 is examined in turn; together they afford us a rare glimpse of one of the earliest encounters between Langi and Europeans.

Odora was born in about 1880. He was brought up near Teboke, on the Okole river, as the son of Angole Acak, who belonged to the Arak

---

[79] Anderson to Wilson, 3.1.08, UNA SMP/4/08; Speke to Leakey, 27.3.08, UNA SMP/1005/08.   [80] Knowles to Wilson, 30.5.08, UNA SMP/1005/08.

me Oyakori clan. Angole Acak was not the leader of his clan section, but in about 1895 he led a sector of the Jo Oyakori away from Teboke to Tarogali, a locality on the Nile, where he had marriage-ties with the leader of the Jo Ogora Atar.[81] Tension soon arose between the Jo Oyakori and their powerful northern neighbours, the Jo Ocukuru of Ibuje. A series of incidents culminated in a major battle: Arum led the Jo Oyakori to complete victory, and many of the Jo Oyakori were killed, including Angole Acak himself. The remainder of the clan section fled south-westwards to Kungu which they reached between 1899 and 1901 (Map 7).[82]

It is a measure of the extremity to which the Jo Oyakori were reduced that they migrated to such an infertile and unhealthy site, abounding in tsetse and mosquitoes. The only merit of Kungu was that, being surrounded on three sides by the Nile, it could more easily be defended against attack from the land. There were no other Langi living in Kungu, and no allies near by on whom the Jo Oyakori could rely.[83] However, by the end of the 1890s there were a few Banyoro living there, and Kungu was also one of the regular access points for Banyoro traders entering southern Lango. These contacts encouraged some of the Jo Oyakori to look across the Nile for friendship and security. Proximity to the kingdom of Bunyoro and its new European overlords was the only asset which the Jo Oyakori possessed in an otherwise very bleak predicament.

By 1903 they had already put their contacts with Bunyoro to use, for when the missionary Albert Lloyd stopped at a village on the left bank of the Nile and invited the Langi of Kungu to visit him, they

[81] Peter Enin, vernacular MS. (1967), translated by J. N. Odurkene as 'The Life of Chief Odora Arimo of Lango', typescript in Department of Religious Studies, Makerere University, pp. 1–4; Reuben Ogwal, 'Bino a Muni kede Mwa i Lango', vernacular MS., summary translation in Makerere University Library, p. 7; Yusto Oweno, vernacular MS., translated as 'The Life of Daudi Odora', type-script in Department of History, Makerere University. Interviews: Isaya Ajoba, Sira Okelo.
The exact identity of Odora's father is disputed. According to one tradition (Enin, Ogwal, Ajoba), Odora was born the son of Ogwok, but Ogwok was killed shortly afterwards and Odora was adopted by his uncle, Angole Acak. According to the other tradition (Okelo, Oweno), Odora was the actual son of Angole Acak. All sources are, however, agreed that Odora was brought up by Angole.
[82] Interviews: Sira Okelo, Okelo Abak, Pilipo Omwa Ayo, Peter Enin, Yakobo Gaci, Andrea Ogwang. The dating of the Kungu migration given here fits the oral record, but is in fact determined by two documentary observations: Evatt to Ternan, 19.1.00, UNA A4/25, and Grant to Wilson, 20.10.04, UNA A12/5.
[83] Their relations with the Jo Ogora Atar had cooled somewhat by this time. Interviews: Sira Okelo, Okelo Abak.

were able to converse in Lunyoro and were aware of Lloyd's un-official status and his movements in Bunyoro.[84] It was while these first contacts with the Banyoro were being made that Odora emerged as leader of his clan section. As Angole Acak's son he naturally had a claim on the leadership, but he did not take over immediately because he was very young; at the time of the battle with the Jo Ocukuru he can have been no more than nineteen or twenty, and he did not even take part. The clan section was led to Kungu by a lineage brother of Angole Acak. In fact, Odora began to take the limelight not because of military prowess, but because of his skill in dealing with the Banyoro. This would not normally have been much of a recommenda-tion, but in the situation of the Jo Oyakori it was an important asset. When Lloyd invited the Kungu people to visit him in 1903, two 'chiefs' came; but as relations with Bunyoro were more assiduously cultivated, Odora came to dominate the elders of the clan.[85]

Odora's first visit to Hoima, the administrative capital of Bunyoro, was late in 1903 or early in 1904, when he went to see Lloyd again.[86] This visit probably convinced him that the best chance of restoring the fortunes of his clan section lay in securing the help of the authori-ties in Bunyoro. Some help was plainly needed, as the Jo Ocukuru were continuing to harass the Jo Oyakori. In December 1903 they attacked Kungu, spearing eight Banyoro, and a year later Odora's men were again attacked.[87] Faced with this threat, Odora resolved on a dramatic gesture of submission to Bunyoro. In October 1904, on another visit to Hoima, he attended the British Collector's *baraza* (meeting); he declared that henceforward he wished to have all disputes among his people settled by the Bunyoro *lukiko* (council); and as an earnest of his good intentions, he there and then handed over to the *lukiko* one of his own men who was accused of killing a Munyoro.[88] With this flourish, Odora thrust himself on the attention

---

[84] Lloyd, op. cit., pp. 123–5. Interview: Peter Enin.

[85] Interview: Sira Okelo. Lloyd, op. cit., pp. 123, 125. Judging by Lloyd's account, only one 'chief' appears to have been included in the group of Langi who visited Hoima a few months later, so this may have marked an important stage in the consolidation of Odora's position within the Jo Oyakori.

[86] Lloyd, op. cit., pp. 124–5.

[87] Prendergast to Wilson, 8.12.03 and 9.12.03, UNA A12/5; Speke, Report on Masindi District for December 1904, UNA A12/5. The attackers in the first case are described as Langi from Itao; this can only mean the Jo Ocukuru. The provenance of the second group is not recorded.

[88] Grant to Wilson, 20.10.04, UNA A12/5; Unyoro District Annual Report for 1904–5, UNA A6/18.

of the British administration as a 'progressive' and an ally of colonial rule.

Odora now made frequent visits to Hoima, bringing gifts to Anderea Duhaga, the *omukama*, and sometimes staying as his guest for a month at a stretch.[89] All the time he was preparing the ground for a government intervention which would confound the Jo Ocukuru and establish himself as a chief outside his own clan. The tradition current in Odora's family is that the Europeans agreed to come and help Odora avenge his father's death.[90] This was certainly not Fowler's intention when he entered Lango in January 1905. His main concern was to remove the Banyoro living on the right bank, but it is likely that during his visits to Hoima Odora had stressed the role played by the Jo Ocukuru in Lango attacks on the Banyoro. To some extent, therefore, Odora probably influenced Fowler's movements. While Fowler was on Lango soil, Odora identified himself with him as closely as possible. When the Sub-Commissioner landed on the right bank at Kungu, Odora presented himself with eighty warriors, and helped in evacuating the Banyoro to the left bank.[91] Fowler was soon joined by seventy officers and men of the K.A.R. (King's African Rifles); accompanied by Odora, he then proceeded northwards to Ibuje. If Odora had hoped for a full-scale attack on the Jo Ocukuru, he was disappointed. Arum had prior warning of their approach; when Fowler arrived, he and his co-leader, Gongi, laid down their spears and submitted. Several Banyoro women and children were recovered, livestock was confiscated, and shots were fired, but there was only one casualty. Odora's demand for the death of Amori Okwelobo, his father's killer, was ignored.[92]

Yet if Odora's desire for revenge was not fully satisfied, the favourable impression he had made on Fowler paid immediate dividends. When Fowler left Lango in February, Odora asked if he might take over the government earthwork in Kungu, which had been occupied briefly in 1899 during operations against the Sudanese mutineers. Fowler not only agreed to this, but sought permission from Entebbe to lend Odora rifles, on the grounds that this would be an economical

[89] Unyoro District Annual Report for 1904–5, UNA A6/18.
[90] Enin, op. cit.; Ogwal, op. cit.
[91] Fowler to Wilson, 8.2.05, and 8.3.05, UNA A12/6.
[92] Fowler to Wilson, 6.2.05, UNA A12/6; Captain Archer, Report of Tour in Bukeddi, 25.3.05, appendix to Uganda Intelligence Report No. 25, PRO CO/879/782; Oweno, op. cit. Interviews: Sira Okelo, Peter Enin, Anderea Ogwang, Yakobo Gaci.

alternative to building a fort on the Nile. Twelve Sniders and 1,200 rounds of ammunition were then made over to Odora, on condition that they were used only for defensive purposes.[93]

The combined effect of Odora's occupation of a former government earthwork and his possession of fire-arms was to give his local standing an immense boost. During the years 1905–7 his following was swollen by migrants from other clan sections in south-west Lango to approximately double its former size.[94] The fire-arms, far from being saved for defence, enabled Odora to switch over to the offensive. He began to raid the hinterland for food supplies and ivory,[95] and also to pay off old scores, particularly in Ibuje.[96] His raids took him as far as Akokoro and even Awir, on the Okole river.[97] British officials in Bunyoro were aware that Odora was interpreting rather liberally the terms on which he had been lent the firearms, but disapproval of his methods was outweighed by the hope that his expanding influence would facilitate the opening of administration.[98] Odora played up to this hope, and during 1905 he conveyed the impression that his influence was being extended by leaps and bounds. By October 1905 Jervoise, the Assistant Collector at Masindi, believed that Odora had a hold over chiefs who lived between three and six days' journey from Kungu.[99] This estimate was wildly exaggerated. Even Awir, the furthest extent of Odora's raids, was no more than three days' journey (forty-five miles) from Kungu, and although Odora was feared over much of the country between the Okole and Lake Kwania, he exercised no regular authority outside Kungu, nor did he command other clan leaders in battle. The evidence strongly suggests that during 1905 Odora went out of his way to deceive Jervoise at Masindi about the territorial reach of his authority; perhaps he was already thinking in terms of an official paramountcy when formal administration began.

[93] Fowler to Wilson, 15.2.05, UNA A12/6; Grant to Wilson, 26.4.05, and attached minutes, UNA A12/6; Anderson, Report on Unyoro District for July and Aug. 1905, UNA A12/7.

[94] Jo Arak me Ococ, Jo Along, and Jo Ogora Atar are among the clan sections mentioned (Interviews: Sira Okelo, Yusto Oweno). For population estimates of Odora's sphere, see Grant to Wilson, 20.10.04, UNA A12/5, and Anderson to Spire, 8.12.07, UNA SMP/34/08.   [95] Interviews: Peter Enin, Matayo Aman.

[96] Interviews: Anderea Adoko, Matayo Ayika.

[97] Anderson, Report on Unyoro District for July and Aug. 1905, UNA A12/7. Enin, op. cit. Interview: Matayo Aman.

[98] This view was first expressed in May 1905: Grant, Unyoro District Annual Report for 1904–5, UNA A6/18. See also Wilson to Commissioner, 14.10.05, A12/7.   [99] Jervoise to Anderson, 2.10.05 and 4.11.05, UNA, A12/7.

Odora did not confine his dealings with the Government to advertising—or exaggerating—his power as a chief. He seized every opportunity to co-operate and to establish his reputation as a 'progressive'. In September 1905, without any prompting from above, he sent back across the Nile a number of Banyoro who had ignored Fowler's ban on settlement east of the river.[100] Soon afterwards he expressed his readiness to begin tax collection, thus prompting the Government to reconsider the opening of a station in Lango.[101] Early in 1907 he obliged Jervoise by providing a large amount of grain to help meet a famine emergency in Bunyoro.[102] From 1906 onwards too, Odora was playing host to Protestant evangelists from Bunyoro—the first Lango to do so.[103] Confronted by so rare a degree of understanding, officials were inclined to overlook the reckless expenditure of ammunition during beer-feasts, and other symptoms of Odora's 'state of barbarity'.[104]

The most spectacular instance of Odora's early skill in exploiting Europeans occurred in November 1907, when Winston Churchill, then Under-Secretary for the Colonies, stopped briefly at Mruli on his way down the Nile from a tour of East Africa. After getting permission to greet the distinguished visitor, Odora and nearly 400 of his warriors crossed the Nile and 'promised their everlasting loyalty to England', in consideration of which they requested help against their hostile neighbours.[105] Churchill rose to the occasion and, without consulting the local officials, promised British protection in the future, and an immediate addition of six Sniders to Odora's arsenal.[106] It is hardly surprising that, as one of Churchill's party later wrote, 'A few words . . . from Mr Churchill put them in the wildest spirits.'[107] No more surprising was the chilly reaction provoked in Entebbe by Churchill's essay in African diplomacy.[108]

[100] Jervoise to Anderson, 2.10.05, UNA A12/7.
[101] Jervoise to Anderson, 4.11.05, UNA A12/7.
[102] Interview: E. B. Haddon (Mr. Haddon was stationed at Masindi under Jervoise for six months in 1907).
[103] Jervoise to Leakey, 4.2.06, UNA A12/7; R. M. Fisher, 'Other Sheep', *Church Missionary Gleaner*, 35 (Jan. 1908), p. 3.
[104] Leakey to Commissioner, 15.2.06, UNA A12/7.
[105] Anderson, Report on Masindi District for November 1907, UNA SMP/317/07.
[106] Anderson to Spire, 8.12.07, UNA SMP/34/08; Churchill to Bell, 8.12.07, UNA SMP Conf./47/10.
[107] F. A. Dickinson, *Lake Victoria to Khartoum with Rifle and Camera* (London, 1910), pp. 80–1. See also W. S. Churchill, *My African Journey* (London, 1908), pp. 146–7.   [108] CS to Anderson, 3.1.08, UNA SMP/34/08.

Odora's attempts to manipulate European officialdom culminated in Sub-Commissioner Knowles's tour of western Lango in April 1908. This tour, during which firm administrative plans were at last drawn up, came not a moment too soon. Odora had been running into difficulties: on the one hand, officials were beginning to be sceptical of his claims to enlightenment,[109] and even to regret the encouragement given to him in the past;[110] on the other hand, the Government's delay in implementing its long-advertised intention to step in was undermining Odora's local prestige.[111] The Sub-Commissioner's tour dispelled most of the doubts about Odora and restored his prestige. Knowles was by no means uncritical: he felt that Odora was exploiting the administration in order to discomfit his enemies, and he established that Odora had no influence north of the Aroca river. But he came away from Lango convinced that Odora controlled the country to the south as far as Lake Kwania and that his position there should be officially recognized.[112] The crucial factor would appear to have been Knowles's decision to proceed northwards, starting at Kungu and taking Odora with him. This choice of itinerary was a timely reminder of Odora's special relationship with the Government. The last European whom Odora had accompanied outside Kungu had been Fowler in 1905; Odora's enemies—notably the Jo Ocukuru—doubtless feared that they might be penalized as before, if they did not allow Odora to stage-manage the tour. This is the most likely explanation for Odora's *tour de force*, a large *baraza* held at Itao, close by the settlements of the Jo Ocukuru. The assembled leaders agreed with Knowles that a paramount chief over the country between Lake Kwania and the Aroca was required, and they 'elected Dora as the man they should chose'.[113] At the same time a site for the District headquarters was selected near Ibuje hill. Knowles did not enlarge on the reasons for his choice, but Odora may well have swayed the decision. Clearly Kungu itself was quite unsuitable; Ibuje, on the other hand, was reasonably central to the new District, while still within Odora's allotted sphere. Ten months later Knowles returned to introduce the first Assistant District Commissioner of

---

[109] Leakey, Report on Bachope and Bakeddi incidents, 18.1.08, UNA SMP/1528/07.
[110] Wilson to Bell, 28.2.08, UNA SMP/1528/07.
[111] Speke to Leakey, 27.3.08, UNA SMP/1005/08.
[112] Knowles to Wilson, 30.5.08, and attached Diary of Tour, UNA SMP/1005/08.
[113] Ibid.

Palango.[114] Odora moved his own headquarters to Ibuje,[115] where he retained his special relationship with the Government, and where he was well placed to press his claims to even greater authority. Compared with his near-desperate straits only six years before, Odora's position as a government chief was a giddy eminence indeed.

The lessons to be drawn from Odora's experience were not lost on other clan leaders in western Lango, though none of them equalled his understanding of European attitudes and requirements. Arum, the leader of the Jo Ocukuru, against whom Odora had been so incensed, learnt quickly from his confrontation with Fowler in 1905. His immediate reaction was to play Odora's game, and to prejudice Fowler against Odongo Aja, just as Odora had prejudiced Fowler against Arum.[116] Over the longer term, Arum appears to have realized that Odora's reputation with the Government was firmly established, and that nothing was to be gained from opposition. It may be that, as Jervoise believed, Arum hoped that friendliness towards the Government would be repaid with the loan of rifles, as in Odora's case.[117] At any rate, he allowed the impression to grow in government circles that Odora had a hold over him: whereas he was described in 1906 as one of the three important Lango chiefs along the Nile, Knowles regarded him two years later as a mere 'headman' under Odora.[118] And at the crucial *baraza* at Itao in 1908, Arum kept in the background and made no objection to Odora's 'election' as chief.[119] During the years 1905–8 the Jo Ocukuru were certainly troubled by Odora's raids, but there is no evidence that Arum was in any sense subject to Odora. His submissive behaviour was determined by political judgement rather than necessity. During Odora's residence at Ibuje from 1909 to 1911, Arum continued to co-operate, and in so doing he strengthened his position *vis-à-vis* his co-leader of the Jo Ocukuru, Gongi, who resisted the administration.[120] Arum's policy paid off in 1911 when, with Odora's move to a new headquarters,

[114] Paske Smith to Grant, 11.3.09, UNA SMP/519/09.
[115] Interviews: Zakalia Isengeze, Saida Apio Alit, Yakobo Adoko.
Odora's village was described in 1910 as lying a little to the north of Palango ation. Melland and Cholmeley, *Through the Heart of Africa*, p. 225.
[116] Fowler to Wilson, 27.2.05, UNA A12/6.
[117] Jervoise, Report on Masindi District for 1905–6, UNA SMP/314/06.
[118] Ibid.; Knowles to Wilson, 30.5.08, UNA SMP/1005/08.
[119] Ibid.
[120] In November 1909, Gongi attacked a Muganda agent. Fox, Report on Lango District for November 1909, UNA SMP/872/09.

Arum became the sole chief in Ibuje and was issued with five government rifles.[121] So far as officials could see, the same process of reconciliation was taking place in Aber, if more haltingly. In view of the clashes with the Baganda in 1895–6 and with Delmé-Radcliffe in 1901, the leaders of the Jo Arak in Aber were more antagonistic to the Government than most.[122] Odongo Aja refused to have any dealings with Fowler in 1905.[123] However by April 1906 his attitude had softened; he now declared his readiness to pay hut-tax, and he made two visits to officials in Bunyoro before his death later in the year.[124] This accommodating stance was continued by his successor Otwal, who visited Masindi in December.[125] It is unlikely that the change of attitude among the Jo Arak betokened a taste for government rule. Almost certainly Odongo Aja regarded the opening of a station near Patiko early in 1906 as evidence that the Government was set on bringing the right bank of the Nile under direct control, and he decided that it would pay him to be less hostile. This interpretation is suggested by the fact that, when Patiko station was abandoned early in 1907, no more overtures were received from Otwal. Indeed, there were signs that the old pattern of Lango raids on the administered area was being resumed, for in December 1907 a war-band landed at Foweira and abducted a chief in broad daylight.[126]

The impression in Aber that the Government was in retreat was finally removed by Knowles's tour in April 1908. From Otwal's point of view, the auguries for his meeting with Knowles were hardly propitious; for besides the recent deterioration in his relations with the Government, Knowles had just visited the Adok clan section of Kidilande, who had given him a very one-sided version of their feud with the Jo Arak. Nevertheless, Otwal dispelled all doubts. He was able to set the record straight on the feud with the Jo Adok, and he said that he would like a trading depot to be set up at Foweira. Most remarkable of all, he convinced Knowles that his territory extended fifty miles east of Foweira, as far as the upper reaches of the Okole

[121] List of Baganda Agents and their posts in Lango District, September 1911, UNA SMP/519/09.
[122] Speke, Report of Tour in Chopi district in Nov. 1904, UNA A12/5.
[123] Fowler to Wilson, 27.2.05, UNA A12/6.
[124] These conciliatory moves are recorded in a sequence of reports on Masindi District by Jervoise: Report for 1905–6, UNA SMP/314/06; Report for July 1906, UNA SMP/515/part 1; Report for Oct. 1906, UNA SMP/515/part 2.
[125] Jervoise, Report on Masindi District for Dec. 1906, UNA SMP/515/part 2.
[126] Anderson to Wilson, 3.1.08, UNA SMP/4/08.

river (a wild exaggeration), and he had himself designated 'responsible chief' of the area between the Aroca river and the Acholi border.[127] Knowles soon realized that to give Otwal authority over the Jo Adok of Kidilande was impractical, and so the Okole was defined as Otwal's southern border.[128] All the same, the administrative divisions made in 1908 were a striking indication of the confidence placed in Otwal—a confidence which Otwal himself had done nothing substantial to justify.

These three case-histories—Odora, Arum, and Otwal—prompt the question of why clan leaders in western Lango showed such sureness of touch in manipulating the colonial authorities—a skill which is not often conceded by historians in the case of small-scale, fragmented societies.[129] The question is all the more insistent in view of the continued manipulation of British officials by Lango leaders during the inter-war years;[130] the methods were different, but they revealed the same insight into the colonial power-structure as Odora's actions had done. A total explanation is doubtless impossible, but part of the answer surely lies in the historical relationship between western Lango and the kingdom of Bunyoro. For at least fifty years before the arrival of the British, the Langi had enjoyed close military and commercial relations with Bunyoro. This experience had made them familiar with a political system radically different from their own— hierarchical, deferential, and relatively centralized. It is a reasonable surmise that the success of the Langi in gaining the benefits of contact with Bunyoro at so little cost to themselves enabled them to approach the British with some confidence that they could profit from the encounter. This confidence must have been strengthened by the fact that the European presence originally impinged upon western Lango as an aspect of relations with Bunyoro: Odora's first recourse was to the *omukama*, from whom it was a short step to the resident British official. The Bunyoro dimension also helps to explain the different response of the south-eastern Langi to the colonial power. The most important factor was clearly the difference between the representatives of Protectorate authority in the two areas—between Europeans in the west and Baganda or Banyara in the south-east. Yet there was also a

[127] Knowles to Wilson, 30.5.08, and Wilson to Knowles, 22.6.08, UNA SMP/ 1005/08.   [128] Knowles to Wilson, 6.10.08, UNA SMP/1520/08.

[129] It is denied, for example, in T. O. Ranger, 'African reactions to the imposition of colonial rule in East and Central Africa', in *Colonialism in Africa*, vol. I, ed. L. H. Gann and P. Duignan (Cambridge, 1969), p. 304.

[130] See below, Chapters 7 and 8.

significant contrast as regards pre-colonial relations with Bunyoro. Although all parts of Lango had participated in trade and military campaigns, south-eastern Lango had experienced nothing like the same intimacy of contact as the west. In the eyes of the easterners, the British arrived as associates not of the friendly Banyoro, but of the hated Baganda, with whom no accommodation had proved possible.

The new District of Palango[131] was inaugurated in March 1909. A site called Palango had already been selected as District headquarters near Ibuje hill. It was staffed by forty African police and by two Assistant District Commissioners, the senior of whom, Paske Smith, was responsible to the District Commissioner in Hoima.[132] The Government confined itself for the time being to the country within twenty miles of the Nile.[133] As a result of friendly contacts with Odora and others, officials faced their task with some confidence. Certainly the ground had been better prepared than in Miro District. Those clan leaders who had obstructed Knowles's tour had by February 1909 submitted, and a handful of leaders ten to fifteen miles inland had also indicated their support.[134] Knowles had already made a straightforward division of the country into three sections according to the main rivers, and he had appointed chiefs over two of them: Odora over the country between Lake Kwania and the Aroca, and Otwal for the stretch between the Ayago and the Okole.[135] During the inaugural tour, Okelo Adak of the Jo Adok was appointed to rule the intervening stretch between the Aroca and the Okole.[136] As far as Knowles could see, it was only a matter of time before a Paramount Chief of Palango was appointed.[137]

This initial confidence in the capacity of Lango chiefs had to be qualified almost immediately. In the first place, it soon became clear that territorially the claims made by Odora and Okelo Adak were much exaggerated. More important was the realization that, even

---

[131] The District was officially known as 'Lango', but to avoid confusion with the Lango District of 1911 onwards (which included both 'Lango' and 'Miro'), I refer to it as 'Palango', which was the name of the headquarters.

[132] Paske Smith to Grant, 11.3.09, UNA SMP/519/09.

[133] Tomkins to Knowles, 22.9.08, UNA SMP/1520/08.

[134] The more distant Leaders were from Cegere, Apac, and Loro. Knowles to Wilson, 30.5.08, UNA SMP/1005/08; Knowles to Wilson, 8.7.08 and 22.7.08, UNA SMP/1003/08; Paske Smith, Report on Masindi District for Jan. 1909, UNA SMP/280/09.   [135] Knowles to Wilson, 30.5.08, UNA SMP/1005/08.

[136] Knowles to CS, 16.3.09, UNA SMP/1520/08.

[137] Knowles to Wilson, 30.5.08, UNA SMP/1005/08.

within his acknowledged sphere, the kind of authority exercised by a clan leader was very different from that of European stereotypes. The fact that government orders were conveyed through recognized leaders did not make the ordinary clansman any more inclined to obey. 'The chiefs themselves', observed Paske Smith, 'are afraid to enforce their authority, stating that if they attempted to do so, they would be driven out of their villages or speared.'[138] During the first months of administration, evidence of the incapacity of the appointed chiefs accumulated. Tax evaders from Bunyoro continued to be offered refuge in Lango;[139] there were raids against the Jopalwo;[140] and—most serious of all—clan leaders near the Nile continued to attack their enemies to the east, in the knowledge that the injured parties would not dare to travel through their territory in order to complain to a District Officer.[141] Although the three appointed chiefs had originally agreed to clear their respective portions of the proposed road down the Nile from Kungu to Kamdini,[142] in practice the enlistment of forced labour was a task beyond them. The truth was that, as in the south-east, the basic administrative tasks of maintaining order and mobilizing labour resources were quite unacceptable to the Langi.

Officials were in little doubt as to how this problem should be tackled in the short term. The obvious example was the Eastern Province, where Baganda agents had been used in similar circumstances, and apparently with striking results. Even at the inauguration of Palango District, it had not been supposed that the appointed chiefs would be able to manage without on-the-spot assistance, and Knowles secured the chiefs' approval for a proposal to bring in Baganda agents.[143] But rapid disillusionment with the appointed chiefs caused Paske Smith to lay much greater stress on the need for agents.[144] He was supported in blunt terms by Grant, the responsible official in Hoima, who had previously served in the heart of the agent country at Mbale; in a letter to the Chief Secretary he wrote:[145] 'The Lango . . . are raw savages. The only system on which these people can be dealt with is through the use of intelligent Agents, as has been

[138] Paske Smith to Grant, 17.5.09, UNA SMP/519/09.
[139] Henry, Report on Masindi District for April 1909, UNA SMP/280/09.
[140] Henry, Report on Masindi District for 1909–10, UNA SMP/671.
[141] Paske Smith to Grant, 5.10.09, UNA SMP/872/09.
[142] Knowles to CS, 16.3.09, UNA SMP/1520/08.
[143] Knowles to CS, 16.3.09, UNA SMP/1520/08.
[144] Paske Smith to Grant, 20.6.09 and 8.7.09, UNA SMP/872/09.
[145] Grant to CS, 26.5.09, UNA SMP/519/09.

done in Bukeddi, and until these Agents are established throughout the District, I fear progress will be slow'. And so in July and August 1909 the first two agents were posted to Akaka in Aber, and to Okelo Adak's village in Kidilande, with a dozen or so followers each.[146] In the next nine months four more agents were posted—to Cegere, Apac, Akokoro, and Ocini (Map 8).

Paske Smith's expectations about the agents' prospects were as illusory as Knowles's confidence in the appointed chiefs. In forwarding his request for agents in March 1909, he observed that 'a tactful Muganda' from Bukedi 'should find no difficulty in managing the people here without any display of force';[147] he was under the impression that the Baganda would be able to start with a clean slate, 'as the Lango have never had any dealings with the Waganda before'.[148] It was true that the western Langi had been spared harassment by Kakungulu and Kazana, but many of them had had unpleasant experiences of the Baganda during the years 1894–6. At Apac the installation of an agent in January 1910 provoked the most serious hostility yet encountered. A large number of villages on both sides of the Aroca, assisted by one from the Okole, carried on what Paske Smith described as 'guerrilla warfare' against the official party. Within a month the agent had deserted his post, and further resistance was offered when a new agent was installed in June.[149] In Aber—the scene of the most serious clash between Baganda and Langi in the mid-90s—the posting of an agent to Akaka destroyed the toleration with which the Jo Arak had hitherto viewed the Government. Until the agent arrived, Otwal's attitude continued to be friendly. But in February 1910 three of the agent's followers were killed in Kamdini. Otwal took to the bush with Owiny Akulo, and while they were still at large, another thirteen Baganda were killed on their way through Ocini. Order was restored in Aber only after vigorous police action and the removal of both Otwal and Owiny Akulo from the District.[150]

The scale of the administration's difficulties greatly increased with the removal early in 1910 of the Governor's twenty-mile limit. Between

[146] Paske Smith to Grant, 2.8.09 and 5.10.09, UNA SMP/872/09.

[147] Paske Smith to Grant, 11.3.09, UNA SMP/519/09.

[148] Paske Smith to Grant, 17.5.09, UNA SMP/519/09.

[149] Fox to Paske Smith, 21.2.10, and Paske Smith to Grant, 12.3.10, UNA SMP/1859/09; Paske Smith, Reports on Lango District for January and February 1910, UNA SMP/193; Tufnell to Grant, 6.7.10, UNA SMP/1876/09.

[150] Paske Smith to Grant, 14.3.10, UNA SMP/201; Fox to Tufnell, 16.6.10, UNA SMP/1860/09. Interviews: Leoben Okodi, Kosia Ato, Erisa Olugo, Edwardi Olir, Yakobo Olugo.

June and October 1910 Captain Tufnell established eight more posts, which extended the Government's range to between twenty-five and forty miles' distance from the Nile.[151] So rapid an expansion was not achieved without violence to the niceties of approved conduct: Tufnell's practice of seizing livestock as a means of effecting quick contact with the owners earned him a reprimand from Entebbe.[152] More important, however, was the added scope which this expansion gave to the Baganda. They were placed in charge of all the new posts, so that the number of agents was more than doubled and the amount of European supervision proportionately reduced. Lango attacks on the Baganda continued, on a wider scale than before.[153] Now, for the first time, officials began to see these clashes in terms of provocation by the Baganda, as well as obstinate resistance by the Langi.[154]

These misgivings were brought to a head in February 1911 by J. O. Haldane, who had just taken charge of Palango District. One tour of the hinterland was enough to convince him that something was seriously wrong. His report[155] prompted the newly arrived Governor, Frederick Jackson, to review the history of administration in Palango. He was appalled by the compromising evidence which he found in earlier reports,[156] and he promptly decided that the agent system should be dismantled in Palango immediately, and throughout the Eastern Province in the near future.[157] The immediate result of Jackson's decision was a spate of correspondence between the responsible officials, in which the system was scrutinized and assessed.[158]

Haldane's outburst was grounded on one solid objection—that the Baganda were not adequately paid. With the exception of the head agent, none of the agents in Palango received more than ten rupees (just over thirteen shillings) per month. Their followers were in an even worse position; despite official recognition that the followers—a

[151] Tufnell to Grant, 28.10.10, and attached map of Lango District, UNA SMP/519/09.
[152] Tomkins to CS, 10.10.10, and Grant to Tufnell, 14.10.10, UNA SMP/1859/09.
[153] Place to Grant, 13.12.10, UNA SMP/193.
[154] Tufnell to Grant, 31.10.10, UNA SMP/519/09; Place to Grant, 13.12.10, UNA SMP/193.
[155] Haldane to Knowles, 6.2.11 (forwarded by Knowles to Entebbe), UNA SMP/519/09.
[156] Jackson's outraged comments appear on several earlier reports from Lango in the SMP/519/09 file.
[157] CS to Knowles, 3.5.11, UNA SMP/519/09; Jackson to Secretary of State, 14.7.11, PRO CO/536/41.
[158] For this debate, see Twaddle, op. cit., pp. 255–74.

Map 8. The Districts of Palango and Miro, 1911 showing all Agents' Posts in Lango Country

dozen or so for each agent—were essential to the system, they received no pay whatsoever. In practice, Haldane concluded, the system was based

upon the *openly unspoken and officially gainsaid* understanding that we concede them the right to live by underhand methods of plunder so long as they employ it discreetly and don't *oblige* us to scrutinize their conduct. It might be suggested that we deliberately countenance peculation on their part as an indirect and economical way of paying them.[159]

This criticism was widely subscribed to by officials in Eastern Province, if in less blunt language,[160] and there is no doubt that Haldane's

[159] Haldane to Knowles, 6.2.11, UNA SMP/519/09.
[160] Jervoise to Spire, 5.6.11, UNA EPMP/Z/44; Watson to CS, 3.11.11, UNA SMP/519/09. See also, Johnstone, 'Past Times in Uganda', p. 9. Johnstone was a K.A.R. officer posted to Lango in 1911; his criticisms of the agent system, written ten years later, are therefore those of an outsider.

attack was justified. In both Palango and Miro, the Baganda agents maintained themselves by compelling the local population to bring them food, and by dispatching raiding-parties to steal anything else they wanted in the way of livestock, grain, or beer.[161] It was a demand for provisions which caused the killing of six Baganda near Bar in May 1911.[162] And the trouble at Aber in 1910 was sparked off in a similar way, as Owiny Akulo's son recounts:

Otwal was drinking beer with some guests—*matoke* beer which some Jopalwo had brought him. Then the Baganda came along and found Otwal drinking beer with his guests, and they seized the beer. Instead of sitting down like the other guests, they just took away what they wanted. Then Otwal's companions said, 'These are not guests, *rwot*; should we fight them?'

Rather than behave quietly until the Langi started to fight, the Baganda shot one man called Ngole Adul, and he fell to the ground. 'He's dead!—He's dead!', the people cried. Ah! Then the young men set upon the Baganda! Some of them, seeing that the Baganda were going towards the Toci river, killed them by the water there. The three Baganda who'd been killed were thrown into the Toci, and the Toci carried their bodies into the Nile.[163]

The predatory attitude of the Baganda compromised their whole role as petty officials. The mere counting of heads could be construed by the Langi as a hostile act.[164] The Baganda had great difficulty in rounding up labour for public works; time and again, they could only persuade people to erect a stockade, clear a road, or prepare a cotton plot by force of arms, which invited counter-action. Of those clashes between Baganda and Langi which were fully reported at the time, the majority were caused by demands for free labour.[165] Taking both Districts up to the middle of 1911, the returns called for by Jackson revealed that the Baganda had expended ammunition against the Langi no less than 118 times; forty-three Baganda and thirteen of

[161] See especially, Johnstone, op. cit., p. 10.

[162] Interviews: Luka Abura, Tomasi Ojuka, Isaya Ogwangguji. The official report on the incident attributed the clash to a demand for forced labour. Jervoise to Spire, 17.5.11, UNA SMP/1960.

[163] Interview: Leoben Okodi. The official report, at second-hand, said that the Baganda were attacked when they arrived with a message for Otwal. Paske Smith to Grant, 14.3.10, UNA SMP/201.

[164] Near Loro it precipitated the killing of two Baganda. Haldane, Report on Lango District for March 1911, and Knowles to Haldane, 19.5.11, UNA SMP/193. Interview: Yosia Omara.

[165] In Palango and Miro Districts, eleven incidents of this nature are recorded for the years 1910–12. The reports are in UNA, SMP/2404, SMP/1938, SMP/2020.

Kazana's men had been killed, while the number of Langi killed almost certainly exceeded the sixty-three recorded cases.[166]

The unrealistic rate of pay was the aspect which received most attention at the time, because it was a readily identifiable defect with a straightforward solution. But there were two other considerations which militated against good government by the Baganda. The first was the racial antagonism of the Baganda towards the Langi. The Baganda despised all those of their neighbours who lacked centralized political institutions, and they applied the term 'Bakedi' (naked people) to them without discrimination. This sense of racial superiority seems to have been particularly strong towards Lwo-speakers, whose language the Baganda found great difficulty in learning.[167]

The second defect lay in the circumstances in which the Baganda were recruited for service in Lango. In the earliest areas of the Protectorate to be farmed out to the Baganda, the lead was taken by chiefs of established eminence in the Ganda political system, who took with them their personal clients in the expectation of establishing permanent fiefs; it was therefore in their interests to protect their new subjects against the worst abuses. Broadly speaking, this was the pattern in the annexed areas of Bunyoro during the 1890s, and in Bukedi between 1899 and 1906. But in Lango there were significant differences. In neither Palango nor Miro was it envisaged that the Baganda would remain indefinitely. Nor did the Government entrust overall responsibility to an important Ganda chief; very few of the agents had any pretension to chiefly title at all.[168] In Miro District there was probably some sort of discipline among the Baganda, since most of them appear to have come as followers of Isaka Nziga, who had himself been a senior lieutenant of Kakungulu's. In Palango even this element of control was lacking: agents and followers were simply hired piecemeal as the need arose, being recruited mostly from the police, from the labour force on the Busoga Railway, and from the ranks of other government employees.[169] In general, the Baganda came to Lango not with an eye to prestige or long-term prospects, but

[166] Returns of all encounters between Langi/Kumam and Baganda/Banyara were sent in from Palango and Miro in July 1911. See UNA SMP/2020, 1938. The number of Kazana's men killed actually exceeded thirteen.

[167] For observations to this effect, see: Kitching to Baylis, 31.12.05, CMS Archives, G3/A7/0/1906(a); Pleydell to CMS headquarters, 5.11.07, in *Extracts from the Annual Letters of the Missionaries for the Year 1907* (London, 1908), p. 239.

[168] For an acute observation on this point, see Melland and Cholmeley, op. cit., p. 220.   [169] I owe this point to Dr. Michael Twaddle.

in order to 'get rich quick'. They were no more than petty officials, and frequent transfers from one post to another gave them ample opportunity to line their own pockets.[170]

Jackson's opposition to the agents led him to question the wisdom of installing them in the first place. He felt that virtually no effort had been made to test the capacity of the indigenous 'chiefs', particularly in Palango.[171] This was less than fair to the officials involved. High hopes had originally been placed in the three appointed chiefs along the Nile. That these hopes had proved illusory was only partly due to the bad choice of men; it was mainly due to misapprehensions about the authority enjoyed by clan leaders in general. In Lango as a whole, the only alternative to the use of alien native agents was direct administration by European officials. A solution of this kind could conceivably have been adopted if the Government had been prepared to expand very gradually from a small nucleus, so that officials could directly train and supervise Lango 'chiefs'. But there were strong arguments against such a course, the main one being that the very slowness of the government advance would undermine the progress of already-administered areas: the longer some portions remained un-administered, the more did people from the administered area use them as places of refuge from government demands. There was much to be said for the view that, once a beginning had been made in the administration of an untouched tribe, the whole tribe should be sub-dued as soon as possible. In the case of Lango, where no political boundaries existed, and where ties of clanship or marriage linked each community to at least one of its neighbours, the problem was parti-cularly acute. At every stage of administrative expansion, officials stressed the difficulty of maintaining order in the current marches of the district, when only a few miles away there were Lango settlements outside the pale of government.[172] If any further argument in favour of quick expansion was required, it was that the bloodshed caused by inadequately supervised Baganda was a fraction of the bloodshed which would have occurred had the Langi been left to continue their inter-clan fighting.[173] Given the nature of the Lango political system

[170] For example, Semu Kagwa served at Kidilande, Inomo, Loro, and Ayer between 1909 and 1913.

[171] Jackson to Secretary of State, 14.7.11, PRO CO/536/41.

[172] Ormsby to Boyle, 23.10.08, UNA EPMP/Z/885/08; Jervoise to Spire, 28.2.10, and Jervoise to PCEP, 3.10.12, UNA SMP/2404; Scott to PCEP, 12.5.13, UNA SMP/2404.

[173] Tufnell to Grant, 28.10.10, UNA SMP/519/09.

and the resources of the Protectorate at the time, the use of alien agents was thus almost unavoidable.

Both Haldane and his Provincial Commissioner, Knowles, were alarmed by Jackson's intention to scrap the agent system completely. Haldane had not advocated the withdrawal of the Baganda agents, merely that their terms of service be improved. Knowles pointed out that to withdraw the agents now would be construed by the Langi as a concession to local pressure—and violent pressure at that.[174] An even stronger reaction came from officials in the Eastern Province, with Jervoise, the District Commissioner at Bululu, well to the fore.[175] The unanimous opposition of local officials caused Jackson to modify his stand. He allowed the employment of agents to continue, on the understanding that they would not be retained a moment longer than necessary, and that a start was made on reducing their number at once. Jackson expected that, with the posting of an additional Assistant District Commissioner to each of the affected Districts, substantial reductions would be made. In order to effect a smooth transition, he also made available several companies of K.A.R. for patrol work. Furthermore the agents' followers were in future to be paid at the rate of three rupees per month.[176] These arrangements were further modified under pressure from the local officials, and nowhere more than in Lango where Jervoise took command of the united Districts of Miro and Palango in August 1911. Despite the arrival of a Company of K.A.R. in September, and of another junior official at the end of 1911, no agents were actually withdrawn until March 1913, when the number was reduced by seven to a total of sixteen agents.[177] When the expansion of the District was resumed in 1915 and the Moroto valley opened up, Baganda agents were again used to lay the administrative foundations. The last agent was not withdrawn from Moroto County until 1927.[178]

Despite the successful delaying tactics of the officials on the spot, the upheaval of 1911 nevertheless marked a significant stage in the

[174] Knowles to CS, 6.5.11, UNA SMP/519/09; Haldane to Knowles, 16.5.11, UNA SMP/545.

[175] Jervoise to Spire, 5.6.11, UNA EPMP/Z/44, and 24.7.11, UNA EPMP/Z/1288/09.

[176] Spire to District Commissioners, Eastern Province, 22.8.11, and Memorandum by the Governor, 9.12.11, UNA SMP/519/09.

[177] Spire to CS, 30.9.12, and Jervoise, List of Agents recommended for gratuities, 4.3.13, UNA SMP/519/09; Scott to Spire, 2.8.13, LDA (I am grateful to Dr. Andrew Roberts for showing me his notes on this letter, since lost).

[178] Black, Report on Lango District for 1927, UNA EPMP/N/40/27.

evolution of the colonial political system in Lango. In the first place, the increased European establishment allowed more touring, and while on tour officials were much more vigilant in their scrutiny of the agents' conduct; both reprimands and dismissals became more frequent. Combined with the payment of followers, this more effective supervision was soon justified by a marked decline in the incidence of clashes between Langi and Baganda. From 1911 to the end of 1913 there were no more than about twenty such clashes,[179] and thereafter the only serious incident was the murder of eleven Baganda at Adwari in 1919.[180]

In the second place, the role of the agent was more narrowly defined than before. He was now seen as the District Commissioner's representative, whose job was to teach and advise the local chief. Except in extreme emergency the agent was not empowered to exercise any independent executive or judicial authority; he was not allowed, for example, to try cases on his own unless he was first accepted as arbitrator by both parties to the dispute, and he could only dispatch his followers to arrest a man after consulting the chief and his headmen.[181] Under these conditions, the appointment and supervision of the chiefs became a much more pressing official preoccupation. From 1913 onwards this problem became more acute as agents were withdrawn from the District. In the longest-administered parts of the District the withdrawal was more rapid than the rate of over-all reduction would suggest, since only by releasing agents from those parts could further advances be made in the north-east of Lango. In short, the crisis of 1911 brought the authorities in Lango face to face with the problem of creating an administrative structure staffed by natives of the District. This task had up till then been all but ignored in the south-east, and had received scant attention in the west since the abortive experiment of 1909.

---

[179] This figure is abstracted from reports in UNA SMP/2404. It is impossible to be more precise because in some cases it is not clear whether the ammunition was discharged by agents or by unsupervised Lango chiefs.

[180] J. Tosh, 'Small-scale Resistance in Uganda: the Lango "Rising" at Adwari in 1919', *Azania*, 9 (1974), pp. 51–64.

[181] No detailed definition of the agents' role has survived in official records, but the official attitude emerges clearly from the following reports and entries in Tour Books: Jervoise to Spire, 30.4.12, LDA (I owe this reference to Dr. Andrew Roberts); Scott, Report on Lango District for 1913–14, UNA EPMP/Z/228/13; extracts from letter from Driberg to PCEP, 20.6.18, enclosed in Eden to CS, 4.10.18, UNA SMP/4349; entry for 21.6.18 at Kwera, Dokolo TB (1913–26, part 1); entry for 19.9.23 at Abako, Dokolo TB (1913–26, part 2).

In the meantime, the prospects for a stable administrative system based on local personnel had been prejudiced in several ways. The effect of the many government-inspired incursions into Lango since 1894 had been to arouse a deep resentment of outsiders, without affording evidence of the benefits which might accrue to the Langi from colonial rule. The reputation of the British had been compromised by their association with inadequately supervised auxiliaries, while the tendency for government forces to withdraw quickly after each penetration did nothing to disillusion the Langi about their capacity to oppose the colonial power in the longer term. When the British began the formal administration of Lango country, they were therefore confronted by continuing resistance, and this was all the greater because of the employment of Baganda and Banyara subordinates. That this resistance declined abruptly after 1911 was, for officials of the day, an immensely reassuring and somewhat surprising development. The most important reasons for this improvement were the reform of the agent system and the realization by the Langi that the government was now securely established in their country. However, the tranquillity after 1911 was only relative. Distrust of the Europeans and rejection of their policies were still very strong. The events of the previous twenty years were hardly conducive to a smooth assumption of government authority by locally recruited personnel.

Within this over-all picture, the period of 'pacification' had seen significant variations between one part of Lango and another. Some parts had had almost no contact with the Government as yet—notably the Moroto valley in the north-east. Within the pacified area, there had been a substantial divergence between east and west. For while in the west the predatory activities of the Baganda had been tempered by the concern of European officials on the spot for long-term administrative prospects, the Langi of the south-east had seen only the most unpleasant face of the government in their country; their response was accordingly much less flexible. By 1911 hardly a single clan leader in Miro District had made gestures of accommodation towards the Government, whereas in the west Europeans were already being manipulated by local interests—in Odora's case with striking results. As officials turned to the task of recruiting and training chiefs to administer Lango in place of the Baganda, they faced difficulties everywhere, but nowhere more so than in the south-east.

CHAPTER 6

The Formation of a Chiefly Hierarchy

In their first attempts in about 1912 to recruit local administrative personnel, officials in Lango District had little doubt where their field of choice lay. In the absence of states and chiefdoms, the vital territorial category was quite clearly the village, with its convenient concentration of up to seventy households. It followed that the key to native administration was to be found in the political leadership of the village. Europeans at that time had somewhat confused notions about this leadership; they were slow to recognize that they were dealing with *clan* leaders.[1] But this did not prevent them from identifying the actual men in authority with considerable accuracy. Once identified, the clan leaders could be accorded recognition as village headmen, responsible to the government. However, this simple expedient was in itself no answer to the staffing requirements of an administrative structure: it merely defined the field of choice. For the problem was not one of identification so much as selection. If the two or three British officials stationed in Lango had needed to relay government instructions to all village headmen directly, their task would have been hopeless. From an administrative point of view, the choice of intermediaries was therefore a vital priority. As a result, almost overnight, a new range of executive positions was opened up to clan leaders, giving them access to unprecedented powers and resources. This chapter shows how the new administrative positions were defined, both territorially and qualitatively, and how the first generation of functionaries was chosen.

What officials aimed at in Lango was the division of the District into territorial 'chiefdoms', to which they could appoint men who combined local political standing with some measure of tolerance towards the colonial power. The total number of chiefdoms had to be small enough to enable District Officers on tour to inspect all of them two or three times a year; at the same time, the size of the chiefdom was limited by the need for the chief to maintain contact with all parts of his allotted territory. In September 1912 thirty-three Langi were

[1] Driberg's analysis is a case in point: Driberg, *The Lango*, pp. 204–6.

officially gazetted as chiefs.[2] In 1920, by which time the colonial administrative system was established over the whole of Lango, there were thirty-seven Lango chiefdoms,[3] varying in size between about 2,000 and 6,000 people. Within his territory the appointed chief wielded full executive and judicial powers, and he was removable only by the Provincial Commissioner acting on the advice of the District Commissioner.

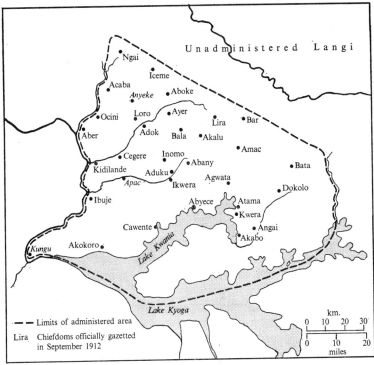

Map 9.   Lango District, 1912, showing sub-counties administered by Lango chiefs

This type of administrative system was not, of course, peculiar to Lango, nor was it limited to Uganda. Throughout British tropical Africa, native administration between the wars was organized along

[2] *Uganda Protectorate Gazette* (hereafter *Gazette*), 30 Sept. 1912.
[3] Thirty-three of these were in Lango District, two were in Gulu District, and two in Teso. Lango District also included seven Kumam and four Bantu chiefdoms. *Gazette*, 31 July 1920.

these lines; in both centralized and acephalous societies, appointed chiefs with executive and judicial authority were the norm. On several significant points of detail, however, the system in Uganda was distinctive. This was because in Buganda, at the centre of the Protectorate, the British found an indigenous chiefly hierarchy which, with some adjustments, was well suited to colonial needs, and which they then extended throughout Uganda. The details of administrative organization in Lango were determined in the first instance by this 'Ganda model'.

On the eve of the colonial period, the Kabaka of Buganda presided over not one category of chief, but three relatively distinct categories, and the high concentration of power in the Kabaka's person was partly due to the dependence of all three on him, and to the tension between them.[4] But during the long minority of Kabaka Daudi Chwa beginning in 1897, the British simplified the government of Buganda and limited the role of the Kabaka. They selected one of the three categories, that of the *bakungu* chiefs, and concentrated all the new functions of government in its hands. The attraction of the *bakungu* category lay in its proximity to the British requirement of graded administrative offices. Pre-colonial Buganda was divided into ten units called *saza*; the *saza* chiefs were appointed, transferred, and dismissed by the Kabaka, and they were bound to attend his court regularly. The Uganda Agreement of 1900 (between Sir Harry Johnston and the Kabaka and chiefs of Buganda) confirmed the *saza* chiefs in their duties and privileges as government servants, and throughout the colonial period the 'county' chiefs, as they were called, were the backbone of the Buganda administration. The British did not, however, confine themselves to squeezing out the other two chiefly hierarchies. They also rationalized the lower levels of the *bakungu* system itself. Under each *saza* chief there had been a number of lesser *bakungu* who administered subdivisions of the *saza*. By two stages these lower positions were simplified and standardized, first in 1908 by the appointment of *gombolola* or 'sub-county' chiefs, and then by the creation of a third position of *miruka* or 'parish' chief in 1916. Every *saza*, *gombolola*, and *miruka* was given precise territorial definition, and the chiefs' powers were fixed by Protectorate

---

[4] For the political system of nineteenth-century Buganda, see C. C. Wrigley, 'The Christian Revolution in Buganda', *Comparative Studies in Society and History*, 2 (1959), pp. 33–48; L. A. Fallers, 'Social Stratification in Traditional Buganda', in *The King's Men*, ed. L. A. Fallers (London, 1964), pp. 64–116.

Ordinance. The end result was a three-tier structure of executive chiefs.[5]

Almost simultaneously, the administration of Busoga and the western kingdoms (Bunyoro, Toro, and Ankole) was adapted in most respects to the Ganda model, and this entailed considerable changes in the position of the chiefs concerned.[6] An even greater local adjustment was needed when the system was extended to the acephalous peoples of eastern Uganda, to whom the notion of formal chiefship was wholly alien. Kakungulu's 'kingdom' of Bukedi was short-lived, but the *bakungu*-type divisions which he created there between 1900 and 1905 provided the basis of British administration among the Iteso and the stateless Bantu peoples to the south.[7] By the time the administration of Lango was set in train, it was virtually inevitable that the Ganda model should be implemented there as well. The need for intermediaries between village headmen and District Officers was met by establishing the three tiers of parish, sub-county, and county. The key position in this hierarchy was the sub-county chief, since he was the most junior African functionary to be entrusted with judicial authority and to be regularly inspected by a European official. Once the days of the Baganda agents in Lango were numbered, the first priority was to select suitable local men as sub-county chiefs. The thirty-three 'chiefs' gazetted in 1912 represented the first attempt to do this. Only later were the other positions in the hierarchy filled; and throughout the colonial period the sub-county chiefs were considered the lynch-pin of native administration in Lango, as elsewhere in the Northern and Eastern Provinces.

Two aspects of the administrative provisions made in Lango in 1912 deserve close scrutiny; the drawing of the sub-county boundaries, and the basis on which sub-county chiefs were chosen. The second of these might appear to be the all-essential issue. In fact it was intimately dependent on the first. For in a situation where the basic unit of administration was in almost every case larger than any territory or sphere recognized in the indigenous system, an individual's chances of being appointed chief in part depended on where he happened to live in relation to the sub-county boundaries. These boundaries were predetermined. In almost every case, the place from which the

---

[5] D. A. Low and R. C. Pratt, *Buganda and British Overrule, 1900–1955* (London, 1960); D. A. Low, 'Uganda: the Establishment of the Protectorate, 1894–1919', in Harlow and Chilver, op. cit., pp. 93–5, 98.

[6] Low, in Harlow and Chilver, op. cit., pp. 95–7.

[7] Twaddle, 'Politics in Bukedi, 1900–1939', especially pp. 136–43.

sub-county of 1912 derived its name and where it had its headquarters was an agent's post, or *boma*. The administrative geography of Lango District dates back not to 1912, but to the years 1908–11. Any inquiry into the politics of colonial Lango must therefore begin with the choice of *boma* sites.

The over-all rate and timing of administrative expansion during those years depended, as the last chapter showed, on wider considerations of government policy. So far as the actual siting of agents' posts was concerned, the only explicit principle was that they should be a convenient day's journey apart.[8] That this principle was not interpreted very precisely is shown by the fact that in 1911 the distance between neighbouring posts varied from seven to twenty miles. Agents also tended to be posted to areas of relatively dense population; this was an important consideration in western Lango, where the population was less evenly spread than in the east, and it resulted in the majority of posts being sited on or near the Nile and its principal tributaries.[9] But even within these guide-lines there was obviously a very wide choice of suitable *boma* sites. By the middle of 1911, twenty-eight posts had been established in Lango country (Map 8). In many instances the circumstances surrounding the posting of the first agent were not recorded in official correspondence, but there is sufficient evidence to suggest that in choosing *boma* sites officials were influenced by three varieties of local political situation.

Firstly—and apparently most frequently—agents were established in localities which had already made trouble for the colonial power. This was clearly so with the first Lango post of all, the one established at Dokolo in 1907. Isaka Nziga was sent into the area which had reacted most sharply against the Kyoga Expedition a few weeks earlier, doubtless on the assumption that if the men of Dokolo were quickly overawed, adjacent areas would give little trouble.[10] In Palango District during 1909 and 1910 four posts were established as a result of local acts of antagonism. At the end of 1909 an agent was sent to Akokoro on Lake Kwania after the Jo Oyima and other clan sections had attacked nearby Banyoro settlements which were under

---

[8] Jervoise to Spire, 30.4.12, LDA (I owe this reference to Dr. Andrew Roberts).
[9] See especially Tufnell's map of Palango District, October 1910, UNA SMP/519/09.
[10] The establishment of the agent at Dokolo was reported in a letter by J. M. Coote; he did not, however, spell out the reasons for his choice. Coote to Grant, 7.8.07, UNA SMP/279/07.

government protection.[11] The posting of agents to Apac and Cegere early in 1910 was preceded by a record of sporadic hostility extending over two years.[12] Further north, the killing of twelve Baganda near Owiny Akulo's village in May 1910 was quickly followed by the posting of an agent to Ocini.[13] A similar pattern can be discerned later in 1910 at Cawente and Ngai, and at Bala in 1911.

At the other end of the spectrum were those cases in which the administration responded to explicit requests for agents. Such requests were not, of course, made out of appreciation of any abstract benefits of colonial rule. They arose from the tensions of inter-clan politics, in the same way that Odora's overtures before 1909 had done. In 1910 Tufnell complied with a request for an agent from Okulo Cagara of Loro, even though Loro was less than ten miles away from two existing posts.[14] Okulo had been objecting to his obligation to perform labour duties for the Cegere agent, among strangers on the other side of the Okole river;[15] his subsequent complaint that outlying villages ignored him suggests that his request may have been motivated by a desire to assert his own clan section's local supremacy.[16] But for his request, it is very unlikely that the Government would have considered posting an agent to Loro. More striking still was the case of Okori Alima, the leader of the Jo Oki me Okabo at Amac, on the periphery of Miro District. Okori had travelled some thirty or forty miles to visit Kakungulu when he was at Bululu; during the eighteen months before an agent was posted to Amac in April 1910, he had been urging that a *boma* should be set up, had entertained officials on tour, and had engaged their sympathies in his feuds with neighbouring clans. When Jervoise at last arrived with an agent, Okori's clan section were alone in providing labour and in standing by the Government when the *boma* was attacked.[17] For a couple of years afterwards, Amac was a major trouble spot: the Baganda were involved in several clashes there; Okori's main assistant was speared, and his

---

[11] Paske Smith to Grant, 29.10.09, UNA SMP/1782/09.
[12] Knowles to Wilson, 30.5.08, UNA SMP/1005/08; Jackson to Paske Smith, 4.5.09, UNA SMP/873/09; Fox to Paske Smith, 30.11.09, UNA SMP/1876/09; Paske Smith to Grant, 12.3.10, UNA SMP/1859/09.
[13] Fox to Tufnell, 16.6.10, UNA SMP/1860/09; Tufnell, Map of Palango District, Oct. 1910, UNA SMP/519/09.
[14] Tufnell to Grant, 28.10.10, UNA SMP/519/09.
[15] Tufnell to Grant, 29.8.10, UNA SMP/1859/09.
[16] Tufnell to Grant, 31.10.10, UNA SMP/519/09.
[17] Jervoise to Coote, 19.3.09, UNA SMP/255/08; Jervoise to Spire, 18.4.10, UNA SMP/624.

own cattle raided.[18] All the evidence suggests that Okori had no influence outside his own clan section, and that he was manipulating the Government at his neighbours' expense. In this he met with considerable success: when his cattle were stolen, the agent recovered them for him;[19] and in 1912 he was appointed chief of Amac sub-county, an office which he managed to retain for seven years.

The third type of situation which affected the siting of *bomas* was one in which—irrespective of hostility or encouragement—an area was found to have one really strong clan section. On the northern side of Lake Kwania, for example, the posts established at Agwata and Abyece in 1910 were close by settlements of the Jo Okide and the Jo Alipa, which were both powerful groups, as well as allies in battle.[20] The choice of what is now Lira town as the site of a post in January 1911 seems to have been determined by the 'considerable sphere of influence' under Olet Apar, leader of the Jo Oki.[21] Official reports are frustratingly silent on the sources of information which were used in identifying significant clan leaders, but the case of Bar may point to a widespread pattern. According to a tradition there, the British established an agent at the village of Oki, leader of the Oki me Abura clan, because Okori of Amac had told them that Oki was the important man in that area.[22]

At the same time, there is no doubt that the siting of many *bomas* was haphazard and arbitrary. Tufnell's hurried expansion into central Lango in the middle of 1910 is a case in point. When agents were established at Aduku, Akalu, and Aboke, Tufnell had no experience of these areas to draw on, since he was the first government representative to visit them. The Aduku *boma* was built not near the village of Lingo, the best-known ritual leader of his day, but on the other side of the Aroca river among the less important Eling clan.[23] The *boma* at Aboke was actually sited at the village of a quite insignificant leader named Atai; eighteen months later it was moved about ten miles away to the territory of the powerful Jo Pukica, who had

[18] The agent was involved in clashes in October 1910, December 1911, and August 1912. Wright to Spire, 15.11.10, UNA SMP/1408; Jervoise to PCEP, 2.1.12 and 3.10.12, UNA SMP/2404.

[19] Jervoise to PCEP, 3.10.12, UNA SMP/2404.

[20] Jervoise to Spire, 28.2.10, UNA SMP/332. Interviews: Israel Alele, Isaka Ojaba.

[21] Haldane, Reports on Lango District for Jan. and Feb. 1911, UNA SMP/193A.

[22] Interview: Lakana Ekin.

[23] Interviews: Yakobo Obia, Lajaro Obia, Enoci Ekak.

attacked the agent soon after his arrival.[24] By and large, however, there was some method in the siting of agents in Palango District. It was in Miro District that the process was most haphazard, particularly during the first two years of administration, when officials were very ill informed about local politics. If the choice of *boma* sites had been no more than a temporary expedient, hasty and ill-informed decisions would hardly have mattered. But the reality was more serious. Whether they appreciated it or not, the officials who posted agents in the years 1908–11 were in fact making detailed provision for the long-term future. Of the twenty-eight sites selected by the middle of 1911, only three have since been abandoned and only one has been moved an appreciable distance.

Later in the colonial period, when the system of native administration in northern and eastern Uganda was under attack, there was a tendency to belittle the status of the first generation of chiefs in Lango. The Baganda were said to have ignored the traditional clan leadership, and to have filled the new positions with their own hangers-on—Langi who had been uprooted from their clan environment to serve as askaris or camp-followers.[25] This interpretation was wide of the mark. Of the thirty-three chiefs gazetted in 1912, not one had worked for the Baganda, and in the next decade there was only one clear instance of the 'camp-follower made good' model.[26] This was in spite of the fact that plenty of Langi did take service with the Baganda. Two of them were actually appointed as agents, but their promotion to sub-county chief was never considered.[27] The truth is that the Baganda agents, like the Lango chiefs who came after them, worked through clan leaders acting as village heads.

It is misleading to concentrate attention here on the Baganda. In those parts of the Protectorate where they were most strongly entrenched, the Baganda did indeed control the recruitment to office of local personnel; this was the pattern in Kakungulu's territory of Bukedi, in eastern Uganda.[28] But in Lango the Baganda were fewer

[24] Place to Grant, 13.12.10, UNA SMP/193; Cator, Report on Lango District for April 1912, UNA EPMP/Z/1329/13.
[25] This view was reflected in the attitude taken by Captain Philipps in 1933–4. See below, Chapter 8.
[26] This was Tomasi Ojuka. For his career, see below, p. 191.
[27] Driberg, entry for 19.5.17, in Dokolo TB (1913–26, part 2), and entry for 12.2.18, in Moroto TB (1918–26).
[28] Personal communication from Dr. Michael Twaddle.

in number, more alienated from the local cultural setting, and altogether less interested in long-term political prospects. And so, in almost every case, the selection of Lango chiefs was carried out by European officials. However defective their understanding of Lango society may have been, it is quite clear from the Tour Books of the period that District Officers on safari took considerable pains to establish the local standing and the qualifications for office of individual clan leaders.[29] This does not mean that the right men were necessarily appointed, but the selection of chiefs was certainly not left to the Baganda. Official policy was consistent: the aim was to appoint the most influential clan leader of the locality, unless there were overriding practical objections. A remarkable degree of success was achieved. Except for one or two cases in which a clan leader deliberately hung back from the limelight,[30] the chiefs gazetted in 1912 were men of local standing.

The selection was most straightforward when the territory round an agent's post contained a dominant clan leader of a co-operative frame of mind. One such case was considered in the last chapter: Arum was made sub-county chief of Ibuje after six years' careful cultivation of Odora and the Europeans.[31] The same pattern held good at Inomo, Iceme, and Lira. The real test of official determination to build on traditional authority lay in those areas where that authority was hostile to the colonial power. Abyece is an example of this. As we have seen, this was one of the most troublesome localities during the first years of Ganda administration. Officials laid the blame squarely on Ebek, the leader of the Jo Alipa.[32] His removal to Mbale and Jinja for a few weeks in 1910 did little to temper his hostility, and the Government had to consider an alternative. The most likely candidate was Ogwal Agir, headman of one of the Alipa villages under Ebek. For a year or two no final decision was made. When government cattle were distributed to twenty-three prominent Langi in February 1912, both Ogwal and Ebek figured among the recipients. In the event Ebek was rejected; Ogwal Agir was the only chief from Abyece to be gazetted in September 1912, and a year later he was clearly recognized

---

[29] Driberg's book, *The Lango*, is also a monument to the local knowledge amassed by officials of the day (1912–18).

[30] This accounted for the appointment of Okelo Adak as chief of the Okole-Aroca division in 1909. Jervoise, Notes on Kidilande, in Koli TB (1912–14, part 1).

[31] See above, pp. 136–7.

[32] His rise to power in pre-colonial Abyece is described above, pp. 69, 72.

by officials as head chief over Ebek.[33] However, Abyece was not typical. By and large, the Government tended to take the risk of nominating fractious clan leaders, particularly if they had shown signs of mending their ways. Thus Onyinge of Cegere was made chief, despite his attacks on agents; and in Aboke Oleny, leader of the Jo Pukica, who had personally organized the killing of fifteen Baganda in 1910, was appointed on the strength of his being 'well-disposed'.[34]

The most striking instance of the Government's readiness to let bygones be bygones was the treatment given to Owiny Akulo of Aber. After the two clashes early in 1910, in which a total of sixteen Baganda had been killed, Otwal, the official chief of the country between the Ayago and Okole rivers, was captured and detained in Hoima, where he died soon afterwards. Owiny Akulo, who had organized the second and more serious incident, was also captured and imprisoned in Jinja.[35] In the immediate aftermath of the killings, District Officers took two actions which were gravely prejudicial to the interests of Otwal, Owiny, and their followers. Firstly, they chose as Otwal's replacement Okelo Abong, the leader of the Ocola lineage.[36] This was a complete contradiction of the traditional distribution of power within the Jo Arak. Otwal, Owiny Akulo, Odongo Aja, and his predecessor as *rwot* had all belonged to the Elwia lineage.[37] In promoting Okelo Abong to be chief of the country north of the Okole, the authorities were not only ignoring local realities; they were also aggravating the existing tension between the two lineages, and in particular between Okelo Abong and Owiny Akulo.[38]

The second action taken in Aber was of greater moment. Otwal's official sphere had extended as far as the Ayago river, which was the western limit of Lango settlement, some twenty-five miles from Kamdini. But Okelo Abong's territory was declared to end at the Toci river. The country to the north, including Kamdini itself, was

[33] Wright to Spire, 3.7.10, and Spire to CS, 12.7.10, UNA SMP/178; List of chiefs given cattle by the government, February 1912, UNA EPMP/N/53/12; Jervoise, Notes on Nabieso, and Scott, entry for 25.8.13, in Kwania TB (1913–19). Interviews: Matayo Ojok, Benedikto Okelo Elwange.
[34] Place to Grant, 13.12.10, UNA SMP/193; Jervoise, Notes on Aboke, in Koli TB (1912–14, part 2). Interviews: Paulo Oyet, Nasan Engola, Bejaleri Ogwang, Israel Opio, Lazaro Okelo.
[35] Fox to Tufnell, 16.6.10, and Tufnell to Grant, 3.10.10, UNA SMP/1860/09; Place, Report on Lango District for November 1910, UNA SMP/193.
[36] Tufnell to Grant, 20.6.10, UNA SMP/1860/09.
[37] For the pre-colonial power structure of Aber, see above, pp. 74–81.
[38] Interviews: Kosia Ato, Matayo Acut, Leoben Okodi, Misaki Oki.

assigned instead to the Acholi chief Lagony.[39] This arrangement was formalized in 1912 by a change in district boundaries: the Toci was made the boundary between Gulu and Lango Districts,[40] and it remained so until 1936 (Map 9). No record of official thinking at the time has survived, but it is hard to resist the conclusion that the boundary change was made on political grounds. The events of 1910 had shown the strength of the Jo Arak as a unit—for example in the co-operation between clan members on either side of the Toci. Officials had been seriously alarmed by the attacks on the Baganda in Aber, and they were apparently now bent on breaking up a major centre of opposition.

The boundary anomaly was not rectified for a quarter of a century, but the favour given to Okelo Abong was soon withdrawn. After just over a year's detention in Jinja, Owiny Akulo was allowed to return home early in 1912. He was presented with a gift of government cattle,[41] and soon afterwards was gazetted sub-county chief of Ocini, which was now detached from Okelo Abong's sphere. In 1916 Okelo Abong was dismissed altogether.[42] A year later Owiny Akulo was appointed first county chief in north-western Lango,[43] and until he became too old he was considered by the authorities to be an exemplary chief. Owiny Akulo's son attributes his father's change of heart to the Christian influences which he encountered in Jinja gaol.[44] In fact the change was not quite so abrupt as it seems. Owiny Akulo never appears to have borne much animus against the Europeans; his quarrel was with the Baganda. He had given them a rough reception in 1895,[45] and fifteen years later he was determined that they should not be allowed to resume their predatory activities. While Owiny was in prison, the maladministration of the agents had been exposed, and it seems likely that the resultant reform and the limit now set on the agents' term in Lango contributed to Owiny's readiness to co-operate on his release. The arrangements made in Aber between 1912 and 1917 were a credit as much to official wisdom as to Owiny Akulo's change of outlook. After the first attack on the Baganda in February

[39] Okelo Abong was gazetted chief 'between the Toshi and Koli rivers' (*Gazette*, 15 Aug. 1910). By January 1911 Lagony had built a post at the mouth of the Toci. Haldane, Report on Lango District for January 1911, UNA SMP/193.

[40] *Gazette*, 15 July 1912.

[41] List of chiefs given cattle by the government, February 1912, UNA EPMP/N/53/12.

[42] Hannington, Report on Lango District for August 1916, UNA EPMP/Z/537/16.   [43] *Gazette*, 30 Apr. 1917.

[44] Interview: Leoben Okodi.   [45] See above, pp. 114–15.

1910, Paske Smith recognized that Owiny had several times before assisted the Government and that in view of this—and in contrast to Otwal—he should eventually be allowed to return to Lango.[46] It says much for the responsible officials that they continued to hold to this view after the more serious events of May. By adhering to the traditional leadership of Aber, the Government secured twenty years of political stability in north-western Lango.

In a very large number of sub-counties—probably the majority—there was no clan leader who stood head and shoulders above his fellows. Here the problem was not whether to risk appointing an important man with a record of hostility behind him, but whom to choose from among several village leaders of equal eminence. In Dokolo a choice had to be made between two men—Okwanga of the Jo Arak and Opige of the Jo Palamyek, both of whom used to lead temporary clan combinatins in cattle-raids on the Kumam.[47] European officials were aware of the importance of these two leaders from 1907 onwards.[48] Their eventual decision to appoint Opige was probably made on several grounds. Okwanga had been the principal victim of the decision to expel Langi living east of the Abalang river, and his attitude to the authorities was probably coloured by this humiliating experience. Opige had ingratiated himself with the Dokolo agent between 1909 and 1913, while Okwanga had mistrusted the Baganda and believed that they would soon leave.[49]

In many sub-counties the field of choice was wider still, and it was in this context that the siting of *bomas* was particularly significant. Other things being equal, clan leaders whose villages were close to the agent's post tended to be co-operative, or at least acquiescent, while those who lived several miles away could afford to be less careful. The odds were therefore in favour of a near-by clan leader taking over as chief when the agent was withdrawn. Apac provides a good example of this. The agent's post on the left bank of the Aroca was used as a base for administering both sides of the river. Tufnell chose four headmen in 1910—two for the left bank and two for the right bank; but it was Okweng, the headman nearest the post, who was made chief in 1912, and even when officials discovered that they had mistakenly chosen a mere 'peasant', Okweng was succeeded not by another of

[46] Paske Smith to Grant, 14.3.10, UNA SMP/201.   [47] See above, p. 81.
[48] According to Jervoise, Coote in 1907 had identified Okwanga, Opige, and two others as local headmen. Jervoise, Notes on Dokolo, in Dokolo TB (1913–26, part 1).   [49] Interviews: Yeromia Otim, Silvesto Otim, Tomasi Ojuka.

Tufnell's nominees, but by the real leader of his own village.[50] If the Apac *boma* had been on the right bank of the Aroca or further upstream, there is little doubt that the choice of chief would have been different. Such was the haphazard procedure for recruiting administrative personnel.

In some places, the kind of informal arrangement which Tufnell had made at Apac in 1910 was maintained much longer, and sometimes even gazetted; in this way a choice could be postponed until the various candidates had had time to prove themselves. In Kwera, at the eastern end of Lake Kwania, three chiefs were gazetted in 1912; one of them was deposed in 1914 and his chiefdom divided between the other two; the following year all Kwera was placed under one chief.[51] In Aduku three chiefs were also appointed in 1912, but by 1915 only one was still recognized.[52] In these places, a genuine effort seems to have been made to test possible chiefs, but even here one suspects that the government officials appointed the man with whom they were most familiar; for in each case the surviving chief was the one nearest the sub-county headquarters.

The most carefully researched initial appointments were made in the Moroto valley, which was the last part of Lango to be opened up. By the time officials turned to this area in 1915, they had learnt a fair amount from their experience in central and southern Lango. They therefore considered the actual siting of the agents' posts in the context of the local distribution of power and the likely choice of chief, which was made in each case within one year of the setting-up of the *boma*. No doubt also the arrangements gained from the fact that most of the *bomas* were sited by J. H. Driberg, whose grasp of Lango politics was exceptional.[53] In Abako Driberg found in 1916 that the area included three significant clan leaders. Two of them, Ocen Ocur and Ogeta, were jockeying for position; during the previous year or two, when District Officers had been on tour near by, each of them had requested an agent to be sent to his village. Instead of responding directly to either of these requests, Driberg established the agent in the intervening territory of the third clan, and he instructed that all

---

[50] Tufnell to Grant, 6.7.10, UNA SMP/1876/09; Jervoise, Notes on Apac, and entry for 31.1.13, in Kwania TB (1913–19).

[51] Notes on Kwera, in Dokolo TB (1913–26, part 1); *Gazette*, 30 Apr. 1914 and 30 Sept. 1915.   [52] Entries for Aduku, in Kwania TB (1913–19).

[53] Driberg opened up Abako, Aloi, and Apala in 1916, and Adwari and Orum in 1918. Ogur was set up in 1915 by another official; Omoro (1915) and Amugo (1917) were opened up from Soroti.

three clan leaders should be treated as equals by the agent until one of them evinced real ability. This proved to be a sensible policy. Within six months it was clear that Ocen Ocur, who had been much the most assiduous in his cultivation of government officials, was in fact the least suited for authority: he refused to take part in public labour and his men frequently took up arms. And so Ogeta was gazetted as chief of Abako in 1917.[54] At Aloi Driberg also chose three headmen, each from a different clan section, though in this case there was little doubt that Ocato, leader of the dominant Jo Oki, would be appointed.[55] The same principle was implemented in 1918 at Adwari, where informal recognition was given to the two most influential clan leaders.[56]

If the procedures adopted by officials in making inaugural appointments to the position of sub-county chief varied in precision and effectiveness, there is no doubt that in the vast majority of cases men of genuine local standing were chosen. In terms of traditional political authority, the decisive break during the years 1912–18 was no so much in personnel, as in the type of authority which the appointed chiefs were called upon to exercise. On paper their powers were transformed in two ways: territorially, they were given authority over clan sections to which they had no prior claim; and qualitatively, the range of circumstances in which they could directly affect their 'subjects' increased beyond recognition. The actual content of these new powers must now be examined.

The powers conferred on sub-county chiefs could be summarized by saying that within the confines of their allotted territories they were responsible for achieving the objectives set by the Protectorate Government. In 1912 these objectives were much as they had been at the start of formal administration four years earlier. The first priorities were still the maintenance of law and order, and the provision of labour for public works.

So far as the physical enforcement of order was concerned, the chiefs simply took over the main instrument of the agents' authority— that is to say, a handful of retainers (called askaris), armed with government rifles. During the transitional period when agents were working alongside Lango chiefs, the chief deployed the Baganda

[54] Driberg, entries for 30.1.16 and 19.7.16 in Dokolo TB (1913–26, part 1).
[55] Driberg, entry for 3.2.16 in Eruti TB (1915–21).
[56] J. Tosh, 'Small-scale Resistance in Uganda: the Lango "Rising" at Adwari in 1919', *Azania*, 9 (1974), pp. 51–64.

followers in consultation with the agent. When the agent was with-drawn, local men were recruited to replace the Baganda followers. They took over their weapons and their rates of pay. By 1919 the allocation had been standardized at three askaris for each sub-county chief.[57] The function of the askaris was to arrest offenders on the chief's orders, to guard them in his lock-up pending trial, and in general to enforce the chief's orders. It is plain from the comments of District Officers that, initially at least, considerable latitude was allowed to chiefs in their use of fire-arms, and no objection was made to the summary killing of offenders who resisted arrest.[58] Until the askaris were reconstituted as chiefs' police in 1920 and given training at District headquarters,[59] the handling of fire-arms was doubtless somewhat inexpert, but the askaris by no means exhausted the chief's resources for enforcing his authority. If there was serious disorder, and especially if any of the askaris was killed or badly wounded, the chief could send for help to a District Officer, who would then arrive on the scene with a detachment of Protectorate police. Government action along these lines was quite common until 1914, and it was always effective.[60]

It was as well for the precarious authority of the chiefs that they were not often called upon to contain raids for cattle and women, of the kind which had been so serious a feature of the period from about 1892 to 1912. Of all the major changes which attended the introduc-tion of colonial administration into Lango, none is more difficult to explain than the prompt achievement of peace in inter-village rela-tions. Cattle numbers had not yet attained their pre-rinderpest level,[61] and the temptation to raid for livestock, while not so overwhelming as during the 1890s, must still have been strong, especially for younger men in need of bridewealth.[62] Certainly inter-village warfare had

[57] Entries to this effect in all current Tour Books by E. D. Tongue in 1919 suggest that the allocation was standardized in that year.

[58] See for example, Driberg, entry for 2.7.18, in Maruzi TB (1912–19).

[59] Tomblings, Report on Lango District for 1920, UNA EPMP/N/121.

[60] Incidents of this kind occurred at Aduku in 1912, Ngai in 1912, Lira, Agwata, and Dokolo in 1913, and Bala in 1914. Jervoise to PCEP, 6.11.12 and 3.10.12, UNA SMP/2404; Scott to PCEP, 12.5.13, 14.5.13 and 10.11.13, SMP/2404; Driberg to PCEP, 10.10.14, SMP/4214.

[61] Driberg, op. cit., pp. 91–2.

[62] The restlessness of the young is stressed in Jackson to Paske Smith, 4.5.09, and Paske Smith to Grant, 5.5.09, both in UNA SMP/873/09. From about 1912 onwards Indian traders did a brisk business selling cattle to the Langi, but they were hardly in a position to meet the demand. See J. H. Driberg, 'The Lango District, Uganda Protectorate', *Geographical Jl.*, 58 (1921), p. 131.

provided a constant headache for administrators between 1908 and 1912.[63] Yet as early as 1913 the District Commissioner reported that in recent months village fights had become infrequent.[64] By 1918 only the south-eastern area round Dokolo was still giving trouble,[65] and two years later Dokolo too had ceased to be the home of 'cattle thieves, murderers, and potential rebels.'[66] The defence of law and order by the new chiefs was therefore conducted largely against individuals rather than whole communities.

The chief's responsibility for law and order was given institutional expression in the court of law over which he presided. These courts took shape during the years 1912–13, when gazetted chiefs were being advised and instructed by Baganda agents. The court, or *lukiko* as it was called from the prototype in Buganda, was composed of the chief and all the village headmen of the sub-county, meeting together at least twice a month to try civil cases and petty criminal cases; its judgements were subject to appeal to District Officers on tour. The *lukiko* functioned not only as a court but also as a council, where matters of public concern could be discussed and Government orders be communicated to the headmen.[67] Procedure was informal, and in both its judicial and its consultative aspects, the early *lukiko* in Lango seems to have depended as much on consensus as on the executive decision of any one individual.[68] Between 1915 and 1918 sub-county courts were set up in every part of Lango except the north-east under the Courts Ordinance of 1911. The sub-county chief's *lukiko* now had original jurisdiction in all civil and criminal cases, and it was to meet regularly once a week. Criminal law was to be administered as laid down by Protectorate law, and civil law as expressed in native or customary law.[69] This formalization of organization and procedure tended to concentrate judicial authority in the chief's hands, but the consultative side of the *lukiko* was maintained. The headquarters of

[63] E.g. Jervoise to Coote, 19.3.09, UNA SMP/255/09; Paske Smith to Grant, 5.10.09, UNA SMP/872/09; Tufnell to Grant, 28.10.10, UNA SMP/519/09; Jervoise to PCEP, 4.12.12, UNA SMP/2404.

[64] Jervoise, Report on Lango District for 1912–13, UNA EPMP/Y/16.

[65] Cator, Report on Lango District for Oct. 1918, UNA EPMP/N/112/18.

[66] Tongue, Report on Lango District for 1919–20, LDA.

[67] Scott, Reports on Lango District for Aug. 1913 and Jan. 1914, UNA EPMP/Z/228/13.

[68] For example, when Akaki of Akokoro was found to be incompetent, the Touring Officer instructed the agent to wait for a suitable successor to emerge from 'a lukiko of equals'. Entry for 3.12.13, Maruzi TB (1912–13).

[69] Proclamation on Lira Native Courts, 9.2.15, and subsequent amendments, UNA SMP/907/08; Standing Orders, 1919, entered in every current Tour Book.

every sub-county chief took the form of a *lukiko* hall with a couple of adjacent offices for the chief and his clerk. On one day the chief would preside over the sub-county court, while on the next day in the same hall he might be hearing the views of the village headmen and other notables on some topical issue.[70]

In time the restraint which a chief could exercise over individuals through his police and law courts became a crucial component of his authority, open to much abuse.[71] Initially, however, the chiefs made an impact on their people less because of their responsibility for law and order than on account of the Government's other top priority—the provision of a labour supply. The chiefs' obligation in this respect touched the daily life of every able-bodied man in the sub-county. Labour demands were of two kinds. There was first of all labour on projects intended by the District authorities to be for the benefit of the community as a whole. During the period of Baganda rule, no practical limit appears to have been set on labour demands, but by 1919 obligations had been standardized. Every year each adult male was liable to one month's unpaid labour, known as *luwalo*, and until 1923 to a further two months' paid labour, known as *kasanvu*.[72] *Luwalo* was mainly used for the building and maintenance of local roads. Paid labour was called upon by Departments of the Protectorate Government for cotton ginneries,[73] major road construction, and above all for 'porterage'—the transport of the countless loads essential to the smooth running of colonial government, ranging from cash-boxes to the Touring Officer's personal effects. The economic significance of these reserves of labour was of course considerable, but in the present context it is their bearing on political authority which matters. The responsibility for enlisting both *luwalo* and *kasanvu* labour lay with the chiefs. It is unlikely that the legal maximum of labour was ever actually called out, and no records were kept as a basis for strict rotation in labour duty. Favour and discrimination were probably practised by the chiefs from the beginning; they were certainly an important feature by the 1920s.[74]

[70] Officials encouraged a close association of these two functions: Tomblings, Report on Lango District for 1920, UNA EPMP/N/121.

[71] See below, chapter 7.

[72] R. C. Pratt, 'Administration and Politics in Uganda, 1919–45', in Harlow and Chilver, op. cit., pp. 492–3. *Luwalo* and *kasanvu* were authorized by the Native Authority Ordinance of 1919.

[73] Entries for 25.5.18 and 8.7.18 in Omoro TB (1915–26).

[74] See below, Chapter 7.

The chief was also entitled to a personal tribute of labour from every man in his sub-county. This was perhaps the most anomalous aspect of the 'Ganda model' so freely exported to the non-centralized societies of the Protectorate. For what had been an integral part of the political culture in the interlacustrine states was seen by the Langi as a degrading imposition. To be liable for personal unpaid service one day a week was hardly less repugnant to a chief's own clansmen than it was to his other 'subjects', since in Lango eyes the principle of labour reciprocity applied as much to the clan leader as to the clan members. There is little doubt that during the first twenty years of colonial rule *arododo*, as it was called (or *busulu* in Buganda), was the most consistently unpopular government requirement.[75] By a convention which in Lango had no explicit statutory basis, chiefs were also entitled to demand a tithe of produce from peasant holdings.[76] How far they actually did so is open to doubt, since few chiefs maintained the large personal followings which could have consumed the proceeds. In view of the fact that pre-colonial clan leadership had carried with it no control over economic resources at all, these forms of tribute and service were a striking—and doubtless highly unpopular —novelty. From the Government's point of view, they could hardly have been avoided at the beginning, when there was virtually no other means of remunerating chiefs; but in allowing *arododo* to continue long after the introduction of taxation, officials were conforming to Protectorate practice at heavy local cost.

The newly appointed chiefs inherited from the agents responsibility for promoting the cultivation of cotton, on which the economic viability of the District was seen by the British to depend. Under the Baganda, cotton-growing had been based on heavy administrative pressure rather than a free market response on the part of the growers. After 1912 enforcement became more rather than less rigorous, for it was now applied to farmers individually instead of the village community as a whole. The communal plots supervized by the agents were abandoned, and every household was now required to grow at least a quarter of an acre, from seed distributed by the chief. Several more years of compulsion were needed before output figures in the early

[75] This is reflected both in contemporary Tour Books and in the personal reminiscences of informants today. The one-day-a-week obligation was written into the Standing Orders of each county in Lango District.

[76] In Buganda this tribute had the weight of tradition behind it, and it was called *envujo*. For examples of the convention in Lango, see: Driberg to Spire, 10.10.17, UNA SMP/4349; Tomblings, entry for 10.2.21 in Maruzi TB (1919–26, part 2).

1920s rose to a level which indicated that cotton had at last become an accepted feature of the Lango agricultural routine.[77]

Stricter enforcement of cotton obligations after 1912 coincided with a determined effort on the part of the administration to place taxation on a sound footing, and here too a heavy burden was placed on the Lango chiefs. In 1914 poll-tax, first applied to Buganda in 1905, was introduced in Lango.[78] The agents had attempted to levy hut-tax in kind in a crude fashion since the beginning of administration, but there was little to show for their efforts as late as 1912.[79] Under the new system every adult male was liable to a fixed payment in cash of three Rupees (four shillings) a year. The first levy of a cash-tax is often taken to have been the point at which the reality of colonial rule was brought home to the rural African. In the case of the Langi, this function was performed by the earlier imposition of labour obligations. While chiefs continued to find difficulty in getting the people to work until well into the 1930s, the annual demand for poll-tax caused very little friction. District Officers sometimes remarked on inefficiency in its collection or embezzlement of the proceeds,[80] but they found little evidence of deep objections on the part of the tax-payers and were gratified by the rapid increase in revenue from taxation.[81] All the same, the beginning of taxation marked an important stage in the evolution of appointive chieftaincy. Even without opposition, collection from every adult male in his sub-county was a major undertaking for the chief. The first generation of sub-county chiefs would probably have failed to come up to administrative requirements had it not been for the 10 per cent rebate on poll-tax which now became their principal remuneration—and an increasingly valuable one as the rate of tax was raised to five Rupees in 1919, and fifteen shillings in 1922.[82]

The setting up of the minimum apparatus of colonial government in

[77] J. Tosh, 'Lango Agriculture during the Early Colonial Period: Land and Labour in a Cash-crop Economy', *Jl. African History*, 19 (1978), in the press. Cf. C. C. Wrigley, *Crops and Wealth in Uganda* (Kampala, 1959), pp. 20, 48; C. Ehrlich, 'The Uganda Economy, 1903–45', in Harlow and Chilver, op. cit., pp. 417–18.

[78] Proclamation under Poll Tax Ordinance, 6.3.14, in *Gazette*, 15 March 1914.

[79] Watson to CS, 20.2.12, UNA SMP/519/09.

[80] Entry for 19.10.21, Dokolo TB (1913–26, part 2).

[81] Figures of Lango tax receipts cannot be given because the official figures (UNA SMP/178, SMP/193, SMP/703) make no distinction between the Langi and the Kumam, who were much more assiduous in their cotton-growing and much more amenable to taxation in the early years than the Langi.

[82] *Blue Books* for 1919 and 1922. The rebate on tax did not replace entitlement to free labour service as a chiefly perquisite.

Lango during the years 1912–14 entailed one other highly important novelty, which represented for the people in general a distasteful restraint, and for the chiefs an additional hold over their subjects: this was the ban on group migration. From an administrative point of view, labour obligations could not be enforced, nor taxes collected, if clan sections retained their freedom to migrate at will. Admittedly, the imposition of colonial rule did not cause a total freeze of existing settlement areas. Colonization of the few extensive bush areas that remained was allowed, so that during the next twenty years the Langi were able to settle in the hinterland of Akokoro and Cawente,[83] and also in the country immediately to the west of Otuke hill.[84] In addition, the Government occasionally ordered villages to move to sites nearer the lines of communication.[85] But otherwise group migration was strongly discouraged. Unauthorized moves were forbidden and punished.[86] And if for some reason a migration seemed not to be entirely out of the question, District Officers tended to leave the decision to the chiefs concerned.[87] Emigration was naturally not favoured by the chiefs, since their pay was directly related to the amount of tax collected. Combined with the Government's own strong preference for a completely settled population, this disfavour effectively placed group migration outside the law. Obligations of service and payment were thus not easily evaded by the ordinary population.[88]

By 1915 the minimum administrative requirements of the Protectorate Government were well on the way to being met in Lango. These requirements were a heavy burden for the ordinary people, requiring adjustment over a period of time. Yet hardly had taxation been successfully begun than further impositions were laid on the Langi, through events outside the Government's control. There was first of all the Great War. In 1917 recruitment to the King's African

[83] Warne, entry for 26.8.13, in Maruzi TB (1912–13); Hannington, entry for 15.8.16, in Maruzi TB (1912–19).

[84] Driberg, entry for 12.2.18, in Moroto TB (1918–26); Rubie, entry for 22.4.32, in Moroto TB (1926–33).

[85] Driberg to Spire, 5.10.17, UNA SMP Conf/340; entry for 8.7.18, in Omoro TB (1915–26).

[86] Scott, entry for 31.1.14, in Koli TB (1912–14); Driberg, entry for 4.2.15, in Kwania TB (1913–19).

[87] Scott, entry for 25.7.14, in Koli TB (1913–19, part 2); Driberg, entry for 8.12.15, in Maruzi TB (1912–19).

[88] It should be noted that the colonial period brought unprecedented opportunities for migration by *individuals*, and this was not discouraged to the same extent.

Rifles and the Carrier Corps was extended to Lango District. In theory recruitment was voluntary, but in practice the chiefs had to co-operate with European officials in mustering a quota of men, whether they volunteered or not. In October 1917 army recruitment occasioned many riots, which—as Driberg pointed out—'but for the tactful conduct of the Chiefs might easily have led to bloodshed'.[89] In all, more than 1,100 men were enlisted into the K.A.R.[90]

The war coincided with, and in part aggravated, an appalling combination of natural disasters. There were epidemics of bubonic plague and smallpox; in 1917 a new disease, cerebro-spinal meningitis, ravaged Lango, to be followed a year later by influenza. Many thousands of people died.[91] The main reaction which these disasters caused among the Langi was a steep increase in witchcraft-accusations and witch-finding.[92] The Government's reaction was to restrict the movement of both people and livestock, and to carry out compulsory inoculation.[93] Both measures required the co-operation of the chiefs in overcoming their people's resentment of highly inconvenient, and apparently irrational, fiats of the Government. These assertions of authority were met with sporadic rioting and general unrest;[94] it is remarkable that no chiefs were killed or wounded as a result.

To add to the ravages of disease, the combination in 1918 of drought and locusts caused famine in every part of Lango except the south-east. The severity of the famine and the cost to the Government of alleviating it (over £11,000) caused local officials to implement permanent precautions against famine: every year in which there was a good yield, a proportion of the harvested grain was to be put aside as a famine reserve and stored in communal granaries at the sub-county headquarters. By the end of 1919 this scheme was in operation.[95] Throughout the colonial period, the levy and maintenance of famine reserves was considered by the Government to be an important part of the chief's duties, especially in drier areas such as Abyece.[96]

---

[89] Driberg to PCEP, 9.5.18, UNA EPMP/Z/862.
[90] Driberg, 'The Lango District, Uganda Protectorate', p. 133.
[91] Driberg, 'The Lango District', p. 133.
[92] Driberg to PCEP, 8.10.17, LDA LDMP/15/17 (noted by Dr. Michael Twaddle and since lost).
[93] Spire, Report on Eastern Province for Sept. 1915, UNA EPMP/Z/441/16; Spire, Report on Eastern Province for June 1917, UNA SMP/1929F.
[94] Spire, Report on Eastern Province for Nov. 1917, UNA SMP/1929F.
[95] Driberg to Eden, 23.3.18, and Special Warrant, 16.4.18, UNA SMP/3942/part 1; Jervoise to CS, 11.11.19, UNA SMP/3942/part 2.
[96] Entries at Abyece, *passim*, in Kwania TB (1926–33). Interview: Pilipo Oruro.

The direct intervention by the Government in public health and famine prevention entailed further restrictions on the liberty of individual Langi and further responsibilities for chiefs. In the period between the Wars there was no comparable crisis in health or food supply, but the Government continued to require compliance with regulations enforced through the chiefs. By 1920 both chiefs and people had been introduced to virtually the full range of government activity as it was practised in the period up to 1939.

By 1920 native administration both below and above the sub-county level had also been systematized. The big increase in chief's duties between 1914 and 1919, and especially the introduction of tax, made it essential to have a clear chain of responsibility and command. When the first chiefs were gazetted in 1912, each village leader in the sub-county was informally designated 'headman'; Okelo Abong of Aber, for example, was recorded as having under him forty-four headmen, whose followings varied from eight to fifty-two adult men.[97] As yet, no hierarchy was established among the headmen, nor were their duties defined; they were merely supposed to sit with the chief in *lukiko* and assist him in the general running of the sub-county. Very soon after 1912—if not before, in some of the longest-administered parts—the traditional settlement pattern began to change. Once cultivators had security against attack by a neighbouring clan section, there was little to be said in favour of the highly concentrated village which kept many of them a mile or more from their own plots. Large villages began to split up and eventually to disperse altogether, until the countryside assumed its present-day aspect of scattered farmers' homesteads, separated from each other by a hundred yards of land or more. This latter stage took some time to be completed, but the splitting-up of villages began early—by 1913 in Kwera for example, and by 1917 in Akokoro.[98] This process led naturally to a proliferation of 'headmen'. Thus, at a time when the range of administrative tasks was increasing sharply, the Government found that the immediate subordinates of the chief were becoming more numerous, and therefore individually less powerful, with every shift in the local settlement pattern. The answer was to erect an intermediate position between that of village headman and sub-county chief. From about

---

[97] Jervoise, List of headmen at Aber, in Koli TB (1912–14).
[98] Jervoise, Notes on Kwera, 1913, in Dokolo TB (1913–26, part 1); Driberg, entry for 8.7.17, in Maruzi TB (1912–19).

1915 the first experiments were made in grouping several headmen under a principal headman.[99] In 1919 a formal distinction was made between parish headmen and village headmen, in accordance with the latest refinement of the *bakungu* prototype in Buganda. In every sub-county between three and six 'parish headmen' were appointed, some of them with authority over more than a hundred households; the ablest of them acted as deputy, or *katikiro* (according to Ganda terminology), to the chief.[100] The village headmen were then organized so that each parish headman had between two and four under him. Even with this adjustment, however, the number of village headmen was often found to be too large, as villages continued to subdivide into yet smaller units. In most places the number of headmen actually recognized by the Government had to be cut down,[101] so that in due course the territory controlled by the official village headman tended to become a somewhat arbitrary category, just as the parish was.

Village chiefs and parish chiefs received a small share of the tax rebates and of the peasants' labour for chiefs (*arododo*),[102] but their appointments were not regarded as full-time by the Government. They had no office or official house, nor did they need to keep records. In two crucial respects their authority differed in kind, as well as in quantity, from that of the senior chiefs. Firstly, they were given no armed retainers; indeed the Government discouraged the keeping of any followers at all, and for this reason refused to allow the junior chiefs to exempt any of their people from labour service.[103] In the second place, parish and village chiefs had no judicial authority. They attended the sub-county chief's *lukiko*, and they might use their influence to bring about an informal settlement of a dispute before it was taken to court, but they could not themselves 'cut cases'. There was no doubt that the main resources of both legal and physical power lay with the sub-county chief. The junior chief's job was essentially to

---

[99] Fox, entry for 5.6.15, in Maruzi TB (1912–19); List of headmen at Iceme, *c*. 1916, in Koli TB (1913–19, part 2); Driberg, List of headmen under sub-chief Ogwal Agir, 1917, in Kwania TB (1913–19).

[100] The Standing Orders and the lists of headmen periodically drawn up in each Tour Book show a consistent pattern.

[101] For example: Driberg, entry for 10.7.18, in Maruzi TB (1912–19); Cator, entry for 26.2.19, in Kwania TB (1913–19); Tongue, entry for November 1919, in Dokolo TB (1913–26, part 1).

[102] Standing Orders (1919), entered in every current Tour Book; entry for 27.7.24 in Moroto TB (1926–33).

[103] Standing Orders (1919), entered in every current Tour Book; Driberg, entry for 17.12.17 in Kwania TB (1913–19); Driberg, Summary of Instructions given at Annual District Baraza, 31.7.18, ADA LDMP/40/15.

pass government orders down the line from the sub-county head-quarters, and to ensure that his people presented themselves for labour service and payment of tax when required.

Concurrently with the internal organization of the sub-county, the administrative structure was capped by the appointment of the first county chiefs. In Buganda the county or *saza* had been much the most important territorial category in the nineteenth-century kingdom, and its chief had been a focus of patronage and power. The county was the first level of the *bakungu* hierarchy to be adapted to the require-ments of colonial government in Buganda. For most of the colonial period, the *saza* chief retained something of the prestige traditionally attached to his office, and the supervision of the lesser chiefs was left almost entirely to him.[104] On paper, the senior chiefs in Lango occupied positions analogous to their prototypes in Buganda; in fact, the model was turned upside down in order to take account of the limited horizon of political action among the Langi themselves. The sub-county was the first tier of the new system to be organized: its boundaries were fixed and its chiefs appointed before the county had any administrative reality at all. And once county chiefs had been appointed, District Officers on tour continued to spend the bulk of their time supervising directly the sub-county chiefs. Though not actually superfluous, county chiefs always had a somewhat ill-defined function in the administration of Lango District.

The first county in Lango District to be given precise form was Kyoga. The demarcation of this county was determined by the per-sonal ascendancy which Kazana had established among the Kumam and in Namasale peninsula. Kazana was formally gazetted county chief in 1912. Except for a few years when Awelo and Aputi on the southern shores of Lake Kwania were included under Kazana's juris-diction, Kyoga county was the concern only of the Kumam, Banyara, and Baruli in the period up to 1935. In Lango proper, the first experi-ments in county administration were made in 1913 in response to two factors: the special position of Odora, and the total withdrawal of the Baganda agents from south-west Lango.

When Odora took up residence near the new station of Palango in 1909, his position was hardly any more defined than it had been during the period of sporadic contact with the Government since 1904. While the other two 'chiefs' appointed by Knowles in 1909 con-tinued to live in their own villages and to exert what influence they

[104] Low and Pratt, op. cit., pp. 219–23.

could further afield, Odora left the day-to-day leadership of his clansmen at Kungu to others, and concentrated instead on consolidating
his position with the European authorities. Outside Ibuje he exercised
virtually no authority. But Odora continued to seize every opportunity
of making an impression on his superiors: in 1910 he was recruiting
porters for European service,[105] and in the same year he responded to
the Government's preoccupation with cotton by preparing a nine-
acre plot near District headquarters as an advertisement of how
cotton should be grown.[106] This remarkable sensitivity to official
aspirations soon paid dividends: when the chief of the country
between the Aroca and the Okole was dismissed, Tufnell recommended that Odora should add that sphere to his own.[107] And in
January 1911 Odora was instructed to take up his headquarters at
Aduku, on the upper reaches of the Aroca.[108]

For the time being Odora's enlarged responsibilities were as empty
as his official role at Ibuje had been. North of the Aroca as well as
south, the Government relied on Baganda agents. The exception was
Aduku itself, which the agent vacated on Odora's arrival. Far from
district headquarters and free from on-the-spot supervision, Odora
was able to assert control over the locality which was to be his headquarters for fifteen years. He was a complete stranger to Aduku. If
there were any of his own clan, the Jo Oyakori, already living there,
they were very few in number.[109] Odora was therefore obliged at first
to rely exclusively on his own askaris. These numbered about fifty,
though not all had guns. A few of them were Banyoro or Baganda;
the majority were Langi from the south-west, with a strong element
of Jo Oyakori.[110] Odora ruled without any semblance of legitimacy or
local consensus. His unpopularity broke surface in September 1912,
when two of his askaris were killed, and the whole area was found to
be in 'a truculent state' and in need of punitive action by the District
Commissioner.[111] At that time, Odora found himself obliged to move
about 'closely followed by several armed followers'.[112]

[105] Melland and Cholmeley, *Through the Heart of Africa*, pp. 224, 233.
[106] Fox, Report on Lango District for May 1910, UNA SMP/193.
[107] Tufnell to Grant, 17.10.10, UNA SMP/1325.
[108] Haldane, Report on Lango District for Jan. 1911, UNA SMP/193A.
[109] Interviews: Peter Enin, Yakobo Obia, Lajaro Obia, Enoci Ekak.
[110] Interviews: Yakobo Adoko, Lajaro Obia.
[111] Jervoise to PCEP, 6.11.12, UNA SMP/2404; Jervoise, entry for 5.10.12, in
Kwania TB (1913–19).
[112] Warne, entry for 8.8.13, in Kwania TB (1913–19) (referring to the period
before April 1913).

Odora might be unpopular in Aduku, but no other Lango of his day had so much experience of Europeans and their requirements. There was much to be said for taking advantage of this flair. Odora's chance to prove his skills in a wider arena came in March 1913, with the permanent removal of Baganda agents from Apac, Cawente, and Abyece.[113] In place of supervision by agents, the Government substituted supervision by Lango county chiefs, who were to be remunerated on the same basis as the sub-county chiefs—by tax rebate and labour services. Odora was appointed county chief of Kwania, with headquarters at Aduku. To the west, a county was formed out of Ibuje, Akokoro, and Kungu. It was called Maruzi county and placed under Arum.[114] Since his move to Aduku, Odora had ceased to exercise any authority in that area, and the arrangements made in 1913 were a simple recognition of this fact.

Officials at the time acknowledged that Odora's position was something of an anomaly; he was 'really more of an agent than a chief',[115] —a *parvenu* even.[116] It was Arum's position in Maruzi which provided the model for county development in Lango as a whole during the next five years. In each case one of the existing sub-county chiefs, a native of the area, was picked out for promotion. In Arum's case, and in the counties of Atura and Kole created in 1917, this was done by appointment from above. When the first county chiefs were appointed to Erute and Dokolo at the end of 1918, the assembled sub-county chiefs were asked to elect one of their number (Map 10).[117] The first county chiefs were sometimes allowed to administer directly their own sub-counties. Odora did so in Aduku from 1917 to 1918, and Arum from 1913 to 1917. But thereafter the appointment of a county chief automatically brought about a vacancy at sub-county level. County chiefs were expected to devote their time to supervising the administration of the county as a whole.

Although the demarcation of sub-counties was somewhat haphazard, several of the resultant units bore at least some relationship to pre-colonial spheres of inter-clan dominance. By contrast, the counties were almost totally artificial. Between four and six sub-counties was regarded as the right size, and within this framework the boundaries

---

[113] Notes on Abyece, Cawente, and Apac, in Kwania TB (1913–19).
[114] Scott, Report on Lango District for June 1913, UNA EPMP/Z/228/13.
[115] Jervoise, Notes on Aduku, in Kwania TB (1913–19).
[116] Scott, Report on Lango District for 1913–14, UNA EPMP/Z/228/13.
[117] Driberg, Report on Lango District for Nov. 1917, UNA EPMP/Z/1326/17.

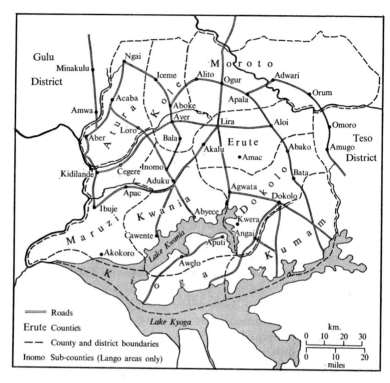

Map 10. Lango District, 1920

were worked out according to ease of communication, the administrative capacity of the first county chief, and other bureaucratic
criteria. As if to emphasize the artificiality of the idea, most of the
counties were given politically neutral names referring to prominent
natural features of the landscape.[118] The county headquarters was
sited in the place which enjoyed the easiest access to the county as a
whole, so that two of the county chiefs had to live and work some
distance from their home areas.[119] Furthermore, county boundaries
were changed several times in the period up to 1939; Kwania, for
example, 'lost' Apac in 1916, but 'gained' Inomo in 1917 and both
Awelo and Aputi in 1918. Of course the artificiality of so large a unit

[118] Kyoga and Kwania were named after lakes; Erute and Maruzi after hills;
Kole and Moroto after rivers.
[119] Owiny Akulo of Atura had to live at Loro, and Olong Adilo of Kole at
Aboke.

as the county was virtually inevitable, but some account could have been taken of pre-colonial categories, however vaguely defined they had been. A little investigation might have revealed the extent of the regional spheres of military influence which had collapsed less than a generation before. During the very years (1913–17) that the counties were being set up, Driberg was uncovering the fourfold division of Lango for purposes of the age-organization,[120] but no account was taken of his discovery. The nearest approach to a pre-colonial unit was Atura county. This corresponded quite closely to the area east of the Toci river which had acknowledged Odongo Aja's military leadership during his last years, and from 1917 until 1939 the county chief was Owiny Akulo, in effect Odongo's successor; but the pre-colonial association broke down on the fact that the area of Odongo Aja's influence *west* of the Toci was now part of Gulu District.

The artificiality of the county boundaries was matched by the total novelty of the county chief's function. His office carried no direct, everyday authority over the local inhabitants, but was concerned mainly with the supervision of administrative subordinates. The county chief presided over a county *lukiko*, which met twice a month as a consultative body and—more important—as a court of appeal from the sub-county courts. Every county chief also had a lock-up for offenders and five (or sometimes eight) police to guard the gaol and to assist in difficult arrests. To begin with, appeals to the county court were few in number, but in time the judicial powers vested in the county chief became very important.[121] The county chief was also responsible for inspecting the work of the sub-county chiefs in their own areas. During his first four years in charge of Kwania county, Odora chose to do this by posting personal representatives to each sub-county headquarters; this amounted to an informal survival of the discarded agent system—the more so since Odora was inclined to employ Banyoro and Baganda for the purpose.[122] Arum used the same method in Maruzi.[123] By 1919, however, both Odora and Arum

---

[120] Driberg, *The Lango*, p. 245.

[121] Eden, Report on Eastern Province for 1919–20, UNA SMP/703I; Standing Orders (1919) entered into every current Tour Book; Driberg, 'The Lango District', p. 129.

[122] Between 1913 and 1917, Odora had two Baganda at Abyece, and two Banyoro at Cawente; at Apac his own brother acted as agent. These men were referred to by the Lunyoro/Luganda word for agent or deputy, *omusigire*. Notes on Abyece, Cawente, and Apac, in Kwania TB (1913–19).

[123] Arum had a Bantu agent at Akokoro from 1914 to 1917, and a Lango agent at Apac from about 1916 to 1918. Entries in Maruzi TB (1912–19).

had abandoned the use of personal agents, and no other county chief resorted to this expedient. Instead, supervision was carried out by frequent touring, during which court records, cash books, and public works were inspected. The touring routine, which consumed a large part of both the county chief's and the District Officer's time, summed up much that was novel in the colonial political system: the hierarchical ordering of functionaries, the specificity of tasks allotted to them, and the importance attached to the accurate recording of petty transactions.

The seal was set on the administrative structure by the choice of an official vernacular terminology for the four grades of chief. From 1917 onwards, the county chief was referred to as *rwot*, the sub-county chief as *jago*, and the village chief as *won paco* ('guardian of the village'); two years later, the newly created parish chief was called *won magoro*, or more usually *amagoro* (literally 'guardian of the waste').[124] No record of how this terminology was arrived at has survived. Official inquiries cannot have been very searching. The only title which remotely corresponded to a pre-existing category was *won paco*. The term *paco* referred both to the family household and to the concentrated village of which it regularly formed a part, and so *won paco* could mean either a household head or a village leader. In the latter sense, the term was near enough to the lowest tier of the official hierarchy as it was originally constituted; but when the concentrated village broke up, leaving the *wang tic* as the basic local community, the officially defined *paco* and its chief lost the appearance of continuity. The most unsatisfactory term in the new vocabulary was *jago*. Among most Lwo-speaking peoples, including the Acholi, this term referred to the leader of a non-royal corporate lineage.[125] The Langi on the other hand lacked both the distinction between royal and commoner lineages, and the position of *jago*.[126] Had officials wanted a vernacular term for the sub-county chief with some traditional legitimacy, they would have done better to chose

---

[124] Driberg, Summary of instructions given at Annual District Baraza, 28.3.17, ADA LDMP/40/15; Standing Orders, 1919, entered into every current Tour Book. Later in the colonial period, the term *won magoro* was changed to *janjago*.

[125] Crazzolara, *The Lwoo*, p. 72; Southall, *Alur Society*, p. 47.

[126] The term *jago* is hardly ever used by informants today when describing pre-colonial politics, whereas *rwot* is used frequently. As pointed out in Chapter 3, Driberg's picture of a traditional hierarchy of *jagi* and *rwode* appears to be completely without foundation. Driberg, *The Lango*, p. 206.

rwot. Instead this term was reserved for the even more artificial rank of county chief.[127]

By 1920 officials in Lango District had erected a structure of native administration which conformed to the general requirements of colonial government, and to the specific model most readily to hand— the consolidated *bakungu* hierarchy of Buganda. We have stressed how alien to Lango conceptions of political order the new structure was. Both territorially and qualitatively, positions of authority were radically transformed. It is easy to see the administrative system as something imposed on an inert and passive population, as a manifestation of the Leviathan which had consumed the Langi and their neighbours during the previous twenty years. Yet local political activity did not cease; it merely entered new channels. The fact that the Uganda Government had to deploy its material resources at a very parochial level, and to entrust these resources to local personnel, brought the colonial power structure firmly within the purlieu of inter-clan politics. The graded chiefly positions quickly became an object of intense rivalry between clan sections. This was partly because chiefships were attractive in themselves as a potent source of political leverage, but it was also because of a more profound conditioning of political conflict. In pre-colonial Lango inter-clan tensions had been resolved in one of two ways, either by fighting or by group migration. Neither of these expedients was permitted by the colonial government. Inter-clan tensions had now to find expression within fixed administrative boundaries, with the result that the allocation of power within these units assumed a crucial political significance.

This chapter has shown that government chiefships were conferred on men who already enjoyed an established position in Lango society. To this extent, there was continuity between the old order and the new. To a large degree, however, the continuity was an illusion. Many clan leaders received no recognition at all, since administrative requirements set a limit on the number of Langi who could be accommodated in the colonial power structure. Furthermore, the creation of a four-tier chiefly hierarchy entailed at every level favouring one clan leader at the expense of his peers; in most cases the

---

[127] In the chapters that follow, I deliberately adhere to the English terminology despite its cumbersomeness. To use the vernacular would imply a spurious degree of traditional legitimacy; it would also lead to confusion between an individual's pre-colonial role and his government position, especially in the case of a *rwot*.

existing distribution of power gave no clear-cut indication of who should be promoted above the level of village headman, with the result that recruitment to senior positions tended, in traditional terms, to be quite arbitrary. Above all, new opportunities for personal power and enrichment meant that the political game was now played for much higher stakes. It is in this setting that politics in Lango during the 1920s and 1930s have to be considered.

CHAPTER 7

Power and Patronage in the Colonial Bureaucracy

THE success of the first-generation government chief in Lango depended on his fulfilling the expectations of the Protectorate authorities without alienating his 'subjects'. This task was complicated by the ambivalent nature of European expectations. During the first half of the twentieth century District Officers in Uganda, as elsewhere in British Africa, viewed 'tribal' institutions with a certain respect, even humility. Only a small minority identified strongly with the local culture, the sole instance in Lango being J. H. Driberg;[1] but most officials assumed that their task was not to erase indigenous institutions, but to adapt them; traditional positions of authority, such as chief or clan head, should be incorporated into the colonial power structure, rather than discarded in favour of a corps of petty officials. These views were not the creation of Indirect Rule theory, which only gained currency in East Africa during the 1920s; they were part of the intellectual equipment with which informed British people approached African issues from the First World War onwards.[2]

Tolerance of indigenous institutions did not, however, extend to the manner in which political authority had been exercised in pre-colonial days. British officials might hesitate to by-pass traditional leaders, but they insisted upon conformity with certain standards of public administration which were by then taken for granted in Britain. In a word, these standards may be described as 'bureaucratic'. A fully developed bureaucracy implies that authority relations are impersonal, authority pertaining to the office rather than the office-holder. It also implies that authority is conferred from above rather than conceded from below, and that it is exercised with impartiality. Admittedly, the colonial power did not expect all attributes of bureaucratic authority to be reflected in the conduct of African

---

[1] The extent of Driberg's identification with Lango culture is clearest in his light-hearted autobiographical work, *Engato the Lion Cub*.

[2] H. F. Morris and J. S. Read, *Indirect Rule and the Search for Justice* (Oxford, 1972), pp. 12–15.

chiefs, or at any rate not immediately. Impersonal administration was not anticipated—indeed it was the intimate ties between the traditional leader and his people which recommended him so highly for a place in the colonial hierarchy. But other bureaucratic assumptions could not be dispensed with. A chief was required to discharge his office without regard to kinship obligation or ancient rivalries. He must only use force as a last resort, when judicial and administrative channels had been exhausted. And in the long run the chief's duty to pass orders down from the District Office must undermine his legitimacy in the eyes of his people: his authority would be seen to be imposed from above, as the means whereby an alien power made itself felt at grass-roots level.

It is a commonplace that these external standards were far removed from the indigenous political systems of Africa during the colonial era, and that chiefs with one foot in each system were subject to irreconcilable expectations.[3] The grafting of bureaucratic institutions on to an acephalous society posed especially acute problems. Some continuity with the traditional order could be maintained in terms of personnel, but so far as the functions of political office were concerned, the break was complete. In Lango the gap between the old order and the new, so far from narrowing, in fact widened during the early colonial period. The way in which political offices were filled rapidly departed still further from pre-colonial practice; the chiefs increasingly exploited their offices for personal or factional ends; and the ordinary population became alienated from the administrative structure. This chapter traces these developments up to 1933. In that year native administration was for the first time since 1911 subjected to serious reappraisal. The resulting exposure of abuses, and the reforms brought in to remedy them, form the subject of the final chapter.

The difficulties which the first generation of sub-county chiefs experienced in enforcing their government-conferred authority turned on two distinct problems. The population of every sub-county fell into two categories: the chief's own clansmen—usually the minority—on the one hand, and on the other all the remaining clan sections—usually the vast majority. Each category presented its own problems. So far as his own clansmen were concerned, the chief had to reconcile

---

[3] The classic account of this conflict for Uganda is Fallers's study of Busoga: L. A. Fallers, *Bantu Bureaucracy* (Cambridge, 1956).

their expectations of his role with those of the Government. The contrast between the informal and only occasionally enforced leadership of a clan head and the full executive powers vested in a government chief was, of course, immense. Some chiefs reacted by opting out of their newly ascribed role altogether. Such a man was Anyuru, the chief of Adyegi sub-county, on the Okole river. His father had been killed by a Muganda agent in 1909, and Anyuru had succeeded him as leader of the Omolo clan.[4] After he had served as chief for eight years, he and his headmen were reported to have not 'the slightest influence over their peasantry. They never will until they show them that they are the masters, *not* their drunken companions, in which latter respect, the Jago himself sets the worst example.'[5] By 'influence' the District Officer meant administrative authority in the European sense. Anyuru was simply continuing to live according to the values of clan leadership, with its emphasis on egalitarian conviviality.

In the long run, however, this response was dangerous. The chief who made no attempt to exact labour duties and tax from his clansmen and who made light of his official authority was sure to be dismissed, with the likelihood that the chiefship would be given to the leader of another clan section in the locality. This indeed was what happened to Anyuru; he was removed in 1920, and his sub-county was divided up between Aber and Loro, which at that time were ruled by the leaders of the Jo Ongweo and the Jo Inomo respectively.[6] The lesson was plain: it was better for clansmen to concede in some measure the distasteful demands made upon them by a chief of their own clan, than to have these demands imposed with much less indulgence by a chief from another clan section. There was undoubtedly scope for a certain amount of discrimination along clan lines in the allocation of duties and payments, but a chief who went too far was placing his whole clan section at risk.

Much the more onerous task for the sub-county chief was the assertion of his authority over clan sections other than his own. His appointment was likely to be construed as an assertion of his clan's hegemony over theirs, and to be resented as an arbitrary arrangement imposed from above. For these other clan sections, the moment of truth must often have been the final withdrawal of the Muganda

---

[4] Scott, entry for 31.1.14 in Koli TB (1912–14, part 1). Interview: Koranima Ayena.
[5] Long, entry for 13.10.20, in Atura TB (1920–6).
[6] Tomblings, Report on Lango District for 1920, UNA EPMP/N/121.

agent and his followers from the sub-county. From then on, there could be no doubt that orders were coming from the chief rather than the agent, and at the same time the *boma* was losing the most tangible expression of the Government's power to crush resistance. In the first areas to be freed from supervision by the Baganda in 1913, the result was reported to be a breakdown of chiefly authority, with village and parish chiefs preferring not to meet in *lukiko* for fear of coming to blows. Intensive touring by officials was required in order to stress the continuing, and threatening, presence of the colonial power.[7]

Over the longer term, the extent to which the sub-county chief's authority was tolerable to clan sections other than his own depended on two factors, one negative and the other positive. The negative element was the extent to which the chief had become personally identified with the Baganda. Some association between them was inevitable. Nearly every gazetted chief continued to have the advice of an agent for a year or two after his appointment, and it was some years after that before there were any Langi qualified to step into the shoes of the Baganda clerks at sub-county and county headquarters.[8] But the crucial question was the nature of the chief's own relations with the Baganda. In Iceme the unruffled calm of the early colonial period undoubtedly owed something to the fact that the Baganda had been kept away altogether; agents had been posted to Aboke and Ngai, but not to Iceme itself, with the result that Chief Olong Adilo lacked any connection with the Baganda at all. In Aber, local indignation against the Baganda had been very strong, but Owiny Akulo had been completely identified with the opposition, both in 1895 and in 1910, and he therefore escaped the taint of being associated with their regime.

Other clan leaders were more accommodating towards the Baganda at the start, and they paid the price of forfeiting local support. Around Lira, for example, the most powerful clan section when the Government arrived was the Jo Oki, led by Olet Apar.[9] Olet was consistently co-operative, and in 1912 even warned the District Com-

[7] Scott, Reports on Lango District for Aug. 1913 and for 1913–14, UNA EPMP/Z/228/13; Scott to PCEP, 12.5.13, UNA SMP/2404.

[8] A school for Lango clerks was opened in Lira in 1921. Eden, Report on Eastern Province for 1921, UNA SMP/703K.

[9] Interviews: Isaya Ogwangguji, Elia Olet. Driberg, *The Lango*, pp. 252–3; M. J. Wright, 'The Early Life of Rwot Isaya Ogwangguji, M.B.E.', *Uganda Jl.*, 22 (1958), p. 131. The exact scope of Olet's influence is difficult to determine, partly because of the very great influence which his family has since obtained in the Lango District Administration.

missioner against an impending attack on the agent.[10] Since he was already an old man, Olet gave his son to the Baganda for training. This son, Ogwangguji, was even more closely identified with the Baganda. He accompanied them on missions outside the *boma*, and on one occasion when they were attacked, he 'personally helped to carry the dying Muganda'.[11] As his father's youthful assistant, he displayed a high-handed arrogance towards village chiefs which was only too typical of the conduct of the Baganda.[12] The result of this co-operation was that Olet Apar and Ogwangguji had great difficulty in enforcing their authority as government chiefs. In April 1913 Jervoise reported that Lira was the only part of Lango where there had been frequent village fights during the previous year, which suggests that Olet exercised no authority in *lukiko*.[13] When his son was formally appointed to succeed him in 1915, he fared even worse. In 1917 Ogwangguji narrowly escaped being speared to death after his followers had been ejected from a near-by village, and at the same time an abortive attack was made on the chief's headquarters by men from another part of the sub-county.[14] These disturbances were symptomatic of Ogwangguji's estrangement from the local people, and one may surmise that there would have been much more evidence of this rift if the District headquarters with its detachment of Protectorate police had not been transferred to Lira in 1914.

The positive factor influencing the extent to which a chief's authority was accepted by his subjects at large was the relationship between the sub-county and the pre-colonial sphere of inter-clan dominance. Here again, Aber and Iceme are striking examples of the potential for reasonably uneventful rule. After Owiny Akulo's release from prison, the distribution of power in Aber south of the Toci river was almost exactly in line with pre-colonial divisions: Owiny Akulo ruled in Ocini, and Okelo Abong in Akaka. In each of the two sub-counties, the population was predominantly Jo Arak, and the remaining clan sections were already accustomed to a subordinate position. Not surprisingly, Aber was one of the earliest areas where

[10] Jervoise to PCEP, 4.12.12, UNA SMP/2404.

[11] Scott to PCEP, 12.5.13, UNA SMP/2404.

[12] 'I have impressed on him [Ogwangguji] his extreme youth and the undesirability of his making himself universally hated before the time is ripe for him to become of active assistance to the Government'. Scott, Report on Lango District for Oct. 1913, UNA EPMP/Z/228/13.

[13] Jervoise, Report on Lango District for 1912–13, UNA EPMP/Y/16.

[14] Driberg to Spire, 10.10.17, UNA SMP/4349.

the chiefs were 'able to settle cases and enforce decisions'.[15] In Iceme, the Jo Olwa had on the eve of the colonial period achieved a dominant position over all the clan sections which were to be brought into the sub-county. The Olwa leader, Olong Adilo, was appointed chief, and there was little evidence of resentment against the new authority.[16] In both these cases, much of the chiefs' success was due to the fact that *lukiko* procedure was not entirely unfamiliar. In Aber and Iceme the right of the dominant *rwot* to settle inter-clan disputes in the area had come to be accepted by the time the British arrived, and regular meetings at his village had provided a forum for adjudication.[17] The similarity between the *lukiko* and these traditional gatherings was increased by the Government's policy of upholding clan—as opposed to individual—liability in both civil and petty criminal proceedings.[18] It would seem that the habit of dependence was sufficiently ingrained to prevent overt resistance to the new demands of colonial government.

As we saw in Chapter 3, however, this degree of inter-clan authority was the exception rather than the rule in Lango at the beginning of the twentieth century. Elsewhere judicial authority tended to be less developed; inter-clan dominance was more restricted to the cattle-raid and the battle field, and its territorial range was smaller. The implications of this were evident in the administrative arrangements made in central Lango, to the east of Lira. In both Bar and Aloi, the dominant clan section was the Jo Oki me Abura. They had lived in the area for two generations, and during the 1870s their *rwot*, Ogwal Abura, had been an important regional leader. By the time the Government arrived, all that remained of this eminence was the lead taken in cattle-raiding by Ogwal's son, Oki, in the Bar area, and by Ocato, Oki's clan brother, in Aloi. Both men were appointed chiefs, but Driberg's intention in 1916 was that the clan connections should be turned to advantage and the two areas placed under Oki, who had shown himself 'able and strong in dealing with his own men'.[19] When this plan was implemented in 1920, however, the new sub-county was

---

[15] Jervoise, Report on Lango District for March 1913, UNA EPMP/Z/1329/13.

[16] The only apparent resentment came from the Jo Arak me Ongoda. Entries for 1914–15 at Iceme, in Koli TB (1913–19, part 2).

[17] See above, pp. 77, 81 n.

[18] This policy is evident from tour book entries in other parts of Lango; Tongue, entry for 10.5.20, and Tomblings, entry for 2.2.21, in Maruzi TB (1919–26, part 1); Lawson, entry for 2.8.22 in Moroto TB (1918–26).

[19] Driberg, entry for 3.2.16, in Eruti TB (1915–21). Interviews: Luka Abura, Erieza Oyaka, Tito Omara.

found to be unwieldy, and after two years it was split into two again.[20]

The establishment of chiefly authority was most difficult in south-eastern Lango, where every circumstance conspired against it; inter-clan dominance was least strong, and the impact of the Baganda and Banyara had been most traumatic. Conditions were worst in Dokolo, whither many of the Langi expelled from east of the Abalang river had migrated. The Kyoga Expedition of 1907 had done most damage there, and—the crowning insult—discharged agents and their fol-lowers were allowed to settle.[21] Here, there was almost no basis for widespread co-operation with the Government. Opige, the official choice for chief, had thrown in his lot with the Baganda, and for four years was 'educated' by the local agent. When the agent was removed in 1913, Opige was soon in trouble. He was subjected to threats by his people,[22] and he had great difficulty in recruiting reliable askaris to handle his five rifles. Within a few months the askaris had precipitated a clash in which a villager was killed, and in July 1914 Opige himself was dismissed because he had used his askaris to carry out raids to the north and to oppress the people of Dokolo itself.[23]

Opige's case illustrates an important general feature of chiefly rule in its early years. Opige was dismissed by the District officials because in their eyes he had grossly exceeded his powers. Authoritarian rule of this kind was almost inevitable in a stateless society, where a chief was required to assert authority with no indigenous models to guide him. He had constantly to demonstrate to his people that he had the force of the administration behind him and that he must be obeyed.[24] He saw his various statutory powers as being all of a piece, and interpreted contradiction of any one of them as a challenge to his personal authority. When minor offences were committed by his sub-jects, the chief tended to lack a sense of proportion and to punish them much too severely. In Lango there were cases of men being

[20] Long, entries for 2.6.20 and 14.2.21, in Eruti TB (1919–26); entry for 15.3.22, in Eruti TB (1920–25).

[21] Twenty-three Baganda were allowed to settle in Dokolo in 1915. Driberg, entry for 7.8.15, in Dokolo TB (1913–26, part 1).

[22] Scott, Report on Lango District for Sept. 1913, UNA EPMP/Z/228/13.

[23] Driberg and Cox, entries for 25.7.14, in Dokolo TB (1913–26, part 1). In using his askaris in this way, Opige, in the words of his son, 'wanted to act as the Baganda had done'. Interview: Ekoc Opige.

[24] For a succinct discussion of this point, see J. A. Barnes, 'Indigenous Politics and Colonial Administration with special reference to Australia', *Comparative Studies in Society and History*, 2 (1960), pp. 133–49.

sentenced to forty-eight lashes or beaten to death, when a small fine would have been more appropriate.[25] Arum, the county chief of Maruzi, was criticized in 1920 for being 'apt to take anything that happens contrary to Standing Orders as a personal affront', and for adopting 'the attitude rather of the Eastern potentate towards his "subjects" '.[26]

This pattern of chiefly rule posed a major difficulty for the European officials in charge of Lango. They well knew that in a situation where administrative authority was so tender a growth, every official encouragement was needed for the chief who was prepared to exercise it in the face of local opposition.[27] E. L. Scott, who acted as District Commissioner in 1913, took the view that official reprimands must be delivered in private, since public evidence of disagreement with Europeans was 'calculated to endanger even the life of a Lango chief who stands alone as the symbol of discipline and authority in the midst of a people who care for neither of these things'.[28] Officials also realized that in some measure the exceeding of statutory powers on the part of the chief was inevitable. Commenting on the situation in Dokolo in 1913, Scott reported, 'Opigi and his headmen must be supported at almost all costs at this present stage, or they will be unable to control their people. No decision by them should be reversed, if possible, even at the risk of occasional injustice. A little oppression even need not be a bad thing.'[29] At the same time, as Opige's case showed, there came a stage when abuse of authority could be tolerated no longer, when arbitrary rule threatened to compromise the standing of the colonial government. The only course then open to officials was to dismiss the chief.

In the period up to 1919, a great many changes had to be made in sub-county appointments. Dismissal was resorted to not only when, as with Opige, chiefs grossly overstepped the limits of abuse, but also when, like Anyuru of Adyegi, they opted out of their role in order to retain the full esteem of their own clansmen. Of the thirty-seven sub-county chiefs appointed in 1912, only nine were still on the payroll in 1919. One had died in office, fourteen had resigned or retired; in many

[25] Driberg, entry for 7.9.17, in Koli TB (1913–19); Lawson, entry for 4.6.22, in Koli & Atura TB (1919–26).

[26] Tomblings, Report on Lango District for 1920, UNA EPMP/N/121.

[27] See for example: Driberg to PCEP, 10.10.14, UNA SMP/4214.

[28] Scott, Report on Lango District for Sept. 1913, UNA EPMP/Z/228/13.

[29] Scott, entry for 10.9.13, in Dokolo TB (1913–26, part 1).

cases this was due to old age or ill health, but some chiefs certainly resigned under pressure, either in order to make way for a more suitable choice, or so that their sub-counties could be merged to form larger units. Thirteen chiefs were actually dismissed between 1914 and 1919. When allowance is also made for comparable changes in chiefdoms which had been set up since 1912, and for promotions to county chiefships, the total replacements which had to be found for sub-county chiefs between 1913 and 1919 amounted to thirty.[30] So far as the emerging political system of colonial Lango was concerned, a great deal depended on the way in which these second appointments were made.

In choosing successors to displaced sub-county chiefs, officials did not apparently work according to any clearly defined objectives. In most cases however, the choice was resolved in one of two ways. In the first place, wherever possible a close agnatic kinsman of the displaced chief was chosen, preferably a son. The hereditary principle was not only integral to clan leadership, which had been taken as the guide-line in most initial appointments to sub-counties. It also corresponded to British conceptions of how in general African peoples were, or ought to be, ruled. Perhaps unconsciously, social and political stability was seen to be tied up with the predictable continuity of hereditary succession. British respect for the hereditary principle is particularly evident in the attitude taken to Odora's family. When Odora in 1916 allowed his adopted son, Elia Adupa, to become a catechist in Acholi, he was told that this was not a suitable occupation for a county chief's son; Adupa's rightful place was held to be at his father's side, and a few months later the District Commissioner gave him a seat in the county *lukiko*,—and this despite Odora's complete lack of any 'traditional' claim to rule in Kwania county.[31]

Many of the first sub-county chiefs were therefore succeeded by their sons. Among the earliest sub-counties where this happened were Aboke and Cawente in 1917, followed by Agwata and Aduku in 1918. Officials were prepared to stick to the hereditary principle even when this entailed the appointment of a very young man. When Akaki of Akokoro retired in 1916, a son in his twenties named Adoko was

---

[30] These figures are abstracted from the official *Gazette*, the Tour Books, and official correspondence.

[31] Driberg, entry for 14.3.16, and Hannington, entry for 7.8.16, in Kwania TB (1913–19). In 1926 Adupa was appointed sub-county chief of Aduku.

appointed, the Government having rejected as unsuitable two candidates previously suggested by Akaki.[32] No doubt from the Government's point of view, the experience which Adoko had had as an askari under Odora and Arum was an asset, but it is very likely that some of the tension in Akokoro during the next few years[33] was due to resentment against a mere stripling, who had been absent from home for several years before his appointment. The Akokoro example emphasizes an important limitation which applied in some measure to all cases of hereditary succession. A son might succeed his father, but it was the officials and not the clan elders who made the choice; given a wide field, the two were unlikely to come to the same decision. Whether or not the hereditary principle was observed, the appointment of a new chief had more the character of a decision imposed from above than a free popular choice.

The second response which officials made to sub-county vacancies was to appoint a prominent figure from a different clan. This happened most frequently in those sub-counties which lacked a single dominant clan section, and above all in south-eastern Lango, where the number of clan leaders to choose from tended to be bewildering. In Amac, for example, the success of Okori Alima in getting the colonial authorities to bolster his clan's shaky position[34] did not survive his tenure of office. When he was dismissed in 1919, he was succeeded instead by a man of the Jo Palamyek.[35] In Dokolo sub-county two changes were made in the space of five years. The discredited Opige was succeeded in 1914 by Owiny Aleka, who was a nephew of Okwanga, Opige's main rival on the eve of the colonial period; and when Owiny Aleka was himself promoted in 1918, he was replaced—much to his own annoyance—by a son of the recently deceased leader of yet another clan section.[36]

Hereditary succession and the selection of alternative clan leaders together accounted for the vast majority of second appointments to sub-counties during the years up to 1919. Both approaches took some account of traditional concepts of legitimacy. But a handful of appointments departed radically from such concepts, and it was these which set the tone for recruitment to office during the 1920s and

[32] Driberg, entry for 7.3.16, in Maruzi TB (1912–19). Interview: Yakobo Adoko.
[33] Long, entry for 14.8.20, in Maruzi TB (1919–26).
[34] See above, pp. 155–6
[35] *Gazette*, 31 Oct. 1919. Interview: Yeromia Otim.
[36] Interviews: Tomasi Ojuka, Yeromia Otim, Silvesto Otim. Cator, entry for 29.10.18, in Dokolo TB (1913–26, part 1).

1930s. When a sub-county chief was promoted to county chief, his successor tended to be a man with little claim to the sub-county chiefship except a close association with his immediate predecessor. In four out of the six counties erected between 1913 and 1918, county chiefs were able to take office with a secure hold over the sub-counties from which they had been promoted. It seems that the Government consulted them about the choice of their successors, and they responded by nominating their own followers. At Ibuje, Arum, after combining the posts of sub-county and county chief for four years, secured in 1917 the appointment of an unimportant village elder who had been under his 'personal tutelage' before promotion.[37] In Aber and Iceme, Owiny Akulo and Olong Adilo were both succeeded by close kin.[38] The most remarkable instance of a personal dependant taking over was at Lira, vacated in 1918 by Ogwangguji's appointment as county chief of Erute. Instead of being succeeded by one of his many brothers and cousins, Ogwangguji chose an askari called Ojuka. This man had been born near Lake Kwania, had taken service with the Baganda, been brought to the *boma* at Bar, and had then escaped unharmed when six Baganda were killed there in 1911; he had then been befriended by Ogwangguji and given employment as askari and interpreter; at the time of his appointment, he had lived in Lira for no more than seven years.[39]

The significance of this exercise of personal patronage by county chiefs was that during the next ten years, from being a rare occurrence, it became a fairly widespread basis for appointments to all official positions below county level. The somewhat limited administrative function of the county chiefs was compensated for by their rise to a position of real influence, from which they were able to manipulate both their subordinates and the European administrative staff.

Initially District Officers viewed with some suspicion attempts by county chiefs to install their own nominees in junior positions. The early administrators set considerable store by the local standing of candidates for chiefships. They were accordingly quite prepared to reject the county chief's candidate if he seemed to be a choice imposed from outside. This happened at Aboke in 1917,[40] Kidilande in 1920[41]

---

[37] Entries for 24.11.16 and 13.7.17, in Maruzi TB (1912–19). Interview: Yakobo Gaci.   [38] For a fuller discussion of these two cases, see below, pp. 200–2.
[39] Interviews: Tomasi Ojuka, Isaya Ogwangguji.
[40] Driberg, entry for 5.9.17 in Koli TB (1913–19, part 2).
[41] Tongue, entry for 12.5.20 in Maruzi TB (1919–26, part 1).

and Agwata in 1922.[42] As the 1920s wore on, however, officials participated less and less in the selection of chiefs below county level. Increasingly the choice was left either to the county chief personally,[43] or to his *lukiko*[44]—which came to much the same thing.

Up to a point, District Officers were a willing party to the concentration of political patronage in the hands of the county chiefs. During the 1920s the range of administrative concerns grew steadily; as pacification gave way to 'improvement', the Government began to step up expenditure on medical, veterinary, and agricultural services.[45] Administrators were obliged to spend more time in their offices at District headquarters. Touring became more infrequent and more hurried, with the result that less time was devoted to assessing the political atmosphere and the standing of prominent individuals in each sub-county. Officials were therefore less qualified to make decisions on chiefly appointments.

Much more significant, though, was the appropriation of missionary education by the county chiefs and their clients. When the first sub-county appointments were made in 1912, literacy was not an issue, since contact between the Langi and the missionaries had by then occurred only on a superficial level. But by the mid-1920s schooling had become available to the Langi, and it was now regarded by the District authorities as an important qualification for office, in view of the growing complexity of native administration. The fact that most of the men so qualified were dependants or close relatives of the older chiefs was a crucial element in the continuity of chiefly personnel during the inter-war period. In order to understand why this was so, some attention must be given to the circumstances in which Christianity entered Lango.

The pattern of early evangelization in Lango was broadly similar to the penetration of the colonial power, in that two thrusts were made, one from the west and the other from the south-east. They were made concurrently, and both were under the auspices of the Church Missionary Society (C.M.S.), the dominant Protestant interest in

[42] Tomblings, entry for 16.3.22 in Dokolo & Moroto TB (1918–26). Interview: Israel Alele.

[43] This tour book entry at Ibuje for 13.12.25 is typical: 'Rwot to find successor, recommends Jemusi, W.M. [parish chief] of Kidilande.' Maruzi TB (1919–26, part 2).

[44] Tongue, Report on Lango District for Aug. 1920, UNA EPMP/N/39/20.

[45] Pratt, 'Administration and Politics in Uganda', in Harlow and Chilver, op. cit., II, pp. 484–6.

Uganda. But the two campaigns were conducted with different tactics, different personnel, and varying degrees of success. In the south-east, Baganda catechists were sent in the wake of Baganda agents, and had reached Dokolo by 1910. At first they were more concerned to minister to their fellow countrymen than to make converts among the Langi. The pioneer catechists did not venture out into the villages, and any Langi wanting instruction had to attend at the agent's post and be taught in Luganda. Baptism would appear to have been a token of co-operation with the hated Baganda, and few Lango converts were made at this early stage.[46]

In western Lango, the central intermediary in early missionary contact, as in early government contact, was Odora of Kungu. During his early visits to Hoima in 1904 and 1905 he had been introduced to the local missionaries by the *omukama* of Bunyoro, who was a keen convert. It is plain that Odora's main interest at this stage was not in Christianity, but in military help against his enemies. Nevertheless he agreed to a suggestion by the *omukama* and the Revd. Arthur Fisher that catechists should be sent to Kungu, and early in 1906 two Banyoro arrived.[47] They were soon disillusioned, probably by Odora's lack of interest in anything except reading and writing,[48] and returned to Bunyoro within a year. Odora, however, continued to value the services of catechists, and Fisher continued to send them.[49] When Odora moved to Ibuje in 1909, a Munyoro catechist came with him,[50] and more teachers followed him to Aduku, where in 1913 Odora was at last baptized.[51] By that time there were ten 'out-stations' of the CMS in western Lango, staffed by Banyoro and Acholi catechists, many of whom had been sent from Aduku to other sub-county *bomas*.[52] A year after Odora's baptism, Arum of Maruzi followed

[46] Kitching to CMS H.Q., 22.12.11, CMS Archives G3/A7/0/1911(b); Jervoise, Report on Lango District for 1912–13, UNA EPMP/Y/16. Interviews: Tomasi Ojuka, Erieza Olwol.

[47] Jervoise to Leakey, 4.2.06, UNA A12/7.

[48] Ibid.

[49] Fisher to Manley, 1.11.13, copy in the Fisher Papers, CMS Archives Interview: Zakalia Isengeze.

[50] This was Daudi Bitatule, the first Munyoro to be baptized in Hoima (in 1900). M. M. L. Pirouet, 'The Expansion of the Church of Uganda (N.A.C.) from Buganda into Northern and Western Uganda between 1891 and 1914', unpublished Ph.D. thesis, University of East Africa, 1968, p. 376; J. G. Huddle, 'The Life of Yakobo Adoko of Lango District', *Uganda Jl.*, 21 (1957), p. 186.

[51] Scott, entry for 24.11.13, in Kwania TB (1913–19); R. M. Fisher, 'The Awakening of a Nile Tribe', *Church Missionary Gleaner*, 41 (June 1914), p. 91.

[52] Fisher to Manley, 3.9.13, CMS Archives G3/A7/0/1913 (b).

his example, and from then on the number of converts rapidly increased.[53]

This responsiveness to local conditions, coupled with reliance on African personnel, was typical of the CMS evangelization of Uganda as a whole. It sprang from the zeal displayed by the Baganda in proselytizing outside their own country, and from a readiness on the part of the European missionaries to give the Baganda—and other African evangelists—their head.[54] But there is an added twist to the Lango story. In most new mission fields in Uganda, pioneer African catechists were quickly followed by a handful of Europeans, to supervise their work and to staff institutions such as schools and hospitals. In Lango there was a time-lag of twenty years: not until 1926 was Protestant missionary work directed from within the District.[55] In the case of the Roman Catholics, whose impact before the Second World War was small compared with that of the Protestants, the delay was still greater: only in 1930 did the Verona Fathers establish a mission station in Lango. Until 1926 European supervision by the CMS was restricted to occasional safaris from Gulu, and from Ngora in Teso. Finance and training facilities for catechists were limited, so that in 1925 the number of catechists was still modest.[56] The limited scale of missionary activity and the absence of Europeans gave the chiefs great scope for controlling the evangelizing process. Catechists were in practice dependent on the good offices of the chiefs, and if they had wanted more independence they could hardly have achieved it without European support on the spot.

In the event, the deployment of catechists was controlled by the chiefs from the beginning. The prior agreement of the chief was normally secured before a catechist was posted to his area. The chief's support was enlisted most often by one of his peers, and here Odora played an important role, both by his own example and by personal contact with chiefs like Omara of Loro and Ogwangguji of Lira.[57]

[53] R. M. Fisher, op. cit., p. 91; H. T. Wright, 'Pioneer Work in Mid-Africa', *Awake*, 25 (May 1915), p. 51.

[54] The authoritative account is Pirouet, op. cit.

[55] Early in 1910 W. G. Innes opened a mission station at Kalaki in Kumam country, but he died of blackwater fever later that year and was not replaced. Wright to Spire, 30.9.10, UNA SMP/178.

[56] Between 1925 and 1926, however, the number of catechists working in Lango increased dramatically from thirty to sixty. Notes by T. L. Lawrence in *Church Missionary Outlook*, 53 (Apr. 1926), p. 81.

[57] Interviews: Yosia Omara, Isaya Ogwangguji.

Once in residence, the catechist was under the chief's orders. The two of them co-operated to their mutual advantage, and to the confusion of those Langi who were less familiar with the distinction between Church and State. The catechist lived at the *boma*, taught and worshipped there, and beat the *boma*-drum to summon the faithful.[58] In some cases the catechumens themselves were encouraged to settle round the *boma*.[59] Catechists and their pupils tended to be exempt from labour services,[60] while the labour service of the non-Christian community was drawn on for building chapels and schools.[61]

The District administration disapproved of these practices on the grounds that a rigid distinction ought to be maintained between Government and missions, and from 1913 onwards rules were formulated to this effect. These rules went considerably further than administrative practice elsewhere in Uganda. Chiefs were forbidden to make public labour available to catechists and to excuse 'readers' from labour calls, and the catechist was forbidden to use the chief's headquarters for any religious purpose.[62] Between 1913 and 1918 the rules were rigorously enforced, especially by Driberg, who combined strident secularism with a romantic attachment to 'the savage as he really is'.[63] Driberg actively discouraged chiefs from taking Christian instruction,[64] and he burnt down mission buildings if they were constructed too close to a chief's headquarters.[65] His behaviour provoked a high-level protest from the Bishop of Uganda in 1917.[66]

After Driberg's departure from Lango in 1918 the restrictions on catechists, though still on the rule book, were not enforced to the same extent. The association between chiefs and Protestant evangelists remained close. In Kwania county under Odora, the exemption of

---

[58] Scott, entry for 19.10.13, in Dokolo TB (1913–26, part 1); Driberg, entry for 6.2.15, in Kwania TB (1913–19).
[59] Driberg, entry for 14.3.16, and Hannington, entry for 7.8.16, in Kwania TB (1913–19).   [60] Hannington, entry for 7.8.16, in Kwania TB (1913–19).
[61] Driberg, entry for 6.12.15, in Kwania TB (1913–19); Driberg, entry for 15.4.18, in Koli TB (1913–19, part 1).
[62] Fisher to Millar, 18.6.13, copy in Fisher Papers, CMS Archives; Hannington, Baraza Instructions, 6.4.16, and Driberg, Baraza Instructions, 28.3.17, ADA LDMP/40/15; Standing Orders, 1920, entered into every current Tour Book.
[63] *The Savage as He really is*, title of book by Driberg (London, 1929).
[64] Wright to CMS H.Q., 21.11.19, copy in Fisher Papers, CMS Archives. Interviews: Isaya Ogwangguji, Isaya Ajoba, Peter Enin.
[65] Driberg, entry for 14.3.16, in Kwania TB (1913–19), and entry for 15.4.18, in Koli TB (1913–19, part 1).
[66] Willis to Jackson, 21.5.17, UNA SMP/4844, cited in F. Carter, 'Education in Uganda, 1894–1945', unpublished Ph.D. thesis, London University, 1967, pp. 86–7.

'readers' from all labour services became standard form.[67] Both in
Kwania and elsewhere, sub-county chiefs often connived at enforced
school attendance.[68] In the context of chiefly control of education,
two aspects of this continuing association between chiefs and catechists were important.

The first aspect was the use of the chief's household as an educational centre. This practice was started by Daudi Odora, who derived
it from Bunyoro. In the interlacustrine kingdoms, great chiefs habi-
tually maintained large households to which youths were sent for
training, either with a view to obtaining a position in the chief's gift,
or simply as a means of being educated in etiquette and the ways of
the world.[69] Odora himself was entertained many times at the court
of the *omukama* of Bunyoro, who had incorporated Christian
teaching into the regime of his household. Partly from delusions of
grandeur—Odora is said to have aspired to be 'Kabaka' of Lango[70]—
and partly because of its value as a lever of patronage, Odora built up
a household on these lines within a few years of his move to Aduku in
1911. He maintained in his compound a large number of 'boys',
known as *ogaragara*, from the Lunyoro word for a chief's attendants,
abagaragara. The boys received food and clothing in return for performing the many domestic chores needed to maintain Odora in the
dignity which he felt befitted a great chief. Some of the boys were
close kinsmen of Odora himself; a few came from afar; the majority
appear to have come from villages in Aduku sub-county. It is not
clear what proportion of the *ogaragara* attended any form of instruction. But a significant number were catechumens who picked up the
rudiments of literacy from the Acholi and Banyoro teachers in
Aduku, and it was these *ogaragara* who after two or three years'
service could look forward to posts as askaris, clerks, and village
chiefs.[71]

On a less grandiose scale, Odora's household was emulated by
other county chiefs in western Lango during the 1920s. Arum of Ibuje
was quick to follow his example, in this as in so many other matters.

[67] Interviews: Yakobo Obia, Pilipo Oruro, Matayo Ojok.
[68] Interviews: Enoci Ekak, Isaka Ojaba, Ibrahim Lodo, Barikia Opie, Ezekeri
Olwa, Yokana Engola, Yeromia Otim.
[69] L. Mair, *Primitive Government* (Harmondsworth, 1962), pp. 190–6; J. Beattie,
The Nyoro State (Oxford, 1971), pp. 124–8, 134–5.
[70] Interviews: Peter Enin, Reuben Ogwal. Huddle, op. cit., p. 186.
[71] Interviews: Peter Enin, Elia Adupa, Reuben Ogwal. Enin estimates that at
one stage Odora maintained around sixty *ogaragara*.

He recruited 'boys' for service at his headquarters from all over Maruzi county during his official safaris, and as early as 1926 two of them had secured chiefly appointments.[72] A comparable household was maintained by Olong Adilo, chief of Kole county.[73] Whether or not the catechist was actually a member of the chief's household hardly mattered when so many of his pupils were recruited by the chief and were lodged in his compound.

However, the amount of education which catechists could provide in Lango was very limited. Catechumens were expected to be able to write their own names, and some certainly took advantage of the better-qualified catechists to learn how to read as well. In addition to the catechists, missionaries sponsored a large number of African school teachers. By 1926 there was a total of ninety-one Protestant and seventy-four Roman Catholic bush schools (known as 'sub-grade' schools) in the whole of Lango District (i.e. including the Kumam area)[74]—figures which indicate that some of the teachers taught at schools away from chiefs' headquarters. But the most that these schools aspired to teach was basic literacy in the vernacular. No schooling beyond that was to be had within the District until 1933 when the CMS opened its Central School at Boroboro, near Lira. In the meantime the only educational openings lay outside Lango.

This restriction provided the county chiefs with their second means of control over educational recruitment. Prospective pupils had to enrol at the CMS High Schools at Masindi, Ngora, or—the usual choice—Gulu. Only a tiny number could contemplate such a possibility, and they were mostly limited to the sons and protégés of county chiefs. This was partly because of the schools' declared preference for chiefs' sons. Gulu High School, for example, was founded in 1913 by the District Commissioner and the senior local missionary with chiefs' sons in mind, and when the School's catchment area was extended to Lango in 1914 it was the chiefs who were canvassed. The élitist composition of the schools was promoted by the high fees, and perhaps too by the daunting prospect of residence among foreigners.[75] County

[72] Anderea Ojuka was parish chief of Tarogali, and Jesmusi Bura sub-county chief of Ibuje. Interviews: Andrea Ogwang, Yakobo Gaci, Yakobo Oluma, Eria Olet.   [73] Interview: Paulo Oyet.   [74] *Blue Book* for 1926.

[75] For Gulu High School, see T. Watson, 'A History of Church Missionary Society High Schools in Uganda, 1900–24', unpublished Ph.D. thesis, University of East Africa, 1968, pp. 456–64. During the 1920s fees at the CMS High School at Ngora in Teso were running at sixty shilling p.a. J. Vincent, 'Colonial Chiefs and the Making of Class: a Case Study from Teso, Eastern Uganda', *Africa*, 47 (1977), p. 151.

chiefs, on the other hand, could afford to pay school fees several times over, while sponsored official visits to neighbouring districts[76] helped to overcome any doubts they may have entertained about the safety of their sons among the Acholi or Banyoro. The first Lango to attend Gulu High School was Daudi Odora's adopted son, Elia Adupa, who was there from 1914 to 1916.[77] Odora sent several other close kinsmen to school in Gulu and Masindi, as well as at least six former *ogaragara* who were not related to him.[78] His example was followed by chiefs Ogwangguji, Owiny Akulo, and Olong Adilo, each of whom had several sons or close kinsmen at Gulu High School between 1915 and 1925.[79] At that time it was rare for anyone not connected with a county chief to attend school outside Lango.[80]

Once having spent several years at school outside Lango, the protégés of county chiefs soon entered government service, and tended to be quickly promoted to sub-county level. A few served an apprenticeship as clerks[81] or interpreters,[82] but most began their careers as village and parish chiefs in their patrons' home areas. In this way a county chief could build up a pool of young men who could be put forward to fill sub-county vacancies anywhere in the county. By 1928 at least five High School graduates had become sub-county chiefs, and three of these were no more than thirty years old.[83] Among European officials there was some prejudice against 'mission boys'; the 'jumped up clerk'[84] seldom won the personal respect which officials showed towards some of the older untrained chiefs, but from an administrative point of view the advantages of appointing an educated man were compelling.

The success of the county chiefs in having their own nominees accepted was paralleled by their ability to get objectionable chiefs dismissed. This was an important weapon, since on the one hand a personal nominee might take a more independent stand once in office, while on the other hand the county chief might wish to remove a man

[76] E.g. Jervoise, Report on Eastern Province for April 1919, UNA SMP/1929H.
[77] Watson, op. cit., p. 461. Interview: Elia Adupa.
[78] Interviews: Elia Adupa, Peter Enin.
[79] Interviews: Misaki Oki, Elia Olet, Mohammed Okec, Nasan Engola.
[80] Exceptions were: Pilipo Oruro (parish chief's son), Reuben Ogwal and Zedekia Angulo (sub-county chief's son). Interviews: Pilipo Oruro, Reuben Ogwal, Misaki Oki.
[81] Elia Adupa and Enoci Igwel (a protégé of Owiny Akulo's) were examples of this.   [82] Elia Olet, cousin of Ogwangguji, was an example of this.
[83] The three were: Elia Adupa of Aduku, Kosia Ato of Aber, and Misaki Oki of Ngai.   [84] Rubie, entry for 22.4.32, in Moroto TB (1926–33).

who had been appointed against his wishes in the first place. Here again government policy became more accommodating with the years. It was not originally intended that county chiefs should be able to remove their subordinates at all. When Olong Adilo attempted to do so shortly after his promotion in 1917, he was roundly told that 'the making and breaking of s/chs is not in his hands and that the present s/chs will certainly not be broken just because he does not like their relations or their faces, and that as County Chief it is his duty to work with the sub/chs appointed by the government.'[85] Blatant attempts by county chiefs to get personal *bêtes-noires* removed continued to be resisted by officials, but in practice an astute chief could exploit his position as administrative overseer of the county. Unfavourable reports on a sub-county chief, combined with more frequent access to officials, could achieve the desired effect. The most successful exponent of this technique appears to have been Arum of Maruzi. In the space of six years between 1919 and 1925 he had three sub-county chiefs dismissed from Ibuje, the first two being former protégés and the last apparently a government nominee from outside; in the first instance Arum chose to interpret a temporary suspension as a definite dismissal and harried the sub-county chief out of the county altogether.[86] In a few cases the objectionable chief was transferred to another county rather than dismissed, but from the county chief's point of view, the effect was the same; in 1926 and 1927 the incumbents at Aboke and Dokolo were disposed of in this way.[87]

In addition to dismissals and transfers induced by the county chiefs, many sub-county chiefs were dismissed on the initiative of District Officers for failure in their official duties. The cumulative result of this combination of pressures was a fairly high turn-over of sub-county chiefs. The average duration of a sub-county chief's term of office was in the order of three or four years. The contrast with the county chiefs could hardly have been greater. The majority of the first county chiefs remained in office for a very long time: Odora and Olong Adilo for fourteen years, Arum for seventeen, Owiny Akulo for twenty-two, and Ogwangguji for a remarkable thirty-nine years. This staying power can partly be explained by the fact that in each county the ablest man had been chosen, and by and large the first county chiefs

[85] Driberg, entry for 7.9.17, in Koli TB (1913–19).
[86] Cator, entry for 22.5.19, in Maruzi TB (1912–19); entries for 6.9.24 and 13.12.25, in Maruzi TB (1919–26). Interview: Yakobo Gaci.
[87] Iwai of Aboke was transferred to Adwari in 1926, and Ogwal Ajungu of Dokolo to Aduku in 1927.

were very able men indeed. But the disparity in tenure was also due to the nature of the offices involved. It was the sub-county chief, rather than his superior, who had direct responsibility for imposing government demands on a diffident or resentful peasantry; slackness or partiality was therefore more easily detected in his conduct. And so, whereas it was relatively easy for the county chief to have his subordinate dismissed, it was extremely difficult for a sub-county chief to discredit his superior in the eyes of the Government.

As a result of their long survival in office, their privileged access to educational opportunities, and the discretion allowed them by officials, it was possible for the county chiefs to establish themselves as the fount of patronage, from which chiefships were dispensed to cliques of their own placemen. By 1933, out of thirty-six Lango sub-county chiefs,[88] at least eleven were personal nominees of the county chiefs, while many others were amenable to influence and pressure from above. The patronage of the county chiefs was most marked in four out of the seven counties,[89]—Atura, Kole, Erute, and Maruzi. A brief account of the first two may serve to illustrate the analysis so far.

Atura county, to which Owiny Akulo was appointed in 1917, consisted of Acaba, Ngai, and Loro, besides Owiny's home area of Aber. As the unquestioned leader of the Jo Arak, the traditionally dominant clan on the lower Toci, Owiny's influence in Aber was considerable, and despite the siting of county headquarters some ten miles away at Loro, Owiny kept a close grip on affairs there. For the first nine years, Aber sub-county was ruled by a nominee of Owiny's called Amolli. He was the leader of the Jo Ongweo, which had acknowledged the dominance of the Jo Arak since the days of Odongo Aja, and his mother came from the Jo Arak.[90] During Amolli's tenure of office, Owiny sent to Gulu High School two of his own sons, one adopted son, one of Odongo Aja's sons, and a boy from the junior lineage (Jo Ocola) of the Jo Arak. By the time that Owiny had turned against Amolli and secured his dismissal in 1926, four of these young kinsmen already held village or parish chiefships in Aber subcounty.[91] Amolli was completely overshadowed by the eldest of them,

---

[88] This leaves out of account the ten Kumam and two Bantu sub-counties also included in Lango District.

[89] Seven, not counting Kyoga county, which was predominantly Bantu, and the two Kumam counties of Kalaki and Kaberamaido.

[90] Interview: Leoben Okodi.

[91] Atura TB (1920–6), *passim*. Interviews: Leoben Okodi, Misaki Oki, Kosia Ato, Matayo Acut.

Enoci Igwel, who acted as his *katikiro* (deputy chief).[92] Igwel succeeded Amolli as chief, and when a District Officer dismissed him in 1928, another of the High School 'boys', Kosia Ato, stepped into his shoes, to be followed by yet another, so that from 1926 until 1940 Aber was ruled continuously by Owiny's closest clan associates.[93] In the county at large, Owiny's influence was based partly on existing clan alliances, and partly on the appointment of his own nominees. Until 1935 Loro was ruled by the son of Okulo Cagara, who had been an ally in battle of Odongo Aja.[94] In Ngai the original chief served until 1927, when he was succeeded first by one of Owiny Akulo's High School protégés, and then by another.[95] From Owiny's point of view, the position was least satisfactory in Acaba where Apil, leader of a clan traditionally antagonistic to the Jo Arak, was chief from 1918 to 1936. Yet the fact that Apil's son was a school-friend of Owiny's own children at Gulu and was then appointed to a parish chiefship in Aber, would suggest that the rift between the two clans had been patched up by the late 1920s.[96]

The neighbouring Kole county, which was created at the same time as Atura, comprised Iceme, Aboke, Ayer, and Bala. Olong Adilo of Iceme built up a county dominance comparable to Owiny Akulo's, though he was slower to take advantage of educational openings. In Iceme itself, Olong was for several years frustrated by the Government's refusal to dismiss chief Odyek Arima. Odyek was Along's *okeo* (sister's son); he had been brought up as an orphan in Olong's own household, and he was Olong's personal choice in 1917, yet almost immediately the two men fell out.[97] The ill-feeling between Odyek Arima and Olong's clan, the Jo Olwa, accumulated until Odyek could no longer arrest debtors for fear of being assaulted; it was at that stage that officials decided in 1927 that Odyek should be removed.[98] His successor, Yokonia Ogwal, though not a member of the Jo Olwa, was nevertheless Olong's nominee. He came from neighbouring Alito,

[92] Peyton, entry for 21.8.21, in Atura TB (1920–6).

[93] A District Officer remarked of Aber in 1932: 'This is Owiny's own stamping ground, Kosia is a son, Leobeni Okodi (katikiro) is also of the family and so is anyone of any importance.' Rubie, entry for 2.9.32, in Atura TB (1926–33).

[94] Interview: Yosia Omara.

[95] Misaki Oki (adopted son) from 1927 to 1932; Kosia Ato (son) from 1932 to 1935.

[96] Interview: Misaki Oki. Rankin, entry for 28.1.28, in Atura TB (1926–33).

[97] Driberg, entry for 3.9.17, in Koli TB (1913–19, part 2). Interviews: Nasan Engola, Anna Awor, Ezekeri Olwa.

[98] Mitchell, entry for 20.6.27, in Koli TB (1926–33).

which had just been added to Kole county; his father had been an ally of the Jo Olwa against the Acholi, and the two clans had close marriage links.[99] By 1930 Olong Adilo's control over Iceme sub-county was completely restored, two of the three parishes and three of the seven villages being in Jo Olwa hands.[100] Outside Iceme, Olong also took time to assert his control. In Aboke, where county head-quarters was situated, the dominant clan section had been enemies of the Jo Olwa before the Government arrived, and for nine years Olong had to tolerate a member of this clan as sub-county chief; not until 1926 was he replaced by the brother of one of Olong's wives.[101] In the next year one of Olong's closest clan associates, Olwa Akoli, who had worked as a police instructor in Lira for several years, was appointed sub-county chief of Ayer. Thus by the time Olong retired because of ill health in 1931 he had built up a strong position in most of the county. His success was capped by the Government's decision to accept his own choice of successor: Olwa Akoli was appointed county chief after only five years as a parish and sub-county chief, and he was succeeded at Ayer by yet another member of the Jo Olwa.[102]

It was in the two most easterly counties that county chiefs had been least successful in building up patronage systems by 1933. In the case of Moroto this can largely be explained by the relatively recent appointment of a Lango chief in this, the last area to be pacified. Not until 1927 was the Muganda county-agent replaced by Enoka Acol of Omoro. In 1929 he managed to get a clansman appointed to Adwari sub-county,[103] but two years later he failed in a similar attempt in his home area of Omoro, and had to accept instead a complete outsider from western Lango.[104] In Dokolo county, the growth of a patronage network was hindered by a change in the county chiefship in 1923; Owiny Aleka of Dokolo was dismissed and succeeded by Odur Acar of Angai.[105] Like Enoka Acol, he was compelled to accept an outsider as chief of his home area—in this case a Kumam.[106] Part at least of the explanation for this divergent pattern in eastern Lango lies in the

[99] Interview: Yokonia Ogwal.

[100] Lists of Iceme headmen, 1926 and 1933, in Koli TB (1926–33).

[101] Interviews: Mohammed Okec, Tamali Adur Apio, Nasan Engola, Onap Awongo, Jemusi Okot.

[102] Interview: Yokana Engola. Entries for 1931, in Koli TB (1926–33).

[103] Entry for 27.10.30, in Moroto TB (1926–33). Interview: George Apenyo.

[104] Rankin, entry for 23.3.31, in Moroto TB (1926–33).

[105] Entries for 7.3.23 and 1.5.23, in Dokolo & Moroto TB (1918–26).

[106] Enoci Eturu, appointed in 1932. His background is described in Hunt to PCNP, 5.4.34, ADA NPMP/274E.

limited impact of Christianity there. In Dokolo county especially, the first catechists had been Baganda, and acceptance of their teaching was probably seen as identification with the agents. Such prejudices died hard. According to the 1931 Census, the proportion of baptized Christians in Dokolo county was much lower than elsewhere in Lango—3·7 per cent of the population, as against 7·5 per cent in Erute, and 11 per cent in Atura.[107] Both Owiny Aleka and Odur Acar were pagans, and neither of them patronized the CMS school at Ngora, in Teso District. The fact that the pool of semi-literate and educated men in Dokolo—and up to a point in Moroto too—was so low helps to explain why District Officers tended to appoint outsiders to chiefly positions in eastern Lango.

The county chiefs were by far the most important source of political patronage in Lango District during the 1920s and 1930s, but they did not exercise a monopoly over appointments, not even in the most homogenous counties like Atura and Kole. Opportunities to manipulate the colonial power structure were shared to a lesser extent by the sub-county chiefs, especially when it came to parish and village posts. Both in appointments and in dismissals they had a good deal of discretion. By the late 1920s District Officers on tour hardly concerned themselves with chiefly positions below sub-county level; their role was confined to the retrospective approval of dispositions already made by the sub-county chiefs.[108] In some cases, the sub-county chief took a leaf out of the county chief's book by exploiting missionary education for patronage purposes. During the 1920s hardly any of them could afford to send boys outside the District for schooling,[109] but the link between chapel and boma enabled some of them to control recruitment to the catechists' classes and then to give minor appointments to converts.

Yakobo Adoko, chief of Akokoro sub-county from 1916 until 1930, was the most successful exponent of this approach. Soon after his appointment, he started to maintain a household along the lines

[107] Census Returns for 1931 (Entebbe, 1933).

[108] Thus at Dokolo in 1932 the touring officer, in noting that chief Alele had sacked three subordinates, commented that Alele should be supported in his attempt to take this problem area in hand. Slaughter, entry for 26.10.32 in Dokolo TB (1926–33).

[109] One of the few who did was Anderea Apil, chief of Acaba from 1918 to 1936; but it may be that his son, Zedekia Angulo, was supported at Gulu High School by the county chief, Owiny Akulo. Interview: Misaki Oki.

of Odora's at Aduku. Until the mid-20s no Christian teaching was given outside the *boma*, and by that time Adoko had available a group of semi-educated men whom he placed with great skill;[110] by 1931 five out of the seven parish and village positions in Akokoro were in the hands of his protégés.[111] Adoko's position was not, however, built up without antagonizing the county chief of Maruzi, Ibrahim Arum. For several years before Arum's death in 1930, the two were at odds.[112] Adoko prevented Arum from installing any of his own nominees in Akokoro, and he was probably already hoping to become county chief. In such a situation, any county chief would have agitated for Adoko's removal, and Arum was no exception.[113] In this instance, however, the Government never seriously considered transferring Adoko, partly because of his record as a competent administrator, and partly because of the special problems posed by the poly-ethnic nature of Akokoro's population.[114] Adoko stayed at the helm, and when Arum died, he succeeded him as county chief. The long-standing tension between Arum and Adoko was highly exceptional. Elsewhere, sub-county chiefs who remained in one posting for a long time did so mainly because they were on good terms with their immediate superiors. And even these were few in number: Abyece (1912–26), Loro (1912–35) and Acaba (1918–36) were the only not-able cases, apart from Akokoro.[115] The European requirement of high bureaucratic standards, combined with the county chiefs' reluctance to allow alternative sources of patronage to emerge in their own counties, ensured a rapid turn-over in the ranks of the sub-county chiefs.

The opportunity for sub-county chiefs to consolidate their local power bases was further constricted by two changes in government policy. In the first place, less emphasis was now placed upon heredi-tary succession. In the early days, personal defects had often been overlooked in order to keep chiefships in the same lineage, but by the mid-20s the tendency was to look elsewhere unless the chief's family included a candidate of outstandingly 'progressive' stamp. At Orum in 1926, for example, the son whom the retiring chief had been

[110] Interviews: Isaya Ajoba, Zakalia Ocam, Zakalia Adoko, Yakobo Adoko.
[111] List of Akokoro headmen, 1931, in Maruzi TB (1926–33).
[112] Maruzi TB (1919–26, part 3) and Maruzi TB (1926–33), *passim*.
[113] Undated entry in Maruzi TB (1919–26, part 3).
[114] Lukyn Williams, entry for 27.4.29 in Maruzi TB (1926–33). Besides Langi, Akokoro sub-county included a sizeable Bantu-speaking population.
[115] The chiefs concerned were Ogwal Agir, Yosia Omara, and Anderea Apil.

grooming for the succession was passed over as 'unsuitable'—even though he was a Christian convert—in favour of a man from a different clan.[116] By the early 1930s there were very few cases of unbroken hereditary succession in sub-county chiefdoms[117]—except, that is, for the home areas of county chiefs.

This move away from hereditary succession coincided with the second change in government policy, which tended to bureaucratize still further the position of sub-county chief. During the years 1927–8, something of a purge was carried out in the ranks of the sub-county chiefs, in an effort to increase the efficiency of native administration. In all, a total of twenty-six changes was made. Some of the new appointments were made in consultation with the county chiefs concerned, as had been standard form hitherto. But in a large number of cases officials pursued a policy of their own: they promoted younger, educated men, even though there might be no vacancy in their home areas, and they began to use the transfer as a reprisal against unsatisfactory chiefs who did not yet merit outright dismissal; five chiefs were even transferred out of their own counties altogether. Despite reluctance to move and requests for re-transfer on the part of the chiefs,[118] the experiment was maintained. The result of this change of policy was that the number of sub-county chiefs serving away from their birth-places increased from seven to fifteen between 1926 and 1927, and it remained at around this level until 1933.[119]

In this respect, the county chiefs presented a striking contrast. They owed their wealth and patronage not only to their long tenure of office, but also to the fact that they administered their home counties —and without fear of transfer. Between 1913 and 1933 the only county chief to rule outside his home area was Daudi Odora, whose circumstances were unique. Paradoxically, District Officers continued to apply their notions of traditional legitimacy to county chiefships for several years after they had abandoned them at sub-county level; and they did so despite the fact that, of all native functionaries, the county chiefs had least connection with the pre-colonial political

---

[116] Black, entries for 29.3.26 and 14.8.26 in Moroto TB (1918–26).

[117] Only two such cases have come to light: Bar, ruled by the Jo Oki me Abura from 1912–31, and Abyece, ruled by the Jo Alipa from 1912–34.

[118] See, for example: entries for 24.1.32 and 30.5.33 in Maruzi TB (1926–33); Rubie, entry for 17.11.32 in Kwania TB (1926–33).

[119] These figures are abstracted from the *Gazette* and the County Tour Books. See also Black, Report on Lango District for 1927, UNA EPMP/N/40/27.

system. When Odora retired from Kwania county in 1927, the District Commissioner felt that none of the local sub-county chiefs was suitable for promotion; but, rather than appoint an outsider, he installed a Muganda as county agent instead; the chiefship itself was reserved for a local man.[120] A similar policy was pursued towards Atura county, where by 1930 chief Owiny Akulo was considered to be overdue for retirement. For several years touring officers commented on the need for a new broom,[121] but Owiny Akulo stayed in office because his family, who dominated the county, appeared to include nobody of county chief calibre; for a time in 1933 the appointment of a caretaker Ganda agent was seriously considered,[122] but at no stage were the claims of outstanding sub-county chiefs elsewhere in the District taken into account.[123] Secure in the knowledge that their own local ties were approved in official quarters, the county chiefs were free to take advantage of the opposite policy which was being pursued towards subordinate chiefships. At a time when chiefly office in Lango was becoming increasingly bureaucratic, the county chiefs retained intact their personal influence and their freedom from administrative control.

The anomalous position of the county chiefs was the more remarkable because by the 1930s bureaucratization had spread down to the lowest level of all—the village. There too the chief was tending to be a man who lacked any local ties apart from his office. In most of Uganda during the colonial period, village chiefships were firmly grounded in tradition; there was often territorial continuity, and the chiefship was either hereditary or elective.[124] In Lango the situation was quite different. The last chapter showed how the change in settlement patterns after 1912 quickly caused the official village boundaries to become somewhat arbitrary. No doubt this was one reason why, almost from the start, village chiefs were designated from above. The District Officers who made these appointments at least restricted their choice to men of the village concerned. But once junior appointments were delegated to the senior grades of chief, this limitation ceased to

[120] Ibid.

[121] Temple-Perkins, entry for 23.11.30, and Bradley, entry for 23.9.31, in Atura TB (1926–33).

[122] Philipps to PCNP, 13.11.33, ADA LDMP/unnumbered.

[123] A chief who was recognized to merit promotion was Tomasi Ojuka of Lira, 'the best Jago in the District'. Entries for 8.5.32 and 22.6.33 in Eruti TB (1930–3).

[124] Audrey Richards (ed.), East African Chiefs (London, 1960), especially pp. 13–14.

apply, and the village chiefship was caught up in a web of patronage which extended over the whole sub-county, and often into the county as well. Before 1939 it was very rare for chiefly protégés, however well qualified, to be drafted directly into sub-county posts; they nearly all served as parish chiefs, and usually as village chiefs also. In addition to these aspirants to higher office, there were the lesser place-men for whom a junior chiefship was a desirable end in itself. By 1933 the majority of junior (i.e. parish and village) chiefs were probably men whose homes lay outside their petty chiefdoms. The first village heads, appointed during the years 1912–19, had been regarded as natural leaders of their own communities; their successors in the 1930s, by contrast, occupied the bottom rungs of a career ladder.

In this way, recruitment to political office in Lango had become completely divorced from traditional patterns. The breakdown was partially obscured by the fact that the most senior chiefs enjoyed considerable status apart from their colonial roles. No doubt it was reassuring to officials to see a veteran war-leader like Owiny Akulo still at the head of Atura county. To groups such as the Jo Olwa in Kole, the Jo Oyima in Maruzi, and the Jo Arak in Atura, the distribution of power probably seemed fair and proper. But outside this charmed circle, the bulk of the population had little cause to identify themselves with the colonial administrative structure and those who staffed it. Political authority was conferred from above, and the recipients tended increasingly to be men who lacked any territorial or clan links with the area allotted to them. And, just as the 'man-on-the-shamba' saw his chief as an outsider with no status apart from his office, so the chief tended to treat his 'subjects' without any of that restraint which kinship affiliation would have imposed. The few years that he was with them were a time for currying favour with the administration and an opportunity to line his own pocket. During the inter-war period, this last aspect loomed large in relations between the chief and his people.

The most obvious way in which chiefs expressed their acquisitive streak was by using askaris for the arbitrary seizure of livestock. Both county and sub-county chiefs are known to have behaved in this way.[125] Arum ranged over the whole of his county of Maruzi, 'making

[125] For example: Lawson, entry for 4.6.22 in Koli & Atura TB (1919–26); entry for 11.12.23 in Kwania & Maruzi TB (1919–26); Mitchell, entry for 13.4.26 in Kwania TB (1926–33).

eagle-pounces on his people's property, sometimes with legitimate cause, but more often not', in what appeared to one official to be a 'general civil-war against the people'.[126] However, predatory confiscation of this kind was not so easily concealed from District Officers, and during the 1920s chiefs evolved subtler means of enrichment, by taking advantage of the new cotton economy and their right to labour services.

The amount of personal labour, or *arododo*, which chiefs of each rank could call upon was carefully defined by regulation, but no abuse came to the attention of touring officers so frequently as extortion of labour above the legal maximum.[127] There were cases of chiefs using unpaid labour for long periods in order to build private residences for themselves; in 1920–1 Arum kept 250 men working for three months on a two-storey house at Ibuje.[128] *Arododo* was also used for the cultivation of subsistence crops, which for a chief who maintained a large household of *ogaragara* was no mean requirement. But the real significance of private forced labour lay in the opportunity which it gave chiefs to amass large incomes from cotton, especially from the early 1920s when the crop's commercial appeal was recognized by the Langi for the first time and output reached significant levels.[129] Direct evidence is lacking,[130] but there can be little doubt that in this respect Lango conformed to the pattern in Eastern Province as a whole. Looking at the cotton-growing areas of the Province during the 1920s, Wrigley concludes that 'a large part, perhaps a major part, of the total crop long continued to be grown by unpaid labour for the profit of the chief.'[131] In Lango these exactions were enforced by heavy punishments, such as fines and beating, either ordered by the chief in *lukiko*, or carried out without any legal process at all.[132] In the drier, less fertile parts of Lango, like the south-west,

[126] Tomblings, entry for 16.2.21 in Kwania & Maruzi TB (1919–26).

[127] For example: Driberg, entry for 14.3.16 in Kwania TB (1913–19); Tomblings, entry for 10.2.21 in Maruzi TB (1919–26, part 2); entry for 27.2.24 in Moroto TB (1926–33).

[128] Tomblings, entry for 16.2.21 in Kwania & Maruzi TB (1919–26).

[129] J. Tosh, 'Lango Agriculture during the Early Colonial Period: Land and Labour in a Cash-crop Economy', *Jl. African History*, 19 (1978), in the press.

[130] Unforunately data do not exist in Lango for calculating roughly what proportion of the District's cash resources was creamed off by the chiefs. For Teso, see Vincent, op. cit., pp. 151–2.

[131] Wrigley, *Crops and Wealth in Uganda*, p. 49.

[132] Entry for 11.12.23, Kwania & Maruzi TB (1919–26); Mitchell, entry for 3.5.27 in Maruzi TB (1926–33); Rankin, undated entry [1927] in Moroto TB (1926–33).

labour demands actually endangered subsistence cropping by the ordinary population.[133] The abuse of free labour became so evident to officials that in 1926 they decided to abolish it; from the following year, peasants were to pay a commutation fee, and chiefs of all grades were to receive fixed salaries, financed by the commutation fees and by the proportion of poll-tax which had hitherto been reserved for personal rebates to the chiefs.[134]

Although this reform was intended to reduce the opportunities for exploitation, in practice the chiefs were hardly worse off than before. The abolition of *arododo* merely encouraged them to misappropriate public labour (*luwalo*) instead.[135] And—more important—the Great Depression soon necessitated a partial return to free personal labour for chiefs.[136] Consequently at the beginning of the 1930s, excessive labour demands and illegal punishments were as prevalent as before.[137] Moreover, a fresh abuse of economic power was now added: some chiefs deprived peasants of a fair price for their cotton; the chief would compel his peasants to sell their crop to a particular Indian trader at a low price, in return for which the trader would buy the chief's own crop at well above market price.[138]

It is easier to establish the main categories of abuse in native administration than to identify the victims. What sort of people had their cattle seized and their time taken up by inordinate labour demands? One possible answer is that these impositions were handed out quite indiscriminately. With the growth of arbitrary appointments and transfers in the late 20s, this probably became an increasingly widespread pattern. Yet as late as 1933 there were still many chiefs of all grades who continued to rule their home areas, and prior to 1927 their number was even larger. In these cases, the chief's treatment of his 'subjects' was guided by loyalty to his own clan and antagonism towards its traditional rivals. And throughout the inter-war period, there was one other potential check on the impartiality of a chief: the

[133] Entries for 10.2.21 and 6.9.24 in Maruzi TB (1919–26, part 2).
[134] Black, Report on Lango District for 1927, UNA EPMP/N/40/27; Wrigley, op. cit., pp. 54–5; Fallers, op. cit., p. 150. Elsewhere in Eastern Province the chiefs still retained some rights to labour service.
[135] Entry for 5.5.27 in Maruzi TB (1926–33).
[136] Ingham, 'British Administration in Lango District, 1907–35', p. 165.
[137] Wrensch, entry for June 1930 in Maruzi TB (1926–33); Temple-Perkins, entry for 20.10.30 in Dokolo TB (1926–33); Slaughter, entry for 10.10.32 in Moroto TB (1926–33).
[138] Oswald, entry for 25.1.32 in Maruzi TB (1926–33); Philipps to PCNP, 13.12.33, ADA NPMP/unnumbered.

presence of his superior's kin, whether clansmen or affines; this was a particularly serious matter if the county chief's own family was represented.[139] In both the allocation of labour duties[140] and in his court judgements,[141] a chief could easily succumb to pressure from his own or his superior's kin. An interesting light is cast on the prevalence of this abuse by an opinion expressed at Omoro in 1931. A vacancy had just occurred in the sub-county; the county chief, Enoka Acol, suggested one of his own clansmen, but the peasants were opposed to the idea, one of them saying that they wished to have an outsider from no closer than Bar, over twenty miles away.[142] For some Langi at least, impartiality was preferable to local ties in a chief. How prevalent this attitude was—or the abuses from which it stemmed—it is impossible to say.

Lack of specific evidence confronts any assessment of the prevalence of these abuses. That they were all practised at one time or another is not in doubt, and in a handful of sub-counties autocratic rule is well documented.[143] But elsewhere lack of evidence cannot be construed as lack of abuses. Certainly the silence of oral testimony is by no means conclusive; misuse of power by government chiefs of only a generation or so ago is far too delicate a matter to be discussed freely by Lango elders today. As for contemporary evidence in government records, the difficulty here is that a great deal of maladministration never reached the ears of District officials. In some measure, this can be attributed to less thorough supervision of chiefs from the 1920s onwards, already mentioned. But a much more important factor was the deliberate obstruction on the part of the chiefs themselves. When in 1933–4 a searching inquiry was at last conducted into native administration in Lango, it revealed that communication between officials and the ordinary population was being impeded on two fronts: the first judicial, and the second administrative.

In theory, miscarriage of justice was guarded against by the right of appeal: from the court of first instance to the county court, and thence to the Native District Court in Lira, presided over by the

[139] Philipps to PCNP, 11.12.33, ADA NPMP/274E.

[140] This aspect is unusually well documented for Akokoro: entries *passim* in Maruzi TB (1919–26, part 2). See also: Philipps, Notes on abuses worth watching, 18.2.34, ADA NPMP/274E.

[141] Philipps to PCNP, 11.12.33, ADA NPMP/274E.

[142] Rankin, entry for 23.3.31 in Moroto TB (1926–33).

[143] Akokoro and Ibuje are the best examples, as frequent reference to Maruzi county in the foregoing footnotes indicates.

District Commissioner. In practice, the chiefs could, if they wished, frustrate this procedure completely. Since they controlled the courts of first instance, they could subject plaintiffs to inordinate delays before even allowing a preliminary hearing.[144] And since they were responsible for initiating the appeal procedure, they could also prevent cases going any further. This kind of obstruction was naturally more frequent in cases where the chief himself was an interested party.[145] It was thus well nigh impossible for the victims of chiefly maladministration to secure redress through judicial channels.

The breakdown in communication was almost as complete in the administrative sphere. The purpose of regular touring was not only to inspect the work of the chiefs, but also to meet the people. But whereas in the early years of colonial rule District Officers travelled on foot at a leisurely pace, by the late 1920s they sped from one sub-county headquarters to the next by motor-car and spoke to few people outside the *boma*.[146] The touring officer's contact with the ordinary population was limited to the *baraza*, a formal gathering at the chief's headquarters where instructions could be given and complaints—in theory—received. It was only too easy for the chief to stop such complaints. Sometimes he omitted to advertise the time of the *baraza* altogether.[147] More often, he assembled an adequate audience, and relied on the common fear that those who spoke out against him would be victimized later. The administration of Adwari by Okuk Awira, a clan brother of the local county chief, presents a striking example. In July 1933 the official who visited Adwari reported, 'everything in the Gombolola is in good order and running well, and there is a marked absence of complaints'.[148] A mere five months later, the Government's widely announced intention to investigate complaints provoked a quite different response in Adwari: it took the District Officer four days to listen to complaints of theft and summary imprisonment brought against Okuk by over a hundred people.[149] During the early and middle 1920s, officials had encountered cases of local maladministration quite frequently, but by the early 30s the

[144] One of the few documented instances before 1933 of refusal to hear cases in *lukiko* was at Adwari in 1927. Rankin, undated entry in Moroto TB (1926–33).
[145] Philipps to PCNP, 23.2.34, and 17.11.33, ADA NPMP/274E.
[146] Philipps to PCNP, 23.2.34, ADA NPMP/274/E.
[147] Entries for 25.8.23 and 25.10.25, in Maruzi TB (1919–26, part 2).
[148] Greenwood, entry for 7.7.33 in Moroto TB (1926–33).
[149] Steil, entry for 1.12.33, ibid.

gagging of protest had become more efficient, and it was rare for chiefs to be challenged in *baraza*.

Apart from judicial appeals and *baraza* complaints, there was one other index of oppression—unauthorized migration out of the sub-county. This reaction was a much more difficult one for the chiefs to stem, and touring officers commented on it quite frequently. Migration entailed a breach of kinship ties and the surrender of territorial rights; it was the last resort of victimized individuals who found the legitimate channels of redress barred to them; they went with their families either to a neighbouring county, or else outside the District altogether.[150] Some evidence of the number of emigrants can be gleaned from the 1931 Census. In that year 17,797 Langi were recorded as living outside the District. Of these, the 10,244 resident in the Paranga county of Gulu District (Acholi) probably belonged for the most part to those Lango villages west of the Toci river which had been detached from Lango in 1912.[151] The remaining 7,553 were almost all living in counties adjacent to Lango where there was no economic inducement such as a demand for migrant labour. The absence from Lango of these people—over 4 per cent of the total Lango population—was almost certainly due to unfavourable conditions at home.[152] Some migrants of course were fugitives from justice in the normal sense, but there is no doubt that many were refugees from the oppression of particular chiefs. This was amply demonstrated when the dismissal, transfer, or promotion of a chief was followed by a reversal of the flow, with natives of the sub-county returning under more equitable conditions, as at Omoro in 1931 and Akokoro in 1933.[153]

Emigration provides one of the few clear indications of peasant attitudes towards authority. Together with the enthusiastic popular reaction to the Government's reforms after 1933, it suggests that most chiefs were unpopular, and that sub-county chiefs, who bore the brunt of enforcing rules and regulations, were especially so. This unpopularity was so widespread that some chiefs regarded it as an occupational hazard of their job. Yakobo Adoko, for example,

[150] The following are typical: entries for 12.8.20 and 6.9.24, Kwania & Maruzi TB (1919–26); Lawson, entry for 12.11.21, Maruzi TB (1919–26, part 2); Bradley, entry for 9.11.29, Atura TB (1926–33); Temple-Perkins, entry for 25.10.30, Moroto TB (1926–33).   [151] See above, pp. 159–60.

[152] *Census Returns, 1931* (Entebbe, 1933).

[153] Slaughter, entry for 10.8.31 in Moroto TB (1926–33), and entry for 31.5.33 in Maruzi TB (1926–33). Interviews: Anderea Okadde, Elia Olet.

admits that he was hated in those days, but says simply, 'Government employment makes enemies' (*tic okelo amone*).[154]

This reaction against the chiefs was a fairly common phenomenon in East Africa between the wars. It reflected the fact that, under colonial rule, formal political leadership had departed radically from pre-colonial norms—so radically that the powers of chiefship, whether abused or fairly enforced, were often viewed from below as intolerable. It is usually at this stage that recent historians, their eyes trained on the later growth of mass political action, begin to identify competition from other types of leadership: sometimes 'progressive', in that educated elements began to assert themselves; sometimes 'traditional', in that ancient forms of leadership were adapted to new purposes.[155] In Lango, however, there was no hint of these developments until the Second World War; least of all was there an educated or 'progressive' leadership waiting in the wings.[156]

As we have seen, education itself was manipulated by the chiefs. Recruitment to schools outside Lango was done in such a way as to ensure that the pupils would enter the local administration as dependants of the senior chiefs. Not even the catechists working in the District posed a threat, since most of them were not Langi. As for the new sources of economic power, these too were effectively controlled by the chiefs. The system of free labour enabled them to derive large incomes from cotton, while preventing anyone else from doing so, with the result that no class of wealthy cash-crop farmers emerged. Cotton-buying and the retail trade were at this time almost exclusively in the hands of the Indians, who were not above making special arrangements with chiefs in order to protect their own position.[157] One other potential catalyst of political change was likewise without significance in Lango—the returned migrant labourer. For most of the inter-war period, Uganda was divided for purposes of economic policy

---

[154] Interview: Yakobo Adoko. *Tic* in Lango means simply 'work' of any kind, but with reference to the early colonial period it is widely used to mean employment with the Government.

[155] For a stimulating commentary on this issue, see J. M. Lonsdale, 'Some Origins of Nationalism in East Africa', *Jl. African History*, 9 (1968), pp. 119–46.

[156] The first sign of a 'progressive' challenge was the emergence of the Young Lango Association in 1944. Even after the War, however, 'new-style' politicians were for the most part closely connected with existing networks of chiefly patronage: Milton Obote, for example, was nephew of chief Yakobo Adoko. For an introductory account of this period, see C. Gertzel, *Party and Locality in Northern Uganda, 1945–1962* (London, 1974), pp. 24–55.

[157] Philipps to PCNP, 13.12.33, ADA NPMP/unnumbered. See above, p. 209.

between materially-productive areas and labour-providing areas. In West Nile, for example, the development of a cash-crop economy was held back in order to release migrant labour for work in Buganda.[158] Lango, on the other hand, had been seen from the beginning as a cotton-growing zone. Some Langi did travel south for employment, but they were never a significant proportion of migrant labour in Uganda as a whole, nor were they numerous enough to exercise influence when they returned home.[159] Educational and economic attainment were alike unable to provide the basis of an alternative political leadership between the wars.

The role of traditional forms of leadership is rather less straight-forward. There is no doubt that outside the official hierarchy such forms of leadership survived, and in some cases they flourished even when the local chief tried to encroach on their preserve. At Ngai the sub-county chief was unsuccessful in laying claim to the traditional office of *won arum*, or 'master of the hunt,' despite his close ties with the county chief of Atura.[160] More important was the continued vigour of ritual leadership. The Baganda agents had tried to stamp out some of the local ceremonies, especially those which called for attendance by many people from different neighbourhoods; in so doing, they had administered the *coup de grâce* to the regional *ewor* ceremonies.[161] But other public rituals survived, above all the rain-making ceremonies which, under the direction of Lingo of Aduku, were if anything more important than before. It was during the 1920s that this celebrated rain-maker consolidated his position; he trained young men of his own clan in the lore of rain-making, and then posted them to other parts of the District; Lingo's role as initiator of both the rain-dance (*myeolo kot*) and the final burial-rite (*apuny*) was also being increasingly accepted all over Lango.[162] Yet outside the

[158] For the development of Protectorate labour policy, see P. G. Powesland. *Economic Policy and Labour* (Kampala, 1957).

[159] A more obtrusive element might have been the soldiers demobilized at the end of the First World War, but the policy of compelling them to disperse to their villages and former occupations appears to have been effective. Driberg, Notes on Lango Baraza of 31.7.18, ADA LDMP/40/15.

[160] Hayley, *The Anatomy of Lango Religion and Groups*, p. 149. The account of the Lango informant whom Hayley quotes does not give the chief's name, but the event evidently refers to either 1927 or 1932; in both years a newly-appointed kinsman of the county chief arrived in Ngai.

[161] Interviews: Anderea Okadde, Omara Ekak, Erieza Olwol. Hayley, op. cit., pp. 71, 80. For the role of *ewor* during the nineteenth century, see above, pp. 57–60.

[162] Hayley, op. cit., pp. 63, 75. Interview: Tomasi Ojuka. For Lingo's pre-colonial position, see above, pp. 91–2.

sphere of ritual, Lingo himself never competed with official authority; indeed for many years he served as a parish chief.[163] Right up to his death in 1936, he appears to have made no effort to turn his immense prestige to political advantage.

In the last resort, it was not the ritual authorities who would have wished to supplant the Government chief, so much as the families of those clan leaders who had received no place in the official hierarchy. The last chapter showed how the creation of such a hierarchy entailed, even at the lowest level, a process of selection which was often quite arbitrary. The historical record is inevitably more illuminating about the jockeying for position inside the official hierarchy, than about the manoeuvres of groups outside. We are dealing here with one of those obscure and elusive undercurrents of early colonial rule, where reliance must be placed more on reasoned inference than on solid evidence. Doubtless those leaders who were unplaced hardly cared at first, regarding their existing roles as more valuable than any that the Government could offer. But as appreciation of the power and privileges conferred by appointment spread, unrecognized clan leaders became resentful of their low status in official eyes. Of course, the first clan sections to be singled out for chiefly appointments did not, in most cases, achieve a monopoly, and many other clan sections were subsequently brought into the ranks of the native administration. But as late as 1933 there were still important clan sections who had received little or no taste of office.

One such group was the Jo Ogora of Ibuje. In terms of length of settlement and numerical strength, this clan section had as good a claim to dominate the sub-county as the Jo Ocukuru did; indeed, it is said that the leader of the Jo Ogora remonstrated with the Government that he had a better right to be sub-county chief than Arum of the Jo Ocukuru, because his clan had settled in Ibuje first.[164] Once in power, Arum did his best to exclude the rival clan from all chiefships, even in their own locality of Tarogali. From 1915 until 1933 no Ogora man received an official position, except for a brief interlude in the early 20s.[165] The clan section as a whole showed little interest in Christian teaching, despite the fact that Ibuje had well above the average number of catechists, and its leaders appear to have devoted

[163] He was *won magoro* of Ikwera until 1928. Kwania TB (1926–33).

[164] Interview: Okelo Abak. See below, p. 269.

[165] Interviews: Yusto Oweno, Okelo Abak. As late as 1936, an official on tour noted that the Jo Ogora held no chiefships in Ibuje. Entry for 26.6.36 in Maruzi TB (1934–54).

more attention to the upkeep of rain-making and other ceremonies in the neighbourhood.[166] The Jo Ogora plainly had more cause for complaint than most in Ibuje, yet there is no indication that their leaders spoke up against the rule of Arum and his family. 'Out-groups' like the Jo Ogora were potentially a focus for popular agitation against the existing political order. Yet in most of Lango no effort was apparently made by the leaders of these neglected clan sections to articulate grass-roots protest.

Part of the explanation of this silence lies in the high concentration of power in the chiefs' hands: if any attempt was made by local clan leaders to challenge chiefly authority, it was stifled before it reached the ears of the District Officers. But there was another reason. By the 1930s grass-roots political leadership was itself in a state of flux. For some time after the assertion of colonial control, the principal position of indigenous authority had continued to be clan leadership, exercised either in conjunction with a government chiefship, or—more commonly—quite separately. However, the practical importance of clan leadership was diminishing, not just because some of its traditional functions were obsolete, but also because the clan section itself was becoming less relevant to ground-level politics. The crucial determinant here was the changing pattern of local settlement. The last chapter showed how the establishment of colonial law and order was quickly followed by the dissolution of the traditional village, with its high concentration of homesteads and its heavy proponderance of a single clan section. This left, as the basic unit of territorial organization, the *wang tic*, or 'neighbourhood'—the largest group within which labour resources were regularly pooled. At the same time, greater security of life and limb weakened the individual's dependence on his local clan section and enabled him to seek land elsewhere.[167] This acted as a further check on the preponderance of a single descent group in any given area. Descent groups of every kind were counting for less and less in the setting of the *wang tic*. It was for this reason that clan leadership, while retaining great prestige, declined as an effective political force. In due course it was to be superseded by new positions, based explicitly on neighbourhood, but during the 1930s these posi-

---

[166] Interview: Okelo Abak. In July 1969, the present writer participated in a rain-making ceremony in Tarogali which was presided over exclusively by elders of the Jo Ogora.

[167] For a short case-history of this pattern of settlement, see Curley, *Elders, Shades, and Women*, pp. 34–5.

tions were only just beginning to appear.[168] Around 1930 there appears to have been something of a vacuum in grass-roots political leadership. As a result, the chiefs had little cause to fear a challenge to their power from below.

In only one sub-county was there a clear case of well-organized and effective popular protest: this was Omoro, in Moroto county. Chief Danieri Awio, who came from neighbouring Amugo, was already noted as unpopular with the peasantry soon after his appointment in 1927.[169] In 1930 the *baraza* was filled with complaints that Awio was misappropriating cattle and imprisoning without trial.[170] A year later Awio was dismissed, and in response to popular demand, the District Officer appointed as his successor a stranger from western Lango, rather than the relative whom the county chief had proposed.[171] Before 1934 there appears to have been no other instance of serious pressure being brought to bear on chiefs in the localities they ruled. For the most part, neither traditional interest groups nor progressive 'modernizers' were in a position to bring about political change, even in a small way. And when significant change did occur, it was imposed from above, rather than demanded from below.

For a long time, officials showed no wish to change the rules of the game which their predecessors had laid down before 1919. They were aware that maladministration occurred, but the limited scale on which it actually came to light encouraged in them the belief that it was only individuals who were at fault, not the system itself. At the same time, their underlying expectations of the chiefs did change. At the end of the First World War, chiefs were still seen as 'of the people', natural leaders who, as Driberg put it, did not 'stand coldly aloof in the isolating attitude of the parvenu'.[172] By the late 1920s, on the other hand, the growing complexity of administration had led to a contrary emphasis on impartial and distant authority. To take a trivial but revealing aspect, frequent participation in communal dancing, which Driberg had seen as laudable in a 'democratic' chief,[173] was now disapproved of as a distraction from paper-work.[174] This change of attitude on the part of the Government had, it is true,

---

[168] The key position was that of *adwong wang tic*, or 'neighbourhood leader'. Curley, op. cit., pp. 21–3, 25.
[169] Rankin, entry for 23.9.27 in Moroto TB (1926–33).
[170] Moss, entry for 15.3.30, ibid.   [171] Rankin, entry for 23.3.31, ibid.
[172] Driberg, 'The Lango District, Uganda Protectorate', p. 129. His comments refer to 1918, the last time when he had served in Lango.
[173] Ibid.   [174] Bradley, entry for 15.9.31 in Atura TB (1926–33).

occasioned the one major reform of the period 1919–33—the introduction of chiefs' salaries in 1927. It had even prompted harsh words
about the calibre of younger chiefs: Captain Black reported from the
District in 1927 that, 'the newcomers . . . are very inclined to let the
welfare of their people suffer while they seek personal gain and to give
a superficial impression of efficiency which is not founded in fact.'[175]
But officials continued to accept this 'superficial impression'. Not even
the frequent cases of emigration from misrule prompted them to look
below the surface of orderly tax-returns and compliance in *baraza*. As
a result, popular feeling was more and more alienated from all grades
of native administration.

[175] Black, Report on Lango District for 1927, UNA EPMP/N/40/27.

CHAPTER 8

The System Scrutinized

TOWARDS the end of 1933, in the space of just over four weeks, the Provincial Commissioner of Uganda's Northern Province[1] received from his subordinate in charge of Lango District no less than five letters on the subject of native administration.[2] Every one of them was highly critical. The District Commissioner had begun a personal inquiry into the conduct of the chiefs by encouraging the peasants to address their grievances directly to him, without reference to the local courts. By the middle of December he had uncovered enough scandal in south-eastern Lango to confirm his own worst fears and to appal his superiors. The abuses inherent in the chiefs' control of appeal procedure and in the system of personal forced labour were exposed, together with intimidation reminiscent of the 'methods of medieval Inquisition'.[3] The offenders were tried by a Native District Court specially set up at Kaberamaido. The District Commissioner chose to interpret his findings in a dramatic light. He went so far as to raise the spectre of rebellion—all that was lacking, he suggested, was a 'pagan Mahdi' to fan the flames.[4] And he also spelt out the implications for Britain's standing as an enlightened colonial power: 'My attitude', he declared in his last letter,[5]

is consistent, straightforward, and quite simple. So long as our representatives at Geneva give to the world firm and formal assurances of the total abolition throughout our 'colonies' of any form of unpaid forced labour, so

[1] In 1932 Lango District was transferred from Eastern Province to Northern Province.
[2] The five letters from J. E. T. Philipps to B. Ashton Warner are dated: 13.11.33, 17.11.33, 27.11.33, 11.12.33, and 13.12.33, ADA NPMP/274E. The Northern Province Archives (now combined with the Acholi District Archives in the DC's office at Gulu) are confused and incomplete, but they have the only accessible record of the Philipps/Ashton Warner correspondence. All trace of the letters in the Lango District Archives has vanished. Copies may survive in the Uganda National Archives, but they are not yet open to inspection.
The Philipps episode was first covered in a brief account by Professor Ingham: 'British Administration in Lango District, 1907–35', pp. 166–8.
[3] Philipps to Ashton Warner, 11.12.33.
[4] Philipps to Ashton Warner, 27.11.33.
[5] Philipps to Ashton Warner, 13.12.33.

long one can only see to it that their position should not be falsified behind their back and any form of such labour should be uncompromisingly and honestly eradicated, thus allowing for no shadow of reproach.

The author of these extraordinary letters was Captain J. E. T. Philipps. For all the impression he conveyed of being a youthful fire-brand, Philipps was in fact an experienced administrator, with a record of service in the Sudan, as well as Uganda. He had nevertheless made a habit of exposing abuses. As early as 1922, he had warned a London audience of the opportunity which heavy-handed govern-ment offered to 'pan-African agitators'.[6] He had on several occasions pushed through major changes in native administration—among the Azande of the Southern Sudan,[7] in Teso District, where he had first become aware of malpractices over the border in Lango,[8] and twice in Kigezi.[9] For his investigations in Teso in 1927, Philipps had been commended at the highest level.[10] However, with the years he became increasingly carried away by his self-appointed role as scourge of the wicked—and these included, in his view, not just unscrupulous African underlings, but also negligent and stupid Europeans. The language of his official correspondence grew more intemperate and provocative (as well as less grammatical). His campaign in Lango District created a greater stir than any of his previous efforts. It was also to be his last.

Ashton Warner, the official to whom Philipps's outbursts were addressed, was cast in a more conventional mould. As Provincial Commissioner for the next five years, he was an important steadying influence on administration in Lango, which was disrupted by fre-quent changes of European personnel,[11] as well as by the prevailing 'state of apprehension'.[12] He shared the typical District Officer's

[6] J. E. T. Philipps, 'The Tide of Colour', *Jl. African Society*, 21 (1922), pp. 129–35, 309–15.

[7] J. E. T. Philipps, 'Development of Indirect Administration in the Southern Sudan, Bahr-El-Ghazal Province' (1925), MS. in Balfour Library, Pitt Rivers Museum, Oxford.

[8] J. C. D. Lawrance, *The Iteso* (London, 1957), p. 35; J. Vincent, 'Teso in Transformation: Colonial Penetration in Teso District, Eastern Uganda, and its Contemporary Significance', in *Government and Rural Development in East Africa*, ed. L. Cliffe, J. S. Coleman and M. R. Doornbos (The Hague, 1977), pp. 75–6, 80, n. 59. See also Ingham, op. cit., p. 166.

[9] D. J. N. Denoon, 'Agents of Colonial Rule, Kigezi 1908–30', University of East Africa Social Science Conference Proceedings, January 1968 (mimeo).

[10] Sir William Gowers to Sec. of State, 28.2.28, PRO CO/536/148.

[11] Between August 1933 and October 1935, Lango had three District Com-missioners.   [12] Ashton Warner to Chief Secretary, 8.8.34, ADA NPMP/274E.

pride in imperial achievement and respect for establishing practice. He also disliked Philipps intensely. But he saw that decisive action was needed, in which case Philipps must submit orderly reports instead of formless manifestos. In his reply to Philipps's five letters, Ashton Warner took the gravest view of the situation in Lango: it pointed, he declared, to 'a complete breakdown of the Native Court System'. But he felt bound to emphasize that, for all their imperfections, the existing courts must be associated with the handling of complaints, if the established order was not to be completely discredited. For the same reason, restraint was to be exercised in punishing errant chiefs. In an effort to stem the flow of correspondence, Ashton Warner requested concise reports on every county in Lango.[13]

Philipps wasted no time in replying. He accepted his instructions, but he felt bound to point out the difficulties that stood in the way of using the chiefs' courts; the members of these courts, he said, 'cannot yet be trusted too long to resist luscious and bovine bribes which affluent defendants, before Court by day, dangle temptingly before them by night.'[14] As requested, Philipps continued his investigations county by county, though with less energy than before. He had begun with the Kumam areas of Kaberamaido and Kalaki. In December 1933 he had investigated Dokolo and Kwania, while an Assistant District Officer covered Moroto county.[15] Philipps now turned to Maruzi and Erute, but although his findings were broadly similar they were based on more superficial inquiries.[16] Atura and Kole appear to have been completely ignored. Then, towards the end of February, he submitted his considered findings, on which reform was to be based.[17]

Philipps began by listing again the several scandals which were disfiguring Britain's good name in Lango District. There were no surprises here. Misappropriation of livestock, torture to extract confessions, the blocking of appeals, and the 'packing' of the county with relatives of the county chief, were by now well-aired abuses. He then went on to identify the historical causes of this fall from grace. His fundamental point was that the Langi (and the Kumam) lacked any traditional idea of chiefs, or of judicial bodies beyond the informal

[13] Ashton Warner to Philipps, 23.12.33, ADA NPMP/274E.
[14] Philipps to Ashton Warner, 28.12.33, ADA NPMP/274E.
[15] Steil, entries for December 1933 in Moroto TB (1926–33).
[16] Philipps, untitled memorandum, 13.2.34, ADA LDMP/unnumbered.
[17] Philipps to Ashton Warner, 23.2.34 (subtitled 'Report on Conditions in Lango (Kumam), including counties of South Kwania and Dokolo'), ADA NPMP/274E.

gathering of village elders. From this, everything else stemmed. The Government had imported a Bantu hierarchical system of administration which was, in Philipps's view, 'quite alien to the genius, social practice and stage of development of this Nilotic people'. In order to staff the new organization, the Government had recruited a Lango Civil Service, whose members it had quite misleadingly termed 'chiefs'. For a time these local officials had been supervised by disinterested Baganda 'tutor-mechanics'; but the Baganda had been removed prematurely, and Lango chiefs had then assumed the character of a 'clan or caste of officialdom', equipped with 'a loaded rifle' in the form of the native courts, and in practice answerable to nobody save themselves. The already wide gulf between rulers and ruled had been worsened by the recent increase in chiefs' salaries, as compensation for the abolition of forced labour, to which tribal custom had anyway never entitled them. Finally, Philipps stressed the lack of contact between European officials and the population at large. He attributed this to the divided loyalties of interpreters and clerks, the Province's reliance on 'a top-heavy façade of 'paper', and the advent of the motor-car, which had induced slap-dash touring.[18]

This analysis shows that, for all his tendency towards verbose exaggeration, Philipps had a shrewd grasp of Lango administrative history. In only two particulars was he at fault. In the first place, he white-washed the Baganda and therefore glossed over the very real dilemma confronting the Government in 1911: should they rely on corrupt foreign agents or on untrained local men? His second and more significant error lay in supposing that Lango chiefs had attained the solidarity of a caste or class. As recipients of by far the largest African salaries in the District and as principal beneficiaries of the cash-crop economy, chiefs in Lango undoubtedly evinced some of the economic characteristics of class. But they lacked the crucial consciousness of being a class which arises from the need to defend common interests against other groups in society, because that need did not yet exist. For a chief what counted was not loyalty to, or identification with, his chiefly peer-group, but his ability to manipulate clan loyalties in his home area for political ends. Between different patronage networks there was real emnity, as events after 1934 were to show.[19]

[18] Ibid.
[19] Cf. J. Vincent, 'Colonial Chiefs and the Making of Class: a Case Study from Teso, Eastern Uganda', *Africa*, 47 (1977), pp. 140–59.

Philipps concluded his report with a plan of action. In view of the fact that he had obtained a total of some 200 convictions of chiefs in the Native District Court,[20] he may once have contemplated a draconian purge. But by this time his prescription was more modest in scope. Indeed, it scarcely measured up to the situation. Philipps raised the possibility of dismissing or transferring 75 per cent of all sub-county chiefs, only to discount it. Instead, he merely suggested an exchange between three pairs of county chiefs, as 'an immediate and decisive check to the nepotic system'.[21] To cope with maladministration at a lower level, he proposed attaching sub-county chiefs to the few remaining Baganda chiefs in the District—two of whom he had himself appointed.[22] The collapse of the Native Court system was to be dealt with by reducing court fees, limiting the powers of the courts, and nominating lay assessors to assist the chief in court. The paperwork carried out by District Officers on tour was to be drastically reduced, as a step towards the 'complete rehumanization' of relations between Europeans and Africans. Philipps ended his report on a characteristic note of self-righteous pessimism:

Both the abuses and their remedy lie very deep. It is, at bottom, a matter of both the secular psychology of this group of African peoples entrusted to our Protection, and British African policy as, in practice, applied to them. Having seen what one has seen, throughout the greater part of Africa and to some extent beneath the surface, one can only beg leave to remain somewhat pessimistic and despondent.[23]

Philipps's superiors agreed that reforming action was required. They not only carried out most of his suggestions; they also made further policy changes of their own. To this extent Philipps was vindicated. But the senior officials probably felt that the implementation of reform and the reassertion of normal controls could not easily be carried out by Philipps himself, since he was associated in the popular mind with an 'anti-chief' stance; a steadier hand was needed. Philipps was anyway more adept at uncovering abuses than at suggesting how they should be checked.[24] Combined with the dislike

[20] Philipps to Ashton Warner, undated [Jan./Feb. 1934], ADA NPMP/274E.
[21] Same to same, 23.2.34, ADA NPMP/274E.
[22] Daudi Mwanga at Ibuje, and Kezekia Atate at Abyece. Philipps had prescribed the same remedy in Teso District in 1926–7. Lawrance, op. cit., p. 35.
[23] Philipps to Ashton Warner, 23.2.34, ADA NPMP/274E.
[24] This view was expressed by the Governor, Sir Bernard Bourdillon, whose opinion is cited in: Sir Cecil Bottomley to P. E. Mitchell, 29.8.35, PRO CO/536/186.

in which he was held by his colleagues, these considerations were enough to get him removed. Shortly after submitting his special report, he was replaced as District Commissioner. A year later, he was retired from the Colonial Service, under protest. A brilliant man who 'did not exactly fit into Colonial administration', ran one official verdict.[25]

The initiative now passed to the Provincial Commissioner, Ashton Warner. At the beginning of March 1934, he held a *baraza* for the whole of Lango District, at which stress was for the time being laid on the punitive aspect of the Government's programme. He told the assembled chiefs: 'Your district is at present like a house which is beautifully white-washed outside but is very dirty inside.'[26] The dismissal or demotion of seventeen sub-county chiefs was announced: eight were Kumam, seven were Langi, and two were Bantu. As for the county chiefs, six were transferred as Philipps had recommended; one was demoted; and Kwania county was split into two, the southern half (Namasale peninsula) forming the new county of Kioga, with a predominantly Bantu population. Ashton Warner told the *baraza* that in future chiefs would be appointed on merit, and that county chiefs would not normally serve in the county of their birth. He made it plain that the intention was to stop certain big families filling positions with their own members.[27]

Ashton Warner's detailed instructions for the reform of native administration were contained in a long letter which he wrote shortly afterwards to Philipps's successor, R. O. Hunt.[28] A number of regulations were formulated to deal with practical abuses. The seizure of peasants' livestock was to stop; personal labour for chiefs was abolished for good; court fees were to be revised; and appeals to the District Commissioner were to be eased. Ashton Warner shared Philipps's faith in the efficacy of more intensive touring by European officials; he therefore instructed that tours should be slower, and less taken up with the inspection of chiefs' paper-work; officials on tour should also leave the beaten track from time to time, and for this purpose 'shooting and fishing by Administrative Officers' were to be encouraged.[29]

More important, however, were the structural reforms designed as a long-term check on oppressive rule. Here, the crucial issue was the

[25] Ibid.
[26] Ashton Warner, text of speech to Lango District Baraza, March 1934, ADA NPMP/274E.   [27] Ibid.
[28] Ashton Warner to Hunt, 7.3.34, ADA NPMP/274E.   [29] Ibid.

recruitment of chiefs. If the chiefs had no hereditary claim to their positions—a point on which Ashton Warner was by this time clear— then 'the alternative was to regard them as civil servants and appoint them on merit without regard to territorial considerations'.[30] The Provincial Commissioner had already adumbrated this approach at the District *baraza*; he now filled in the details. The policy against chiefs serving in their home areas was to apply not only to the county chiefs, but also to the sub-county chiefs; wherever possible, they were to serve outside the county of their birth. With this end in view, a number of transfers of sub-county chiefs was to be carried out; six transfers were actually made in 1934, and most of the promotions occasioned by dismissal or retirement were in effect transfers as well. But the most radical reform concerned the lowest office in the official hierarchy: henceforth the village chief was no longer to be regarded as a government chief; he was to be a local and unpaid headman, elected by the villagers to convey their views to the Government. This policy, which brought Lango District into line with most of Uganda, was in operation by April 1934.[31] A clear break was thus effected between the village chiefship, which was to be a non-official and 'democratic' position, and the three grades of the government hier-archy, which were to assume a strictly 'bureaucratic' nature.[32]

Ashton Warner capped his programme with two reforms, both designed to involve the layman in public affairs. The first of these was a Native Council, to advise on matters affecting the welfare of the whole District, and to include other persons besides chiefs. The Council was constituted along these lines during 1935 and began work in 1936. The second reform was one which Philipps too had advocated: on an experimental basis, four 'non-officials' in selected counties were to be appointed to the bench by the District Commissioner, to serve as assessors in the native courts; they were to represent the more 'progressive and educated' elements.[33] At the same time, however, Philipps's suggestion regarding Baganda agents was ignored. No agents were appointed, and the two Baganda chiefs whom he had installed were soon removed.[34]

[30] Ibid.   [31] Hunt, entry for 19.4.34 in Maruzi TB (1934–54).
[32] Ashton Warner to Hunt, 7.3.34, ADA NPMP/274E. The words 'democratic' and 'bureaucratic' were not actually used in official correspondence of the time. For a time, Ashton Warner intended to make the parish chiefship an elective position also, but this idea was never put into practice.   [33] Ibid.
[34] Kezekia Atate of Abyece was dismissed in 1935; Daudi Mwanga of Ibuje retired in 1936.

This was the only one of Philipps's proposals which was not actually carried out; and several reforms which he had never even hinted at were vigorously pursued. Taken as a whole, Ashton Warner's programme was remarkably innovatory. It involved the biggest upheaval in Lango administration since the gazetting of the first chiefs in 1912. Philipps himself had been rejected, together with his insinuations against the integrity of British rule; but, so far as practical reform went, he had been outdone by a more senior, and by nature a much more cautious, official.

Nor did the changes of 1934 mark the end of official scrutiny of native administration in Lango. The late 1930s were a time of reform and re-appraisal in northern and eastern Uganda generally.[35] In Acholi there was a short-lived attempt in 1937–8 to re-draw the administrative map in accordance with traditional clan groupings,[36] while in Teso the establishment of representative councils at every level proved to be of lasting importance.[37] Furthermore, for the first time since the days of Frederick Jackson, the impulse towards reform now emanated from the highest level, in the person of Sir Philip Mitchell, Governor of Uganda from 1935 to 1940. Mitchell came to Entebbe from Dar es Salaam, where for ten years he had been closely involved in the adaptation of native authorities in Tanganyika to Indirect Rule. Unlike his predecessors, he took a close interest in the details of native administration, as well as its underlying philosophy.[38] In this atmosphere, officials in Lango were encouraged to keep their reforms under constant review; and District and Provincial reports of the time dealt more fully with the tenor and practice of local administration than ever before.

However, it was one thing to place reforms on the rule-book, but quite another to see that they were enforced. The first task was to convince the ordinary population that the Government meant business

---

[35] The critical attitude towards government chiefs in these areas is reflected in L. P. Mair, *Native Policies in Africa* (London, 1936), p. 176: in Nilotic Uganda, she wrote, 'chiefs entrusted with the operation of a foreign system which has no place in the society to which they belong use their new powers largely for their personal advantage.'

[36] Bere, 'Land and Chieftainship among the Acholi', pp. 50–1; Girling, *The Acholi of Uganda*, pp. 196–7.

[37] Lawrance, *The Iteso*, p. 36; J. C. D. Lawrance, 'The Position of Chiefs in Local Government in Uganda', *Jl. African Administration*, 8 (1956), p. 189.

[38] P. E. Mitchell, 'Indirect Rule', *Uganda Jl.* 4 (1936), pp. 101–7; *Native Administration: Note by the Governor* (Entebbe, 1939).

in seeking to end abuses which had the sanction of twenty years' practice behind them. There is little doubt that Philipps's original initiative in 1933 met with an enthusiastic popular response. He found himself 'literally beseiged by aggrieved persons'.[39] For the people of Angai in Dokolo county, the opportunity to air their grievances appeared as 'water in a thirsty land'.[40] At Adwari, the District Officer found over 100 people ready to voice their complaints against the sub-county chief.[41] Having once opened the doors to unimpeded litigation against salaried officials, the Government could not easily close them again. Long after Philipps had left Lango, actions continued to be brought against chiefs: 1935 was the peak year, after which the volume of litigation slowly dropped.[42]

These signs of popular enthusiasm strongly suggested that Philipps's indictment of native administration had been justified, but they hardly settled the more difficult question of whether serious misrule by chiefs had actually been eradicated. Here there is little evidence to go on. The only positive indication that conditions had materially improved was the reversal of the trend of migration out of mis-governed sub-counties: by the end of 1935 large numbers of Langi had returned from Bunyoro and Buganda to settle at home once more.[43] This was certainly a most significant development, but it is the only one which can be elicited from contemporary sources. The remaining evidence is negative: the fact that migration out of Lango was never resumed on any scale, and the almost complete absence from the Tour Books of cases of oppressive rule by chiefs.[44] This last piece of evidence must plainly be handled with caution, in view of the failure of touring officers in the 1920s and early 30s to perceive the true state of native administration. All the same, the greater thoroughness of touring after 1933, combined with the more acute awareness of the possible abuses and deceptions, suggests that the

[39] Philipps to Ashton Warner, 17.11.33, ADA NPMP/274E.
[40] Philipps to Ashton Warner, 11.12.33, ADA NPMP/274E.
[41] Steil, entry for 1.12.33 in Moroto TB (1926–33).
[42] Ashton Warner's report in *Annual Reports of the Provincial Commissioners, Eastern, Northern and Western Provinces, on Native Administration for 1937* (Entebbe, 1938), p. 27.
[43] Ashton Warner's report in *Annual Reports . . . for 1935* (Entebbe, 1936), p. 17.
[44] In the aftermath of Philipps's investigations, some of the older chiefs proved unable to change their methods. Enoka Acol, transferred from Moroto to Kwania county, was an example. Cox, entry for 16.6.34 in Kwania TB (1934); Richards to Bell, 22.1.35, ADA LDMP/unnumbered.

absence of reported complaints may be taken more or less at face value. In this respect, the reforms of 1934 were effective.

However, Ashton Warner had aimed at more than a clean-up of day-to-day administration. His measures had also been designed to open up the political system, at the expense of the family blocs which had hitherto held most power. It was in this sphere that the strongest resistance to reform was encountered. If the ordinary population was now spared the worst excesses of chiefly misrule, the hopes for less restricted recruitment to office and for lay participation in public affairs proved to be largely illusory. When the dust had settled and orderly administration had been resumed, many of the old faces still survived, and some of the patronage networks to which they belonged were hardly less influential than before. In part, this was due to the skill and resilience of experienced chiefs; it was also due to uncertainty and confusion among officials.

Philipps and Ashton Warner had rightly identified the county chiefs as the focus of powerful patronage-groups based on kinship. The straight swap between three pairs of chiefs was a neat way of breaking up these groups at one blow. In the event, however, this programme was never fully carried out. Within days of his announcement at the Lango District *baraza*, Ashton Warner modified the proposed changes: only two pairs of chiefs were to be switched after all; Olwa Akoli of Kole county and Ogwangguji of Erute county were to remain at their posts.[45] There is no record of what caused the Provincial Commissioner to change his mind over Olwa Akoli; but in the case of Ogwangguji his reason was that he had, as he put it, 'received a remarkable demonstration of his popularity with all classes'.[46] It is impossible to say whether this demonstration was genuine or not. Ogwangguji was undoubtedly adept at hoodwinking authority; he needed to be, since his county headquarters was situated barely a mile from the District Commissioner's office. But, whether or not it was based on a misapprehension, the decision to leave Ogwangguji *in situ* ran against Ashton Warner's own policy. According to this policy, county chiefs were not intended to serve in their home counties; Ogwangguji's supposed popularity might show that he was a good chief, but it could hardly justify his indefinite rule over Erute county, where he had been born and where all his government service had been performed. The same consideration applied in the case of chief

---

[45] Ashton Warner to DC Lango, 6.3.34, ADA LDMP/unnumbered.
[46] Ashton Warner to CS, 8.3.34, ADA NPMP/274E.

Owiny Akulo of Atura, whom not even Philipps had suggested should be transferred, and who also survived unscathed.[47] The result of this retreat was that, of the four most cohesive county cliques of the early 1930s, three retained their leaders after 1933. Only Yakobo Adoko was compelled to abandon his power-base in Maruzi by moving to Moroto county, at the other end of the District; and even he was to find ways of sustaining his role as patron. Of the seven Lango county-chiefs in office in 1939, four were ruling their counties of origin.[48] So much, then, for the hope that county chiefs would become senior civil servants, without any deep local ties. The Government's determination had flagged at exactly the point where increased bureaucratization would have had most effect.

Ashton Warner's policy towards sub-county chiefdoms was watered down in a similar way, though more gradually. The transfers and promotions of 1934 were not questioned immediately, but by the middle of 1935 the District Commissioner, J. R. Bell, had his doubts, which crystallized round two points. The first of these was sensible enough. One result of the changes of 1934 had been that several Kumam chiefs found themselves among the Langi, and vice versa; in Moroto and Dokolo counties there were four Kumam sub-county chiefs.[49] Bell therefore submitted a number of transfers with a view to separating Kumam and Langi.[50] But his proposals went one stage further, in a direction totally at odds with the policy laid down in 1934. Bell wished to restore a number of chiefs to their home areas. Now it is true that in some cases he was doubtless bowing to the inevitable. This certainly happened at Akokoro: the dominance of the Oyima clan there was so entrenched that the outsider whom Philipps had installed as chief could make no impression—he merely fell in line with the 'family caucus' of junior chiefs;[51] Bell therefore replaced him with a brother of Yakobo Adoko, 'a popular appointment' as he noted with relief.[52] However, Akokoro was the exception,

[47] Ashton Warner to DC Lango, 6.3.34, ADA LDMP/unnumbered.
[48] Owiny Akulo (Atura), Olwa Akoli (Kole), Ogwangguji (Erute), and Tomasi Ojuka (Dokolo). This last was a rather marginal case, since Ojuka had not lived in Dokolo county since he was a boy.
[49] At Dokolo, Kwera, Omoro, and Adwari. Also one county chief was transferred from Kumam to Lango in 1934: Yakobo Engwau succeeded Yakobo Adoko in Maruzi.
[50] Bell to Ashton Warner, 8.5.35, ADA LDMP/unnumbered.
[51] Bell, entry for 9.5.35 in Maruzi TB (1934–54).
[52] Bell to Ashton Warner, 18.9.35, ADA LDMP/unnumbered. The new chief was Stanley Opeto, father of Milton Obote (Interview: Stanley Opeto).

rather than the rule. There is no evidence of comparable local pressure in the other two sub-counties to which local men were appointed in 1935.[53] The trend was continued by Bell's successors; in 1938, for example, two local men were appointed to sub-counties in Dokolo county.[54] In addition, a few sub-counties—Aber, Acaba, and Ogur—saw no break in local control from 1933 until the end of the decade. In the ten sub-counties for which we have reliable information,[55] 39 per cent of the chiefs who ruled between 1933 and 1939 were local men.

Like his earlier decision to leave Ogwangguji as county chief of Erute, Ashton Warner justified this change of policy by reference to what he took to be grass-roots opinion in Lango. In this case, the obstacle confronting his original policy was the popular preference for 'some form of territorial or clan leadership'.[56] Ashton Warner would have been wise to have refrained from acting on evidence of this kind. For, despite the reforms of 1934, there was still no way in which officials could test grass-roots opinion. Any canvassing of views tended to be selective and arbitrary, and this allowed powerful interests to 'prime' opinion in advance. What ordinary people actually felt—if, indeed, they shared a common reaction at all—is impossible to tell.

One of the ways in which the Government should have been able to assess grass-roots opinion was through the popularly elected village chiefs. But this, too, was a reform which barely got off the ground. In areas such as Dokolo, where bitter experience had led people to distrust—and if possible ignore—government institutions, there was no popular interest in elections.[57] More typically, the representative character of the village headship was subverted not by local apathy, but by the intervention of the senior chiefs. One county chief of the period recalls that election meetings were always attended by the county chief and the sub-county chief; and although they did not speak in public, they could easily make their preference known beforehand.[58] Officials were aware of this danger. The District Commis-

[53] Abyece (Pilipo Oruro) and Akalu (Muca Ogwal).
[54] Dokolo (Joseph Okelo) and Angai (Gideon Odwongo).
[55] The official *Gazette* gives the names of chiefs, but for their personal origins and early careers, reliance has to be placed principally on oral sources. These ten areas represent just over a quarter of all Lango sub-counties in 1939.
[56] Ashton Warner's report in *Annual Reports . . . for 1937* (Entebbe, 1938), p. 32.
[57] Richards, entry for 3.3.35 in Dokolo TB (1934–54).
[58] Interview: Elia Olet (county chief of Maruzi from 1936 to 1941).

sioner reported in 1936 that a 'popular choice', as submitted by the chiefs, was rarely confirmed by the people afterwards.[59] Sometimes District Officers attended elections and indicated from which clans candidates ought to come forward, in an attempt to limit control by one family caucus.[60] Yet inevitably, the number of elections over which officials could preside was a small proportion of the whole. For the most part, senior chiefs could expect to have their placemen 'elected', provided their interference was not too blatant. The result was that dominance of a sub-county by one family continued to occur.

In Aber, for example, Misaki Oki, who had been chief since 1932, continued to install his own clansmen in junior positions, despite warnings from above against favouritism.[61] In 1939 the clan still held three of the four parish chiefships and four of the twelve village headships.[62] This dominance was perhaps predictable in view of the fact that Misaki Oki was the adopted son of chief Owiny Akulo, whose county included Aber. More revealing is the case of Akokoro, in Maruzi county. Yakobo Adoko had been county chief of Maruzi, but after 1934 he was no longer in a position to exert direct pressure on his home sub-county of Akokoro. Nevertheless, his Oyima clan maintained as strong a hold on petty chiefships there as it had at the end of 1933.[63] The success of the Jo Oyima was partly due to their skilful propaganda: in May 1935 a touring officer left Akokoro with the impression that about 90 per cent of the population was descended from Adoko's grandfather,[64] which was a wild exaggeration. Faced with the kind of situation which prevailed in Akokoro and Aber, officials simply passed the buck to the peasantry: people not related to the dominant group were urged to turn up in force when there was an election; and if the democratic will was overruled, it was up to them to report the matter to a District Officer.[65] Whether the democratic element in village headships was equally weak elsewhere in Lango is hard to say, in view of the thin coverage of contemporary evidence. But it is clear that Sir Philip Mitchell's prediction—that Lango county chiefs would in due course be chosen from men who had

[59] DC's report, quoted by Ashton Warner in *Annual Reports . . . for 1936* (Entebbe, 1937), p. 32.
[60] Entry for 26.6.36 at Ibuje, in Maruzi TB (1934–54).
[61] Entry for 12.5.36 in Atura TB (1934–9).
[62] List of chiefs in Aber, 1939, in Oyam TB (1939–53).
[63] Lists of chiefs, and entries for Akokoro, in Maruzi TB (1934–54).
[64] Entry for 9.5.35 in Maruzi TB (1934–54).
[65] Entry for 12.5.36 in Atura TB (1934–9); entry for 15.10.37 in Maruzi TB (1934–54).

begun as popularly elected headmen—was wide of the mark.[66] Much more than the stroke of a pen was needed to implement a radical change at the expense of strong vested interests, and at the level most distant from administrative scrutiny.

A similar fate overtook Ashton Warner's other venture into the field of democratic reform—the Lango Native Council, with its prescribed lay representation. This council was not the first central organ of African opinion in Lango District. In 1919 a council of county chiefs had been set up; it was to meet quarterly in order to discuss matters of public concern and to recommend changes in customary law.[67] Five years later, this council had been given an additional role as Native District Court under the District Commissioner's presidency.[68] Both these bodies had been the exclusive preserve of the county chiefs. The proposed constitution of the Lango Native Council could therefore be construed as a threat to their primacy. This was certainly how Ashton Warner had intended it. However, the precise composition of the Council was left to the District Commissioner, and the principle of independent members was soon modified, to the advantage of the county chiefs. Bell decided that the Council should be made up of all ten county chiefs, ten of the sub-county chiefs, and up to ten 'non-officials'; the last two groups were to be nominated by the county chiefs, and of the nine 'non-officials' actually chosen, eight had at one time served as government chiefs.[69]

Bell's superiors were a little perturbed by the scope for control which his provisions gave to the county chiefs. Mitchell observed that, since the Lango Native Council was not a customary body, its members could reasonably be nominated by officials; but these must be *British* officials.[70] In practice, all this proviso meant was that the Provincial Commissioner's approval was required before the county chiefs' choice could take effect.[71] When the Lango Native Council was reconstituted in 1938, the non-official element was subdivided into five 'clan heads', or *wegi atekere*, and six educated people nominated

[66] Mitchell to Bottomley, 23.5.36, PRO CO/536/186.

[67] Eden, Report on Eastern Province for 1919–20, UNA SMP/703I; Ingham, op. cit., p. 164.

[68] Ingham, op. cit., p. 165.

[69] Bell to Ashton Warner, 18.6.35, UNA NPMP/ADM/21/L.

[70] Mitchell's remarks were cited in Chief Secretary to Ashton Warner, 23.11.35, UNA NPMP/ADM/21/L.

[71] Ashton Warner to DC Lango, 5.11.35, UNA NPMP/ADM/21/L. Responsibility for choosing the sub-county chiefs' representatives was in fact shifted from the county chiefs to the sub-county chiefs themselves.

by the District Commissioner.[72] The term *wegi atekere* was completely misleading. The District Commissioner claimed that they had, 'except by rare coincidence, no official status'.[73] But, since the 'clan heads' were to be chosen by the county chiefs, he could not ensure that they were outside the web of chiefly patronage: of the five 'clan heads' who attended the Council's next meeting in January 1939, four had previously held office as sub-county chiefs, and two of these had been dismissed by Philipps for gross misrule.[74] Until the end of the Second World War, the county chiefs were strikingly successful in ensuring that grass-roots opinion did not make itself heard at District level.

The topics aired in the Lango Native Council were seldom of great moment.[75] But the Council was none the less politically important in that the 'feel' of Lango opinion was conveyed to European officials mainly through the county chiefs and their henchmen. The prominence of the county chiefs in all deliberations at District level confirmed a trend already apparent before 1934—their greater access to European administrators. This was evident in the sphere of senior appointments. Before 1934 so few changes of personnel had occurred at county level that no procedure had been devised for selecting new chiefs. After 1934 such vacancies arose more frequently, and they were filled in such a way as to entrench existing interests. For example, when the county chief of Maruzi was transferred in 1936, the District Commissioner consulted the other county chiefs about the vacancy, with the result that Elia Olet, a cousin of Ogwangguji's ,was chosen in preference to any of the other 'progressive' sub-county chiefs.[76] As regards sub-county appointments, county chiefs were able to advance the interests of their families as before: Olwa Akoli of Kole had his son made chief of Alito in 1936, while Ogwangguji installed a brother

[72] Tucker to Ashton Warner, 25.6.38, and Ashton Warner to Tucker, 13.7.38, UNA NPMP/ADM/21/L.

[73] Tucker to Ashton Warner, 25.6.38, UNA NPMP/ADM/21/L.

[74] The Council's members are listed in Rogers to Sandford, 27.2.39, UNA NPMP/ADM/21/L. The two who had been dismissed by Philipps were Israel Alele (Dokolo) and Danieri Okuk Awira (Adwari).

[75] In January 1939 the Council's resolutions concerned the following: (1) regret at transfer of Kumam areas to Teso District, (2) proposed school in memory of King George V, (3) payment of bridewealth, and (4) the regulation of adultery and fornication (the majority of resolutions). Minutes of Lango Native Council, 6.1.39, UNA NPMP/ADM/21/L.

[76] Interview: Elia Olet. Olet's claim was admittedly strengthened by his education at King's School, Budo (the only Lango of this time to have been there) and his experience as interpreter in the DC's office.

at Apala in 1939.[77] In that year there were at least eleven sub-county chiefs in Lango who were personal protégés of county chiefs. This total represented no fall-off from the pre-1934 figure. The only difference was that placemen were now less likely to find themselves in the same county as their patrons. From the point of view of opening up the Lango political system, the reforms of 1934 had very meagre results. Some of the smaller patronage groups probably went to the wall. But the really powerful ones survived. They not only retained their hold on local appointments, but became increasingly effective at the District level, where they were able to press their candidates' claim to vacancies anywhere in the District.

It remains to consider two negative implications of this continued prominence of established interests. At the time of the 1934 reforms, officials had not speculated on who would benefit from the predicted break-up of the existing patronage networks. But there were two categories which in retrospect might have been expected to gain substantially. The first was dependent on the 'bureaucratic' aspect of the reforms, and the second on the more democratic objective of grass-roots involvement.

Ashton Warner's preference for appointment on merit without regard to territorial or clan considerations, if carried to its logical conclusion, entailed the promotion of 'new men', dependent on education rather than patronage connections. Before 1934 'rootless' men had gained important positions, but only because they had entered the orbit of senior chiefs. Thus Tomasi Ojuka, who had begun as a camp-follower of the Baganda, became a sub-county chief through Ogwangguji's patronage.[78] From 1934 onwards, it was no longer impossible for a *parvenu* to gain advancement on his own merits. Erieza Olwol, who had been a Protestant catechist and a clerk, was appointed by Philipps to a Kumam sub-county, and was then transferred to Apala in 1935.[79] Joseph Okelo grew up in Dokolo and received five years of Catholic education, before serving first as a clerk and then as a sub-county chief from 1935.[80] Neither of these men came from clans of any significance, and they both later became county chiefs. In part, their careers reflect the increasing scale of missionary activity, which the chiefs could not control so successfully

[77] Interviews: Yokana Engola, Isaya Ogwangguji.
[78] Interviews: Tomasi Ojuka, Isaya Ogwangguji.
[79] Interview: Erieza Olwol.
[80] Interview: Joseph Okelo.

as before.[81] Yet, even in the late 1930s, such cases were still very much the exception. The fact that educational standards among chiefs were improving did not as a rule indicate a loosening of the patronage nexus. The second category who might have been expected to profit from the upheaval of 1934 were the 'out-groups'—those clan sections for whose leaders no place had been found in the chiefly hierarchy. The Government had the opportunity of filling some of the vacancies caused by Philipps's investigations with men from these groups. There is no evidence that such a policy was considered, and it must be admitted that to appoint to a sub-county chiefship a man with no previous experience of administration would have been a risky course. At all events, none of the unplaced clan leaders was appointed. Alternatively, 'out-groups' might have entered the system through election to village headships. For all the machinations of the senior chiefs, it is probable that some of them did gain village headships. But to achieve recognition in this way was no guarantee of entry into the system. The village headship lay outside the three-tiered government hierarchy, and admission to this hierarchy continued to be mainly at the discretion of the senior chiefs. It would seem a reasonable surmise, therefore, that the changes in the method of recruitment to chiefships after 1933 did nothing to halt popular alienation from the official hierarchy. The successful eradication of abuses doubtless tempered the resentment of the 'man-on-the-shamba' towards government chiefs, but he could still not think of them as the natural spokesmen for his own community.

It will be plain from the foregoing account that this outcome, which fell so far short of the hopes entertained in 1934, was due in large measure to the manipulative skill of the chiefs themselves. But it also reflected the confusion and vacillation of official policy, particularly when this turned on European perceptions of 'bureaucratic' and 'traditional' authority in an acephalous society. Captain Philipps had been in no doubt about the real status of senior chiefs in Lango: they were no more than 'native officials'.[82] Sir Philip Mitchell was if anything blunter: chiefs in areas like Lango were 'a subordinate black administrative service', comparable to the discredited akidas of

---

[81] A big expansion followed on the establishment of a CMS headquarters at Boroboro in 1926 and a Verona Fathers Mission at Ngeta in 1930.

[82] Philipps to Ashton Warner, 17.11.33, ADA NPMP/274E.

German East Africa.[83] What Philipps's indictment boiled down to was that in Lango civil servants had been treated by the Government as though they were traditional rulers; and these civil servants, lacking the restraints which an indigenous position of authority would have imposed on them, had not unnaturally used their immense powers for personal enrichment and patronage.

If this analysis was accepted, there were only two possible remedies: either the chiefs should be subjected to the controls appropriate to salaried civil servants, or the whole structure of native administration ought to be reconstituted in the light of the indigenous social organization. Ashton Warner had begun by settling for the first alternative. When, however, he drew back from a rigorous programme of bureaucratization by transferring chiefs back to their home areas, he justified himself on the grounds that the Langi appeared to favour 'some form of territorial or clan leadership'.[84] Whether or not this preference really reflected the popular view, the way in which Ashton Warner acted on it showed considerable confusion in his mind about Lango society. For, if clan leadership was to be the model, then much more was required than the appointment of local men to existing chiefships; the boundaries of pre-colonial clan combinations would have to be reconstructed, and the views of the elders canvassed as to the identity of the most important clan leader.[85] A reform along these lines was actually attempted in Acholi District in 1937, though it was short-lived.[86] In Lango, the recasting of the village chiefship might be interpreted as a step in this direction, but otherwise a restructuring of local administration was never considered. All that happened as a result of Ashton Warner's change of heart was that the bureaucratic element in appointive chiefship was diluted, to the profit of the existing chiefs and their families.

Of course, the difficulties which stood in the way of reorganizing native administration from the bottom upwards must not be underestimated. The basis of indigenous political organization had eluded the very first officials stationed in Lango. By the 1930s their successors had in addition to contend with the distorting effect of an alien type of government, which had overlaid traditional forms for twenty years or more. As the follow-up to the much discussed Women's Riots of 1929

[83] Mitchell to Bottomley, 25.5.36, PRO CO/536/186.
[84] Ashton Warner's report in *Annual Reports . . . for 1937* (Entebbe, 1938), p. 32.
[85] It is doubtful, in fact, whether such an investigation would have been successful, in view of the declining importance of clan leadership, described in Chapter 7.   [86] Bere, op. cit., pp. 50–1.

in Eastern Nigeria showed, patient research was required in order to uncover the indigenous political organization of 'submerged' acephalous peoples.[87] If more than superficial results were to be obtained, anthropologists had to be employed, or administrative officers seconded for full-time research, and the Uganda Government could not afford such luxuries. At the same time, some of the difficulties were of the officials' own making. Whatever the theoretical appeal of a reorganized administration, District Officers were in practice reluctant to dispense with a set of chiefs who, tyrannical and corrupt though they might be, smoothed the path of government. They preferred a system which was fairly standard throughout Uganda to the unpredictable task of devising a new form of native administration for a single District. This conservatism was strongly reinforced by the European officials' own terms of service; frequent leaves and changes of posting encouraged them to content themselves with the efficient conduct of routine administration. This was a common pattern in the Colonial Service.[88] The impetus for reform usually came, not from within the provincial administration, but from agitation below, or from a shift in policy at Secretariat or metropolitan level.

So it was in Lango. Radical change, when it came in the 1950s, was the result of a change of course which affected the whole of Uganda. The essence of the new policy was that control over the chiefs, together with some of their administrative functions, should be transferred to elected District Councils. This was in response to the Colonial Secretary's dispatch of 1947, which declared that democratic local government on the English model was now the objective in the African dependencies. In Uganda, an Ordinance of 1949 transferred the power to alter native law from the chiefs to the councils; and by another Ordinance in 1955 the District Council was recognized as constituting the District Administration, with power to appoint and remove chiefs.[89] It is true that by 1947 representative councils had already been introduced in many parts of Uganda, including Lango, where a three-tier system had been set up below District level in 1946,[90] and where the District Council could be traced back to the

[87] M. Perham, *Native Administration in Nigeria* (London, 1937), pp. 241–8.
[88] Ibid., pp. 351–2.
[89] For the development of these new institutions, see F. G. Burke, *Local Government and Politics in Uganda* (Syracuse, 1964), pp. 38–72; and Gertzel, *Party and Locality in Northern Uganda*, pp. 15–23.
[90] Lord Hailey, *Native Administration in the British African Territories*, part 1 (London, 1950), pp. 64–5.

reforms of 1934; but until the change of policy in London, these bodies showed no sign of evolving beyond an advisory capacity. Only when the councils were charged with executive functions was the power of the chiefs significantly reduced. As a result of the innovations made between 1947 and 1955, native administration in Lango was recast for the first time since 1912, and the rules of the political game were rewritten. Some of the patronage factions which had grown up since 1920 continued to flourish, but they did so in a different atmosphere and by different methods.[91]

It may seem remarkable that, throughout the discussions among administrators about what changes ought to be made in Lango during the 1930s, hardly any reference was made to theories of colonial government. Captain Philipps himself, for all his delight in pronouncing on broader issues of colonial policy, was not measuring Lango against the requirements of Indirect Rule, nor was he calling in question the value of that doctrine; he merely observed that the undesirable terms of service which senior chiefs enjoyed in Lango owed their currency to the way in which Indirect Rule was being implemented elsewhere.[92] At the Colonial Office, Philipps's investigations were construed as an attack on Indirect Rule,[93] but in Uganda his activities were frowned upon for more down-to-earth reasons. Until Mitchell's Governorship (1935–40), theory and doctrine had little place in the native administration of Uganda.

During the inter-war period the Langi were not, of course, governed in accordance with the principles of Indirect Rule. In the first place, the powers allowed to them were too restricted in certain areas, notably the financial. Indirect Rule implied a native government with its own treasury, empowered to initiate expenditure on a wide range of public concerns. In Lango, on the other hand, all taxes were paid in to the Protectorate Government; only the most trifling sums were entrusted to African authorities, and these only at sub-county and county levels. In the second place, the administration of Lango could not be said to have been carried out by indigenous authorities, except in the most superficial sense. Initially some identity had been achieved between government chiefs and clan leaders, but the connection soon

---

[91] In the early 1950s, control of the African Local Government in Lira was hotly contested between Isaya Ogwangguji and Yakobo Adoko, each of whom served a term as paramount chief (*rwot adwong*). For an introduction to the postwar period in Lango, see Gertzel, *Party and Locality in Northern Uganda*, pp. 24–55.   [92] Philipps to Ashton Warner, 23.2.34, ADA NPMP/274E.
[93] Minute by J. E. W. Flood, 8.6.36, PRO CO/536/186.

became tenuous. Besides, continuity of personnel was less significant than continuity of territory and function, and here the official positions were radically different from the clan leadership that had gone before—and different, too, from the regional leadership which had perished a generation earlier. Clan leaders invested with government office found themselves ruling villages over which they had no vestige of natural authority, and exercising powers which were totally alien to their experience.

Indirect Rule rested on the assumption that indigenous institutions could be adapted to the requirements of 'civilized' administration. That these institutions should be authoritarian was not integral to the theory, but during the early colonial period it was deemed essential that they be so in practice. The exponents of Indirect Rule had great difficulty in separating their theory from the highly authoritarian institutions through which it had first seen the light of day in northern Nigeria. This is evident from the experience of the Tiv of central Nigeria, whose traditional political organization was egalitarian and parochial. In 1909, and again in 1933, individual British officials attempted to recast local administration along indigenous lines by the use of councils; in each case the experiment failed because of the overwhelming preference in official quarters for African subordinates with undiluted executive authority.[94] The only significant exception was in south-eastern Nigeria among the Ibo and Ibibio peoples. Here, Sir Donald Cameron's abolition of the Warrant Chiefs in favour of a multiplicity of councils, based on the indigenous village organization, proved more durable, largely because the Government had been so shaken by the Women's Riots of 1929.[95] As a general rule, Indirect Rule in practice prevented any institutional continuity in acephalous societies.

So far as Lango was concerned, considerations of general theory had anyway not entered into the original provisions for administration. The institutions of government established between 1912 and 1919 were authoritarian and hierarchical—and thus contrary to traditional forms—because at that time there appeared to be no other way of securing the enforcement of administrative demands. Broadly speaking, the system was maintained over the next thirty years for the

[94] D. C. Dorward, 'The Development of the British Colonial Administration among the Tiv, 1900–49', *African Affairs*, 68 (1969), pp. 316–33.
[95] Perham, op. cit., pp. 206–54; H. A. Gailey, *The Road to Aba* (New York, 1970), pp. 135–55.

same reason, except that the expansion of government services set if anything a great premium on the 'Ganda model'. The men who set up these institutions in Lango District were under few illusions about the new departure which they entailed for the Langi themselves; because they realized how little experience the 'chiefs' had of administrative authority, the earliest officials kept them on a tight rein. Their successors were less prudent. Without being obliged to conform to Indirect Rule—or to any orthodoxy at all—they nevertheless succumbed to the common tendency to regard administrative systems as in some sense hallowed by tradition. As a result of both Protectorate policy and improvisation at District level, powers were accorded to chiefs in Lango which might have been appropriate to traditional rulers, but which were quite unjustified in the case of a recently established civil service. The underlying attitude was that, in Lango as elsewhere, rule by chiefs was part of the natural order, and that the British were administering the Langi through their own leaders. This misconception increased the reluctance of officials to tamper with the system. Had they recognized the real status of the chiefs, they would perhaps have been more sympathetic to the idea of radical change. Not until after the Second World War were changes made which materially diminished the power of the chiefs. Only then was the authoritarian character of the political system in Lango tempered by an element of democratic control.

Conclusion

THE preceding chapters amount to a case-study of political change in an African stateless society over a period of nearly a century and a half. Within this timespan, the most revolutionary changes were brought about by the imposition of British control; as a result, Lango society experienced for the first time the exercise of specialized political authority, indigenous forms of leadership being transformed by the bureaucratic requirements of the colonial power. Bureaucratization was not, however, applied to a static political system, but to one which was of relatively recent origin and which had undergone since then a number of changes.

The most important of these changes stemmed from the final stage in the settlement of Lango country by its present stock at the very beginning of the nineteenth century. The process whereby Nilotic Lwo and Para-Nilotic Iseera combined to form the Lango people is beyond recall, but the long-term results may be discerned. The segmentary lineage organization of the Lwo was so disrupted that it ceased to be a mechanism of political co-operation above the level of the village cluster. At the same time, the age-organization of the Iseera became less and less effective as a mechanism of social control and military co-operation. Consequently by the late nineteenth-century Lango society lacked those 'incipient structures through which organised large communities could be brought into existence when the need arose'.[1] Compared with acephalous communities based on segmentary lineage systems (such as the Nuer) or on age-groups (such as the Jie), Lango society could fairly be described as 'amorphous'.[2]

Secondary migration and settlement within the confines of Lango country continued on a large scale until the 1880s, and to a lesser degree right up to the beginning of colonial rule. Throughout this period new clans were being formed, and most clans were becoming divided between an ever increasing number of separate locations. By the beginning of the twentieth century there were probably around six hundred localized clan sections, with an average adult male

---

[1] Colson, 'African Society at the Time of the Scramble', p. 53.
[2] Ibid., p. 52.

membership of one hundred. Each localized section acknowledged its own clan leader (*rwot*) but it did not exist in isolation. The political community typically comprised several clan sections, bound together by ties of neighbourhood and marriage rather than a common clan identity (since the sections usually belonged to different clans), and recognizing the primacy of one of the constituent clan sections and its leader. A *rwot* whose leadership encompassed two or three clan sections spread over a dozen villages was by no means uncommon. It was explained in Chapter 3 why it is inappropriate to describe such a leader as a chief.[3] But the influence enjoyed by clan leaders made them the most important actors on the political stage at the close of the pre-colonial era.

The flourishing condition of clan leadership at the turn of the century was in marked contrast to the fate which had overtaken the other main authority position in pre-colonial Lango—regional leadership. This position may have originated as a feature of the age-organization, but by the late nineteenth century it depended more on strength of personality and the attractions of foreign campaigning. It was the regional leaders who led the Langi across the Nile in armies several thousand strong, and who organized resistance against the Sudanese freebooters who descended on Lango during the 1870s. Their authority was not, however, very resilient. Under the stress of military defeats abroad and the disastrous rinderpest epidemic at home, regional leadership collapsed in the early 1890s, and with it the social conventions which had limited the severity of inter-clan conflict.

During the pre-colonial era, then, the Lango political system clearly underwent considerable modifications. But it can hardly be said to have been moving in the direction of state formation, or to have experienced an enlargement of political scale—indeed, rather the reverse. The history of pre-colonial Africa includes a number of instances in which acephalous societies evolved more formal institutions of government. Sometimes political differentiation was a consequence of successive layers of settlement, the tension between immigrant and indigenous groups being resolved by the subordination of one to the other. The interlacustrine kingdoms and the Shilluk

---

[3] See above, pp. 68, 87. For a more accommodating view on the application of the concepts of 'chief' and 'state formation' to the Lwo-speaking peoples of northern Uganda, see J. M. Onyango-ku-Odongo and J. B. Webster (eds.), *The Central Lwo during the Aconya* (Nairobi, 1976).

monarchy have been explained along these lines, with the Lwo in each case acting as the catalyst.[4] There is no hint of this kind of development in Lango history, notwithstanding the prominent part played by the Lwo. Stateless societies have also in the past been profoundly modified by their involvement in overseas or long-distance trade. Provided the influx of trade goods was large enough, those groups or individuals who could monopolize relations with the traders were equipped with a formidable power-base. This, at least, is part of the explanation for the origin of the Niger Delta states.[5] The Langi, on the other hand, received no more than a trickle of exotic imports during the nineteenth century, and control over their supply was never an important issue. Alternatively, political differentiation, instead of arising from economic or social stresses within an acephalous society, might be imposed from without by an expanding state. This possibility merits consideration in the case of the Langi because of their contacts with the interlacustrine kingdoms. During the nineteenth century Bunyoro, the nearest of these kingdoms, would undoubtedly have preferred to deal with the Langi as subjects, whose military aid could be demanded as of right instead of being solicited with gifts. Yet not even Kabarega, the most powerful of Bunyoro's kings, made good the claim to rule Lango. His failure demonstrates that stateless societies were not always at a disadvantage in their dealings with strong African kingdoms.

In the event, it proved to be the British who incorporated the Langi into a centralized political system. They did so under conditions which rendered Lango acquiescence highly improbable. The first generation of colonial officials made little effort to overcome their ignorance about Lango society; and initially they depended for the basic spadework of administration on under-paid and under-trained government agents from Buganda, who not only shared British ignorance of local conditions but regarded their service in Lango as an opportunity for speedy enrichment. The response of the Langi was generally, though not uniformly hostile; for some twenty years the incoming colonial power was violently obstructed by countless small clan combinations.

[4] B. A. Ogot, 'Kingship and Statelessness among the Nilotes', in *The Historian in Tropical Africa*, ed. J. Vansina, R. Mauny, and L. V. Thomas (London, 1964), pp. 284–302.
[5] R. Horton, 'Stateless Societies in the History of West Africa', and E. J. Alagoa, 'The Niger Delta States and their Neighbours, 1600–1800', both in *History of West Africa*, vol. I, ed. J. F. A. Ajayi and M. Crowder (London, 1971), pp. 78–119, 269–303.

It is not immediately obvious, perhaps, that uncoordinated and inter-
mittent resistance of this kind posed serious problems for imperial
rule. The hostility of a state like Bunyoro was clearly a weighty
matter.[6] So too was the resistance of an acephalous society able to
draw on new resources of leadership, such as prophetic power.[7] It has
also been conceded that a society based upon a comprehensive segmentary lineage system could effectively close ranks against an
aggressor who appeared to threaten its way of life.[8] But historians
have not given much attention to those small-scale societies whose
resistance always remained parochial in range.[9] The Lango case shows
that such resistance, repeated again and again in first one part of the
District and then another, was not to be made light of. For a government whose representatives were very thin on the ground, it was in
some ways more taxing and more demoralizing than a full-scale
rebellion would have been.[10]

In one respect Lango resistance had tangible results. It brought
about in 1911 a drastic reappraisal by the Government of its administrative methods in Lango and neighbouring districts: the use of
Baganda agents was to be restricted and a definite limit set on their
term of service. But for the incessant hostilities of the previous three
years, the Baganda might well have remained in Lango until the
1920s or even beyond, as they were to do elsewhere in Uganda.[11] In
this way the British were faced with their second major political
problem in Lango: the creation of a district administration staffed by

---

[6] Hemphill, 'The British Sphere, 1884–94', pp. 423–7. This episode still awaits
the treatment in depth which it deserves.

[7] See, for example, A. King, 'The Yakan Cult and Lugbara Response to
Colonial Rule', *Azania*, 5 (1970), pp. 1–25. Cf. R. Waller, 'The Maasai and the
British 1895–1905: the Origins of an Alliance', *Jl. African History*, 17 (1976),
pp. 529–53.

[8] Colson, op. cit., pp. 52–3.
Segmentary lineage organization was an important factor (though not the only
one) in the prolonged resistance of the Nuer to the Condominium Government of
the Sudan between 1902 and 1929. An important work on this topic is being prepared by Douglas H. Johnson.

[9] See, for example, Ranger, 'African Reactions to the Imposition of Colonial
Rule in East and Central Africa', pp. 296, 304.
A notable exception is S. Marks, 'Khoisan Resistance to the Dutch in the
Seventeenth and Eighteenth Centuries', *Jl. African History*, 13 (1972), pp. 55–80.

[10] For further consideration of this issue, see Tosh, 'Small-scale Resistance in
Uganda: the Lango "Rising" at Adwari in 1919'. For observations to the same
effect, see Munro, *Colonial Rule and the Kamba*, p. 31.

[11] A. D. Roberts, 'The Sub-Imperialism of the Baganda', *Jl. African History*, 3
(1962), pp. 435–50.

local personnel. Both prior experience in centralized polities such as Buganda, and the practical requirements of colonial government, demanded that a wide range of powers be entrusted to 'chiefs', accountable to—and fully supported by—European officials. Confronted by societies which lacked chiefs, the colonial government did not improvise an alternative system; instead, as Fortes and Evans-Pritchard observed of the inter-war period, 'it makes use of any persons who can be assimilated to the stereotyped notion of an African chief'.[12] In Lango these persons were the clan leaders.

From the point of view of colonial administration, Lango clan leadership left a great deal to be desired. In almost every instance its territorial range was less than the size of the 'chiefdom' regarded by officials as the minimum unit. Its functions were limited to the military and the judicial. Above all, it was inhibited by the values of an egalitarian society: a strong element of consensus entered into all decision-making, and the clan leader did not enjoy those rights to labour service which were regarded as an essential part of a chief's remuneration in the early colonial period. It was men accustomed to exercise leadership of this restricted kind who, from 1912 onwards, were selected as government chiefs. On grounds which were wholly arbitrary so far as the Langi were concerned, between thirty and forty clan leaders were suddenly invested with formidable new powers. Chiefship endowed them with unprecedented public authority and personal privilege, and it gave them sway over communities to which they had no prior claim. Lacking the guidance of indigenous models of conduct, the chiefs not unnaturally used their powers in an arbitrary way.[13] This situation called for tactful and frequent supervision. The officials who set up the system were well aware that 'political education' must be provided for chiefs performing completely new roles. Yet even before the depletion of staff caused by the First World War, the size of the District's European establishment was inadequate. Nor was supervision intensified after the War, since by then District Officers—unlike their pre-war predecessors—were beginning to assume that the chiefs were traditional authorities who should be disturbed as little as possible. The chiefs in turn exploited this assumption to conceal their arbitrary use of power, to line their own pockets,

---

[12] Fortes and Evans-Pritchard (eds.), *African Political Systems*, editors' Introduction, p. 15.
[13] Cf. Barnes, 'Indigenous Politics and Colonial Administration with special reference to Australia'.

and to construct patronage networks which placed a stranglehold on the local administration.[14]

Viewed as an essay in colonial rule, the British record in Lango up to 1939 was hardly an unqualified success. How far it should be judged a failure is not easy to determine, since British officials seldom expressed their objectives clearly. Broadly speaking, there were two standards of judgement which—in Lango as elsewhere in British Africa—co-existed uneasily in the official mind. The first was the bureaucratic standard—that is, a concern that native administration should be efficient, honest, and impartial. Initially valued for their own sake, these attributes were by the 1920s seen as the indispensable foundation on which ambitious schemes of welfare and development could be built. It is clear that, up to 1934 at least, chiefly administration fell far short of British expectations. Captain Philipps's findings in 1933 shocked his superiors because they had begun to take minimum bureaucratic standards for granted. Now the effectiveness of twenty years of British protection was suddenly being called in question.

Philipps's outburst had an important bearing on the second criterion applied by the British to local administrations of their own creation: that power should be exercised by traditional authorities enjoying the broad support of their people. This area of official thinking was strongly affected by self-deception and half-truths. No district in Uganda between the Wars was administered according to 'Indirect Rule' in the classic formulation of Lord Lugard. This truth was sufficiently obvious.[15] But it was assumed by Protectorate officials that, as a general principle, indirect rule had been applied throughout Uganda. Indeed, there was a case for saying that the prototype of indirect rule in British Africa was to be found, not in the emirates of northern Nigeria, but in the arrangements made for Buganda at the turn of the century.[16] Officials were extremely reluctant to recognize that, outside the interlacustrine states, Uganda was governed through an administrative system which had been exported from Buganda, irrespective of local conditions. In reality, a

[14] Cf. R. L. Tignor, 'Colonial Chiefs in Chiefless Societies', *Jl. Modern African Studies*, 9 (1971), pp. 339–59; Munro, op. cit., ch. 4; J. Vincent, 'Colonial Chiefs and the Making of Class: a Case Study from Teso, Eastern Uganda', *Africa* 47 (1977), pp. 140–59.

[15] D. A. Low and R. C. Pratt, *Buganda and British Overrule, 1900–1955* (London, 1960), part 2.

[16] M. Perham, 'Some Problems of Indirect Rule in Africa', *Jl. Royal Society of Arts* (May 1934), reprinted in M. Perham, *Colonial Sequence, 1930 to 1949* (London, 1967), pp. 93–4.

system which in Buganda could be interpreted as one version of indirect rule assumed a totally different character in districts like Lango. The results, as Sir Philip Mitchell pointed out in 1939, amounted to 'direct rule'.[17] But the majority of British officials did not see so clearly. Instead, chiefs in Lango were erroneously regarded as traditional authorities; they were therefore allowed a latitude quite out of keeping with their real status as junior officials.

The main purpose of this book, however, has been not to assess the effectiveness of British colonial policies, but to analyse the political changes sustained by an acephalous society. Official policy was itself, of course, an important source of change. But the colonial political system also reflected the response of Lango society to the occupying power, and in particular it reflected the manipulative skill of local interests. Manipulation of colonial authority had started from the moment the British began actively to concern themselves with the Langi; one has only to think of Daudi Odora's early career, or the way in which individual clan leaders influenced the siting of government posts. In different forms manipulation continued throughout the colonial period, and with striking results: key positions in the chiefly hierarchy were held by the same families throughout the interwar years, being virtually unaffected by the official attempt at reform in 1933–4. And when during the 1950s national political parties made their appearence in Lango, the local branches fell under the control of the same senior chiefs.[18] Such continuity of political leadership argues a formidable ability to exploit the external sources of power, be they colonial or nationalist. Collaboration was not only practicable but paid high dividends. This conclusion is at variance with recent writing on the African response to colonial rule. Terence Ranger has denied to small-scale societies the benefits which accrued from collaboration to kingdoms and chiefdoms; he suggests that for the former the choice between resistance and collaboration scarcely existed.[19] To be sure, societies like Lango did not evince a consistent or united response. The choice between resistance and collaboration was not exercised by the society as a whole, but by important groups within it; taken together, their impact was considerable. The political

---

[17] *Native Administration: Note by the Governor* (Entebbe, 1939), p. 19.

[18] Milton Obote (U.N.C., later U.P.C.) began as the protégé of Yakobo Adoko, who had first gained chiefly office in 1916. Isaya Ogwangguji, some of whose family were prominent in the Democratic Party, had received his first appointment in 1915.

[19] Ranger, op. cit., p. 296.

system of colonial Lango was profoundly influenced by these groups, through their skilful manipulation of the colonial authorities.

What was at stake in this interplay between Lango chiefs and British officials was control over the new resources of wealth, education, and power which the imperial connection made available to the Langi. By the early 1930s an excessive proportion of these resources was being appropriated by the senior chiefs and their respective clan sections. The effects on the mass of ordinary Langi were serious. It has been maintained that, in those parts of Uganda where the British imposed an administration modelled on Buganda, the new institutions were soon regarded by the local people as traditional.[20] The Lango case does not support this conclusion. It would indeed have been remarkable if the immense formal differences between colonial chiefship and pre-colonial clan leadership had been forgotten within a generation. What was most resented at grass-roots level, however, was the dictatorial rule and personal enrichment of the senior chiefs. These traits were an affront to the egalitarianism of Lango society—all the greater because contact with the outside world in the late nineteenth century had not brought about any measure of political differentiation in Lango society. British officials had hoped that, once overt resistance had ended, the Langi would acknowledge the legitimacy of the colonial order in their midst. These hopes were confounded because the discrepancy between the indigenous political culture and the actual exercise of administrative authority was too great. Recent research on other African stateless societies under colonial rule would suggest that the Lango case was not atypical.[21]

In this context, the upheaval in Lango District of 1933–4 should be interpreted as a reassertion of egalitarian values against a powerful minority which lacked traditional legitimacy. That the Government did not interpret events in this light was due in part to the less than total spontaneity of the anti-chief protests; the suspicion remained that these were induced by an eccentric District Commissioner with an axe of his own to grind. The reforms carried out from 1934 on-

[20] A recent example is Morris and Read, *Indirect Rule and the Search for Justice*, p. 142: 'If, in fact, historically this system of chiefs, together with their courts, was largely an importation from the lacustrine kingdoms, the local people soon came to look upon it as part of their traditional heritage.'

[21] Afigbo, *The Warrant Chiefs: Indirect Rule in Southeastern Nigeria* (for the Ibo); Dorward, 'A Political and Social History of the Tiv People of Northern Nigeria, 1900–1939'; King, 'A History of West Nile District, Uganda', (for the Lugbara).

wards did not, therefore, introduce fundamental changes; they merely trimmed some of the more obvious abuses of chiefly power.[22] As a result, ordinary Langi continued to feel alienated from the administrative system through which they were governed. At the district level, the chiefs were still successful in preventing the discontent which they aroused from finding political expression. Those groups, such as teachers and 'progressive' farmers, which elsewhere articulated this kind of discontent,[23] had not yet emerged as distinct interests in Lango: both educational opportunities and the new wealth from cash crops had been largely appropriated by the chiefs and their dependants. Another, closely related, symptom of chiefly dominance was the fact that for the Langi themselves the District hardly counted as a political arena. As a cultural identity, 'Lango' was rooted in the historical experience of the Lango people in the course of the nineteenth century. However, during the early colonial period (1908–39), when so many new political aggregations were taking shape in East Africa,[24] there were few signs that this identity was perceived by the Langi as having a political dimension, either *vis-à-vis* other ethnic groups, or as a means of pressing sectional interests with the district administration.[25] The only exception was the chiefs themselves. It was they who went on official visits to neighbouring districts; it was their sons whose sense of Lango identity was sharpened by attending schools in Acholi or Teso; and it was they who registered indignation at the Government's bias in favour of the Acholi dialect of Lwo at the expense of the Lango dialect.[26] Not until the mid-1940s was the first popular interest in district-level politics expressed and the Young Lango Association formed.[27]

[22] This was in marked contrast to events in south-eastern Nigeria a few years earlier. There, the Women's Riots of 1929 were not only entirely spontaneous but constituted a serious breach of the peace. The Government's response was to sweep away the chiefs altogether, and to model local administration on the village councils which were indigenous to the Ibo and Ibibio. See Perham, *Native Administration in Nigeria*, pp. 206–54.
[23] Lonsdale, 'Some Origins of Nationalism in East Africa'.
[24] D. A. Low and J. M. Lonsdale, 'Introduction: Towards the New Order, 1945–1963', in *History of East Africa*, vol. III (Oxford, 1976), ed. D. A. Low and A. Smith, pp. 24–32.
[25] Important constraints here were the limited extent of labour migration from Lango, and the lack of a sizeable 'reference group' of non-Langi resident in the District. Cf. Twaddle, ' "Tribalism" in Eastern Uganda', p. 196.
[26] Entry for 16.11.38 in Maruzi TB (1934–54); Ogwal Ajungu, untitled vernacular history (1936–7), MS. in the possession of Dr. T. T. S. Hayley, Preface.
[27] Gertzel, *Party and Locality in Northern Uganda, 1945–1962*, pp. 13, 28, 31.

At the grass-roots level, however, there was some indication as the inter-war years drew to a close of a positive reaction against the official order. It was during the 1930s that the *wang tic*—the 'neighbourhood' based on co-operative labour—began to evolve a political leadership of its own. The position of 'neighbourhood leader' had not existed in pre-colonial times, but was a response to the diminishing importance of clan membership and to changes in the pattern of rural settlement. Above all, it was consistent with the egalitarian politics of consensus; in this sense, at least, it was comparable to the clan leadership of the pre-colonial era, and a reaction against the authoritarianism of the chiefly hierarchy. Other aspects of the colonial order—notably the cash-crop economy—have been assimilated to the Lango way of life, but to this day the Langi may be said to be unreconciled to the institution of chiefship.

APPENDIX 1

The Origins of the Langi

THE debate on the question of Lango origins goes back more than fifty years,[1] and in that time very different solutions have been proposed. The great progress in elucidating the early history of the Nilotes has not included the Langi. Indeed, the debate has centred on the more basic question of whether the Langi should be seen as Nilotes at all, there being many features of Lango culture which suggest a Para-Nilotic attribution.[2] It is because of this ambivalence that, as recently as 1967, Ogot referred to the issue of Lango origins as 'one of the most difficult and unsolved questions in the pre-European history of Uganda'.[3]

The earliest attempts to solve the problem were committed exclusively to one side or the other. Driberg saw the Langi as being of purely Nilotic stock, while Tarantino later declared that they were fundamentally Para-Nilotes (or 'Nilo-Hamites', to use his term).[4] Such monolithic explanations are out of fashion. Recent authorities have tended to see the Langi as a fusion of two principal stocks, an earlier Lwo substratum having been over-laid by Para-Nilotic immigration from the east.[5] This interpretation dove-tails neatly with our knowledge of Lwo migrations as a whole, but—as Ogot points out—the deciding factor must be the traditions of the Lango clans.[6] These traditions are as yet imperfectly known, mainly because of the bewildering number of Lango clans. But, when set alongside the history of neighbouring peoples, those traditions that are known yield a clear and convincing picture.[7]

While the debate has centred on the roles of the Lwo and the Para-Nilotes, it has not been supposed that these were the first inhabitants of

[1] The first contribution was Driberg, 'The Lango District, Uganda Protectorate'.

[2] See above, p. 25.

[3] Ogot, *History of the Southern Luo*, vol. I, p. 48.

[4] Driberg, *The Lango*, pp. 23–33; Tarantino, 'The Origin of the Lango'.

[5] Crazzolara, 'Notes on the Lango-Omiru and on the Labwoor, and the Nyakwai'. R. Oliver, 'Discernible developments in the interior *c.* 1500–1840' in *History of East Africa*, vol. I, ed. R. Oliver and G. Mathew (Oxford, 1963), pp. 173–9; Ogot, op. cit., pp. 48–62.

[6] Ogot, op. cit., p. 53.

[7] Lango traditions of origin are the subject of another recent study, B. R. Mugane, 'The Origins of the Langi of Uganda: a case study in migrations and ethnic fusion', unpublished Ph.D. dissertation, University of California, Berkeley, 1972. Mugane's approach is somewhat different from that taken here; it is difficult to assess her work since she does not give a full account of her fieldwork methods. The techniques of lexicostatistics have also been applied to the Lango problem: R. T. Curley and B. Blount, 'The Origins of the Langi: a Lexicostatistical Analysis', *Jl. Language Association of Eastern Africa*, 2 (1971), pp. 153–67.

Lango country. Middle Stone Age artefacts have been found at the Nile–
Chobi confluence in the extreme west of the Lango settlement area,[8] and
doubtless plenty more will come to light in other places. But so far no
archaeological survey has been made of Acholi and Lango. Until this has
been done, any reconstruction of the area's history before the Lwo migrations of the fifteenth century must be speculative in the extreme, and only
one scholar has seriously attempted it. In Lango, as in Acholi, Crazzolara
sees the pre-Lwo population as having consisted of two elements—Madi,
and 'western Lango', by which he means Para-Nilotes akin to the Didinga
of the Southern Sudan.[9] So far as Lango is concerned, Crazzolara's evidence
consists almost entirely of clan names and place names, without reference
to the traditions surrounding them.[10] The attribution of these names to the
Madi or 'western Lango' rests on guess-work, and in the absence of
supporting evidence it cannot command much confidence. Furthermore, if
some Lango place names are indeed Madi in origin, then it must be pointed
out that these names could just as probably have been given at a later date
by Lwo groups which had absorbed Madi during their southward migration. For southern Lango, D. W. Cohen cites Banyara traditions from south
of Lake Kyoga to show that, besides Madi, there were probably Bantu-
speakers north of the Lake who retreated southwards when the Lwo
appeared.[11] Both these suggestions have some plausibility, but at present
they are hardly more than guide-lines for further inquiry.

The Lwo settlement

During the fifteenth century, the Southern Lwo began their southward
advance from a camping area in the Nile valley, near Nimule. Most groups
followed the valley of the Nile until they reached Pubungu at the north end
of Lake Albert. Here a dispersion occurred. Some entered Bunyoro, where
they established the Bito dynasty and became the dominant element in
eastern Bunyoro (Chope). Some remained on the right bank of the Victoria
Nile and slowly expanded into Acholi. Others at a later date crossed into
what is now Alur country in West Nile District. Meanwhile a smaller
section of the Southern Lwo had stayed behind in the Nimule area, and
from there they gradually spread over north Acholi. Such was the migration
pattern over a period of two centuries.[12]

This pattern extended to Lango as well. Crazzolara and Ogot, drawing
mainly on Acholi and Padhola traditions, have shown that, broadly
speaking, the Lwo groups which entered Lango can be placed in three
categories: those who migrated south from Nimule and the Agoro massif,
at some distance from the Nile valley; those who stopped their southward

---

[8] B. M. Fagan and L. Lofgren, 'Archaeological Sites on the Nile–Chobi
Confluence', *Uganda Jl.*, 30 (1966), pp. 201–6.

[9] J. P. Crazzolara, *The Lwoo* (3 parts, Verona, 1951–4), pp. 81–2, 340–1, 551.

[10] Crazzolara, 'Notes on the Lango-Omiru', pp. 179–90; *The Lwoo*, p. 548.

[11] D. W. Cohen, *The Historical Tradition of Busoga* (Oxford, 1972), p. 158.

[12] Crazzolara, *The Lwoo*, parts 1 and 2; Oliver, op. cit., pp. 171–80; Ogot, op.
cit., pp. 40–7. See also now J. M. Onyango-ku-Odongo and J. B. Webster (eds.),
The Central Lwo during the Aconya (Nairobi, 1976).

migration at Pubungu, without crossing the Victoria Nile; and groups from Pawir or Chope, in eastern Bunyoro.[13] However, as is so often the case with pre-colonial African migrations, it is easier to enumerate the groups who entered an area than to determine which ones remained there over a long period. There is no doubt that Lango country was part of the broad stage across which the Southern Lwo were migrating from the fifteenth-century onwards, but it is more difficult to distinguish the Lwo groups still there at the end of the eighteenth century, when the first Para-Nilotes arrived from the east, especially since so many Lwo had migrated still further south to Padhola and Nyanza. In order to assess the extent of Lwo settlement, we must turn to Lango traditions and the evidence of Lango clan names.

Three areas of Lango attracted permanent Lwo settlement: the Nile valley on either side of Karuma Falls, a portion of the Moroto valley, and the Lake Kwania region. The picture is clearest in the Nile valley. From the earliest days of Lwo settlement, it seems that the Lwo colony of Pawir in eastern Bunyoro in fact included both banks of the Nile. The distribution of clan names indicates that, on the right bank of the Nile, Lwo country stretched from the Ayago river almost as far upstream as the Aroca.[14] At its greatest extent, this Lwo sphere stretched at least twenty miles up the Okole river, and perhaps as far up the Toci also.[15] In this region, the Langi have never maintained that they were the first inhabitants.[16]

Further east, Crazzolara's inquiries in Ogur and Alito have shown that, before the easterners arrived, there was a Lwo population which complemented the one north of the Moroto river, in Awere and Puranga. Probably the strong concentration of the Alira clan round modern Lira town should be included in this group.[17]

More problematic is the Lake Kwania–Kyoga area, since this was one of the principal migration 'corridors' of the Padhola, whose traditions mention Kacung and Kaberamaido as early stopping-places.[18] Conceivably, *all* Lwo from this area had moved further east by the time the Langi finally settled there in the 1870s, and some traditions lend support to this view.[19] But the abnormal density of population noted there by the first European visitors[20] suggests that the Langi had in fact absorbed a previous population. Lango informants do not admit as much, but some of them say that when the

---

[13] Crazzolara, *The Lwoo*, pp. 78–80, 563–4; Ogot, op. cit., pp. 55–61.

[14] The relevant clan names are: Acore, Atik (not to be confused with Atek), and Alwaa. In most cases, these names survive today in conjunction with Para-Nilotic clan names, e.g. Okarowok me Acore (found in Minakulu and Aber).

[15] Interviews: Bartolomayo Okori, Matayo Acut.

[16] Driberg, *The Lango*, pp. 25–7; Tarantino, 'Notes on the Lango', p. 148.

[17] Crazzolara, *The Lwoo*, p. 563; Crazzolara, 'Notes on the Lango-Omiru', p. 194. See also: Anywar, *Acoli Ki Ker Megi*, pp. 117–18; Reuben Ogwal, 'A History of Lango Clans', p. 24.   [18] Ogot, op. cit., pp. 68–9.

[19] It is often said that the Langi reached this area to find potsherds and excavated iron-ore, but no people. Interview: Tomasi Ojuka; J. A. Otima, 'Atek of Oumolao Clan and its leaders in Kwera and Aputi in the nineteenth century', undergraduate research essay, Department of History, Makerere University, 1970.

[20] Grant to Boyle, 1.7.07, UNA SMP/751/07; A. R. Cook, 'The Story of a Camping Tour in Equatorial Africa', *Mercy and Truth*, 13 (1909), p. 280.

Langi first reached Abyece, Awelo, and Dokolo, they had to chase away 'Kumam'.[21] The Kumam are a small tribe who today live mainly in Kaberamaido county in south-western Teso; the problem of their origin is similar to that of the Langi, in that they too speak a form of Lwo while evincing many typically Para-Nilotic features. Now Kumam tradition completely denies any settlement west of the Abalang river.[22] It seems likely, therefore, that Lango traditions about 'Kumam' settlers in south-eastern Lango refer to a Lwo group quite distinct from either the Langi or the Kumam. Some of these Lwo may indeed have joined the Kumam as refugees, but it is equally probable that others were assimilated by the Langi.

During the period 1500 to 1700, Lwo settlement was not, of course, static. Small bands of migrants were probably joining those already there until well into the eighteenth century, while others were pressing further inland from the Nile and the Moroto river. Even so, it is clear that the Lwo colonized only a small part of what was to become Lango country (Map 3). Ogot's statement that 'most of the Lango clans formed part of the migrating group of the Southern Luo' cannot be accepted,[23] for there are only ten clan names in Lango with reasonably clear affiliations to the north and west, rather than the east.[24] In short, there is no evidence that all, or even most, of Lango was settled by the Lwo.

This being so, the standard explanation[25] that the Para-Nilotes from the east assimilated the language and some of the social institutions of their Lwo predecessors seems scarcely tenable. The first European observers in the 1860s and 1870s placed the Lango language in the same category as other Lwo languages such as Jopalwo, Acholi, and Shilluk.[26] The possibility that the Para-Nilotes had within two generations of their first westward migration adopted the Lwo language could perhaps be entertained, had they been an immigrant minority obliged to take wives from a comfortably entrenched existing population.[27] But, in view of the very limited extent of Lwo settlement and the likelihood that the easterners were in the majority, so fast a rate of linguistic assimilation is inconceivable. Clearly another explanation for the infusion of Lwo culture must be sought. The most obvious alternative is that the fundamental fusion of Lwo with non-Lwo did not take place in Lango at all, but in the land of the Para-Nilotes to the east. The evidence brought to light by recent research now makes this interpretation inescapable.

[21] Interviews: Isaka Ojaba, Amnoni Abura, Ekoc Opige.

[22] Personal communication from Mr. Mathew Odada, of Canon Lawrence College, Lira, who is engaged on research in Kumam history.

[23] Ogot, op. cit., p. 52.

[24] The clan names are: Acore, Atik, Alyec, Obala, Ojimo, Amor, Ayom, Abol, Alira, and Alwaa.

[25] See Oliver, op. cit., pp. 176–9, and Ogot, op. cit., pp. 61–2.

[26] Grant, A Walk across Africa, p. 291; Linant de Bellefonds to Gordon, 24.3.75, in Shukry, Equatoria under Egyptian Rule, p. 238.

[27] Compare, for example, the case of the Ngoni of Malawi. M. Read, 'Tradition and prestige among the Ngoni', Africa, 9 (1936), pp. 453–83.

The migrations of the Para-Nilotes

Due consideration of the Lwo factor in Lango history has been inhibited by the almost universal tradition of the Langi themselves that they migrated from Otuke, the imposing hill which marks the boundary between Lango and Labwor. The statement, 'We Langi came from the east', has been seen as pointing exclusively to a Para-Nilotic origin.[28] Insufficient attention has been given to Lango traditions about migrations before Otuke. Now it is true that the majority of elders today are unable to elaborate on the Otuke statement; but a significant minority can. Broadly speaking, the traditions fall into two categories: the first and largest group refer to Teso, Karamoja in general, or Jie in particular,—that is, to areas which for a long time have been predominantly Para-Nilotic in speech.[29] The second group refer to several locations in the south-eastern Sudan. The places of origin are re-called only in the most general terms, but the essential common ground is that some of the Langi at Otuke had migrated not from the east, but from the north.[30] The number of informants who can recount traditions of this second category is small, but they gain weight from one conclusion reached by Driberg some fifty years ago. According to him, the Lango tribe origina-ted near the Agoro range of hills on the Uganda–Sudan border, due north of the Lango country; they then migrated southwards, and settled for a time in the area immediately north-east of Lango District, before moving into their present homeland.[31] The ethnic and linguistic associations of this second group are far more open to debate. Lango traditions do not indicate whether this group was composed of Lwo or Para-Nilotes, nor do they say how or when the easterners and northerners at Otuke combined to form a single people.

For enlightenment on these questions, we have to refer to the traditions of the Jie people, which have recently been the subject of an exhaustive study by Lamphear.[32] Two aspects of his reconstruction of Jie history are

[28] Tarantino, 'Origin of the Lango', p. 14.

[29] This explanation runs through the migration traditions collected by Canon Ogwal. R. Ogwal, op. cit.

[30] Didinga, Lotuko, and Shilluk are mentioned. Interviews: Edwardi Olir, Tomasi Ojuka, Lazaro Okelo; N. Engola, 'Olden Times in Northern Lango', translation of undated vernacular MS., Department of History, Makerere University, p. 1; R. Ogwal, op. cit., pp. 46, 47, 55.

[31] Driberg, *The Lango*, pp. 27–30. Traditions about Agoro should not be taken to imply any connection with the other, very small tribe called Lango, which lives near the Agoro range, between the Lotuko and the Didinga. The name 'Lango' is not their own, but was given them by their Lwo-speaking neighbours to the south. C. G. and B. Z. Seligman, *Pagan Tribes of the Nilotic Sudan* (London, 1932), p. 346.

[32] J. Lamphear, *The Traditional History of the Jie of Uganda* (Oxford, 1976). The next two paragraphs are drawn from chapters 3 to 5 of this work; his con-clusions can be given here only in the form of a bald summary.

Some of the same ground is also covered in J. B. Webster and others, *The Iteso during the Asonya* (Nairobi, 1973), but there are several divergences of inter-pretation between this work and Lamphear's. See also now, Onyango-ku-Odongo and Webster, *The Central Lwo during the Aconya* [sic], in which the

relevant to Lango: the identification of *two* layers of Para-Nilotes, distinguished originally on grounds of subsistence economy; and the indications of substantial Lwo infiltration into Jieland. The Jie have usually been
seen as originating from a concentration of pastoral Para-Nilotes in the
Koten–Magos area of Karamoja, above the Rift Valley Escarpment which
today forms the frontier between Kenya and Uganda.[33] While this group
certainly played a very important part in Jie evolution from the time of
their westward migration in the mid-eighteenth century, it is now clear that
they were not the first Para-Nilotes to inhabit either Jieland or Karimojong
country. The Koten–Magos group arrived to find a well-established Para-
Nilotic population, which for its livelihood depended less on pastoralism
than on the traditional crop complex of northern Uganda—millet, simsim,
ground-nuts, and above all sorghum. These agriculturalists are known to
Jie tradition as 'Ngiseera' or 'Iseera'; they had probably originally migrated
from the region of the Agoro hills in the southern Sudan. When the
pastoralists first reached central Jieland from Koten and Magos, a significant proportion of the Iseera migrated to the south-west. They stopped
first at the Kotidani river, north of the Labwor Hills, and then continued
through Labwor to the vicinity of Otuke hill.

The Iseera themselves, however, were something of a composite group.
This was on account of Lwo influence which affected them at every stage
of their migration. Before the Koten–Magos group arrived in central
Jieland around the middle of the eighteenth century, there had already been
Lwo infiltration from the west—so much so that the Iseera are said to have
become bilingual in Ajie and Lwo before their departure to the south-west.
By this time, there was also a significant Lwo population along the
Kotidani river itself; so when the Iseera settled there, they were exposed to
still more Lwo influence, absorbing both new people and new cultural
traits. At the same time, some of the original Iseera migrants from Jieland
were disheartened by famine at both Kotidani and Otuke, and they retraced their steps to settle alongside the Koten–Magos group. As the westward migration of the Iseera continued, therefore, the number of Lwo
increased, while the Para-Nilotic speakers became fewer. This process probably continued at Otuke, since there are Acholi traditions about Lwo
groups who migrated south-eastwards as far as Otuke.[34]

So far from conflicting with Lango traditions, this general picture conveyed by Jie sources in fact complements them. Jieland is given by several
accounts as the Lango homeland,[35] while mention of locations in the

relevance of western Karamoja to the settlement history of Acholi is stressed by
several contributors.

[33] P. and P. H. Gulliver, *The Central Nilo-Hamites* (London, 1953), pp. 10–11,
28–9.

[34] Crazzolara, *The Lwoo*, pp. 305, 534, 541, 552. Acholi traditions describe
these groups as having retraced their steps to Acholiland proper, but it is reasonable to suppose that not all of them left Otuke for the north.

[35] Ogwal Ajungu, untitled vernacular history (1936–7), paragraph 84; R. Ogwal,
op. cit., p. 7. Interviews: Joseph Orama, Yokonia Ogwal, Kezekia Okelo,
Yakobo Gaci.

Southern Sudan by some Lango sources can readily be interpreted in the light of the probable Iseera migration from the Agoro area. The Langi say that when they lived at Otuke they already grew millet, sorghum, and simsim,[36] and already spoke their present language, though bilingualism continued for some time.[37] According to Lango traditions, the Langi and the Jie separated at Otuke because of ill-feeling caused by food scarcity: the Langi enjoyed a surplus, while the Jie were short, and the Jie were obliged to sell their children to the Langi in return for food; the two came to blows, and the Langi decided to move away. This tradition is sometimes recounted with reference to the Karimojong or the Labwor, rather than the Jie—an understandable confusion, in view of the likelihood that these labels had as yet no meaning in the late eighteenth century.[38] None of this conflicts with the Jie tradition that at Otuke there was a division among the Iseera, some returning to Jieland on account of famine, and others pressing forward to the south-west.

Beyond indicating an easterly origin in general, the evidence of Lango clan names is more difficult to assess. Among the 250 or so clans identified to date, there are many which on present evidence have no affiliations with any other clan in Lango or elsewhere. However, at least 100 clans, and possibly as many as 200, are associated with six names representing the original clans from which they sprung: Oki, Bako, Atek (or Atekit), Arak (or Arakit), Ober, and Okarowok.[39] Three of these clans—Atek, Arak, and Okarowok—are found among several Central Para-Nilotic-speaking peoples. Lamphear has shown convincingly that these 'universal' clans belong to the Iseera, or agricultural Para-Nilotes, and that their prevalence in each of the tribes varies according to the historical contribution of the Iseera to the present-day population.[40] Lamphear also includes in this group one other clan, Otengoro, which is found among the Langi, but is much less widespread than the basic six.[41] The three remaining clans of the Lango 'core' do not appear to correspond to any groups elsewhere. This is not in itself an argument against the theory of an Iseera origin for the Langi. Jie elders today recall only the names of those clans which contributed to the return migrations from Kotidani and Otuke; they shed no light on the identity of those Iseera clans which continued their journey westwards without any of their members returning to Jieland. It is these clans which in the Lango story are particularly important, and it seems reasonable to suppose that Oki, Bako, and Ober represent Iseera clans which decamped *in toto* from Karamoja to Otuke, and thence to Lango country proper.[42]

[36] Interviews: Tomasi Ojuka, Anderea Okadde, Luka Abura, Adonia Ecun.

[37] Interview: Anderea Okadde. In the 1930s some elderly Langi could still remember how to speak Ajie. Tarantino, 'Origin of the Lango', p. 15.

[38] Interviews: Ekoc Opige, Nasaneri Owino, Anderea Okadde, Yubu Engola, Adonia Ecun. Tarantino, 'Notes on the Lango', pp. 147–8.

[39] See above, p. 46.   [40] Lamphear, op. cit., pp. 84–5, 92.

[41] ibid., p. 85. The Oremakori clan, a minor group in Lango, is also classified as an Iseera clan. ibid., p. 135.

[42] I owe this suggestion to Dr. Lamphear. The name 'Ober' would appear to be Lwo in origin, and to point to the Lwo infiltration of Kotidani and Otuke,

The traditions of the Lango clan sections themselves do not greatly help in this respect, since pre-Otuke migration routes are not recalled with sufficient precision to allow identification with any one of the different groups in Jieland or Labwor. The details of Lango migration are thus tantalizingly vague at present—and will perhaps remain so—but the general outline emerges clearly enough from Jie traditions, substantiated on a few crucial points by Lango sources. The assimilation between Lwo and Para-Nilotes was well under way by the time that the Langi left Otuke. They began their westward migration into Lango already equipped with a know-ledge of the Lwo language, and already practising a mixed economy of seed-agriculture and pastoralism which was well suited to their new environment.

Besides linguistic and economic adaptation, there is one other problem which has been seen to stand in the way of a theory of eastern origin for the Langi: the problem of population growth. The 1959 Census showed that Lango has about two-and-a-half times as many people as Karamoja. This contrast reflects the big disparity in natural endowment between the two Districts, a disparity which has probably not changed radically during the last 200 years. The problem of reconciling the demographic picture with migration traditions is aggravated by the fact that important elements of the Iteso trace their origin to the same area. Faced with the almost total lack of evidence, all that can be done is to comment on such population statistics as exist, and to offer a few tentative suggestions.

The really spectacular growth in the Lango population has taken place since 1931, and is associated with greater material prosperity and the growth of medical services. Until the 1930s the improved conditions of the colonial period did not make much of a demographic impact. Census figures for the early colonial period are not a very accurate guide, being liable to serious under-enumeration; but assuming a roughly equal discrepancy in the first two Censuses of Lango District (1921 and 1931), it appears that the Lango population increased by 3 per cent in ten years, to something probably well over the official figure of 176,000.[43] There are two reasons for thinking that the rate of growth may have been higher than this during the pre-colonial era. The first is that an expanding pioneer society can reproduce more rapidly than a settled society which has reached the practical limits of territorial expansion. The second reason is more peculiar to Lango. During the nineteenth century, the Langi were constantly raiding their neighbours, and they sometimes engaged in quite distant campaigns. There are good grounds for supposing that the Langi were extremely effective warriors, and

discussed above. Outside the central core of six, a few other Lango clans can be classified: Ararak (not to be confused with Arak) occurs also in Teso and Turkana; Omolo and Inomo appear from Teso evidence to be Lwo clans. Lawrance, *The Iteso*, p. 55; Webster, op. cit., p. 5.

[43] *Census Returns, 1921* (Entebbe, 1921); *Census Returns, 1931* (Entebbe, 1933). District population figures for this period have to be broken down into their tribal constituents, since the Lango settlement area did not then coincide with Lango District.

The inadequacy of population statistics for the early colonial period is stressed in R. R. Kuczynski, *Colonial Population* (Oxford, 1937), pp. vii–xiv.

that the balance of success lay with them.[44] Now an important feature of these campaigns was the taking of captives, especially women and girls. In a polygynous society these were easily absorbed, and the natural result would have been to increase the average number of offspring of each married man.

Turning to Karamoja, there is one item of material evidence for large population movements in a westward direction. In the area of the Kotidani river, Lamphear has discovered several hundred grinding-stones which Jie tradition ascribes to the Iseera group, most of whom went on to Otuke. This would suggest that the migrants themselves were numbered in thousands.[45] The constant reference in tradition to Otuke, a dry locality, presents no major difficulty. It is clear from Lango traditions that 'Otuke' stands as a symbol for the whole Labwor area, access to which is by way of Otuke hill; the more detailed traditions current in eastern Lango mention several other localities deep into Labwor—Morulem, Nangolebwal, Awila, and Loyoroit.[46] Compared with the surrounding areas of eastern Acholi and Jieland, the Labwor hills are fertile and healthy. It can tentatively be suggested that the Iseera group from Jieland entered a region where the pressure of expanding population was already building up to a crisis, and that the sudden addition of new settlers from the east set in train a steady exodus to the south-west. Much depends here on how large were the Lwo groups which joined the Iseera at Kotidani and Otuke, and on the size of the existing Lwo population in Lango itself. On all these points of detail, further evidence is needed; but the main outline of events up to 1800 is now reasonably clear.

[44] See above, chapter 4.   [45] Lamphear, op. cit., pp. 149–51.

[46] Interviews: Yubu Engola, Anderea Okadde. R. Ogwal, op. cit., *passim*; Tarantino, 'Notes on the Lango', p. 146. ('Awila' here does not, of course, refer to the village of that name in Akokoro sub-county.)

APPENDIX 2

The Organization and Conduct of Fieldwork in Lango District

I spent ten months in Lango District, from January to November 1969. Seven months were devoted to the collection of oral tradition. It was clear from the outset that the first task must be one of selection. Although the exact nature of the pre-colonial political system was as yet obscure, I knew that traditions were conveyed in a clan setting, and that clans were very small. The only way in which every clan could have been reached during the time at my disposal was by use of a questionnaire. At the best of times this is a somewhat inflexible and superficial device, and since it was not even obvious what questions would be relevant it seemed a particularly unwise approach. I therefore concentrated my research on a handful of the forty-two Lango sub-counties, with a view to producing case-studies of political development, from which a more general analysis could be abstracted. In order to take account of regional variations—an important issue, as it turned out—I included sub-counties in every quarter of the District. This geographical spread also enabled me to consider the impact of the very varied peoples whose territories are adjacent to Lango. In addition, documentary sources from the early colonial period provided a guide as to areas which had been particularly accommodating towards the British, areas which had put up strong resistance, and areas from which the crucial first generation of county chiefs had been recruited. In all, nine sub-counties were chosen. If any bias crept into the selection, it was in favour of the extreme west of Lango, near the Nile, since here the supporting documentary evidence was richer than anywhere else (Map 11).[1]

It is extremely difficult to strike the right balance between in-depth case-studies and over-all coverage, and doubtless mine was not the perfect answer. Given time, there were other areas which I would like to have studied. Even within the case-study area, informants had inevitably to be selected according to their clan alignment, their reputation as experts on the past, and their accessibility. My understanding of certain topics might have been deepened had I conducted a completely thorough investigation of one village. Otherwise, the results of fieldwork tended to justify both the over-all balance and the actual choice of case-study areas.

The time spent in each of the nine selected sub-counties varied from four to ten days of continuous interviewing, and the number of people interviewed from seven to twenty, depending on the speed with which good informants were identified, and on the complexity of the historical material.

[1] The nine sub-counties chosen were: Akokoro, Ibuje, Aber, Iceme, Abyece, Dokolo, Bar, Adwari, and Omoro.

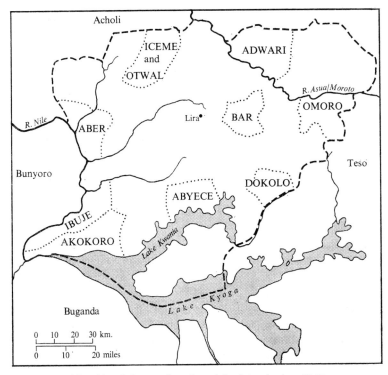

Map 11. Sub-counties selected for interviewing, 1969

So far as my standing in the eyes of informants was concerned, much depended on my relationship with the Lango District Administration. I could not have carried out fieldwork without government permission, and everyone in Lango knew this. Apart from that, I was anxious to disclaim any connection with the Government, and in the early stages I resisted any involvement by the chiefs in my research. These efforts proved in vain. Except for the missionaries, any European working in rural Lango is assumed to be associated with the Government, and the information that I was a student did nothing to remove this impression. The mere presence of a European was taken to be the business of the authorities—from the District Office down to the village chief. In due course, I accepted the logic of this situation; I sent the sub-county chief advance notice of my arrival, and accepted his help in contacting good informants, especially those who were not easily reached at their own homes. So far as I could tell, the closer involvement of the chiefs did not inhibit my informants. My semi-official status was established from the start, and by acting on it I was not making myself any less acceptable to informants.

Throughout my research, informants were interviewed singly, rather than in groups. Since the group method has been favoured by some historians of acephalous societies,[2] it is worth explaining why I rejected it. If a group testimony takes the form of an agreed version conveyed through a spokesman on behalf of a definite social group, then it can be regarded as valid.[3] But when recent historians have advocated the group method, this is not usually what they have meant. In practice, the initiative for a group interview tends to come not from the informants, but from the historian himself, for whom it is a means of coping with the multiplicity of historical sources in a non-centralized society. Undoubtedly group interviews enable the researcher to cover the ground more quickly, with less repetition and less disagreement among informants. But there are serious disadvantages. The discrepancies between related traditions, which may be obscured or suppressed in the group interview, are a vital part of the historian's source material, because they show up the various views which different social groups have of the same events. Of course, a group interview is not necessarily free from argument among the informants; but, even if the historian is proficient enough in the language to follow the cut-and-thrust of debate, he will still be losing something, since many informants naturally defer to those with strong personalities or political influence. The basic objection to the group interview, as usually practised, is that it partially removes from the historian's hands the weighing of conflicting evidence. So far as Lango is concerned, there was never any suggestion from informants that a group meeting should be called. A rewarding number of informants—and not always the most forceful personalities—gave testimonies of outstanding value which might never have come to light in a group interview. The use of the private interview exploited to the full the knowledge and goodwill of the individual informant, and allowed his testimony to be completely grasped on the spot. The group method might be appropriate for certain purposes and under carefully controlled conditions, but the bulk of any historical research among the Langi should be done by individual interviews.[4]

The conduct of the interview was determined by the piecemeal way in which clan traditions are usually transmitted. With very few exceptions, informants were unable to hold forth for more than a few minutes without prompting. The basic form of the interview was therefore question-and-answer. On account of the concentration required from all concerned, this pattern placed a limit on the length of the interview, which hardly ever exceeded two hours. Such a situation calls for considerable skill on the part of the researcher. A courteous and deferential manner must be maintained, loaded questions must be avoided, and the informant's answers must not meet with an unduly prejudiced response—either of enthusiasm or incredulity.

---

[2] By Ogot among the Luo, for example (Ogot, *History of the Southern Luo*, vol. 1, pp. 23–5). While I was in Lango, J. B. Webster was collecting traditions among the Iteso; he used group interviews almost exclusively.

[3] J. Vansina, *Oral Tradition* (London, 1965), p. 28.

[4] A similar view is taken in G. Muriuki, *A History of the Kikuyu, 1500–1900* (Nairobi, 1974), pp. 11–12. See also D. W. Cohen, *The Historical Tradition of Busoga* (Oxford, 1972), p. 35.

These requirements make it particularly important for the researcher to be in full control of the interview. Complete command of the language is something which few Europeans can hope to attain, particularly when time is limited, but some knowledge is essential. Six months' tuition in London had introduced me to the grammar, and to the peculiarities which distinguish Lango from other, better-documented dialects of Lwo. Once in the field, it did not take long to acquire some knowledge of both the stock phrases of everyday conversation and the fairly restricted vocabulary used for recounting the past. This meant that I could respond directly to informants from time to time, and towards the end of my stay I could sometimes manage without on-the-spot translation. Most important of all, I was able to control my interpreter—to ensure that his manner towards informants was appropriate, and to check any tendency on his part to sift information or run the interview. In the event, my interpreter's ease of manner greatly contributed to a good interviewing atmosphere, and for the most part he restricted himself to a detailed translation into English of what was said. Interviews were recorded on tape, and I also took notes in summary form.

The interviewing atmosphere was generally relaxed and friendly. This was partly due to the fact that most interviews took place in the informant's own home, where he felt most at ease. The interview often became a social event in itself, as friends and kinsfolk gathered from nearby homesteads. I do not think that my informants were preoccupied by thoughts of material gain. Although I always gave a small present—usually tea and sugar or cigarettes—I never offered any payment, a salient point which had probably reached the ears of many people before I arrived to request an interview with them. For most informants it appeared to be enough to know that their testimony would contribute towards a book about the Langi which their descendants would be able to read. The fact that a stranger should be interested in their past did not usually provoke surprise or suspicion. Unlike other academic subjects, history is regarded by the Langi as a self-explanatory and innocent preoccupation, though this attitude is admittedly confined to 'olden times' (*kare acon*) prior to the colonial era. The enthusiasm with which informants were prepared to endure a long interview—and sometimes two or three—meant that the collection of traditions was in itself an enjoyable and rewarding experience.

As research in each of the nine localities was completed, the testimonies were transcribed from the tape-recorder on to paper and then rearranged according to their content. Verbatim transcription seemed inappropriate to informal traditions of the kind current in Lango, and only a minute proportion was given this rigorous treatment; it was reserved for testimonies with a strong narrative element and a few others which contained precise descriptions of pre-colonial political institutions. For the rest, the final written record always entailed an element of paraphrase and summary, in which my own questions and any repetitious matter were omitted.[5] In addition, about one-quarter of the interviews, amounting to some sixty-five

[5] The transcripts are in manuscript, and will remain in my possession until arrangements have been made for their deposit or publication.

hours, was retained in an edited form on tapes; these are deposited in the Library of the British Institute in Eastern Africa, Nairobi.

Early on in the collection of testimonies, certain strengths and weaknesses in Lango tradition became apparent. The most important point was that the oral evidence proved to be more plentiful and more consistent than I had been led to expect. An informant's testimony generally began with a brief account of his clan section's origin and migration route to its present locality. Then came a description of the organization of the clan section, with special attention to its leadership. Informants were encouraged to give the fullest possible details about particular battles and disputes, since these shed light on the content of clan leadership and on the relationship between the clan section and its neighbours—both Langi and non-Langi. The bulk of any interview was taken up by these topics, on which the informants' knowledge was fullest, and the results were impressive.[6] The catch came in the fact that these descriptions as a rule referred only to the last generation before the colonial occupation (i.e. the period from about 1880 to 1910)— usually the lifetime of the fathers of today's elders. Within this span, traditions were fairly precise as regards their sequence and their place in clan genealogy, so that chronology presented few problems. Once informants moved further back in time, however, their testimonies were much more difficult to evaluate. There was nothing like the same amount of detail, nor could events and personalities be easily put in context. For different reasons, which I discuss in the Introduction, informants were unable to offer much oral evidence on the colonial period.

One way of interpreting the oral material which I had gathered would have been to treat it impressionistically, and to abstract points of detail in conformity with an over-all analytical plan. I decided instead that material collected on a case-study basis was best kept in that framework, at least during the first stages of interpretation. Accordingly each case-study was written up in turn, using only the evidence relating specifically to that area —whether oral or documentary. This was an extremely time-consuming task. Meticulous cross-checking was needed between informants of the same area, and between the traditions of different areas with shared experiences (for example, battles or common migrations). The measure of agreement between sources was on the whole reassuring.

Two of the nine areas—Bar and Adwari—failed to produce good material over the range of topics found in the other research locations. The informants in these places were usually confused and imprecise. I might have discovered the reasons for this, or possibly have identified more promising sources, if I had spent more time there; but I could only have done so at the cost of excluding other areas altogether. In the remaining seven locations, detailed and consistent pictures of pre-colonial history were obtained.[7] Only when all the case-studies had been fully examined was the shape of the present work determined in detail.

[6] Two summarized testimonies are reproduced as examples in Appendix 3.

[7] No case-study has been reproduced *in toto* in this book, but parts of the same case-history apear at different stages and are fully cross-referenced. The most extended examples are taken from Aber and Akokoro. See above, pp. 50–2, 74–81.

APPENDIX 3

Two Oral Testimonies

REPRODUCED below are two summarized testimonies. They are summaries in only the most technical sense. The questions put to the informant have been omitted; the testimonies have been pruned of repetition; and in some places the sequence has been rearranged according to chronology (the informant's, not mine) or theme. But in both cases every substantial item of historical information has been included. Each summary was made soon after the interview ended, the information being carefully transcribed from the tape-recording. The summaries which follow may therefore be regarded as full and accurate records. The rest of the interviews which I conducted in Lango were recorded in a form similar to that presented here. As stated in Appendix 2, the transcripts at present exist only in manuscript form and are in my possession.

The two informants represented here have been chosen with a view to their contrasting credentials as informants. The first one, a senior elder of no education at all, is as immersed in traditional culture as it is possible for a Lango to be today. The second informant is a much younger man with considerable experience of government employment; his clear and articulate exposition was the result of a more deliberate concern with the past.

(1) INTERVIEW WITH OKELO ABAK, 30 JUNE 1969

Early migration of the Jo Ogora Atar

Okelo's father, Abak Omoti, was born near Alito rock.[1] He led the people from Alito to Orem (in Aduku), then to Oporowie (Apac), and then to Tarogali. While the Jo Ogora Atar were in Alito, their leader was a man called Omare, who was Abak's elder brother; their father was called Omoti. Omare sent Abak away to find his own hunting tract, because he was a strong young man, and so Abak left Alito. Long before they lived at Alito, while they were still near Otuke, the Jo Ogora Atar and the Jo Ogora Acol[2] were one and the same clan; but a fight broke out between them, and so they separated. The clan got their name 'Atar' (white) because a very old woman once slept in the ashes and came out all white.

Another group of the Jo Ogora Atar branched off and migrated to Apoi (in Akokoro), where the Jo Okabo lived. This section was led by a lineage brother of Abak's, called Olila. When Olila's men were chased away from

[1] Alito rock is situated in north-central Lango, between Lira town and the Acholi border.
[2] This clan is more frequently called the Jo Ocukuru, and is now the dominant clan in the Ibuje area.

Apoi by the Jo Okabo, they settled in Kwibale (also in Akokoro). Olila's son was killed there. When Abak heard that his brother's son had been killed, he went and brought Olila's people to settle near him in Tarogali. Their place was called Oding.

The settlement of Tarogali

Abak settled in Tarogali because there was so much game and fishing there. In the other places along the way from Alito there had been animals in plenty, but there had been other homesteads as well. Tarogali was the only place that Abak really wanted to settle in. He possessed no cattle when he arrived, because he was a poor man; he simply came on account of the game. He had to fight his way to Tarogali—fight and then press forward.

Abak did not direct the people exactly where to settle. They knew where to put their own houses. The village was very large, with very many houses close together in one compound. Each group within the village ate its own food separately—say about ten households in a group.

With Abak there came nine men; they were all lineage brothers, and they all brought wives and children. They were: Bamma, Elida, Oguta, Atala, Obura, Ekwom, Amuca, Ongom, and Pole. Other members of the clan then followed them from Alito.

Members of the Jo Ogora Atar in Tarogali used to visit other branches of the clan at Amac and Aduku.

The arrival of other clans in Tarogali

At the time when the Jo Ogora Atar settled in Tarogali, there were no other people there, or anywhere in Ibuje. The Jo Ocukuru came a long time afterwards. Nor were there any Langi living further west (towards the angle of the Nile at Masindi Port). The Jo Oyakori arrived later, and Abak told them to go further west and settle in a place where there were no other people; the place where they actually settled was Te Acoda (also in Tarogali); they stayed there for a long time, until the death of their leader, Angole Acak. The two clans were related, because while they were both in Alito, Angole's son, Ocika, had married the sister of Amare.

When Abak arrived, there were no Baruli living on this side of the Nile; but when the Baruli saw that Abak had settled here, they came across one by one. The reason they came was that they feared the wild animals on their own side, especially the wild pigs. They settled peacefully, farming and fishing, and Abak had no objections. They came from a place called Carana, nearly opposite Tarogali on the other bank of the Nile. This was when the Jo Ocukuru had already settled in Ibuje.

Before they arrived in Tarogali, the Jo Ocukuru were already related by marriage to the Jo Ogora Atar. So there was no fighting when they came to settle. They were the first clan to join Abak, to be followed by the Jo Arak me Oyakori. Then the Jo Atek me Omwara settled in Tarogali. Other clans who came at one time or another were: the Jo Arak me Otwal who came and intermarried with the Jo Ogora Atar, but who later joined the rest of their clan in Aber; and the Jo Okabo, who later moved on to Apoi (in Akokoro).

The border between the Jo Ogora Atar and the Jo Ocukuru is marked by a swamp between the villages of Alenga and Tarogali.

A pre-colonial battle

On Ibuje rock there were two clans which were very strong—the Jo Arak me Ococ and the Jo Obanya. They once attacked the Jo Ocukuru, killing many of them. So Arum, one of the important men in the Jo Ocukuru, ran to Tarogali, to ask for Abak's help. Abak told him that he was just like a woman: the people who had attacked him were so few that Arum should have chased them away like goats, and now he was running away. All the same, Abak sounded his horn to summon his men, and they asked where the fight was; Abak answered that Arum had appealed for help. So they went and defeated Arum's enemies. During the battle, Abak was challenged by a man on the other side called Eryong; but Abak marked out a line on the ground with magic medicine and dared the enemy to cross it; when they did, they lost all their strength and were defeated.

The Jo Arak me Ococ were chased away to Apac. However, some of the Ococ people had helped Arum in the battle; they had avoided killing their fellow-clansmen, and had killed men of the Jo Obanya instead. When the rest of the Jo Arak me Ococ were chased away to Apac, these people stayed behind with Arum in Ibuje.

The extent of Abak Omoti's authority

Abak used to settle disputes between members of the Jo Ogora Atar. He never took cases to anyone else. Other clans like the Jo Atek me Omwara used to bring their disputes to him.

Abak wore a special skin garment, and two iron bracelets on each arm, which were called *okom*. He was the only man in the clan who could wear *okom*.

Abak was a rain-maker (*won kot*).[3] When he held a rain-making ceremony, other clans used to come along, but they did not participate. They did not shake the tree which the Jo Ogora Atar shook.[4] They came only for the beer which was served at the end of the ceremony. Okelo Abak succeeded his father as *won kot*, and the ceremony today is the same as it was in Abak's time.[5]

[3] This combination of clan leadership and ritual authority in the same person was very rare in pre-colonial Lango.

[4] One of the main features of the ceremony of *lamo kot* ('praying for the rain') is the pouring of water into the branches of a tree, followed by the shaking of the tree; both men and women may participate in this stage of the ceremony.

[5] Two days after this interview, I participated in the *lamo kot* ceremony at Okelo Abak's invitation. South-western Lango was badly hit by drought at this time.

Relations with the Banyoro

Abak only went to Bunyoro once, and on that occasion he was speared by a gun.[6] Langi came from the east on their way to Bunyoro, and they took Abak along with them. All the important men in the Jo Ogora Atar went, and also Arum of the Jo Ocukuru. When they reached the Nile, they found people from the other side waiting to ferry them over. The boats were at Kungu, Aganga, Rwekasaza, Palango, and Ibuje. Ogwal Atigo was the leader who took the Langi across the Nile, but he did not rule the Langi. They went to help a Munyoro called Odongo, who lived at Doyo rock; this man was not a Muchope.[7]

Abak also once purchased a Munyoro girl who had been brought over to Otwal's place at Kamdini (in Aber) and was then brought to his home.

When Kabarega ran away to Lango, Abak did not help him. He stayed in Itao for only a few days before continuing to Kamdini. His pursuers did not pass this way, though they were not far away; when Okelo Abak was a boy, he remembers hearing the sound of the guns.

Relations with the Jo Arak me Oyakori

Abak Omoti and Angole Acak, the leader of the Jo Oyakori, were friends and in-laws. But later on, there was trouble. A he-goat belonging to the Jo Ogora Atar strayed into the village of the Jo Oyakori; the Jo Ogora saw it when they went for a dance there, and they asked to have it back. But the Jo Oyakori said it was their own goat and refused to return it. So there was a fight. Angole Acak's brother, Ongom Adilo, was speared on the neck, but he was protected by the bracelets which he wore round his neck. The two clans did not kill each other because they were related by marriage.

The ceremony of ewor (or iwor)

At the time of *iwor*, people used to gather together and then follow a route to a certain place, and then return. On their way, if they met any children they would just push them aside; but if they met a grown man, they would beat him. It all used to start in the east. The people who lived near Otuke did not go right across Lango, but only as far as the next village; those people would go to the next place, and so on. The people of Tarogali used to go to Aganga and return, and then the people of Aganga went to the next place. When a group of people like this reached their destination, they brought with them news of *iwor*; the other people gave them beer-flour which they took home with them; and then they danced.[8]

Forced labour under the Government

When the Government arrived, they made Abak an important man. People were ordered to work in his fields. In the old days, people only went

[6] Presumably a bayonet.

[7] My question here was prompted by the fact that Odongo is a Lwo name; in this instance it must have been a Lango nickname for a Munyoro.

[8] This confused and unilluminating account is typical of oral descriptions of the age ceremonies in Lango.

into other men's fields when beer was going to be made. But after the Government had arrived, people were forced to work. They came individually, by turns, to work in Abak's fields. Previously there had not been this compulsion.

Abak's relations with Arum

Abak and Arum both went to Kungu to meet the Europeans. Arum was appointed chief (*rwot*), but it should have been Abak, since he had been the first one to settle anywhere in Ibuje sub-county. In fact, Abak asked to become chief, but instead the Government appointed Arum. Abak became his deputy (*katikiro*). After that, Abak forgot about his ambition to be chief, and was friends with Arum. He served as Arum's deputy for a long time. When there was a small case, Abak used to settle it. But when there was a difficult case, he sent it to Arum; but the parties to the case still had to come to Abak first.

Abak Omoti never had instruction from a catechist. He was succeeded as clan leader of the Jo Ogora Atar by Adupa, who was the son of Abak's brother, Onyac.

Okelo Abak's experience of the Government

Okelo read at Alwala. But he was never baptized, because someone falsely accused him of illicit intercourse and speared him; he then stopped reading. For two years Okelo worked as *askari* for Arum. His job was to collect chickens, which the people were forced to give.

(2) INTERVIEW WITH YUBU ENGOLA, 13 NOVEMBER 1969

The Langi at Otuke

While the Langi were living at Otuke, they lived peacefully alongside the Karimojong, without trouble. But later on the Karimojong had a famine, and they stole food from the Lango granaries. The Langi felt that they must migrate to another place if they were to avoid losing their food-supplies.

At that time, the Langi were living on the Morolem[9] side of Otuke hill. The Karimojong lived further east, while the Jie were further north. There was a certain rock which separated the Langi from the Karimojong. The Langi and the Labwor lived on either side of a swamp called Ongolebwal;[10] the Langi and the Labwor each had their own settlements in different places, the Labwor living near a rock called Oyoroit.[11] It was said that the Langi originally came from the Karimojong country.

At the time when the Langi left Otuke, they had no trouble with the Labwor. Later on, the Labwor were troubled by famine, and they used to bring their children to the Langi to sell in exchange for food, while others just stole food.

[9] Morolem is deep in Labwor country, i.e. east of Otuke, and is now the site of a large Verona Fathers Mission. [10] Nangolebwal hill, near Morolem. [11] Loyoroit river, in northern Labwor.

Separation of clans and migration

When the Langi were at Otuke, they were already divided into the clans of Atek, Okarowok, Otengoro, Arak, and a few more; but there were not as many clans as today. Clans split up because people married their clan-sisters.

All the Langi left Otuke at the same time, because of the trouble with the Karimojong. Then they separated and migrated along a number of different routes; but all the Langi went westwards as far as the Nile. When they found they could go no further, they started to retrace their steps and passed through Lira.

Informant's family connections

Engola belongs to the Jo Oki me Wonadyang. His father was Opio Amak, who was son of Okwir Odingo Aleng, who was the son of Won Adyang, who was the son of Kode who migrated from Otuke. Opio Amak's mother (Engola's grand-mother) was a Karimojong war-captive. Engola's mother was the daughter of Oyanga Apenyo, the leader of the Jo Otikokin.[12] Oyanga Apenyo also had a son called Okuk Awira,[13] and it was he who told Engola about the past.

Early migration of the Jo Oki

Kode, of the Jo Oki me Wonadyang, left Otuke and seems to have died somewhere near Lira. He was succeeded as leader of the clan by his son, Won Adyang. Actually, up to that time, the clan had been called Jo Oki me Atek. Won Adyang himself owed his name to the fact that he used to exchange any bull calves he had for cow calves, so that his herd would multiply. The Jo Oki me Wonadyang split off from the rest of the Jo Oki me Atek because they sat down to eat *apuny*[14] with the Jo Otikokin. The rest of the Jo Oki me Atek ate *apuny* with the Jo Ober, and they changed their name to Jo Atek me Ober. The Jo Wonadyang do not marry with Jo Atek me Ober or with Jo Atek me Odyekowidi, but they can intermarry with Jo Otikokin—witness Engola's own father.

Wonadyang died in Akia.[15] He was succeeded by Okwir Odingo Aleng, who settled in Alebtong, near Aloi. Oyanga Apenyo of the Jo Otikokin was also living there. Okwir was killed while hunting on the southern side of the Moroto river. In those days Omoro itself was all bush.

Settlement in Omoro

When Oyanga Apenyo migrated from Alebtong to Omoro, several important men of the Jo Oki me Wonadyang went with him. These were Opio Amak, Atyang Aluko, and Olwit Amuko. They all migrated

---

[12] The Jo Otikokin were one of the two most important clans in Omoro on the eve of the colonial period.

[13] Danieri Okuk Awira was chief of Adwari sub-county from 1929 to 1934.

[14] *Apuny* was the final burial rite, held every two or three years. Since it was an *etogo* function, several clans took part.

[15] Akia is a *paco* near Lira, in Adekokwok sub-county.

together and were led by Oyanga Apenyo, who was Atyang Aluko's *okeo* (sister's son). The reason for the migration was that a disease had killed many of the Jo Oki and Jo Otikokin, including Oyanga Apenyo's own children. The two clans settled together in Amuk village; there were three cattle pens, belonging to Oyanga Apenyo, Acuru Aryam (Jo Otikokin), and Atyang Aluko (Jo Oki).

Later, they were joined by another group of Jo Otikokin which included Acol, Owuni, Icel, and Okwany Awaitum. This group had been living in the south, at Bata; they had been visiting Oyanga Apenyo, and they decided to migrate to Omoro because there was plenty of land there. After their migration, they stayed for a time as visitors in Amuk village. Then they settled in their own village called Akany, about three miles away.

Other clans in Omoro

When Oyanga Apenyo first settled in Amuk, there were no other Langi living in Omoro. In fact the whole place was actually called 'Oyanga'; it was the Baganda who named the place 'Omoro'. After the Jo Otikokin and the Jo Oki, the first clan to settle was the Jo Atek;[16] they were led by Goi Arop and settled at a place called Inur, now in Angeta *paco*. They were followed by a different Atek clan,[17] who were led by Oyuru Abwango. Then came the Jo Arakit, all of whom settled in Amuk village; their leader was Onyanga Waitum. Next came the Jo Ngurapuc, led by another man called Oyanga. Then came the Jo Ocukuru; they were led by Owiny Agel, and their number also included Odur Onymoi and Arwat Abal; they had come from Bata and settled at Akany village. Lastly, there came the Jo Ober, who were led by Awany Alel (there was another man of the same name who belonged to the Jo Atek me Adyang me Okwerkic).

As men went to live with their wives' families, the clans began to get mixed up. This happened in Amuk, but the Jo Oki and Jo Otikokin still outnumbered all the people who came from other clans to settle in Amuk.

Oyanga Apenyo's authority

Akany village was ruled by Acol.[18] His father, Opita Lobomo, had died in Alapata (in Bata); at that time, Acol had been old enough not to need adoption by another father, but he did not marry until he reached Akany. Although Acol ruled Akany village, he in turn was ruled by Oyanga Apenyo, because Acol was his nephew. Oyanga settled disputes in Acol's village and led him to battle. Each of the other clans in Omoro dealt with its own disputes.

When there was to be a battle against the Iteso, Oyanga Apenyo sent word to Goi Arop who would tell all the other clan leaders to bring their men too. If there was a fight between two different groups in Omoro—say the villages of Angeta and Abukamola—Oyanga would settle the matter;

---

[16] Jo Atek me Okwerowe.   [17] Jo Atek me Okide.
[18] Enoka Acol was later first sub-county chief of Omoro (1916–27) and first county chief of Moroto (1927–34).

Goi Arop might come to Oyanga and tell him that the people were intending to fight among themselves. Then Goi and Oyanga would go and settle the matter before it came to fighting. But in that sort of case, the clans would not have appealed voluntarily to Goi and Oyanga, because they would have had far to travel.

On one occasion, Okwany, the son of Oyanga Apenyo's brother, killed Ogwal Apelo on account of illicit sexual intercourse. This Ogwal was a man of Oyuru Abwango's. So Oyuru came and raided some of Oyanga's cattle. Apart from that, Oyanga Apenyo was never involved in fighting against any of the clans whom he led in battle against the Iteso.

Relations with the Iteso and Acholi

Oyanga Apenyo used to lead the other clan leaders of Omoro against the Iteso. In those days the border with Teso was as it is today, only about $3\frac{1}{2}$ miles from Oyanga's village. The Iteso came and attacked Omara of the Jo Bako, the father of Ikel Abura, but they never attacked Amuk village.

Oyanga Apenyo was never involved with the Acholi, either in trade or in battle.

The defeat of the Arabs

Omato Ali was an Arab who came with the Acholi in order to raid cattle from the Langi. He invaded the area of Ading, which is between Adwari and Apala, and he was killed on his very first visit to Lango. The Arabs had guns. The Langi were led by a man called Oluju (who had no connection with Oluju Akor of Orum). The Langi watched Omato Ali secretly; they waited until he was asleep at night, and then Oluju killed him. The cattle he had robbed were then recovered.

Relations with the Banyoro

Oyanga Apenyo used to fight in Bunyoro under the leadership of Agoro Abwango. He used to lead men from all the clans in Omoro, but some of them stayed behind in order to protect the homesteads. Oyanga would spend between one and three months at a time in Bunyoro. Some of the Langi returned quickly from Bunyoro because of a tick (*kwodo*) disease there: if the man bitten by a tick kept quiet about it, he survived, but if it was mentioned that he had been bitten, then he died from the bite. Kabarega used to present Agoro Abwango with captives if the expedition was successful, and Agoro would then distribute them to the other *rwode* whom he had invited to come with him.

Kabarega also used to give and to sell hoes to Agoro Abwango; Agoro then sold to the *rwode* of Omoro, who would supply the ordinary people with hoes. Banyoro traders did not visit Omoro itself. The hoes were actually called *Ja Olum*, and Engola himself has seen hoes of this kind on Kabarega's grave. However, most of the Langi in those days used sharpened sticks instead of hoes. It is only since the arrival of the Government that hoes have become common among the local farmers.

Trade with the Labwor

The Langi also used to obtain hoes from the Labwor, but this was a dangerous business. Usually the Langi had to go to Labwor to get the hoes, and Engola's own uncle was killed there. The Labwor themselves only came to Omoro when there was famine in their own land; then they would bring their daughters to sell to their Lango friends.

The arrival of the Government

It was Oyuru Abwango of the Jo Atek me Okide who brought the Baganda and the Europeans from Soroti[19] to Omoro. He did so because he wanted to take vengeance on Oyanga Apenyo and recover his cattle, and he appealed to the Government to help him. Oyanga Apenyo had been warned that enemies were coming to seize his cattle, so he sent his cattle to friends in the west. He sent some of them to a clan-brother named Odero Anyanga in Aloi; and he sent the rest to a man of the Jo Arakit called Ocet Abal, who lived at Apado, in Alebtong near Aloi; but these cattle were robbed by chief Ogwangguji of Lira for his own use. The rest of the cattle were pursued to Aloi by the government forces, who had arrived at Oyanga's home to find no cattle there. Oyanga Apenyo was then arrested by the Government. The first man the Government had arrested had been Goi Arop (also known as Obira), whom they had then told to lead them to Oyanga, which he did. The third man arrested was Okeng Ongolomoi of the Jo Atek.[20] The Government also confiscated the cattle belonging to Goi and Okeng and brought them all to the same cattle-pen.

Besides Oyuru Abwango, there was a Kumam called Aoja who claimed that Oyanga had seized some of his cattle, so he was given some of the confiscated livestock. Oyuru Abwango and his clan-brother, Ocet (no connection with Ocet Abal), claimed that they should receive all the rest of the cattle. But the Government said that Oyanga's cattle must not be finished completely, and so he was allowed to keep some of them. Then the leaders were told to remain together in peace, which they have done to this day. The families of Oyanga and Oyuru intermarry, and there is no hatred between them.

During the government expedition, three men of Akany village were killed.

The early colonial period in Omoro

When Opige of Dokolo raided northwards with his government guns, he reached Ongora hill,[21] but he did not get as far as Omoro.

When the Langi of Adwari fought against the Baganda, none of the Omoro men went to help them.

The Baganda who ruled Omoro behaved roughly; they used to use people as seats to sit on when they were drinking beer. Amulani Kewaza

---

[19] There was already a government post nearby at Orungo in Teso country, and until 1923 Omoro was administered as part of Teso District from Soroti.

[20] Jo Oki me Atek.   [21] In Abako sub-county.

was the leader of the Baganda from 1914 until 1926, and after he left there were no more Baganda in Omoro. The Baganda were only rough in the early days, before Enoka Acol was made *jago* [1916]. Acol, known as Acol Amak before he was baptized Enoka in 1932, was the first *jago* of Omoro; Oyuru Abwango was never made *jago*. Acol was a Protestant, and he never joined the *abamalaki*.[22] He was a good chief. After he had retired, he went to live in Okwon village in Omoro, where he died in 1938.

Engola's own father, Opio Amak, was *won paco* of Omarari, under Amulani Kewaza, and died in 1926. Oyanga Apenyo died about two years after Engola himself began to pay poll-tax.

[22] The *abamalaki* were a separatist Christian sect and originated in Buganda. According to F. B. Welbourn (*East African Rebels*, p. 47), Acol was a member.

APPENDIX 4

Oral Sources

IN the footnotes of this book a total of 117 informants has been cited; a further twenty-two were also interviewed during fieldwork in 1969. The reader is perhaps entitled to expect a list of oral sources, comparable to the Bibliography of written sources, which appears below. It has proved impracticable to give full details about informants here. However, in the thesis on which this book is based will be found a comprehensive list of informants, including details of their family backgrounds and careers.[1] When conditions in Uganda once more permit the collection of oral material, this list will be made freely available to researchers in the field.

[1] J. A. Tosh, 'Political Authority among the Langi of Northern Uganda, *circa* 1800 to 1939', London University Ph.D. thesis, 1973, pp. 379–402. The thesis may be consulted in either the Library of the University of London, or at the School of Oriental and African Studies.

Bibliography

A. UNPUBLISHED PRIMARY SOURCES

(1) *Official Documents*

Public Record Office, London: British archives are most useful for the period up to 1905 when Uganda was the responsibility of the Foreign Office. Military and administrative contacts with the Langi during that period are fully covered in the series FO/403 (Confidential Prints). By contrast, the Colonial Office records (CO/536) contain little which is directly relevant to the administration of Lango District.

Uganda National Archives, Entebbe: the administration of Uganda up to 1906 is covered District by District in the 'A' series. The files on Busoga (A10–11), Bunyoro (A12–13) and Acholi (A16–17) were all useful. After 1906 documents are arranged in Secretariat Minute Papers (SMP). These are not numbered in a straightforward sequence, nor are they properly catalogued. It is therefore impossible to be sure that everything relevant to Lango has been consulted; but in the period up to 1919 (the start of the closed period), my coverage appears to have been comprehensive. After 1919 it was difficult to get clearance for any documents apart from quarterly and annual reports.

The Uganda National Archives also hold what is left of the former Eastern Province Archives (EPMP), which mainly take the form of regular reports. The Northern Province Archives (relevant to Lango from 1932 onwards) are divided between Entebbe and the Acholi District Archives at Gulu (see below); the correspondence at Entebbe relating to the Lango Native Council in the 1930s was made available to me.

Lango District Archives, Lira: almost no general correspondence before the 1940s survives, though there are a few District Reports from the earlier period, which duplicate those held in the Uganda National Archives. The principal holding is the County Tour Books (for a general description, see Preface). Up to 1912 touring records were made in a single book, which was lost in Lake Kyoga in that year. Thereafter each county had a separate book. For the counties of Dokolo, Maruzi, Kole, Kwania, and Moroto, the series is complete for the period from 1912 to 1939; in the remaining counties there are gaps, which are particularly bad in the case of Erute.

Acholi District Archives, Gulu: a few items concerning the administration of Acholi are relevant to Lango, particularly the Paranga Tour Book for 1925–6, which contains some useful historical information about the Lango enclave of Minakulu, administered from Gulu until 1936. But the most important files are those which formerly were kept in the Northern Province Archives (NPMP); these include the only accessible record of the

Philipps–Ashton Warner correspondence of 1933–4 and the reforms brought in by the Provincial Commissioner in the next two years.

Teso District Archives, Soroti: the best organized archives in Uganda. The Tour Books dealing with the early administration of the Kumam counties of Kalaki and Kaberamaido were transferred from Lira to Soroti, presumably when these areas were ceded to Teso District in 1939. There are also reports dealing with the early administration of some of Moroto county (Omoro and Amugo) which was part of Teso until 1923. Otherwise the Teso District Archives were not relevant.

(2) Non-official documents and private papers

A. G. Bagshawe, 'Journal of Lango Expedition, April–August 1901', MS. in Makerere University Library. A diary of Delmé-Radcliffe's expedition by the Medical Officer who accompanied it.

Church Missionary Society Archives, Waterloo Road, London. On account of the fifty-year rule, letters from the missionaries who were stationed in Lango from 1926 are not available. But earlier letters from Acholi and Teso may be consulted in the series G3/A7/0.

Papers of the Revd. A. B. Fisher, deposited in the CMS Archives. The papers include correspondence relating to the Gulu Mission in 1913–14.

Field-notes of Dr. T. T. S. Hayley, in his possession. These are the raw material on which Hayley based his book, *The Anatomy of Lango Religion and Groups.* He was resident in Lango from 1936 to 1937. His notes include the original of Ogwal Ajungu's history (see below).

R. H. Johnstone, 'Past Times in Uganda', MS. in Rhodes House Library, Oxford. A record of personal reminiscence, written in 1921. Johnstone commanded a detachment of the K.A.R. in Lango from 1911 to 1912.

Neill Malcolm, 'Diary', MS. in Rhodes House Library, Oxford. A journal covering the period of the Uganda Mutiny (1897–9); Malcolm was an army officer who for several months was based at Foweira on the Nile.

J. E. T. Philipps, 'Development of Indirect Administration in the Southern Sudan, Bahr-El-Ghazal Province (1925), typescript in the Balfour Library of the Pitt-Rivers Museum, Oxford. This gives an account of Philipps's innovations in Zandeland.

B. PUBLISHED PRIMARY SOURCES

(1) Official Publications of the British Government (London)

Parliamentary Papers: the annual reports of the Commissioners (later Governors) of the Uganda Protectorate appeared as Parliamentary Papers up to the report for 1918–19.
Colonial Reports—Annual: from 1919 this was the only form in which the annual reports on Uganda were published.

(2) *Official Publications of the Uganda Government* (*Entebbe*)

Annual Reports of the Provincial Commissioners, Eastern, Northern and Western Provinces, on Native Administration for 1935 (1936). Similar volumes were published for 1936, 1937, and 1938.
Blue Books, published annually from 1907.
Census Returns, 1921 (1921).
Census Returns, 1931 (1933).
Native Administration: Note by the Governor [Sir Philip Mitchell] (1939).
Report on the 1969 Population Census, vol. I (1971).
Uganda Protectorate Gazette, published fortnightly from 1908.

(3) *Non-official publications* (all books published in London, unless otherwise stated).

ASHE, R. P. *Chronicles of Uganda*, 1894.
BAKER, S. W. *The Albert N'yanza*, 2 vols., 1866–7.
———— *Ismailia*, 2 vols., 1874.
CASATI, G. *Ten Years in Equatoria*, 2 vols., 1891.
CHURCH MISSIONARY SOCIETY. *Extracts from the Annual Letters of the Missionaries for the Year 1907*, 1908.
CHURCHILL, W. S. *My African Journey*, 1908.
COOK, A. R. 'The story of a Camping Tour in Equatorial Africa', *Mercy and Truth*, 13 (1909), pp. 181–7, 277–85.
DICKINSON, F. A. *Lake Victoria to Khartoum with rifle and camera*, 1910.
FISHBOURNE, C. E. 'Lake Kioga (Ibrahim) Exploration Survey, 1907–8', *Geographical Jl.*, 33 (1909), pp. 192–5.
FISHER, R. M. 'Other Sheep', *Church Missionary Gleaner*, 35 (Jan. 1908), p. 3.
———— 'The Awakening of a Nile Tribe', *Church Missionary Gleaner*, 41 (June 1914), pp. 90–1.
GRANT, J. W. *A Walk across Africa*, 1864.
GRAY, J. M. (ed.) 'The Diaries of Emin Pasha—Extracts II', *Uganda Jl.*, 25 (1961), pp. 149–70.
———— 'The Diaries of Emin Pasha—Extracts III', *Uganda Jl.*, 26 (1962), pp. 72–96.
———— 'The Diaries of Emin Pasha—Extracts IV', *Uganda Jl.*, 26 (1962), pp. 121–39.
———— 'The Diaries of Emin Pasha—Extracts V', *Uganda Jl.*, 27 (1963), pp. 1–13.
———— 'The Diaries of Emin Pasha—Extracts VII', *Uganda Jl.*, 28 (1964), pp. 75–97.
———— 'The Diaries of Emin Pasha—Extracts VIII', *Uganda Jl.*, 28 (1964), pp. 201–16.
HILL, G. B. (ed.) *Colonel Gordon in Central Africa, 1874–9*, 1881.
JUNKER, W. *Travels in Africa during the Years 1882–1886*, 1892.
KIRKPATRICK, R. T. 'Lake Choga and surrounding country', *Geographical Jl.*, 13 (1899), pp. 410–12.
LAWRENCE, T. L. Notes on mission work in Lango, in *Church Missionary Outlook*, 53 (April 1926), p. 81.

LINANT DE BELLEFONDS, E. 'Voyage de service fait entre le poste militaire de Fatiko et le capitale de M'tesa roi d'Uganda', *Bulletin trimestriel de la Société Khédiviale de Géographie du Caire*, 1 (1876–7), pp. 1–104.

LLOYD, A. B. *Uganda to Khartoum*, 1906.

MELLAND, F. H. and CHOLMELEY, E. H. *Through the Heart of Africa*, 1912.

MITCHELL, P. E. 'Indirect Rule', *Uganda Jl.*, 4 (1936), pp. 101–7.

PERHAM, M. and BULL, M. (eds.) *The Diaries of Lord Lugard*, vol. II, 1959.

PHILIPPS, J. E. T. 'The Tide of Colour', *Jl. African Society*, 21 (1922), pp. 129–35, 309–15.

PIAGGIA, C. 'Sesto Viaggio di Carlo Piaggia sul Fiume Bianco nel 1876', *Bollettino della Società Geografica Italiana*, 14 (1877), pp. 380–91.

SCHWEINFURTH, G. *et al.* (eds.) *Emin Pasha in Central Africa*, 1888.

SHUKRY, M. F. (ed.) *Equatoria under Egyptian Rule*, Cairo, 1953.

SPEKE, J. H. *Journal of the Discovery of the Source of the Nile*, 1863.

SYKES, C. A. *Service and Sport on the tropical Nile*, 1903.

VANDELEUR, S. *Campaigning on the Upper Nile and Niger*, 1898.

WILSON, C. T. and FELKIN, R. W. *Uganda and the Egyptian Soudan*, 2 vols., 1882.

WRIGHT, H. T. 'Pioneer Work in Mid-Africa', *Awake*, 25 (May 1915), pp. 50–1.

C. UNPUBLISHED SECONDARY SOURCES

(1) *Lango Vernacular Histories*

ENGOLA, NASAN, 'Kop Otimere i Lango Ibut Ober', MS. in the author's possession; translated by J. A. Tosh and K. Ochen as 'Olden Times in Northern Lango', typescript copy in the Department of History, Makerere University.

————— 'Rwot Kole Olong Adilo', MS. (incomplete) in the author's possession; translated by J. A. Tosh and K. Ochen as 'Olong Adilo, the Rwot of Kole', typescript copy in the Department of History, Makerere University.

ENIN, PETER, Vernacular history, translated by J. N. Odurkene as 'The Life of Chief Odora Arimo of Lango', typescript in the Department of Religious Studies, Makerere University.

OGWAL, REUBEN, unfinished account, translated by J. A. Otima and W. Okot-Chono as 'History of Lango Clans', mimeo, Department of History, Makerere University.

————— 'Bino a muni kede mwa i Lango', MS. in Makerere University Library; the translated version, 'The coming of the Europeans and the Baganda to Lango', is incomplete and unreliable.

OGWAL AJUNGU, untitled historical account, in the possession of Dr. T. T. S. Hayley; Ogwal, who was a county chief at the time, dictated his account to a literate aide, specifically for Hayley's use, in 1936 or 1937.

OKELO, LAZARO, 'Kit Kop a Kwarowa Acon', MS. in the author's possession; translated by J. A. Tosh and K. Ochen as 'Concerning our

Ancestors', typescript copy in the Department of History, Makerere University.

OWENO, YUSTO, untitled MS. in the author's possession; translated by J. A. Tosh and K. Ochen as 'The Life of Daudi Odora', typescript copy in the Department of History, Makerere University.

(2) *University theses, conference papers, etc.*

CARTER, F. 'Education in Uganda, 1894–1945', Ph.D. thesis, London University, 1967.

CURLEY, A. C. 'Social Process: Clanship and Neighbourhood in Lango District, Uganda', M.A. thesis, Sacramento State College, California, 1971.

DENOON, D. J. 'Agents of Colonial Rule, Kigezi 1908–30', University of East Africa, Social Science Conference Proceedings, Jan. 1968 (mimeo).

DORWARD, D. C. 'A Political and Social History of the Tiv People of Northern Nigeria, 1900–39', Ph.D. thesis, London University, 1971.

DWYER, J. O. 'The Acholi of Uganda: Adjustment to Imperialism', Ph.D. dissertation, Columbia University, 1972.

HERRING, R. S. 'A History of the Labwor Hills', Ph.D. dissertation, University of California, Santa Barbara, 1974.

JACOBS, A. H. 'The Traditional Political Organization of the Pastoral Masai', D. Phil. thesis, Oxford University, 1965.

KING, A. 'A History of West Nile District, Uganda', D. Phil. thesis, Sussex University, 1971.

LONSDALE, J. M. 'A Political History of Nyanza, 1883–1945', Ph.D. thesis, Cambridge University, 1964.

MATTHEWS, T. I. 'The Historical Tradition of the Gwembe Valley, Middle Zambezi', Ph.D. thesis, London University, 1976.

MUGANE, B. R. 'The Origins of the Langi of Uganda: a Case Study in Migrations and Ethnic Fusion', Ph.D. dissertation, University of California, Berkeley, 1972.

ODURKENE, J. N. 'The Langi–Banyoro Relationship, and the Career of Chief Daudi Odora, 1850–1931', undergraduate research paper, Department of Religious Studies, Makerere University, 1968 (mimeo).

OKOT, J. P'BITEK, 'Oral Literature and its Social Background among the Acholi and Lango', B. Litt. thesis, Oxford University, 1963.

OTIMA, J. A. 'Atek of Oumolao Clan and its Leaders in Kwera and Aputi in the nineteenth century', undergraduate research paper, Department of History, Makerere University, 1970.

PIROUET, M. M. L. 'The Expansion of the Church of Uganda (N.A.C.) from Buganda into Northern and Western Uganda between 1891 and 1914', Ph.D. thesis, University of East Africa, 1968.

SOUTHALL, A. W. 'Padhola: Comparative Social Structure', East African Institute of Social Research, Conference Proceedings, Jan. 1957 (mimeo).

TWADDLE, M. J. 'Politics in Bukedi, 1900–39', Ph.D. thesis, London University, 1967.

WATSON, T. 'A History of Church Missionary Society High Schools in Uganda, 1900–24', Ph.D. thesis, University of East Africa, 1968.

D. PUBLISHED SECONDARY SOURCES
(books published in London, unless otherwise stated)

(1) *Works principally concerned with Lango*

COX, T. R. F. 'Lango Proverbs', *Uganda Jl.*, 10 (1946), pp. 113–23.
CRAZZOLARA, J. P. 'Notes on the Lango–Omiru and on the Labwoor and Nyakwai', *Anthropos*, 55 (1960), pp. 174–214.
CURLEY, R. T. *Elders, Shades, and Women: Ceremonial Change in Lango, Uganda*, Berkeley, 1973.
——— and BLOUNT, B. 'The Origins of the Langi: a Lexicostatistical Analysis', *Jl. Language Association of Eastern Africa*, 2 (1971), pp. 153–67.
DRIBERG, J. H. 'The Lango District, Uganda Protectorate', *Geographical Jl.*, 58 (1921), pp. 119–33.
——— *The Lango*, 1923.
——— *Engato the Lion Cub*, 1933.
GERTZEL, C. *Party and Locality in Northern Uganda, 1945–62*, 1974.
GRAY, SIR J. M. 'Gordon's Fort at Mruli', *Uganda Jl.*, 19 (1955), pp. 62–7.
——— 'The Lango Wars with Egyptian Troops, 1877–8', *Uganda Jl.*, 21 (1957), pp. 111–14.
HAYLEY, T. T. S. *The Anatomy of Lango Religion and Groups*, Cambridge, 1947.
HUDDLE, J. G. 'The Life of Yakobo Adoko of Lango District', *Uganda Jl.*, 21 (1957), pp. 184–90.
INGHAM, K. 'British Administration in Lango District, 1907–35', *Uganda Jl.*, 19 (1955), pp. 156–68.
OLYECH, E. 'The Anointing of Clan Heads among the Lango', *Uganda Jl.*, 4 (1937), pp. 317–18.
TARANTINO, A. 'Il matrimonio tra i Lango anticamente e al presente', *Anthropos*, 35 (1940–1), pp. 876–97.
——— 'The Origin of the Lango', *Uganda Jl.*, 10 (1946), pp. 12–16.
——— 'Lango Clans', *Uganda Jl.*, 13 (1949), pp. 109–11.
——— 'Notes on the Lango', *Uganda Jl.*, 13 (1949), pp. 145–53.
——— 'Lango Wars', *Uganda Jl.*, 13 (1949), pp. 230–5.
TOSH, J. 'Colonial Chiefs in a Stateless Society: a Case-Study from Northern Uganda', *Jl. African History*, 14 (1973), pp. 473–90.
——— 'Small-scale Resistance in Uganda: the Lango "Rising" at Adwari in 1919', *Azania*, 9 (1974), pp. 51–64.
——— 'Lango Agriculture during the Early Colonial Period: Land and Labour in a Cash-crop Economy', *Jl. African History*, 19 (1978), in the press.
TUCKER, A. N. 'Some Problems of Junction in Lango', *Mitteilungen des Instituts für Orientforschung*, 6 (1958), pp. 142–56.
WRIGHT, M. J. 'The Early Life of Rwot Isaya Ogwangguji, M.B.E.', *Uganda Jl.*, 22 (1958), pp. 131–8.

———— 'Lango Folk-Tales—an Analysis', *Uganda Jl.*, 24 (1960), pp. 99–113.

(2) *Other works*

ADEFUYE, A. 'Palwo Economy, Society, and Politics', *Transafrican Jl. History*, 5 (1976), pp. 1–20.

AFIGBO, A. E. *The Warrant Chiefs: Indirect Rule in South-eastern Nigeria, 1891–1929*, 1972.

AJAYI, J. F. A. and CROWDER, M. (eds.) *History of West Africa*, vol. I, 1971.

ALAGOA, E. J. 'Oral tradition among the Ijo of the Niger Delta', *Jl. African History*, 7 (1966), pp. 405–19.

———— 'Long-distance trade and the States in the Niger Delta', *Jl. African History*, 11 (1970), pp. 319–29.

———— 'The Niger Delta States and their Neighbours, 1600–1800', in Ajayi and Crowder, *History of West Africa*, pp. 269–303.

ALLAN, W. *The African Husbandman*, Edinburgh, 1965.

ANYWAR, R. S. *Acholi ki Ker Megi*, Kampala, 1954.

BALANDIER, G. *The Sociology of Black Africa*, 1970.

BARBER, J. *Imperial Frontier*, Nairobi, 1968.

BARNES, J. 'Indigenous Politics and Colonial Administration with special reference to Australia', *Comparative Studies in Society and History*, 2 (1960), pp. 133–49.

BEATTIE, J. *The Nyoro State*, Oxford, 1971.

BERE, R. M. 'Land and Chieftainship among the Acholi', *Uganda Jl.*, 19 (1955), pp. 49–56.

BOHANNAN, P. 'The Migration and Expansion of the Tiv', *Africa*, 24 (1954), pp. 2–16.

BURKE, F. G. *Local Government and Politics in Uganda*, Syracuse, 1964.

BUTT, A. *The Nilotes of the Anglo-Egyptian Sudan and Uganda*, 1952.

BUXTON, J. C. *Chiefs and Strangers*, Oxford, 1963.

CLIFFE, L., COLEMAN, J. S. and DOORNBOS, M. R. (eds.), *Government and Rural Development in East Africa*, The Hague, 1977.

COHEN, D. W. 'A Survey of Interlacustrine Chronology', *Jl. African History*, 11 (1970), pp. 177–201.

———— *The Historical Tradition of Busoga*, Oxford, 1972.

———— 'Pre-Colonial History as the History of the "Society" ', *African Studies Review*, 17 (1974), pp. 467–72.

COLSON, E. *The Plateau Tonga of Northern Rhodesia*, Manchester, 1962.

———— 'African Society at the Time of the Scramble', in Gann and Duignan, *Colonialism in Africa*, pp. 27–65.

CRAZZOLARA, J. P. *The Lwoo*, 3 parts, Verona 1950, 1951, 1954.

DENOON, D. and KUPER, A. 'Nationalist Historians in Search of a Nation', *African Affairs*, 69 (1970), pp. 329–49.

DORWARD, D. C. 'The Development of the British Colonial Administration among the Tiv, 1900–49', *African Affairs*, 68 (1969), pp. 316–33.

DRIBERG, J. H. *The Savage as He Really Is*, 1929.

DYSON-HUDSON, N. *Karimojong Politics*, Oxford, 1966.

EHRLICH, C. 'The Uganda Economy, 1903–45', in Harlow and Chilver, *History of East Africa*, pp. 395–475.

EVANS-PRITCHARD, E. E. *The Nuer*, Oxford, 1940.

———— 'Luo Tribes and Clans', *Rhodes-Livingstone Jl.*, 7 (1949), pp. 24–40.

———— *Anthropology and History*, Manchester, 1961.

FAGAN, B. M. and LOFGREN, L. 'Archaeological Sites on the Nile-Chobi Confluence', *Uganda Jl.*, 30 (1966), pp. 201–6.

FAGE, J. D. 'Slavery and the Slave Trade in the Context of West African History', *Jl. African History*, 10 (1969), pp. 393–404.

FALLERS, L. A. *Bantu Bureaucracy*, Cambridge, 1956.

———— (ed.). *The King's Men*, 1964.

FEIERMAN, S. *The Shambaa Kingdom: a History*, Madison, 1974.

FISHER, R. M. *Twilight Tales of the Black Baganda*, 1911.

FORD, J. *The Role of the Trypanosomiases in African Ecology*, Oxford, 1971.

FORTES, M. *The Dynamics of Clanship among the Tallensi*, 1945.

———— and EVANS-PRITCHARD, E. E. (eds.). *African Political Systems*, 1940.

GAILEY, H. A. *The Road to Aba*, New York, 1970.

GANN, L. H. and DUIGNAN, P. (eds.). *Colonialism in Africa, 1870–1960*, vol. I, Cambridge, 1969.

GIRLING, F. K. *The Acholi of Uganda*, 1960.

GOLDTHORPE, J. E. *Outlines of East African Society*, Kampala, 1958.

GOOD, C. M. 'Salt, Trade, and Disease: Aspects of Development in Africa's Northern Great Lakes Region', *International Jl. African Historical Studies*, 5 (1972), pp. 543–86.

GOODY, J. *The Social Organization of the LoWiili*, 2nd edition, 1967.

GRAY, SIR J. M. 'Kakunguru in Bukedi', *Uganda Jl.*, 27 (1963), pp. 31–59.

GRAY, R. *History of the Southern Sudan, 1839–89*, 1961.

———— and BIRMINGHAM, D. (eds.). *Pre-Colonial African Trade*, 1970.

GROVE, E. T. N. 'Customs of the Acholi', *Sudan Notes and Records*, 2 (1919), pp. 157–82.

GULLIVER, P. and GULLIVER, P. H. *The Central Nilo-Hamites*, 1953.

GULLIVER, P. H. 'The Age-Set Organization of the Jie Tribe', *Jl. Royal Anthropological Institute*, 83 (1953), pp. 147–68.

———— *The Family Herds*, 1955.

———— 'The Turkana Age Organization', *American Anthropologist*, 60 (1958), pp. 900–22.

———— (ed.). *Tradition and Transition in East Africa*, 1969.

HAILEY, LORD, *Native Administration in the British African Territories*, part 1, 1950.

HARLOW, V. and CHILVER, E. M. (eds.). *History of East Africa*, vol. II, Oxford, 1965.

HEMPHILL, M. DE K. 'The British Sphere, 1884–94', in Oliver and Mathew, *History of East Africa*, pp. 391–432.

HENIGE, D. P. 'Reflections on Early Interlacustrine Chronology: an Essay in Source Criticism', *Jl. African History*, 15 (1974), pp. 27–46.

HERRING, R. S. 'Centralization, Stratification, and Incorporation: Case Studies from North-eastern Uganda', *Canadian Jl. African Studies*, 7 (1973), pp. 497–514.

HORTON, R. 'Stateless Societies in the History of West Africa', in Ajayi and Crowder, *History of West Africa*, pp. 78–119.

ISICHEI, E. *The Ibo People and the Europeans*, 1973.

———— *A History of the Igbo People*, 1976.

JACOBS, A. H. 'A Chronology of the Pastoral Maasai', *Hadith*, 1 (1968), pp. 10–31.

JAMESON, J. D. 'Protein Content of Subsistence Crops in Uganda', *East African Agricultural Jl.*, 24 (1958), pp. 67–9.

JONES, G. I. 'Time and Oral Tradition with Special Reference to Eastern Nigeria', *Jl. African History*, 6 (1965), pp. 153–60.

KING, A. 'The Yakan Cult and Lugbara Response to Colonial Rule', *Azania*, 5 (1970), pp. 1–25.

KJEKSHUS, H. *Ecology Control and Economic Development in East African History*, 1977.

KUCZYNSKI, R. R. *Colonial Population*, Oxford, 1937.

K.W. 'The Kings of Bunyoro-Kitara', 3 parts: part 1, *Uganda Jl.* 3 (1935), pp. 155–60; part 3, *Uganda Jl.*, 5 (1937), pp. 53–67.

LAMPHEAR, J. *The Traditional History of the Jie of Uganda*, Oxford, 1976.

———— and WEBSTER, J. B. 'The Jie-Acholi War: Oral Evidence from Two Sides of the Battle Front', *Uganda Jl.*, 35 (1971), pp. 23–42.

LANGDALE-BROWN, I. *et al. The Vegetation of Uganda*, Entebbe, 1962.

LAWRANCE, J. C. D. 'The Position of Chiefs in Local Government in Uganda', *Jl. African Administration*, 8 (1956), pp. 186–92.

———— *The Iteso*, 1957.

LEACH, E. R. *Political Systems of Highland Burma*, 1954.

LEVINE, R. A. 'The Internalization of Political Values in Stateless Societies', *Human Organization*, 19 (1960), pp. 51–8.

LEWIS, I. M. (ed.). *History and Social Anthropology*, 1968.

LONSDALE, J. M. 'Some Origins of Nationalism in East Africa', *Jl. African History*, 9 (1968), pp. 119–46.

LOW, D. A. 'The Northern Interior, 1840–84', in Oliver and Mathew, *History of East Africa*, pp. 297–351.

———— 'Uganda: The Establishment of the Protectorate, 1894–1919', in Harlow and Chilver, *History of East Africa*, pp. 57–120.

———— and LONSDALE, J. M. 'Introduction: Towards the New Order, 1945–63', in Low and Smith, *History of East Africa*, pp. 1–63.

———— and PRATT, R. C. *Buganda and British Overrule, 1900–55*, 1960.

———— and SMITH, A. *History of East Africa*, vol. III, Oxford, 1976.

MAIR, L. P. *Native Policies in Africa*, 1936.

———— *Primitive Government*, Harmondsworth, 1962.

MARKS, S. 'Khoisan Resistance to the Dutch in the Seventeenth and Eighteenth Centuries', *Jl. African History*, 13 (1972), pp. 55–80.

McMASTER, D. N. *A Subsistence Crop Geography of Uganda*, Bude (Cornwall), 1962.

MIDDLETON, J. 'Notes on the Political Organization of the Madi of Uganda', *African Studies*, 14 (1955), pp. 29–36.

——— and TAIT, D. (eds.). *Tribes Without Rulers*, 1958.

MORRIS, H. F. and READ, J. S. *Indirect Rule and the Search for Justice*, Oxford, 1972.

MUNRO, J. F. *Colonial Rule and the Kamba: Social Change in the Kenya Highlands, 1889–1939*, Oxford, 1975.

MURIUKI, G. *A History of the Kikuyu, 1500–1900*, Nairobi, 1974.

NALDER, L. F. (ed.). *Tribal Survey of Mongalla Province*, Oxford, 1937.

NYAKATURA, J. W. *Anatomy of an African Kingdom: a History of Bunyoro-Kitara*, New York, 1973.

OGOT, B. A. 'Kingship and Statelessness among the Nilotes' in Vansina, Mauny, and Thomas, *The Historian in Tropical Africa*, pp. 284–302.

——— *History of the Southern Luo*, vol. I, Nairobi, 1967.

——— 'Some Approaches to African History', *Hadith*, 1 (1968), pp. 1–9.

OLIVER, R. 'Discernible Developments in the Interior, *c.* 1500–1840', in Oliver and Mathew, *History of East Africa*, pp. 169–211.

——— and FAGE, J. D. *A Short History of Africa*, Harmondsworth, 1962.

——— and MATHEW, G. (eds.). *History of East Africa*, vol. I, Oxford, 1963.

OMER-COOPER, J. 'Kingdoms and Villages: a Possible New Perspective in African History', *African Social Research*, 14 (1972), pp. 301–10.

ONYANGO-KU-ODONGO, J. M. and WEBSTER, J. B. (eds.). *The Central Lwo during the Aconya*, Nairobi, 1976.

PERHAM, M. *Native Administration in Nigeria*, 1937.

——— *Colonial Sequence, 1930 to 1949*, 1967.

POWESLAND, P. G. *Economic Policy and Labour*, Kampala, 1957.

PRATT, R. C. 'Administration and Politics in Uganda, 1919–45', in Harlow and Chilver, *History of East Africa*, pp. 476–541.

RANGER, T. O. 'African Reactions to the Imposition of Colonial Rule in East and Central Africa', in Gann and Duignan, *Colonialism in Africa*, pp. 293–324.

READ, M. 'Tradition and Prestige Among the Ngoni', *Africa*, 9 (1936), pp. 453–83.

RICHARDS, A. I. (ed.). *East African Chiefs*, 1960.

ROBERTS, A. D. 'The Sub-Imperialism of the Baganda', *Jl. African History*, 3 (1962), pp. 435–50.

——— (ed.). *Tanzania Before 1900*, Nairobi, 1968.

——— *A History of the Bemba*, 1973.

ROBINSON, R. and GALLAGHER, J. *Africa and the Victorians*, 1961.

ROGERS, F. H. 'Notes on Some Madi Rainstones', *Man*, 27 (1927), pp. 81–7.

SELIGMAN, C. G. and SELIGMAN, B. Z. *Pagan Tribes of the Nilotic Sudan*, 1932.

SOUTHALL, A. W. 'Lineage Formation Among the Luo', *International African Institute Memorandum*, 26, 1952.

——— *Alur Society*, Cambridge, 1956.

——— 'Stateless Society', in *International Encyclopedia of the Social Sciences*, vol. 15 (New York 1968), pp. 157–67.

———— 'Rank and Stratification among the Alur and other Nilotic Peoples', in Tuden and Plotnicov, *Social Stratification in Africa*, pp. 31–46.

SWARTZ, M. J. (ed.), *Local-Level Politics*, Chicago, 1968.

————, TURNER, V. W. and TUDEN, A. (eds.), *Political Anthropology*, Chicago, 1966.

THOMAS, H. B. 'Capax Imperii—The Story of Semei Kakunguru', *Uganda Jl.*, 6 (1939), pp. 125–36.

———— and SCOTT, R. *Uganda*, Oxford, 1935.

TIGNOR, R. L. 'Colonial Chiefs in Chiefless Societies', *Jl. Modern African Studies*, 9 (1971), pp. 339–59.

———— *The Colonial Transformation of Kenya: The Kamba, Kikuyu, and Maasai from 1900 to 1939*, Princeton, 1976.

TOSH, J. 'The Northern Interlacustrine Region', in Gray and Birmingham, *Pre-Colonial African Trade*, pp. 103–18.

TOTHILL, J. D. (ed.). *Agriculture in Uganda*, 1940.

TUCKER, A. N. and BRYAN, M. A. *The Non-Bantu Language of North East Africa*, 1956.

———— *Linguistic Analyses: The Non-Bantu Languages of North-Eastern Africa*, 1966.

TUDEN, A. and PLOTNICOV, L. (eds.). *Social Stratification in Africa*, New York, 1970.

TURNER, V. W. *Schism and Continuity in an African Society*, Manchester, 1957.

TWADDLE, M. ' "Tribalism" in Eastern Uganda', in Gulliver, *Tradition and Transition in East Africa*, pp. 193–208.

UGANDA GOVERNMENT. *Atlas of Uganda*, Entebbe, 1962.

VANSINA, J. *Oral Tradition: a Study in Historical Methodology*, 1965.

————, MAUNY, R. and THOMAS, L. V. (eds.). *The Historian in Tropical Africa*, 1964.

VINCENT, J. 'Colonial Chiefs and the Making of Class: a Case Study from Teso, Eastern Uganda', *Africa*, 47 (1977), pp. 140–59.

———— 'Teso in Transformation: Colonial Penetration in Teso District, Eastern Uganda, and its Contemporary Significance', in Cliffe, Coleman, and Doornbos, *Government and Rural Development in East Africa*, pp. 53–80.

WALLER, R. 'The Maasai and the British, 1895–1905: the Origins of an Alliance', *Jl. African History*, 17 (1976), pp. 529–53.

WEBSTER, J. B. *et al. The Iteso during the Asonya*, Nairobi, 1973.

WELBOURN, F. B. *East African Rebels*, 1961.

WERE, G. S. *A History of the Abaluyia of Western Kenya*, Nairobi, 1967.

WRIGHT, A. C. A. 'Notes on the Iteso Social Organization', *Uganda Jl.*, 9 (1942), pp. 57–80.

WRIGLEY, C. C. *Crops and Wealth in Uganda*, Kampala, 1959.

———— 'The Christian Revolution in Buganda', *Comparative Studies in Society and History*, 2 (1959), pp. 33–48.

———— 'Historicism in Africa: Slavery and State Formation', *African Affairs*, 70 (1971), pp. 113–24.

Index

(CL = clan leader; RL = regional leader; CH = government chief)